ALSO BY FOX BUTTERFIELD

China: Alive in the Bitter Sea

The Pentagon Papers
(with Neil Sheehan, Hedrick Smith, and E. W. Kenworthy)

American Missionaries in China
(edited by Kwang-Ching Liu)

ALL GOD'S CHILDREN

For Mary Dunn
With my admiration & best
wishes.
Fox Butterfield

and companions at dinner, 28 April 96

Marta ~ Qué bueno haberla conocido,
Ma. Isabel Véliz

Aïda Donald

Wendy & Phil ~ looking forward to our summer travels
with you & Richard!

In memory of an evening of enormous fun at
Literary Lofts. Jim and Korey Poston.

Romey and Jim Poston

Many New Moons to my favorite "lady of letters"

For Mary Dunn –

historian, librarian,

college administrator, with

affection & esteem,

David Herbert Donald

Mary – Cross paths!

admiringly – Joseph Bruce Ellis

ALL GOD'S CHILDREN

The Bosket Family and the
American Tradition of Violence

FOX BUTTERFIELD

Alfred A. Knopf New York

1995

THIS IS A BORZOI BOOK
PUBLISHED BY ALFRED A. KNOPF, INC.

Library of Congress Cataloging-in-Publication Data
Butterfield, Fox.
All God's children : the Bosket family and the American tradition of violence /
Fox Butterfield. — 1st ed.
p.   cm.
Includes bibliographical references (p.   ) and index.
ISBN 0-394-58286-1
1. Bosket family.   2. Afro-Americans—Biography.
3. Afro-American prisoners.   4. Violence—United States.
5. Racism—United States.   6. United States—Race relations.
I. Title.
E185.96.B98   1995
929'.2'08996073—dc20   95-1540
CIP

Manufactured in the United States of America

First Edition

For my wife, Elizabeth,
for my children, Ethan, Sarah, and Sam,

And for all those Americans
whose lives have been touched by violence

For these are all our children.
We will all profit by, or pay for,
whatever they become.

James Baldwin,
in a concert program to benefit
the Wiltwyck School for Boys

CONTENTS

PROLOGUE

THE BIG CELL DOOR swung open, its spindly passenger splayed out backward against the heavy iron bars. His hands were cuffed and shoved through a slot behind his waist. His feet, in heavy manacles, stuck through an aperture just above the cement floor. An automobile tow chain snaked between his hands and feet.

It was an entrance that promised little dignity. Emerging backside first into the world, his arms and legs stretched taut, Willie James Bosket Jr. looked like an insect pinioned for dissection, like an animal trussed for market. The prison authorities thought this a fitting arrangement for the man they considered the most violent criminal in New York State history. Dr. Hannibal Lecter, they liked to call him.

The shackling ritual was required any time Willie was allowed out for exercise, or on those rare occasions when a visitor called on him. Otherwise, day after day, year after year, he sat alone in his specially designed cage. It was a prison within a prison, the most restrictive confinement of any inmate in America. His private quarters lay far beyond a series of electronically controlled slam gates, past a maze of gloomy corridors where the ordinary convicts were kept—the murderers, the rapists, and the drug dealers—and through a labyrinth of courtyards decorated with gargoylelike carvings of masked bandits, screaming women, and judges wearing wigs from long ago. You came at last to the solitary confinement block, with its smell of chemical disinfectant, and behind that, in back of another great gate opened with an ancient half-foot-long key, was Willie's chamber.

It was perfect isolation. The guards were forbidden to speak to him, so the only sound he could hear, as the head of the Department of Correctional Services was fond of boasting, was the noise of his toilet flushing. Willie's cell lacked even electric outlets. They had been removed after he took to swallowing the lightbulbs. Radio, television, and newspapers were forbidden here. The front of his cell was the standard latticework of thick iron bars. But it had been sheathed in Plexiglas to halt Willie's habit of throwing excrement at his guards. Four video cameras mounted in the narrow, cement-brick corridor outside his cell kept him under surveillance every minute of the day and night, even when he used the toilet or took a shower. The guards who monitored Willie kept a small blackboard on which they chalked the number of days he was condemned to solitary. Any time he bit a nurse who was trying to give him his medication, or whenever he set fire to his cell, the figure increased. At last count, Willie had fifty-five more years in the box, taking him to the year 2046.

Willie did not look dangerous. He is slight, five feet nine inches tall and at most one hundred fifty pounds, when he is not on a deprivation diet of bread, cabbage, and water. He has cherubic features and a quick, boyish grin accentuated by deep puckish dimples at both corners of his mouth. His large, lively eyes convey an infectious enthusiasm. His voice is strong and deep and persuasive. When he was a boy, some of his teachers thought he could have been president, he had so much charm and intelligence. His IQ breached the genius level.

Unhappily, there was the matter of his criminal record. He had first been sent away to reform school by a judge at age nine. That was after he heaved a typewriter out of a school window at a pregnant teacher.

No reformatory or mental institution could hold him for long. He assaulted his social workers with scissors or metal chairs, set other inmates on fire, or escaped by driving off in state vehicles, his legs seemingly too short to reach the controls and his head not high enough to see over the dashboard. Psychiatrists prescribed antipsychotic drugs; they had no effect.

By the age of fifteen, Willie claimed he had committed two thousand crimes, including two hundred armed robberies and twenty-five stabbings. Even allowing for youthful braggadocio, the figure was impressive.

In the spring of his fifteenth season, Willie shot and killed two men on the subway in Manhattan. The murders should not have happened. Willie was supposed to have been under the supervision of the Division for Youth, New York's juvenile justice agency. Afterward, Willie laughed about the killings. "I shot people, that's all," he said. "I don't feel nothing." He was sentenced to the maximum the law allowed—five years in a state training school.

The murders made Willie a celebrity. Mayor Ed Koch branded him "a mad dog killer." More important, the shootings made Willie a precursor of the terrifying surge of children who kill in the waning hours of the twentieth century. In New York, revulsion over Willie's acts and the brevity of his sentence frightened the legislature into swiftly passing a new law that enabled the state to try juveniles as young as thirteen for murder as if they were adults. It came to be known as the Willie Bosket law; it was the first such statute in the country. Soon, as the epidemic of children with guns spread, other states copied the New York model.

As an adult, Willie continued his campaign of terror even while incarcerated. In 1988, he stabbed a prison guard in the chest with a five-and-a-half-inch shank, a homemade stiletto. Willie picked the visiting room for the assault, in front of more than one hundred people. He had never seen the guard before, nor did he know his victim's name, Earl Porter.

At his trial, Willie cheerfully admitted his guilt. "To this day," he told the jury, "the only regret Bosket has is not having killed Earl Porter and spitting on his corpse." The reason for the stabbing, Willie said, was that he had been incarcerated since he was nine years old and prisons had become his surrogate mother. Consequently, Willie proclaimed, "I am only a monster created by the system."

Willie's testimony caught the attention of an editor at *The New York Times*, E. R. Shipp. Shipp, one of the first African-American editors at the *Times*, wondered what made Willie so violent, and she thought his story might provide an insight into why so many young people in our inner cities have taken to killing. Scanning the newsroom for a reporter, for some reason she fixed on me.

I accepted the assignment with misgiving. Little in my professional training or experience, most of which involved fifteen years working in Asia, prepared me for it. I was also ambivalent about Willie. Some journalists, intent on writing about criminals, end up being seduced by them and become their publicists. Still, I had lived as a boy in the old segregated South—when there were "white" and "colored" drinking fountains and chain gangs working the roads in striped pajamas—and I had become enthralled by African-American history, reading as much as was available in the restricted era before the civil rights movement. Perhaps Willie offered an unexpected way to revisit my youthful interest and at the same time to try to come to grips with the topic that was transfixing Americans—why our country is so violent.

Fortuitously, Willie himself had begun to ponder the same question. He knew it was too late to save himself, but he watched with alarm as his favorite niece, a bright, ebullient nine-year-old, started to get into trouble at school. He wanted to do something to stop her and other children from following his path.

So when I wrote to Willie, he answered immediately and arranged a visit, putting me on his short visitors list at Woodbourne Correctional Facility, the state prison where he was kept. "Any so-called civilized society should be extremely concerned with the sociological, criminological, penological, and hereditary implications involved in the Willie Bosket story," he wrote. He had a habit of referring to himself in the third person. It made him seem grander, adding heft to his already large legend.

On inspection, Woodbourne was an odd choice as the place to hold Willie. It was not even a maximum security prison; it just happened to be where the state could construct a super isolation chamber for its most troublesome inmate. From a distance, the prison looked like a medieval monastery, perched in brooding solitude on a bluff above a narrow valley in the Catskill Mountains. The nearest town, incongruously, was named Liberty. This was the epicenter of the Borscht Belt, where generations of Jewish families from New York once came in the summer to rented cabins or big resorts like Grossinger's. It was here that Danny Kaye, Sid Caesar, and Milton Berle got their start. Assimilation and air-conditioning had destroyed that summer world. Now the local economy depended heavily on a newly thriving industry—state prisons.

In preparation for my arrival, Willie had been handcuffed and mana- cled and trundled out aboard his cell door. Three guards had then put him in an adjacent cell, which had been divided in half by a steel wall. This was where he received visits from his lawyers, his mother, and a handful of friends. Each half of the narrow cell was just wide enough for a chair. A small space had been cut in the partition for viewing, and there were a series of pinprick-size holes for talking. Everything had been covered over with an extra layer of Plexiglas and wire mesh thick enough to prevent raccoons from clawing through.

"Welcome," Willie said exuberantly. "I can get you whatever you want. Ginger ale, juice. I run the show here. The guards aren't going to argue with me." To prove it, he yelled for a corrections officer. "Yo, C.O." The guard came promptly. Willie winked knowingly at me.

Willie's hands were padlocked behind his waist to a wide leather belt and his ankles were in leg irons, but he acted as though he was in command. He seemed to relish the situation, despite his confinement in a tiny, shrunken world. It was as if by some feat of prestidigitation, he had altered reality and was no longer the prisoner. He had made prison into his palace.

Recently, he said, lying awake at night, he had the presentiment that there was something inside him that impelled him to act as he did. He wondered if it was his father. Willie had never met his father, who bore the same formal name, Willie James Bosket. All he knew, as a boy, is what his mother and grandmothers told him—that his father was a mur- derer and that he looked just like him. By the time Willie was born, in fact, his father was already in jail awaiting trial for a double homicide. Whenever young Willie misbehaved, his mother scolded him with the imprecation, "You're going to end up just like your father."

There were other coincidences that intrigued him, Willie confided. Both he and his father had been sent to the same reform school at the age of nine, and both he and his father had been taken to Bellevue Hospital for psychiatric evaluation.

Willie had a story to tell about himself. It was a baleful tale of growing up poor in Harlem, of abuse and emotional neglect, of a chaotic juvenile justice system, and of a reckless obsession with violence. But he knew virtually nothing about his family's background, not even where his own father was born. Willie sensed that the mystery of his family's history might hold important clues to his behavior. We all descend from the past, and no individual exists free from his or her patrimony. So Willie suggested I search for his family's origins, a task he clearly could not perform. He would supply the documents he had amassed about himself: hundreds of pages of juvenile criminal records, psychiatric reports, and trial transcripts. These provided a starting point, a cornucopia of normally confidential information. Where there were gaps—and there were many— Willie would also give me permission to seek the declassification of other sealed files about his own life as well as that of his father, who had died in a shoot-out with sheriff's deputies in 1985.

At the outset of this quest, I thought I would be lucky to get a clear picture of Willie's father. Later, as the research progressed, I discovered that his grandfather, too, had a criminal record, and that his great-grandfather was a legendary badman at the turn of the century. Willie and I discussed each new layer as it was unearthed. Little did we imagine that the story could be traced back to slave times before the Civil War and then, eventually, all the way back to the American Revolution.

What emerged was not just a portrait of the Boskets, but a new account of the origin and growth of violence in the United States. Violence is not, as many people today presume, a recent problem or a peculiarly urban bane; and in its inception it had little to do with race or class, with poverty or education, with television or the fractured family—in short, with most of the usual suspects. Rather, it grew out of a proud culture that flourished in the antebellum rural South, a tradition shaped by whites long before it was adopted and recast by some blacks in reaction to their plight. For its adherents, it served almost as a way of life. And at its heart was a lethal impulse.

PART I

CHAPTER I

"BLOODY EDGEFIELD"

Edgefield . . . has had more dashing, brilliant, romantic figures, statesmen, orators, soldiers, adventurers, daredevils, than any county of South Carolina, if not any rural county in America. . . . They gave to their village and county a character that was South Carolinian, more intense, more fiery, than was found elsewhere.

William Watts Bell, *The State That Forgot*

IN EARLY NOVEMBER 1781, with the outcome of the American Revolution much in doubt, Captain James Butler of the South Carolina militia got word that a raiding party of Tory loyalists had seized a herd of cattle and a bevy of horses from his neighbors. His fellow settlers at Mount Willing, little more than a forest clearing in the backcountry wilderness, urged him to lead a force to pursue the marauders. Butler demurred. He had been released from eighteen months in a British jail in Charleston only weeks before. He had suffered enough, he said, and his farm needed tending.

Butler had immigrated to the South Carolina backcountry in the early 1760s over the great wagon trail that led from Pennsylvania through the Shenandoah Valley of Virginia, then the most heavily traveled road in America. With him came his wife, two sisters, and a growing family, which now numbered eight children in all. The Butlers were of Scotch-Irish descent, part of a huge wave of 250,000 immigrants who arrived in Pennsylvania between 1715 and 1775 from the north of England, Scotland, and northern Ireland. They spoke English, not Gaelic, but had a lilting cadence in their voices, an accent preserved in the speech of the South today. These Scotch-Irish were a poor but proud people who had left their homelands after centuries of incessant warfare. In temperament, they were tough, blunt, touchy, hard-drinking, and pugnacious.

The Butlers' new land in South Carolina was promising. It lay halfway between the Blue Ridge Mountains and the Atlantic Ocean in what would become Edgefield County. There were great primeval forests of oak and hickory and endless stretches of longleaf pine. In the spring, the undergrowth was clothed in splashes of pink, white, and magenta by dogwood and azaleas. Swarms of wild turkeys, geese, ducks, and pigeons darkened the sky. Everywhere there was an abundance of small streams and rivers for water. Along their banks, stands of sugarcane grew in profusion, often reaching higher than a man's head. The red clay soil was rich, good for growing corn and grazing cattle and horses. Some of the settlers experimented with cotton, but until Eli Whitney invented the cotton gin across the nearby Savannah River in Georgia in 1793, separating the seeds from the fiber was too difficult to make it a profitable crop. Still, a few of this first generation in the backcountry, including the Butlers, had already acquired enough wealth to buy black slaves.

But if the land was rich, life had proven vicious. Since 1760, spanning the whole time the Butlers had been in South Carolina, the area around them had been engaged in some of the cruelest fighting in American history. The conflict had started with a massacre in 1760 by Cherokee Indians that killed scores of settlers. In one attack, the seventy-six-year-old grandmother of John C. Calhoun, a future vice president of the United States and the greatest of all the Carolinians, was murdered in an ambush with twenty-two other people.

By 1761, when the Cherokee were defeated, much of the backcountry was devastated. Homeless veterans formed outlaw gangs that abducted young women from their villages and tortured wealthy planters and merchants to make them reveal where they had hidden their valuables. Infuriated by this lawlessness, the more respectable settlers formed themselves into "Regulators" to break up the gangs. It was the first organized vigilante justice in America.

The Regulators succeeded. But they were so brutal that the leading historian of the movement, Richard Maxwell Brown, has argued that "they introduced the strain of violence and extremism that was to be the curse of the upcountry and the nemesis of South Carolina" for more than a century. Often they were sadistic. One group of fifty Regulators who captured a "roguish and troublesome" fellow, said to be a horse thief, stripped him and tied him to a tree with a wagon chain. Then they each took turns giving him ten lashes, for a bloody total of five hundred stripes, to the accompaniment of a drum and fiddle.

An uneasy calm ensued in the early 1770s, but the fighting erupted even more violently with the advent of the American Revolution in 1775. Along with the battles between the Continental and British armies, there was a guerrilla war of family against family and neighbor against neighbor; it was carried on by ambush, atrocity, and plunder. "No conflict within the borders of the United States has surpassed the South Carolina Back Country civil war in cruelty and bitterness," it has been said.

Some of the militia on both sides—the Tories and the Revolutionaries, or Whigs—were in the war explicitly for booty. Two of the leading South Carolina Whig officers, Andrew Pickens and Thomas Sumter, made plunder part of their troops' pay. "Each Colonel to receive three grown negroes and one small negro," one set of instructions advertised. "Each Major to receive three grown negroes; Captain two grown negroes; Lieutenants one large and one small negro; the Staff one large and one small negro; the Sergeants one and a quarter negro; each private one grown negro."

The most sanguinary episode in the backcountry feuding came in 1781 as a troop of three hundred Tory militia cavalry under Major William Cunningham, known as "Bloody Bill," moved out of British headquarters in Charleston, passed through the American lines, and advanced up the Saluda River on Mount Willing, where the Butlers lived. In background, Cunningham was much like Captain Butler. He, too, was of Scotch-Irish descent and had emigrated down the wagon trail from Pennsylvania and Virginia, settling with a group of his relatives only a few miles from Mount Willing. He had fought with Butler in some of the same battles against the Cherokee and at the outset of the Revolution had joined the colonists against the British. But he changed sides abruptly in 1778 after he received word that his brother, who was lame and an epileptic, had been whipped to death by a Whig militia captain.

On a vengeful raid, Bloody Bill's troop stole the horses and cattle from Captain Butler's neighbors. Butler's reluctance to join in the pursuit was finally overcome by a plea from his nineteen-year-old son, James, who refused to take part in the expedition unless his experienced father headed it. The Revolutionaries soon overtook a small band of Cunningham's raiders and recaptured their animals. The elated men stopped at dusk at a tavern ten miles southeast of Mount Willing near Cloud's Creek. The creek itself was named for a family that had been killed by the Cherokee a few years earlier. Thinking themselves safe, and unaware of the size of the rest of Bloody Bill's force, the colonists passed the night drinking happily, without posting a sentinel.

Early the next morning, while still drunk, Butler's men were roused by the tavernkeeper's daughter, who saw Cunningham's troops approaching. It was three hundred against thirty, and Cunningham had them surrounded. The Tory major demanded a surrender. But the younger James Butler was suspicious of the enemy commander and told his companions that he "would settle the terms of the capitulation." At that, he fired his flintlock rifle, killing a Tory and setting off a general fusillade. James himself was mortally wounded while he knelt to prepare a second shot. As he lay dying, he handed the rifle to his father, who kept firing until he had exhausted all the balls in his pouch.

An unconditional surrender was arranged. The Revolutionaries were made to stand on a ladder suspended as a bench, and Bloody Bill then ordered that they all be put "to the unsparing sword." Captain Butler grabbed a pitchfork and tried to defend himself, until a saber stroke severed his right hand. Only two of the thirty men escaped.

Cunningham continued his raid up the Saluda River, massacring several more groups of settlers. At Mount Willing, Mrs. Sarah Smith, a sister of Captain Butler's, led a group of wives, mothers, and sisters to bury the dead. Only Captain Butler, with his severed hand, and his son were recognizable. The rest of the men were placed in a common grave, dug by the victims' slaves.

Major Cunningham fled South Carolina after the Revolution; one of his lieutenants, Matthew Love, did not. In November 1784, three years to the day after the Cloud's Creek massacre, Love was pardoned by a judge in accordance with the terms of the peace treaty with England. A crowd led by Butler's oldest son, William, was waiting at the courthouse. While the sheriff watched, the mob took Love outside and hanged him from a tree.

It was not until almost a century later, after the Civil War, that the African-Americans kept as slaves at Mount Willing were publicly identified. Before emancipation, virtually no records gave the surnames of slaves in South Carolina because, by law, slaves were deemed "chattels personal in the hands of their owners." As a South Carolina court succinctly put it, "they are, generally speaking, not considered as persons but as things." When slaveholders referred to their bondsmen at all, on bills of sale or in inventories of their plantations, they listed only the slave's first name. But in 1868, the name of Willie Bosket's great-great-grandfather, Aaron Bosket, appeared on the voter registration rolls for Mount Willing precinct, Edgefield County. It was the first election in which the former slaves were allowed to vote and the first public recording of Willie's family. Willie's ancestors had not chosen to live in Edgefield— they had been sold into slavery there—and legally they did not exist. Nonetheless, they tilled Edgefield soil, and as the years passed and generations of Boskets followed one another, they came to feel that the county was their home as much as it was the Butlers'. Like the white families, they came to be part of Edgefield. Aaron, born into hard servitude, had a phrase for it that he took from an old spiritual: "We are all God's children."

• • •

THE CLOUD'S CREEK MASSACRE and the era of violence in the backcountry from 1760 to the 1780s left an unhappy stamp on the early settlers. The physical destruction alone was awful; Edgefield was a wasteland. A minister who had fled another heavily fought-over district along the coast and returned at the end of the war found that "all was desolation." Every field, every plantation, he wrote, "showed marks of ruin and devastation. Not a person was to be met with in the roads." Society itself, he thought,

> seems to be at an end. . . . Robberies and murders are often committed on the public roads. The people that remain have been peeled, pillaged and plundered. . . . A dark melancholy gloom appears everywhere, and the morals of the people are almost entirely extirpated.

Inland, in the backcountry, it was worse, particularly around Mount Willing. John A. Chapman, a historian who was born in Edgefield early in the nineteenth century, said, "I doubt whether any part of the State, or of the United States, suffered more from the strife between Whig and Tory than did this particular section of Edgefield."

The constant fighting, looting, and killing left many people with a numbed, often casual attitude toward violence. Soon, the county acquired a reputation as "Bloody Edgefield" because of its high number of murders. Judge Thomas J. Mackey, who rode the South Carolina circuit, presiding over the regular fall and spring sessions of court week in Edgefield, said facetiously, "I am going to hold court in Edgefield, and I expect a somewhat exciting term, as the fall shooting is about to start."

Mason L. "Parson" Weems, an itinerant writer best known for the biography of George Washington that invented the pleasant fiction of little George and the cherry tree, visited Edgefield to peddle his books. He was inspired to pen a sensational tract, *The Devil in Petticoats, or God's Revenge Against Husband Killing.* It told the tale of Becky Cotton, an Edgefield lady who murdered her three husbands and deposited their bodies in a pool near her house. "Oh mercy!" Parson Weems began. "What! Old Edgefield again! Another murder in Old Edgefield! . . . Well, the Lord have mercy upon Old Edgefield! For sure it must be Pandemonium itself, a very district of Devils."

Cotton was the name of Becky's third husband. She killed her first spouse by running a mattress needle through his heart; the second she poisoned; Cotton's head she split with an ax. Put on trial in 1806, she "came off clear," Weems discovered. Her tears and beauty, he said, conquered the judge and jury. One juror even became her fourth husband. In the end, though, Becky Cotton was killed by one of her brothers.

Judge John Belton O'Neall, a distinguished South Carolina jurist, recalled attending his first court session at Edgefield not long after the Becky Cotton trial. "The dockets were enormous," he said, with more than two hundred cases, a huge number for an agricultural county with a total population of twenty-four thousand whites and blacks. Edgefield's biggest town was Edgefield Court House, also known as Edgefield Village, with a mere three hundred inhabitants.

Determining crime rates in antebellum South Carolina is necessarily inexact; contemporary judges, juries, and sheriffs had limited interest in keeping statistics. But some rough estimates can be made. One careful study of judicial records for the period from 1800 to 1860 found that the murder rate in South Carolina, an overwhelmingly rural, agrarian area, was four times higher than that in Massachusetts, then the most urban, industrial state. This goes against a central theorem of modern criminology, which predicts higher homicide rates in densely populated urban regions, where crowding and anonymity break down traditional social ties and values. In South Carolina, prosecutions for all crimes of violence—including assault and rape as well as murder—made up almost sixty percent of the court cases, but only eighteen percent in Massachusetts, where the most common criminal acts were theft and public drunkenness. The records also show that the vast majority of people put on trial for violent crimes in antebellum South Carolina were whites; the slaves were thought to be a gentle people.

If the murder rate in South Carolina was high compared with the North, one scholar has suggested it was even higher in Edgefield, perhaps double the state average.

The prevalence of murder in Edgefield in the mid-nineteenth century can be crudely measured through the county coroners' reports of juries of inquest. From 1844 to 1858, the Edgefield coroners officially recorded sixty-five murders. That is probably an undercount, since a number of deaths were attributed to natural causes or "acts of God" that by a less charitable interpretation might have been the result of deliberate violence, such as a person who drowned after being beaten. Nevertheless, that works out to an annual rate of 18 murders per 100,000 inhabitants. In 1992, according to the FBI's Uniform Crime Reports, only one state in the entire country, Louisiana, approached this figure, with a homicide rate of 17.4 per 100,000.

These figures for antebellum Edgefield might be dismissed as an anomaly, given the county's small size. But Edgefield was part of the

South, and every statistical measure in the years that have followed has shown that the South, not the "Wild West" as popularly believed, was the most violent region of the United States. H. V. Redfield, a correspondent for the Cincinnati *Commercial* stationed in the South after the Civil War, was so struck by the frequency of murder there that he put together the first quantitative study of the subject in 1880, using figures gleaned from local newspaper reports. By his calculations, in 1878 the three Southern states of South Carolina, Kentucky, and Texas (which was then settled mostly by Southerners) numbered between 12.2 and 28.8 murders per 100,000 citizens. In urban Massachusetts that year, the rate was only 1.4. Vermont and New Hampshire, two Northern states that were predominantly agricultural, like most of the South, recorded only a single murder between them in 1878, Redfield pointed out. South Carolina had 128. Even New York City averaged only 3 to 7 homicides per 100,000 throughout the nineteenth century. "Have we not here two civilizations?" Redfield asked. He was the first of a series of writers and scholars to suggest that the South had produced a culture of violence.

The statistical differences persisted. In 1933, the year the federal government first published homicide data for the entire country, the ten states with the highest murder rates were all Southern or border states that had been involved in the Confederacy, from Virginia to Texas. South Carolina's homicide rate was almost four times the national average.

Over the years, many theories have been advanced for the South's propensity for violence. One is fanciful—that the region's hot climate produced hot tempers. Others offer what may be parts of the explanation. At least since Frederick Law Olmsted journeyed through the South in the 1850s and penned his three-volume work, *The Cotton Kingdom*, writers have pointed to the persistence of frontier conditions in the South. The frontier bred lawlessness, according to this thesis, and Southern plantation agriculture, with its widely scattered settlements and paucity of roads, bridges, and schools, remained a frontier until after the Civil War. Edgefield, with its early history of backcountry fighting, seems to support the theory. But not all parts of the South shared this gory military history. And recent studies of the American West contradict the stereotypes of pervasive violence in cattle towns there. In fact, the bloodshed that erupted on the Western frontier may have been Southern violence brought in via Texas.

Another contributor to Southern bellicosity was the heavy influx of Scotch-Irish among the region's settlers. These immigrants shocked the good Quakers of Pennsylvania, where they first arrived in the new world. Benjamin Franklin chastised them for being "white savages." Their way of life was an outgrowth of seven centuries of fighting between the kings of England and Scotland over the borderlands they inhabited. They had grown inured to their towns being sacked and burned and their kinsmen tortured to death. Many had been forcibly resettled in Ireland. When they came to America, they brought with them a penchant for family feuds, a love of whiskey, and a warrior ethic that demanded vengeance. Their prevailing principle, "lex talionis," the rule of retaliation, helps explain the Cloud's Creek massacre and the bloodiness of the fighting in the South Carolina backcountry from 1760 to 1785.

One of their favorite sports was a savage form of wrestling, or "wrassling," which evolved in Virginia into "rough and tumble" and in South Carolina into "knock down and drag out." An Irish traveler, Thomas Ashe, described a fight between a Virginian and a Kentuckian. The contestants were asked if they wanted to "fight fair" or "rough and tumble." When they replied "rough and tumble," the crowd roared in approval. The Virginian began by pitching "himself into the bosom of his opponent," sinking his sharpened fingernails into the Kentuckian's head. "The Virginian never lost his hold . . . fixing his claws in his hairs and his thumbs on his eyes," and ripped his opponent's eyes from their sockets. Even after the eyes were gouged out, the fight continued. The Virginian sunk his teeth into the Kentuckian's nose and bit it in two pieces. He then tore off the Kentuckian's ears. Finally, the "Kentuckian, deprived of eyes, ears and nose, gave in." The victor, though maimed and bloodied himself, was carried around the grounds by the crowd.

In an effort to halt this pastime, South Carolina in 1786 made any defendant found guilty of premeditated mayhem subject to the death penalty. Mayhem was defined as "violently depriving" another person of a member of his body, excepting the ears and nose. The ears and nose were excluded because their loss only disfigured the victim. Despite the severity of the law, gouging flourished. Judge Aedanus Burke, who worked the Edgefield circuit, was appalled by the number of one-eyed men in his courtroom. "Before God, gentlemen of the jury, I never saw such a thing before in the world!" he once exclaimed. "There is a plaintiff with an eye out! A juror with an eye out! And two witnesses with an eye out! What a state of society you must have in this part of the country!"

Behind this brutality lay an ethic of "primal honor," brought with the Scotch-Irish to the new world. It had its roots in the blood feuds between families and clans dating to the Middle Ages. Above all, honor meant reputation; a man's worth resided in the opinion of others. Honor also meant valor; a man had to be prepared to fight to defend his honor if challenged or insulted. This concern with honor produced "rough and tumble" and an abundance of assaults and murders among the proletariat in the backcountry.

The slaveholding gentry of Virginia and the aristocracy of low-country South Carolina, along the coast, had developed a similar code in seeking to copy the manners of the English ruling class. "In the sixteenth and seventeenth centuries tempers were short and weapons to hand," Lawrence Stone has written.

> The behavior of the propertied classes, like that of the poor, was characterized by the ferocity, childishness and lack of self-control of the Homeric age. . . . The educational and social system of the age inculcated ideals of honour and generosity. Impulsiveness was not reproved, readiness to repay an injury real or imagined a sign of spirit. . . . Moreover, a gentleman carried a weapon at all times, and did not hesitate to use it.

Thus for the Southern upper class, just as for the lower class, honor became a compelling passion, an overwhelming concern with one's reputation and manliness. For the gentry, honor had an added element of gentility, requiring its adherents to be generous hosts and occasionally to improve their libraries and show religious devotion. But mostly a Southern gentleman was expected to be truthful and to be good at riding horses, playing cards, and handling firearms. Honor brought out both the best and the worst in its apostles. Contemporaries described Southerners as gracious and hospitable, but touchy and pugnacious. For honor required gentlemen to pay great attention to appearances to ensure proper respect, and when that was not forthcoming, violence could quickly erupt. In practice, this meant that it was as intolerable to call a man a liar as to hit or shoot him.

The code of honor reached its apogee in the duel. Dueling had virtually disappeared in the North after Aaron Burr killed Alexander Hamilton in 1804, and even in England, where Southern cavaliers looked for inspiration, dueling declined in the early nineteenth century. But in the South, and especially in South Carolina, the code duello, "affairs of honor," became the accepted means for gentlemen to settle disputes. A gentleman did not go to court; the law was seen as weak. As Andrew Jackson's mother told him when he was young, "The law affords no remedy that can satisfy the feelings of a true man."

There is no record of the number of duels fought, but contemporary accounts suggest they were frequent. William Faux, an English traveler, wrote that in Charleston he had been introduced to thirteen men, eleven of whom "had killed their man" in duels. The editor of the *Gazette* in Camden, South Carolina, saw nothing out of the ordinary in reporting that three duels had taken place there in a single week in 1817.

In 1812, South Carolina outlawed dueling, levying a heavy fine and up to a year in jail for all participants, including seconds. If the duel was fatal, the survivor could be prosecuted for murder. But few men were tried for dueling, and none were convicted of murder. South Carolina law held that homicide could be either "felonious, justifiable or excusable," and juries were always ready to apply the two limitations to the duelist.

The elaborate handbook on which duelists relied, *The Code of Honor*, was written by a former governor of the state, John Lyde Wilson, who deplored the Christian doctrine of turning the other cheek. Such forbearance, he said, is "utterly repugnant to those feelings which nature and education have implanted in the human character." If the antidueling laws were enforced, Wilson insisted, "all that is honorable in the community would quit the country and inhabit the wilderness with the Indians." Duels are necessary, Wilson argued, because "words are no satisfaction for words."

Dueling became a cherished part of culture for many planters. Louis T. Wigfall, the son of a prominent Edgefield family, who had lost one brother in a duel, ran into trouble himself at the University of Virginia when he invited a Southern belle, a Miss Leiper, to dance during a social gathering. She refused, Wigfall was insulted, and so he challenged her escort to a duel. Later, back in Edgefield, he was accused by another young planter, Preston Brooks, of being a coward. Since Brooks was out of town, Wigfall challenged Brooks's father instead. When the older man declined, Wigfall went to the courthouse and, in keeping with the code duello, put up a public notice calling him a scoundrel. He also shot and killed a member of the Brooks clan who tried to tear the note down. Eventually, Wigfall and Preston Brooks met in a duel, leaving both wounded. Each went on to become a Southern hero, Brooks as a congressman from South Carolina, Wigfall as a senator from Texas.

Another of Wigfall's brothers, Arthur, an Episcopal priest, denounced the slaughter produced by all this dueling. "There exists in our country a privileged class, *soi disant*, men of honor, who have established for themselves a higher law," he said in a sermon. "They put their foot upon the criminal code and trample it in the dust. They may and they do commit murder with impunity." Reverend Wigfall had no objection to a privileged class, if it was built on virtue and intelligence. "But we do protest, and shall with our dying breath protest against an aristocracy of crime."

Reverend Wigfall had espied something significant—these cavaliers of honor placed themselves above the law. In the antebellum South, there was a fine line between heroism in the name of honor and criminality, between deeds of valor and acts of violence. Honor could make men brave, or cruel; it could make them nobly rash, or simply self-destructive. Honor was a powerful quotidian force, determining men's destinies and even affecting the course of state and national politics.

THE SAME SENTIMENTS of honor that compelled Louis Wigfall to duel led other citizens of Edgefield into more mundane forms of violence: street fights, drunken brawls, and shootings over card games. These eruptions, known as "personal difficulties," were the most common form of violence in Edgefield and accounted for a large percentage of the county's high murder rate. Southerners' copious consumption of whiskey and the proclivity of most Southern white men to carry firearms, even in the romanticized mint-julep-and-magnolia days of the antebellum period, contributed to the problem. But it took honor, the need to prove one's manhood and protect one's good name, to ignite these fights. "There is no one here but carries arms under his clothes," a young Alabama lawyer told Alexis de Tocqueville in a remark that could have been said in Edgefield. "At the slightest quarrel, knife or pistol comes to hand. These things happen continually; it is a semibarbarous state of society."

In the barroom of Edgefield's Spann Hotel in July 1851, two friends fell into an argument while drinking at the counter. Philip Goode, the more belligerent of the two, accused his friend, William Cloud, of boasting that he could whip Goode in a fight. Cloud denied making the claim and said "he had nothing against him," according to witnesses. One patron recalled that Cloud "tried to retreat as honorably as he could."

But Goode persisted, calling Cloud "a damn liar," the worst offense to honor. Soon, Goode climbed off his bar seat, grabbed Cloud by the coat collar, and fired his "large six barrel revolver" into his friend's chest. The two were so close that the murdered man's coat "took fire from the shot."

"God damn you," Goode swore, standing over the dead man and firing twice more. "That will satisfy you."

The dictates of honor ensnared even members of Edgefield's most esteemed families in "personal difficulties." In July 1856, George Tillman, a lawyer and member of the state legislature, was playing a game of faro in the Planters Hotel. There was a history of violence in his family—his father, a wealthy planter, had once killed a man during a card game, and two of his brothers were shot and killed after insulting gentlemen—and Tillman himself had been in a duel and wounded two men. Now, during the faro game, Tillman got into an argument over how much money he had bet. When a bystander backed his opponent, Tillman denounced him as "a God damn liar" and shot him dead.

At his trial, Tillman was let off with a two-year sentence for manslaughter since the shooting was regarded as unpremeditated. In jail, Tillman was treated more like a guest than a felon; he was given comfortable quarters and allowed the pursuit of a courtship and the resumption of his law practice. Afterward, Tillman was repeatedly elected to Congress. Homicide was no bar to elective office.

Tillman's mild punishment was hardly unusual. In the sixty-five cases of homicide recorded by the Edgefield coroners between 1844 and 1858, only thirty-three people were tried for murder. Eighteen were acquitted, ten were found guilty of the lesser charge of manslaughter, and only five were convicted of murder.

Juries, given the choice of deciding whether a homicide was "felonious, justifiable or excusable," were readily prepared to entertain arguments that a defendant had acted in self-defense or been provoked on a point of honor. They shared the opinion of an Edgefield lawyer who wrote, "We have a sort of honorable crime. . . . Whenever the Southern dagger is drawn, there is something manly and chivalrous in the use of it." Southerners did not think of themselves as lawless; they believed passionately in the Constitution and they took their Bible literally. Both, after all, could be read to justify slavery.

EDGEFIELD TYPIFIED the up-country South, yet there was also something that set it apart, that made Edgefield's residents even more pugnacious, reckless, and prone to shed blood. By the middle of the nineteenth century, mere mention that a person hailed from Edgefield was enough to explain his character to other South Carolinians. During the war between the United States and Mexico in 1846, a South Carolina judge who had volunteered with his state's Palmetto Regiment came across a young soldier busy dodging bullets. "You seem to be rather pert to get out of the way of the bullets," the judge said.

"Wall," replied the soldier, "I don't hanker after bullets as a general thing."

"Then why in the deuce did you come down here?" inquired the judge.

"Wall! you see capen'," replied the stranger, "I b'long to old Edgefield deestrick and I jes' kim here to get away from danger."

A South Carolina journalist later calculated that Edgefield "has had more dashing, brilliant, romantic figures, statesmen, orators, soldiers, adventurers, daredevils, than any county of South Carolina, if not of any rural county in America." Most Edgefield families, he noted,

> were kin, by blood or marriage, and they gave to their village and county a character that was South Carolinian, more intense, more fiery, than was found elsewhere. . . . They seemed to be, if they were not, harder riders, bolder hunters, more enterprising and masterly politicians. Their virtues were shining, their vices flamed. They were not careful reckoners of the future, sometimes they spoke too quickly and so acted, yet in crises an audacity that might have been called imprudence by milder men made them indispensable to the state.

One reason for Edgefield's special character may have been that it was a major point of contact between the up-country Scotch-Irish settlers, who were Presbyterians and Baptists, and the low-country gentry, who were of English stock and Episcopalian. These two peoples each brought its own culture of honor, one coarser, one seemingly more genteel; the resulting mixture was highly combustible, producing a level of tension absent elsewhere in South Carolina.

Edgefield's history also played a role in setting it apart. Many of its famous characters, including George Tillman, descended from the settlers who survived the brutal warfare between 1760 and 1785. They grew up in families where stories of the battles and massacres of that generation were told and retold as a living legacy, and some of them had treasured souvenirs. The eldest son of Captain James Butler, the militia commander killed at Cloud's Creek, narrowly missed capturing his father's nemesis, Bloody Bill Cunningham, in a horse race through the forest; but he did manage to seize the Tory officer's sword and pocketbook. These were handed down in the family. Over time, the early settlers' experiences took shape as legend, and legend grew into the Edgefield tradition. This heritage gave Edgefield a character that made it different from other communities in the South in much the same way that New York is different from Boston, and Los Angeles is different from San Francisco.

It was not just physical violence that Edgefield inherited from the days of the Cloud's Creek massacre. It was also a penchant for political extremism. Edgefield, along with Charleston, South Carolina's only city before the Civil War, produced a disproportionate share of the state's political leaders, most of them "fire-eaters," or pro-secession radicals in the local lexicon. Edgefield was "a breeding ground for the species." Although its white population never exceeded seventeen thousand before 1900, the county turned out ten of South Carolina's nineteenth-century governors. It has also been home to one of South Carolina's two United

States senators for most of the period from 1842 to the present. The incumbent is Strom Thurmond, a native of Edgefield Court House who has been in the Senate since 1954, making him the Senate's most senior member. He originally came to national attention as the rebellious Dixie-crat candidate for president in 1948, opposing Harry Truman as too liberal on civil rights.

During the nineteenth century, these governors and senators, as well as a flock of congressmen from Edgefield, served as key participants at every crucial juncture in South Carolina's radical history. They were ardent advocates of nullification, declaring the tariff of 1828 illegal and proposing to use force against the federal government. In 1860, they helped lead South Carolina and then the South into the Civil War. In 1876, leaders from Edgefield ended Reconstruction in South Carolina by intimidating, killing, and defrauding African-American voters. And in the 1890s, a politician from Edgefield led the effort to impose segregation on South Carolina. Edgefield may have been small in size, but its impact was large. What South Carolina—the hotspur state—was to the nation, Edgefield was to South Carolina.

ONE OF EDGEFIELD'S POLITICIANS was Preston Brooks, the man who fought a duel with Louis Wigfall. Brooks, too, was a descendant of the settlers massacred at Cloud's Creek; his grandmother was a sister of Captain James Butler. Six feet tall, with a proud military record in the Mexican War, Brooks was elected to Congress and once half-humorously proposed that representatives be required to check their firearms in the cloakroom before appearing on the House floor.

On May 19, 1856, he had listened with rising anger as Senator Charles Sumner of Massachusetts, a leading abolitionist, excoriated his cousin, Senator Andrew Pickens Butler, for supporting the pro-slavery govern-ment of Kansas. Speaking from the Senate floor, Sumner branded Butler as the Don Quixote of slavery, a man who "has chosen a mistress to whom he has made his vows, and who, though ugly to others, is always lovely to him . . . the harlot, Slavery." Sumner also mocked the elderly Butler's slight labial paralysis, charging that "with incoherent phrases" he "discharged the loose expectoration of his speech." Brooks was further outraged by Sumner's claim that South Carolina suffered a "shameful imbecility from Slavery."

The Massachusetts senator had "insulted South Carolina and Judge Butler grossly," Brooks wrote to his brother. Under the code of honor, Butler was obliged to flog Sumner, but "this Butler is unable to do," Brooks reasoned, because Sumner was thirty pounds heavier and in more robust health. "Under the circumstances," Brooks concluded, "I felt it to be my duty to relieve Butler and avenge the insult to my State."

Although Sumner's remarks were slanderous, Brooks did not even consider bringing a lawsuit. This was a matter of personal honor. Nor did Brooks think of challenging the Massachusetts senator to a duel, feeling that since an abolitionist was "incapable of courage," Sumner would not accept. But mainly Brooks would not challenge Sumner because, under the code duello, a duel must be between social equals. Brooks did not want to grant Sumner that respectability. The punctilio of honor also ruled out Brooks's using a pistol or sword to punish an insulting inferior. In the end, the instrument he chose was a gold-headed gutta-percha walking stick given him by a friend.

On May 22, Brooks found Sumner at his desk in the Senate, autographing printed copies of his speech for admirers. Brooks was fuming with anger, but honor required that he wait until some ladies who were in the visitors gallery left the chamber. At last, "under the highest sense of duty," he approached Sumner.

"I have read your speech twice over carefully," Brooks began. "It is a libel on South Carolina, and Mr. Butler, who is a relative of mine." Sumner tried to rise from his desk, but his long legs were tucked under it and it was bolted to the floor. Before the senator could move, Brooks gave Sumner "a slight blow" with the smaller end of his cane. When Sumner tried to cover his head with his arms, Brooks felt "compelled to strike him harder than he had intended," raining down blow after blow.

Blood was now streaming from Sumner's head. Finally, with a huge effort, he ripped the desk from the floor and staggered down the aisle semiconscious. "Toward the last he bellowed like a calf," Brooks told his brother. "I wore out my cane completely."

It took Sumner three years to recover from his wounds, and the assault polarized the nation. Northerners were outraged; protest meetings were held in virtually every city and dozens of small towns. In the South, Brooks became an instant hero. "Every Southern man sustains me," he wrote his brother. "The fragments of the stick are begged for as sacred relics." In Charleston, a group of merchants bought a new cane for Brooks, which they inscribed, "Hit him again."

The news even made its way to the slaves on his plantation in Edgefield, where some of them regarded "Marse Preston" as a hero. "One day he marched right in de Senate, wid his gold head cane, and beat a Senator til him fainted," recalled an ex-slave many years later. It was " 'bout sumpin' dat Senator say 'bout him old kinsman, Senator Butler," the former slave remembered. "Dat turn de world up side down."

The House of Representatives moved to expel Brooks but fell well

short of the two-thirds vote required; ominously, every Southern congressman but one supported Brooks. In a gesture of bravado, Brooks resigned
anyway and was reelected overwhelmingly.

The incident underscored how strongly the dictates of honor governed
life in Edgefield. To Northerners, Brooks's attack had been brutal and
lawless, a criminal act. To Southerners, Brooks had been a gentleman,
justifiably defending a relative and his state. As Brooks himself explained,
"Public opinion distinguishes between crime and honorable resentment."
In coming years, the code of honor would persist and deeply influence
all those who lived in Edgefield. Honor, along with violence, was part of
the region's heritage.

CHAPTER 2

MASTERS AND SLAVES

It is African slavery that makes every white man in some sense a lord. . . .
Here the division is between white free men and black slaves, and every
white is, and feels that he is a MAN.

Edgefield *Advertiser*, December 12, 1850

O N A SPRING DAY in 1834, a South Carolina planter's wife recorded in a letter that her aging father had gone to Columbia and
bought a female slave. It was a casual purchase, unplanned and considered
of little consequence by the family. "He bought a negro and paid for her
in cotton," Ann Wadlington wrote about her father, Thomas Bauskett.
"He has to deliver it in Columbia on Monday."

About the same year, Bauskett's son, John, an ambitious Edgefield
planter, acquired a young slave boy named Ruben. John Bauskett, then
forty-five years old, had several sources for buying slaves. Some he purchased at estate sales of his friends or neighbors after their deaths. From
the heirs of Christian Breithaupt, he bought the "Negro Eliza and Vin-
cent" for nine hundred dollars and "Little John" for eight hundred
dollars. Additionally, Bauskett picked up an old horse named "Charley"
for twenty-six dollars, a copy of the *Life of Washington* for ten dollars,
and six bottles of ketchup for twenty-five cents. Slaves could also be
found at sheriffs' sales when a planter was delinquent on a debt. Sheriff
H. Boulware announced in an ad in the Edgefield *Advertiser* that he would
sell six slaves and four horses to settle several lawsuits. The wording of
the ad makes it clear that most of the slaves were being sold individually,
without their families. "Two negro slaves by the name of George and
Spencer" were to be auctioned off in one lot, and "One negro girl slave
by the name of Louisa" in another. In a third lot, a slave mother and
her son were to be sold, "Trulove and her child by the name of Maximil-
lion." No mention was made of the father.

Bauskett was on his way to becoming a very large slaveholder—by

1850, he owned 221 African-Americans—and he needed a steady, reliable means of supply. For this he turned to professional slave dealers, called "Negro speculators," or visited the slave markets in Charleston, Columbia, or Hamburg, a bustling entrepôt on the South Carolina side of the Savannah River just across the stream from Augusta. Many of these speculators specialized in buying slaves in the upper South, the older part of the region, including Virginia, Maryland, and North Carolina, then driving the bondsmen overland in coffles and reselling them in the newer, still expanding reaches of the lower South, from South Carolina and Georgia to Alabama, Mississippi, and Texas. There were at least eight such firms that dealt in the long-distance slave trade in Edgefield, and their ads appeared frequently in the *Advertiser*. "Negroes, Negroes," began one notice. "A fresh lot of likely Negroes will be received every week, through the season by us. We have on hand at this time a first-rate blacksmith and tanner. Give us a call and examine our stock."

It was from one of these slave dealers that Bauskett acquired young Ruben, who had been born in the mid-1820s. Later, Ruben would take the name Bauskett as his own, not out of fondness for John Bauskett but simply because Bauskett was the first master Ruben could recall, and the name gave him a sense of historical identity and family pride. Over the years, it would be spelled in different ways, since the slaves were kept illiterate by law and local whites who kept the records were not particular about how it was written. Eventually, in the early twentieth century, Bauskett became Bosket.

Precisely where Ruben was born is unknown, but it was somewhere in the upper South where his former master sold him off to a dealer, without his mother, father, or any siblings. He was placed in a slave coffle and herded south. Another slave, Charles Ball, who was sold by his master in Maryland about 1805 and marched overland in a coffle for resale in South Carolina, has left a vivid account of the experience. A young father, Ball was sold so abruptly that he was not allowed even to say goodbye to his wife or children. Instead, he was added to a trove of fifty-one other bondsmen.

> The women were merely tied together with a rope, about the size of a bed cord, which was tied like a halter around the neck of each; but the men, of whom I was the stoutest and strongest, were very differently caparisoned. A strong iron collar was closely fitted by means of a padlock round each of our necks. A chain of iron, about a hundred feet in length, was passed through the hasp of each padlock. . . . In addition to this, we were handcuffed in pairs. In this manner we were chained alternately by the right and left hand; and

the poor man to whom I was thus ironed wept like an infant when the blacksmith with his heavy hammer fastened the ends of the bolts that kept the staples from slipping from our arms.

The slave coffles were marched, under the threat of whips and wooden paddles, an average of twenty miles a day.

We had no clothes except those we wore, and a few blankets; the larger portion of our gang being in rags. . . . Two of the women were pregnant; one far advanced—and she already complained of inability to keep pace with our march; but her complaints were disregarded.

When coffles arrived in Hamburg, twenty miles south of Edgefield, they were kept in a large brick building with holding pens. A former slave who saw other bondsmen sold there recalled, "They put 'em up on something like a table, bid 'em off just like you would do horses or cows. . . . They would sell a mother from her children." According to family legend, it was in Hamburg that Ruben was purchased by John Bauskett.

Ruben was part of a huge long-distance traffic in slaves. Between the 1820s, when it can first be measured, and 1860, some 200,000 slaves were sold into the trade each decade. For a slave in the upper South, this meant that the cumulative chances over a lifetime of being sold and shipped to the deep South were about 30 percent. Ruben was typical of those slaves sold into the trade: he was young and strong, "a likely Negro," as the ads proclaimed, who would fetch more by the pound. The speculators had no interest in buying whole families, since they might include bondsmen too young, too old, or too weak to bring maximum profit.

In South Carolina, the danger of being sold was especially high, for not only were large numbers of bondsmen being brought into the state in the early part of the nineteenth century to till the newly opened cotton lands, but by the 1830s, many slaves were also being sold off to the even more promising areas with fresh soil farther south, from Georgia to Texas. In such a state, by the best estimate, it would have been rare for a slave to survive into middle age without being sold either locally or into the long-distance trade.

All this traffic in slaves, and the vast force needed to run a society based on bondage, was another major contributor to violence in the South. Slavery had a brutalizing effect that fell on both the bondsmen and their masters.

Charles Ball noticed it. "It seems to be a law of nature that slavery is equally destructive to the master and the slave," he wrote. "For, whilst it stupefies the latter with fear, and reduces him below the condition of man, it brutalizes the former, by the practice of continual tyranny; and makes him the prey of all the vices which render human nature loathsome."

Slavery had a particularly corrosive influence on South Carolina because no other state was as profoundly involved in the "peculiar institution," as Southerners called it. South Carolina was unique among Britain's colonies on the mainland of North America in that slaves were present from its founding. The first permanent settlers landed near what would become Charleston, named for King Charles II, in the spring of 1670 under the command of an affluent English sugar planter from Barbados, Sir John Yeamans. Among them was "one lusty negro man . . . and an oversear [sic]." By the second summer of settlement, almost half of the whites and more than half of the blacks in South Carolina had come from Barbados, which had been colonized earlier in the seventeenth century. "The Barbadians endeavour to rule all," wrote John Locke, the English philosopher who also served as secretary to the "true Lords and Proprietors" of Carolina, the English nobles who had been given the land by King Charles. In fact, South Carolina became something of an offshoot of Barbados and took on a Caribbean caste, with a heavy reliance on slavery and a political system dominated by a ring of émigré Barbados planters.

This dependence became more pronounced after the discovery in the 1690s that rice could be grown in the marshy, tidal waters of the lowcountry, along the Atlantic Ocean, and exported for immense profits to Europe. So close was the connection between Barbados and South Carolina that even after 1700, English documents occasionally referred to "Carolina in ye West Indies."

The link to Barbados gave Charleston architecture its piazzas for shade and cool breezes in the semitropical heat, to which Englishmen were unaccustomed. It also imparted a more exploitative mentality to South Carolina's slaveholders than existed in the other mainland colonies. And the number of slaves grew dramatically. Sullivan's Island, a sandy spit on the northeast edge of Charleston harbor where incoming slaves were briefly quarantined, became the Ellis Island of black Americans. More than 40 percent of all the slaves imported into the British mainland colonies between 1700 and 1775 arrived in South Carolina. By 1860, on the eve of the Civil War, 59 percent of South Carolina's populace was black, the highest proportion of any state. Equally important, almost half of South Carolina's white families owned slaves, again the highest figure in the country.

South Carolina's heavy dependence on slavery had momentous consequences. It helped make the white inhabitants of the low-country the richest population in British North America, if not the entire world. By an economist's measurement, the mean per capita wealth among whites in the colony's most populous district in 1775 was the equivalent of $126,844 in 1978 dollars.

Such a huge number of slaves also created chronic fears of servile insurrection. With the atmosphere so charged, any division in the white community became anathema, and a culture of conformity spread across the state, tying wealthy planters to poor whites and the old aristocratic low-country to the brash, upstart backcountry areas like Edgefield.

The settlement of the up-country, which came after the devastation of the 1760 to 1785 period, occurred with remarkable speed. The key changes were the invention of the cotton gin in 1793 and the revolution in British textile manufacturing, which together created an enormous world market for short-staple cotton. Up-country South Carolina was fortuitously situated to become the center of the South's first cotton boom. Its loam-covered clay contained many nutrients, and cotton could be shipped down the Savannah River for easy export. White farmers and planters rushed to take advantage of this bonanza. Whereas in 1793 all of South Carolina produced only ninety-four thousand pounds of cotton, and that mostly of the luxurious long-staple variety grown on the sea islands, by 1811 the up-country alone exported more than thirty million pounds of short-staple cotton. It was fitting that a planter from Edgefield, James Henry Hammond, would coin the phrase that came to define the South, boasting that there, "Cotton is king."

Among the farmers who stampeded into the up-country in the 1790s was Thomas Bauskett, then known as Thomas Baskett. Like the Butlers and so many of the up-country settlers, he was of Scotch-Irish heritage. Cotton quickly made him prosperous; by 1810, he had acquired ten slaves. He also changed the spelling of his last name to Bauskett. Perhaps it was an effort to make the name sound Huguenot, since many of the wealthiest families in the low-country around Charleston were of Huguenot extraction, and this lent the rough backwoods farmer more cachet. Or perhaps it was simply a result of the poor level of spelling at the time in the up-country. Andrew Jackson, another Scotch-Irishman, himself born on the western border of North and South Carolina, once declared that he could never respect a man who knew only one way to spell a word.

To solidify his newly won status as a member of the gentry, Bauskett sent his son John to South Carolina College in Columbia, where the offspring of the state's elite were groomed for future leadership. Upon graduation, John Bauskett followed a pattern typical of many aspiring planters—he became a lawyer, invested heavily in land, acquiring thousands of acres, and ran successfully for the state legislature. He was also an early Southern industrialist—he started a bank, operated a privately owned bridge and a ferry, bought one of South Carolina's first cotton textile mills, and tried to win financing for a railroad to link Edgefield with South Carolina's growing network of railways.

The young slave boy Ruben was just one of Bauskett's manifold acquisitions. This was Bauskett's problem. He was too much the entrepreneur, his attention diverted by his business ventures, his law practice, and politics. He acknowledged in a letter to his sister, Ann, that he could only "occasionally superintend" his major plantation, which lay along the Savannah River near Hamburg. He left it in charge of an overseer named Benjamin Franklin. It was to this plantation that Ruben had been sent after his purchase. At one point, Bauskett was so anxious to raise money for a business venture that he risked 138 of his slaves by pledging them as collateral for a small loan that amounted to a mere fraction of their value.

His lack of interest in running a plantation, along with his disappointment that Edgefield was being bypassed by South Carolina's growing spine of railroads, led Bauskett to an important decision in late 1852—to sell his big plantation on the Savannah and move to Columbia, then beginning to boom as a railroad center. Besides, his brother-in-law had just been appointed to direct construction of the new state capitol building, the biggest business project in the state. Columbia, he calculated, was more suited to a man of his ambitions. On December 29, 1852, the following ad appeared in the Edgefield *Advertiser* under John Bauskett's name:

> Valuable Land & Negroes for Sale.
>
> Being about to remove from this part of the country, the subscriber offers for sale his plantation on the Savannah River, in Edgefield District. It is situated about eight or ten miles above Augusta and contains three thousand five hundred acres. On the premises are two settlements or quarters, two gin houses, cotton screws and a grist mill.

Almost as an afterthought, Bauskett added, "To an approved purchaser the subscriber would also sell from one to two hundred Negroes, mostly in families."

FOR THE SECOND TIME, Ruben was being sold, his life subject to the whim of his master. Fortuitously, the purchaser was another Edgefield resident, Francis W. Pickens, who bought the plantation and about one hundred of the slaves. For the time being, Pickens left all the bondsmen in place.

Although Pickens was not born in Edgefield, its tradition and that of the up-country was in his blood. His family were Scotch-Irish, and his grandfather, Andrew Pickens, was one of the South Carolina militia generals in the Revolution who paid their recruits with slaves seized from Tories. One of his grandfather's brothers had been captured by Tories, handed over to the Indians, and burned to death. William Butler, a son of the Revolutionary commander slaughtered at Mount Willing, was an officer under Andrew Pickens and named one of his own sons in honor of the general, Andrew Pickens Butler. It was Andrew Pickens Butler who, years later, as a senator from South Carolina, became the subject of the quarrel between Charles Sumner and Preston Brooks.

Francis Pickens was a man of considerable intellect, though not of prepossessing appearance. A journalist once described him as

> short and squarely built, with a large and squarish head, a broad and flat face, a small and insignificant nose, round and piggish eyes, and broad high forehead. He has a bristly iron-gray moustache and chin whiskers, and wears a brown wig—whereby there is a peculiar and noticeable contrast.

In temperament, he was like many members of the South Carolina gentry. He could be romantic and served as a splendid host at Edgewood, his rambling plantation house, stocked with imported clocks, chandeliers, and china. But Pickens had little personal warmth. John C. Calhoun, his cousin and political mentor, said of Pickens that he "has a strong enfusion of envy, jealousy and vanity in his composition." Pickens himself once confessed, "I believe it is my destiny to be disliked by all who know me well."

Pickens was a staunch defender of slavery and South Carolina, "Mother Carolina," he called it, in accord with the notions of chivalry. As a student at South Carolina College in the 1820s, he became an early apostle of the new doctrine of states' rights and strict construction of the Constitution, arguing that South Carolina should "nullify" protectionist federal tariffs on Northern manufactured goods, which Southern cotton planters thought would ruin them. He confessed he was "for any extreme, even war to the hilt rather than go down to infamy and slavery with a government of unlimited powers."

This was extremism of the kind familiar in the Edgefield tradition, and Pickens would only become more radical as slavery, rather than the federal tariff, soon emerged as the critical issue. In January 1831, William Lloyd Garrison launched the *Liberator*; Nat Turner's slave rebellion took place later that year in Virginia. These developments convinced South Carolinians that they were under assault from the North. Pickens, who had been elected to the state legislature at the age of twenty-five in 1832, sounded the alarm. "We have a peculiar and local institution . . . of great delicacy and momentous concern to the very vitals of our society," he said in a report on a proposed oath of allegiance to South Carolina. "If there be any citizen of South Carolina who . . . should refuse or hesitate to swear allegiance to the mother that has cherished or protected him, he deserves to be an offcast and wanderer upon the earth."

Such militancy made Pickens popular, and with Calhoun's sponsorship, he was elected to Congress the next year, 1833. In Washington, he spent years championing the cause of slavery and making ever more apocalyptic pronouncements. In a speech to the House in 1836, he repudiated the doctrine of the equality of man. "From the days of Moses and the children of Israel, the history of mankind proclaims that there is 'an elect and chosen few,' made the peculiar receptacles of the favors and blessings of an all-wise and all-prevailing providence," he said. "This is the world as we find it," Pickens insisted, and therefore there was no evil in slavery. He also spoke menacingly of "the old appeal to the sword," and in a prophetic summation predicted that if the abolitionists were not stopped, it would finally be impossible to "avoid the contest."

During these years, Pickens was one of the greatest slaveholders in the entire South. At the time he bought Ruben Bosket, he owned as many as 563 slaves; only fourteen planters in the country owned more than 500 slaves, according to the Census of 1860. He had plantations not only in South Carolina, but in Alabama and Mississippi as well.

Unlike John Bauskett, Pickens spent considerable time personally managing his slaves, and he believed he was a beneficent master and had good slaves. "My negroes are nearly all of them family negroes of the very best kind," he recorded in his plantation journal. To ensure that his workers were productive, Pickens laid out careful instructions on how his bondsmen were to be treated. These model rules, no doubt, were genuinely intended, a reflection of Pickens's belief that he was a paternalistic master entrusted with the care of childlike charges. But they could also be read as a rationalization; Pickens, like many slaveowners, sought to justify their peculiar institution in the face of growing criticism from the North. Pickens's first rule, he wrote, was that his slaves "must be well-clothed and fed" and given proper medical attention. "The crop must never be too great. Rather have too little planted than too much," he said. "The women are never to work out at all in the cold wet weather in the winter." Nevertheless, he expected his slaves to work hard. "All must start to work at light in the morning," he commanded, and "There is to be no noise by any negro on the place after 10 o'clock at night. At that time the overseer must see that all go to bed."

The supply of food on Pickens's estates, by all accounts, seems to have been adequate. Matilda Brooks, a former slave of Pickens's, reported that the diet "consisted largely of potatoes, corn bread, syrup, greens, peas and occasionally ham, fowl and other meats or poultry." The slave cabins on Pickens's plantations were typical of those everywhere in the South, small humble residences made of logs or weathered boards, with one room for the whole family. On Saturday nights, recalled Rachel Sullivan, another former slave of Pickens's, there would be dances and frolics, with many of the male slaves going to neighboring plantations to visit their wives, girlfriends, or other family members.

Like most planters, Pickens sought to discourage such visiting, regarding it as disruptive and potentially a means for escape. Hence, Pickens decreed, "No negro must be allowed to go off the place without a pass." Such visits should be kept to a minimum, "except to church every Sunday." He also ordered that "No negro man is to have a wife off of the plantation, and no strange negro is to have a wife on the plantation."

On smaller farms with few slaves, such restrictions could have made life impossible for the bondsmen because they would not have been able to find spouses. But in the late 1840s, when Ruben was in his early twenties, he had courted and won a wife, Caroline Vaughn, right on the plantation. Another former slave of Pickens's years later recalled what weddings were like on one of his plantations. "In dem days all dey hadder do to git married was step ober de broom." There was no preacher to perform the ceremony. "The broom wus de law! . . . Jus' say you wanner be married and da couple git together 'fore witnesses and step ober de broom." It was a simple ceremony, evolved out of necessity and the slaves' strong tradition, dating to their African ancestors, of wanting to have families.

Ruben and Caroline, who were field hands, soon began to raise their own family. Rosa, a daughter, was born first. Then, in 1848, came Aaron, Willie Bosket's great-great-grandfather. Later, there were three more sons, Sicker, Tillman, and William. But the family would not enjoy the comfort of growing up together for reasons once again far beyond Ruben's control.

In 1858, Pickens's own life had suddenly been transformed. He had accepted President Buchanan's nomination to be minister to St. Petersburg. And following the death of his second wife, he had persuaded Lucy Petaway Holcomb, the "Rose of Texas," to be his new bride. She was a prize catch for Pickens, who had married his first two wives for their money. As another leading South Carolina politician described Lucy, "She was preeminent for her beauty, intelligence and accomplishments. She was, most deservedly, the belle of the South." The Confederate government would later emblazon its hundred-dollar bill with her picture. But she did not succumb easily to Pickens's schoolboylike entreaties. "I love wildly, blindly, madly," he wrote her. "It is for you to bless—or turn me, cold—cheerless, without hope and without mercy upon a dark and dreary world." This from a man who was fifty-one, twice her age, and bewigged. Still, there were his vast land holdings and slaves to be considered, and now he could offer her the glamor of life at the czar's court.

They were married at the Holcomb home in Texas on April 26, 1858. On the way to Russia, they had audiences with Queen Victoria in London and Napoleon III in Paris. In St. Petersburg, the thirty-eight-year-old czar, Alexander II, often asked Lucy to dance, and when she became pregnant, there were rumors that he was the real father of her baby. "In a society like this," Lucy wrote to her sister, "where the existence of virtue is not believed in by men, mine has not been an existence free from incidents."

For Pickens, his new life, and wife, were proving expensive. Lucy fancied jewels, furs, fashionable clothes, and European furniture. Calculating his wealth, Pickens found he was in debt. One solution was to sell off some slaves, which he had already begun doing. The buyer was Alfred L. Dearing, the younger brother of Pickens's late second wife, Marion Antoinette Dearing. A few years earlier, Pickens had acted as agent in arranging to sell Dearing a famous plantation near Mount Willing, called Cane Break, that had belonged to Calhoun's son-in-law, Thomas Green Clemson. Dearing had been left a small fortune by his father, and now he wished to add to his holdings of land and slaves at Cane Break.

Pickens prided himself on his paternalism and, like most planters, seldom acknowledged that he engaged in the dirty business of buying and selling slaves. In Southern theology, slave speculation was for an inferior class. So his admission that he had actually sold slaves to Dearing was neatly concealed. It came in a letter written in April 1860 to his best friend, Milledge Luke Bonham. Pickens was describing why he had decided to give up his post as minister to Russia and return to Edgefield. It was only a few months before the critical presidential election of 1860, in which Southerners feared the Republicans would elect Abraham Lincoln and force them out of the Union. "I must go home," Pickens began, "because we are on the verge of seeing great events in our country." Duty and honor required his presence back in South Carolina.

There was another reason, too. "I must return because my private affairs must be managed, as there is nothing so expensive as negroes unmanaged," he told Bonham. Many of his slaves were "children," he said, "and they, like anxious hounds, will devour me unless I attend to them with care and economy."

But the most important factor, Pickens insisted, was his concern for the welfare of his slaves. "I have ever looked to my negroes as part of my family," he wrote, "for numerous of them came by inheritance from my father . . . and I feel a particular attachment that makes it my duty to be near them to protect them kindly." In the middle of this sentence, so filled with good intentions, Pickens inserted in parentheses some other information that must have struck him as less significant. He had "sold to Mr. Dearing $70,000 worth" of slaves that he himself had earlier purchased. It was a good commercial deal, and Pickens saw no contradiction between his professed feelings for his slaves and his simultaneous willingness to sell some of them.

AMONG THOSE PICKENS SOLD and sent to Cane Break about 1858 were Aaron Bosket and his sister, Rosa. Aaron was just ten years old and would not see his father or mother again.

Aaron's new master, Alfred Dearing, was a native of Georgia and as hot-blooded as the members of South Carolina's gentry. While a student at the University of Georgia, he had challenged a prominent professor of mathematics to a duel after the teacher accused Dearing of throwing papers out of his room as a prank.

At Cane Break, thanks to his late father's money, Dearing quickly became a leading citizen. He owned $300,000 worth of slaves, a huge amount for the time. In 1858, Dearing was elected to the state legislature and hired an overseer named Michael DeLoache to run his property. DeLoache was another scion of a Mount Willing pioneer family; the old Edgefield tradition ran deep at Cane Break.

Life at Cane Break was harsher, Aaron soon discovered, than it had been on his old plantation. He and his sister were lodged with another slave family, but they weren't his parents and they didn't treat him and Rosa as their children. It was a family of convenience. Moreover, whereas Pickens occasionally fired an overseer who whipped his slaves too severely, Dearing followed an injunction in the Edgefield *Advertiser*: "Spare the rod and you spoil your negroes."

Sometimes, slaves in Edgefield were whipped to death—a dozen cases were reported by coroners' juries between 1844 and 1858. The fate of a slave named Randal is typical. At 2 p.m. on the afternoon on May 8,

1844, Randal was riding a mule through a freshly plowed field when the overseer, Seabourn Randolph, began chasing him on horseback. Randolph caught the slave, knocked him to the ground, hit him in the face, then had him tied up and given a total of five hundred lashes with a cowskin, a common form of whip. After inflicting the blows, Randolph and another overseer washed Randal with salt and water to make the wounds sting more. But still the slave "appeared to be impudent and did not humble himself," another white witness testified to the coroner's jury. None of the men thought the whipping "was sufficient to endanger the negro's life," they told the jury. The real cause of his death, they insisted, was that he drank too much water afterward, making him throw up and inflaming his stomach. A doctor who performed a postmortem examination reported that Randal had been "severely whipped and bruised, the bruises extending to the depth of, from half an inch to three-quarters of an inch deep, and extending generally over the whole surface" of his body.

The recommended norm for whipping slaves in South Carolina was in keeping with the old biblical injunction of thirty-nine lashes. But the number of slaves whipped to death in Edgefield makes it clear that some whites felt free to use whatever physical violence they wished to discipline a bondsman. A slave named Aaron, "the property of Larkin Swearenghem," was whipped severely for repeatedly venturing onto another plantation, perhaps to see his wife or girlfriend. The stripes left wounds on Aaron's left thigh that became infected, and he died a month later of tetanus.

Michael DeLoache, the overseer at Cane Break, was a member of a coroner's jury that investigated the death of a slave named Dinah, a field hand who was pregnant at the time. Another overseer had stripped her and lashed her seventy times. She miscarried a few days later, and not long after, she died of a fever. But no one thought the whipping caused Dinah's miscarriage or death. Even a physician, Dr. Hugh Boyd, who was called in as an expert, saw no connection. "In some cases seventy-five lashes would excite miscarriage," Dr. Boyd said. But in Dinah's case, he testified, it was "owing to the constitution of the woman entirely," her own physical shortcomings, in other words. DeLoache, as part of the coroner's jury, found Dinah responsible for her own death.

Under South Carolina's slave codes, bondsmen were supposed to be protected against such physical abuse and murder by whites; slaves were valuable property to their owners, with an adult male slave fetching one thousand dollars in 1850 and far more in 1860. In 1821, killing a slave became a capital offense, which stiffened the penalty for such a crime. But the law also provided that if the killing occurred "in heat and passion," the punishment would be only a five-hundred-dollar fine and six months in jail. This offered a sizable loophole, but there was an even bigger one. Slaves could not testify in court, so if a white was accused of cruelty to a slave or of killing a slave, unless there were other white witnesses, the defendant could get off simply by pleading innocent. Judge O'Neall called this "an invitation to perjury."

The result was that few whites were convicted of killing slaves. According to the most authoritative study of South Carolina's surviving judicial records before the Civil War, seventy-one whites were tried for killing slaves, but only sixteen were convicted. Most of these guilty verdicts were for less than first-degree murder, and only one of them carried the death penalty. Jurors were reluctant to find their fellow whites guilty of killing a slave, so much so that in one case the jury foreman declared "he would not convict the defendant, or any other white person, of murdering a slave."

By contrast with this lax punishment of whites, slave crime was treated with great seriousness. For whereas most crimes by whites, like shootings after a quarrel, were seen as merely an excess of passion, crime by slaves threatened the very fabric of South Carolina. Not surprisingly, white juries convicted slaves at a rate double that for whites in the antebellum period. Slaves were also executed at a high and consistent rate in South Carolina, at least eight a year in the eighteenth century, six annually in the nineteenth century.

Here was a double standard of justice that would prevail into the present era. It was a system of justice that added to the aura of violence, just as the code of honor and the Edgefield tradition did. For, as the Edgefield *Advertiser* put it, "slavery makes every white man in some sense a lord." To ensure this arrangement, white men in South Carolina were placed above the law, and a private, extralegal form of justice was created—plantation justice. Most crimes by slaves were summarily dealt with by the planter, who was virtually sovereign. "On our estates we dispense with the whole machinery of public police and public courts of justice," said James Henry Hammond, Pickens's rival as the greatest planter in Edgefield. "Thus we try, decide and execute the sentences, in thousands of cases, which in other countries would go into the courts. . . . If there is any fault in our criminal code, it is that of excessive mildness."

Some serious crimes by slaves did make it into the local courts. But, significantly, only 12 percent of the bondsmen brought to trial between 1818 and 1860 were charged with the violent crimes of assault or murder, a reversal of the pattern with whites. Most slaves were prosecuted for stealing. Bondsmen did not regard stealing from their masters as theft. After all, they had been stolen themselves. They were simply "using" what was rightfully theirs. They worked and did not get paid. "Putting massa's chicken in massa's nigger" was what slaves called petty theft.

There is also evidence that honor was coming to be prized among slaves and that honor bred violence among African-Americans just as it did among white Southerners. Whites believed that slaves had no honor, but the bondsmen did not see it that way. They had been stripped of all their earthly possessions, even their families and their humanity. For many of the slaves, all that was left was personal honor. And it was hard to avoid the constant example of their masters: brutal soldiers like those involved in the Cloud's Creek massacre, duelists like Preston Brooks, and murderers like George Tillman.

The Edgefield coroners' reports contain numerous accounts of insults and quarrels leading to killing among slaves that sound much like those among whites. On Christmas Eve, at the plantation of Francis Pickens's brother-in-law, two slaves, Elbert and Harry, got into an argument over a debt of twenty-five cents. Elbert said "he was as good a man" as Harry and challenged Harry to come outside to let him prove it. Harry grabbed a heavy piece of wood, but Elbert struck first with a knife, killing the other slave. On another plantation, a slave named Anderson became infuriated after a fellow slave named Baze said that Anderson's wife was his mistress. "God damn you," Anderson responded, and killed Baze with an ax.

The records also contain hints of deep slave anger at their masters. John Butler was killed by two runaway slaves after he caught them and had dismounted from his horse to whip them. They stabbed him sixteen times in the chest and stripped his body. One of John Bauskett's in-laws, Dr. William Keitt, was murdered by his slaves in Ocala, Florida, shortly after moving there from South Carolina. Two of the slaves were hanged, and four others were transported out of the state after being whipped.

Before the Civil War, much of this black violence remained hidden from white view. Slaveholders might lock up their smokehouses and corn cribs, but they did not lock their homes or bedroom doors. "At the slaveholding South all is peace, quiet, plenty and contentment," boasted the writer George Fitzhugh. "We have but few in our jails, and fewer in our poor houses." As long as slavery lasted, this might appear to be true. The costs of honor, a weak legal system, and a society built on racial repression remained out of sight. But a cataclysmic change was approaching.

BY THE LATE 1850S, white South Carolinians believed they were living in a state of siege. The steady advance of the abolitionists made them afraid their slave society was in danger of extinction. "Everyone here feels as if we are upon a volcano," Lawrence Keitt, a congressman and in-law of John Bauskett, warned after Preston Brooks caned Charles Sumner in the Senate in 1856. For years, Southern politicians, aware that slavery stirred up intense voter interest, had consciously invoked the slavery issue. As James Henry Hammond, the Edgefield planter, put it, "you have to say but nigger to the South to set it on fire, as one whistles to a turkey to make him gobble." Then John Brown's raid on Harpers Ferry in October 1859 touched off a spasm of fear as the South's worst nightmare seemed to be coming true. The election of Abraham Lincoln in November 1860 was the final blow for South Carolinians; they felt it signaled the North's embrace of the antislavery cause. Extremism and political paranoia were in the air. "Nobody could live in this state unless he were a fire-eater," wrote Mary Chestnut, the wife of a wealthy planter, in her diary.

The code of honor exacerbated the crisis, for honor dictated that the defense of the South and of slavery was the same as the defense of one's personal honor. Brooks had caned Sumner in the Senate to satisfy these strictures of honor. Now honor also suggested a solution to the crisis. An honorable man did not submit; he took swift action. Secession was the only alternative.

Soon after Lincoln's election, Francis Pickens returned from St. Petersburg to Edgefield, the most obstreperous district in the most obstreperous state. He had become one of South Carolina's senior statesmen, and he had long had a reputation as a zealot. During nullification times, when a colleague asked him if he was fearful of his course, Pickens replied, "Fear! I was born insensible to fear." Now, back at home, Pickens was invited to address a pro-secession meeting. "If I know the pulse of South Carolina—if I know the pulse of Southern men—the great heart of the South is beating steadily to the march of Southern Independence," Pickens told the crowd. "Independence, now and forever, rather than bear in peace the ignominious bondage whose shadow is already insultingly thrown over our path." The crowd cheered wildly.

Pickens's radicalism served him well. He was promptly given the honor of addressing the South Carolina General Assembly and spoke passionately of the need to risk war with the North. "I would be willing," he said, "to appeal to the god of battles—if need be, cover the state with ruin, conflagration and blood rather than submit."

On December 12, 1860, only a month after Lincoln's election and only a fortnight after his return to Edgefield, the legislature elected Pickens governor of South Carolina. Eight days later, he announced that a special state convention had unanimously passed an ordinance of secession.

Pickens had led South Carolina, and the South, out of the Union. "We are divorced, North from South, because we hated each other so," Mrs. Chestnut explained in her journal.

Over the next few critical months, as South Carolina and the federal government in Washington maneuvered on the brink of war, Pickens's impulsiveness played a key role. On the evening of December 26, Major Robert Anderson, the Union commander in Charleston, caught the Carolinians napping when he secretly moved his small garrison from Fort Moultrie to the empty Fort Sumter on an island out in the harbor. Moultrie was indefensible; Sumter was heavily fortified. Anderson's action made the rebels' task of removing the "foreigners" much more difficult. Governor Pickens felt further insulted. He immediately dispatched three companies to seize Castle Pinckney, another of the Union fortifications around Charleston. Although Castle Pinckney had a garrison of only two soldiers, it was federal property—Pickens had committed the first act of aggression against the United States. Had he refrained from the attack, the chances are good that President Buchanan, irresolute and without any power, would have ordered Major Anderson out of Fort Sumter and back to Fort Moultrie. But to Pickens, this was a matter of honor that could not wait. When Fort Sumter finally fell on April 14, 1861, after a prolonged bombardment, he crowed from the balcony of the Charleston Hotel, "We have rallied; we have met them . . . let it lead to what it might, even if it leads to blood and ruin. We have humbled the flag of the United States . . . humbled before the glorious little state of South Carolina."

Pickens and his fellow Carolina cavaliers had acted in character. They had been bold, touchy, and violent, and had moved without weighing the consequences. This was the nature of honor. Honor did not calculate risks; it was an ancient warriors' code. Honor was reputation. But in time, this mentality would spread to others in South Carolina, to the Boskets, and in them it would not always be deemed glorious.

CHAPTER 3

AARON

After Freedom

It is dangerous for a black man to live in Edgefield.

John Picksley, an ex-slave, November 8, 1865

THE TROOPS IN BLUE came marching into Edgefield on June 21, 1865. It was more than two months after the Confederate surrender at Appomattox, and marked the first time Union soldiers had been seen in Edgefield since the Civil War began. To the mortification of the local whites and the delirious joy of the African-Americans, the soldiers assigned to occupy the village were a company of the Thirty-third Regiment, United States Colored Troops. Most were ex-slaves, and as they paraded by the neoclassical, white-columned courthouse on the spacious village green, they sang:

> Don't you see the lightning?
> Don't you hear the thunder?
> It isn't the lightning,
> It isn't the thunder,
> It's the buttons on
> The Negro uniforms!

For Aaron Bosket, it was the long-awaited day of Jubilee. At Cane Break plantation, Aaron and the other slaves had been praying secretly for their deliverance. They had heard about Sherman's march across Georgia and then up to Columbia, where the city had been burned. They had heard, too, that Sherman had ordered that the freedmen in the South Carolina low-country be given forty acres of land and a mule. Aaron's master, Alfred Dearing, delayed as long as he could, but he finally called the slaves together to tell them they were free. Aaron was ecstatic. Dearing urged his new freedmen to stay on; the cotton needed tending, and he had no other labor force. But Aaron, a stocky seventeen-year-old with a large square head, felt the urge to move about. After all the years of tight restrictions on slave movements, needing a pass to go off the plantation, he had a compulsion to travel. How could he be sure he was free if he stayed in his place of bondage? So Aaron left Cane Break, the beginning of a quest to make his freedom real.

Most of all, Aaron wanted his own land. He had earned it, he believed. He and his father had cleared the white folks' land and picked their cotton. Blacks owned a mere 2 percent of the acreage in Edgefield, though they made up 60 percent of the county's forty-two thousand residents. Aaron did not know that the new president, Andrew Johnson of Tennessee, had rescinded Sherman's Special Field Order No. 15, which had touched off the rumors that the federal government would provide "forty acres and a mule" by setting aside a large portion of the low-country for the exclusive settlement of blacks. He did not understand why the new federally run Freedmen's Bureau, with an office right in Edgefield, did not distribute the land of the masters who had supported the rebel army. Reluctantly, Aaron agreed to a new arrangement—he signed a labor contract with another white planter in the Mount Willing area. He would farm the land in exchange for a portion of the crop. Here lay the origin of the sharecropper system that would bind Aaron and millions of other rural African-Americans in peonage for decades to come. But he did not realize it at the time. The contract was for only one year, and Aaron thought something better would soon come along. For in March 1867, the Radical Republicans in Congress, led by Senator Charles Sumner, now recovered from his caning by Preston Brooks, passed the Reconstruction Act over President Johnson's veto. As a prerequisite to gaining re-admission to the Union, it required the Southern states to grant the former slaves the right to vote.

Suddenly, voter registrars, backed by Union troops, fanned out everywhere in Edgefield and signed up virtually every black male. In the Mount Willing precinct, African-American voters outnumbered whites 163 to 86. Aaron's name was proudly near the top of the list. Aaron might not own land and he might be illiterate, but he could vote, just like the whites. This new power made the freedmen in South Carolina "irrepressible democrats," said a contemporary writer, Belton O'Neall Townsend. All things now seemed possible. In the 1868 election for the new state legislature, Edgefield picked five Republicans, one white and four black. Truly, the world had turned upside down.

. . .

FOR FRANCIS PICKENS, Aaron's onetime master and the governor who took South Carolina into the Civil War, emancipation was a disaster of unparalleled magnitude. "Our country is dead; my heart is so sad," he wrote to his wife, Lucy. "I pray we may be saved from the horrors of anarchy and reckless negro rule," he said to an old colleague. Edgefield had suffered no physical damage during the Civil War, but almost a third of the 2,137 men from Edgefield who enlisted in the Confederate forces had been killed; many more were wounded or maimed for life. Pickens's own son-in-law, Matthew C. Butler, returned from the war a decorated major-general of cavalry, but minus a leg. With the arrival of the Union troops, the bulk of the fortunes of the county's wealthy families was liquidated in an instant—their slaves were no longer their property. John Chapman, a wounded Confederate veteran who later wrote a history of Edgefield, recalled what it was like to be a white man living through that time. "It was as though the foundations of the great deep were broken up," he said. There was a "great disintegration of the old order of things taking place all around." Pickens himself sought a pardon from President Johnson but, as an arch traitor, was refused and died a man without a country in 1869.

But despite their defeat in the Civil War, most of Edgefield's whites refused to accept emancipation. They were embittered and frightened by their ex-slaves' assertions of equality. The few federal officials stationed in Edgefield to preside over Reconstruction noticed this from the beginning. "As the blacks were not considered as having rights while they were slaves, there seems to be difficulty in having a recognition of the fact that they have them now," the Freedmen's Bureau agent reported from Edgefield soon after the close of the war.

B. O. Townsend, the South Carolina writer, put it bluntly:

> The old relations have not been forgotten. Every one thinks, and every child is trained up in the belief, that the negro is meant for the use of white people, was brought here and should stay here for no other purpose; that he is a half-way sort of animal, an excellent rice or cotton worker . . . but utterly incapable of government or culture; that he should be ruled in all things by the white man and kept in his place.

For whites, the dismantling of slavery thus created a terrifying vacuum. No longer was there a mechanism to control the blacks and, equally important, provide the cheap African-American labor on which they depended. White supremacy had to be reestablished. To do it, Edgefield's whites drew on one of their oldest traditions: violence, the use of personal extralegal justice. "To swallow an insult from a negro would be perpetual infamy," Townsend related.

> Accordingly, the whites do not think it wrong to shoot, stab, or knock-down negroes on slight provocation. It is actually thought a great point, among certain classes, to be able to boast that one has killed or beaten a negro. It is quite impossible to convict a white of a crime against a colored man if there be a white man on the jury.

Given these attitudes, 1865 did not mark the end of the war in Edgefield. Instead, it brought the beginning of a new guerrilla war of terrorism directed against blacks. Ironically, these pogroms were made easier after 1865 because blacks were no longer slaves; they were no longer valuable property protected by their masters.

The Freedmen's Bureau was quickly flooded with reports of "outrages" against the former slaves. One freedman, Elbert MacAdams, who went to visit his wife living on another plantation, was shot three times and had his throat cut because his wife's former master suspected that MacAdams had come to take her away, depriving him of a laborer. The former master, Basil Callaham, was released when nothing could be proved. A Confederate veteran, William Hardy, embittered by having been taken prisoner and consumed with trying to revenge the South's loss, kept strings of ears he'd chopped from blacks tied to the sides of his buggy.

A federal officer stationed in Edgefield reported, "The city . . . is inhabited by thieves, murderers and disloyal men, who promenade the street with six-shooters in their belts and Bowie knives thrust in their boots, and do not hesitate to handle freely the weapons thus displayed." They terrorized the local blacks and white Republicans, the officer said, and he had been warned to leave. Within a few days, one of his troopers was killed on the street. "During the whole of my Military Experience," the officer concluded, "I never traveled so wild and lawless a country."

An ex-slave named John Picksley summed up the situation in a sworn complaint to the Freedmen's Bureau in Edgefield in November 1865. "It is dangerous for a black man to live in Edgefield," he said. "It is almost a daily occurrence for black men to be hunted down with dogs and shot like wild beasts," he explained. "I know of several Freedmen being found dead in the woods and swamps near where I live. My life has been repeatedly threatened and my former master (Marsh Frazier) has told me several times that he could get my brains blowed out for twenty dollars at any time."

Picksley did not describe the reason for his former master's hostility toward him, but much white violence against blacks was prompted by disputes between white planters and black tenants over land and labor. The whites did not want their black laborers leaving their farms, or disputing the meager cash payments given them at "settling up" time after the harvest, or attempting to buy land of their own. Other acts of violence grew out of seemingly trivial incidents as everyday life became charged with political meaning. Some African-Americans were whipped by whites for having a dog and hunting with a shotgun. That was acting like a white man, they thought; it was being impudent and uppity, and putting on airs. Blacks' desire to make their freedom real had run into whites' insistence that emancipation did not make blacks their social equals. In the summer of 1865, in the town of Newberry just north of Mount Willing, a hotel clerk named William Lemons beat a light-skinned mulatto for asking Lemons to hold his carpetbag. Lemons did not know the guest had served in the Confederate army.

The first wave of post–Civil War violence grew sharply worse with the state and federal elections of 1868, after the freedmen had been registered to vote. The new sheriff of Edgefield, John H. McDevitt, a white Republican native of the county, told a committee of investigation from the state legislature in 1869 that during the campaign he had been forced to sleep away from his house because his life was repeatedly threatened. At one Republican rally, a group of white Democrats made an assault on the speaker's stand "with pistols, sticks and rocks, the leader advancing with a drawn pistol" to order the Republicans out of town. In the days leading up to the election, the sheriff testified, "Every day colored men would come in and report the death, also whipping and abusing of persons. I have heard of fully twenty such cases, and have seen the wounds on the parties." But, the sheriff acknowledged, "I have never heard of any action being taken in the matter."

Near Mount Willing, a mob of men dressed in white gowns, with white masks over their faces and white covers over their horses, attacked the home of Pickens Stewart, a black farmer. It was three days after the election, and they intended to punish him for being "too smart, running to town too often to speeches," and having the temerity to vote. When Stewart opened the door to the disguised riders, they "presented pistols at me and told me to come out, which I did. I wanted to return to put on my pantaloons. They told me I need not go back . . . as what I had on would soon be taken off of me."

They quickly seized him, blindfolded him with a towel, and carried him out to a field where he had been plowing. There they beat him and, when he resisted, tied him to a tree stump. Then, Stewart reported, they "beat me until I was senseless."

Incidents like this one marked the first appearance of the Ku Klux Klan in South Carolina. It was not yet well-organized, but like so much in Edgefield, it grew out of local history. "The Ku Klux Klan with its night visits and whippings and murders was the legitimate offspring of the patrol," wrote B. O. Townsend. Before the Civil War, Townsend explained, "Every Southern gentleman used to serve on the night patrol, the chief duty of which was to whip severely any negro found away from home without a pass from his master." Now, after the war, the Klan became a vigilante-style force to restore white supremacy and undo Reconstruction. In Edgefield, as elsewhere in up-country South Carolina, the Klan devastated the local black and white leadership of the Republican Party before President Grant belatedly ordered federal troops into the state in 1871.

BY SOME MEASURES, the freedmen made spectacular progress in South Carolina in the 1870s. In the election of 1872, African-Americans took four of the eight statewide elective offices, including lieutenant governor and attorney general; they captured 106 of the 156 seats in the legislature; they gained both the speakership of the House and the presidency of the Senate; and they won four of South Carolina's five congressional seats. These political victories reflected blacks' 60-percent share of the state's population and their propensity to vote in extraordinary numbers.

Given these facts, Martin Witherspoon Gary, an Edgefield planter, lawyer, and former Confederate officer, devised a plan of "terrorizing the negroes" to "redeem" South Carolina in the election of 1876. His strategy, known as "the Edgefield plan," called upon each white Democrat to "control the vote of at least one negro by intimidation, purchase, keeping him away or as each individual may determine." Remember, Gary counseled, that "argument has no effect on them: They can only be influenced by their *fears*." The sixteenth point of his plan read: "Never threaten a man individually. If he deserves to be threatened the necessities of the times require that he should die. A dead Radical is very harmless."

On July 4, 1876, an incident provided Gary and his militant friends in Edgefield a chance to try out their plan. In Hamburg, where Ruben Bosket was first sold as a slave, what came to be known as the Hamburg Massacre began when two young white farmers in a buggy found their way blocked by the local state militia company celebrating the nation's centennial. The militia were entirely black and under the command of Dock Adams, an African-American Union army veteran. After harsh words were exchanged, the two white men felt insulted "as no white people upon earth had ever to put up with before."

The father of one of the young whites then retained Matthew C. Butler to press charges against Adams. Butler, Francis Pickens's son-in-law and a Confederate general, was also the great-grandson of Captain James Butler, killed at Cloud's Creek. In him were all the traditions of Edgefield. On July 8, Butler arrived in Hamburg, accompanied by a large number of armed whites who were members of local rifle and saber clubs that had recently been formed to suppress blacks. He demanded that Adams apologize to the two white farmers, as a matter of honor, and that he disarm his militia. When Adams refused, fighting broke out and the badly outnumbered black militiamen retreated into their red-brick armory. Hundreds of white reinforcements soon arrived along with a cannon from Augusta, across the Savannah River. At 7:30 p.m., filling the hot summer night with the rebel yell, the whites attacked the armory. Hamburg's black marshal was mortally wounded and twenty-five men were captured. Five of these prisoners were murdered in cold blood, according to some eyewitnesses, with Butler personally selecting the men to be executed. Matilda Evans, a black woman who had grown up in the area, wrote later that the prisoners "were taken out in the streets, before the eyes of their wives and children and shot to death, in the light of a brilliant moon." A mob then ransacked the homes and shops of Hamburg's African-Americans.

The Hamburg Massacre transformed the political atmosphere, encouraging the whites and frightening blacks. Two months later, some of the same members of the Edgefield rifle and saber clubs seized Simon Coker, a black state senator from neighboring Barnwell County. The head of the group was Nat Butler, a one-armed Confederate veteran who was Matthew Butler's brother. Coker was accused of making "an incendiary speech to the negroes, urging them to fight for their rights." Butler led Coker to a clump of bushes by the roadside and told him, "You have but a few minutes to live. Is there anything I can do for you?"

Coker replied calmly, "Yes, sir, here is my cotton house key. Please send it to my wife and tell her to gin the landlord's cotton and pay him the rent as soon as she can."

Butler agreed, then asked, "Is there anything else?"

"Yes, sir, I would like to pray."

"Very well, get at it," Butler said.

Coker dropped to his knees and began to pray. But Butler soon interrupted him. "You are too long; make ready men." The group then cocked their pistols, and Butler ordered "aim, fire" with Coker still kneeling.

One member of the rifle club who took part in the incident was a prosperous young Edgefield farmer named Benjamin Ryan Tillman. Tillman's brother George had murdered a man during a card game, as had his father. The violent campaign of 1876 would give him his start in politics—ultimately, he would become governor of South Carolina and then a senator, and the symbol of unapologetic white racism. Reflecting on Coker's murder years later, Tillman said, "It would appear a ruthless and cruel thing to those unacquainted with the environments. . . . The struggle in which we were engaged meant more than life or death. It involved everything we held dear, Anglo-Saxon civilization included."

The election that November for governor of South Carolina "was one of the greatest farces ever seen," B. O. Townsend wrote. Despite the campaign of intimidation, the Republican candidate, Daniel H. Chamberlain, a Yankee carpetbagger, polled the largest Republican vote in the state's history. But in the up-country, especially Edgefield, the "plan" was put into practice. In Edgefield village, a white Democrat took the ballot box from its customary position on the portico of the courthouse and carried it into an interior room. A mob of armed whites occupied the courthouse and refused to let blacks vote while hundreds of whites from Georgia arrived and stuffed the ballot box. The chicanery in Edgefield provided just enough margin to elect the Democratic candidate, Wade Hampton, a wealthy planter and Confederate general who once told a congressional committee that blacks lacked the capacity for "forethought."

The men who had lost the war now won the peace, through violence. Matthew Butler, the white leader of the Hamburg Massacre, was elected to the United States Senate. Aaron Bosket, who had been able to vote and had served on a jury, would not enjoy these rights again. Reconstruction in South Carolina was over. The state had been "Redeemed."

BEHIND THE CLASH of political parties, Aaron Bosket had slowly, painstakingly built a modest new life for himself. About 1869, he had moved briefly to Columbia, the state capital, in search of a better job. But opportunities for uneducated black farmers were no better there, and he soon returned to Edgefield, where he became a sharecropper, like the vast majority of former slaves, planting and picking a white farmer's cotton in exchange for a third of the crop. Sometime before 1880, Aaron married a woman named Angeline, who was three years younger than he was, and they took in two women boarders to help make ends meet.

Life was a ceaseless struggle. Every December, at "settling up" time, after the fall harvest, the white farmer would calculate what Aaron had earned. But after the farmer deducted money advanced him for seeds, fertilizer, and food for his family, there usually was almost none left over. Then there were Aaron's debts to Zeke Crouch, the owner of the largest general merchandise store nearby. Aaron often gave a lien on his share of the crop to Crouch's store, and that would take the rest of his earnings.

Listening to the white men count his share, Aaron frequently felt he was being swindled. But he was illiterate, he could not read the figures the whites quoted him, and besides, the local authorities were not sympathetic to a black sharecropper. His only recourse was to move after the "settling up," which he did every few years, hiring himself out to still another white farmer. Sometimes, Aaron would repeat a few lines of local doggerel:

> Naught's a naught, and five's a figger,
> All for the white man and none for the nigger.

So year followed year, and Aaron only seemed to become further ensnared in the web of controls that were being built up to reestablish white supremacy after the end of slavery. He never owned any land. And when the county began collecting taxes from poor black farmers, the total assessed value of his property, including any horses, mules, chickens, or pigs, was often as little as ten or twenty dollars.

In spite of these hardships, Aaron remained a genial man of upright character. He became a deacon in his church, the Pleasant Hill Baptist Church, which was formed after 1865 as a separate black church out of the oldest church in the area, the Red Bank Baptist Church. Red Bank was a white church, where white planters had let their slaves attend services. But after the Civil War, the church changed, along with everything else. Aaron and the other African-Americans nearby wanted their own church, to worship in their own way; at the same time, the whites would no longer permit the former slaves in Red Bank. For whites, this grew out of a sense that the races were inherently incompatible if the blacks were no longer slaves. Now they would have to be put in their separate and inferior place.

For Aaron, Pleasant Hill became the most important institution in his community. Benjamin E. Mays, one of the few African-Americans from Edgefield in that era who received an education, recalled later of his own church: "Negroes had nowhere to go but to church. They went there to worship, to hear the choir sing, to listen to the preacher, and to hear and see the people shout. The young people went to . . . socialize, or simply to stand around and talk. It was a place of worship and a social center as well." What Aaron's family remembered most about him was that he was a kind, churchgoing man, so good "he wouldn't hurt a hair on your head." And they recalled his voice on Sundays: "You could hear him sing a mile away."

Aaron was cautious. He still carried with him the hard lessons he had learned as a young slave boy—the need for accommodation, the necessity for humility, and the importance of masking his real feelings in a world controlled by whites. So he did not openly object when whites called him "boy," or later, as he grew older, referred to him as "uncle." No white used the term "Mr." before his name. In turn, he followed the etiquette of racism and spoke to his landlord as "boss" or "captain," terms that replaced "master" after the end of slavery. "Just try and live lowly and humble," he advised his family.

Whether Aaron and Angeline had children is unknown, but they eventually separated. Divorce was unthinkable for a white couple in South Carolina; in fact, it was the only state in the nation with an absolute ban on divorce. The code of honor, chivalry, ruled that women must be protected. But divorce was easier for African-Americans, perhaps a heritage of slave times, when allowance had to be made for the large number of families forcibly separated by sales. A widowed member of a nearby black Baptist church recalled the marriage and divorce customs of the time. "Us had de preacher but us didn't have to buy no license and I can't see no sense in buyin' a license nohow, 'cause when dey gits ready to quit, dey just quits."

Aaron later found another wife in the congregation at Pleasant Hill, Tilda Mobley Pou. Tilda's father was a white man, her mother's master or overseer during slave times, and she had beautiful long, straight black hair, "long enough so she could sit on it," the family remembered. She originally married a black sharecropper named James Pou, by whom she had three children. But in the early 1880s, a prosperous white farmer and Confederate veteran, J. William Merchant, enticed her into a liaison. Some members of the Bosket family say Merchant simply threw Tilda's husband off the farm; a black neighbor, Posey Padgett, said Merchant fell in love with her and set her up in a house with money of her own. "She was a nice-looking girl, and he was nice and social to her and she fell for it," Padgett said. Whatever the truth, Tilda bore Merchant three children, Carrie, Mamie, and Gilbert.

Here was an underside of the Edgefield tradition—white men taking advantage of their superior position to have their way with African-American women. James Henry Hammond, the great Edgefield planter and a senator, had a slave mistress who gave him children. A brother of

Lucy Pickens's, a Confederate cavalry officer, came to visit Lucy on his way back to Texas after the Civil War but stayed to have an affair with one of the Pickenses' former slave women. He never left. Benjamin Mays, in his autobiography, relates that both his wife's father and her maternal grandfather had white fathers, born under slavery.

Eventually, Merchant broke off his relationship with Tilda. She was thirty-four years old and the mother of six young children by two different fathers, one black, one white. Aaron was forty and an impoverished sharecropper. When they began living together soon after the breakup of Tilda's affair with Merchant, their house was not much different from a slave cabin, a dilapidated, unpainted, weatherbeaten one-room frame hut leaning out of plumb in a field of red clay. The windows were covered only by a wooden shutter, without glass or screens; there was no ceiling; the floor was dirt; and the roof leaked. Flour sacks did for curtains. The open fireplace served as the stove, and since the only furniture was a crude bed, the family sat on the floor to eat. The house was hot in the intense heat of summer, cold in the winter. The wind came right through large unfinished chinks in the sides of the house.

The next year, there in that house, their first child was born. They named him Clifton but called him Pud, as in pudding. Pud was Willie Bosket's great-grandfather.

Some African-Americans in Edgefield had grown to hate the county, with its violence, its racial oppression, and its economic misery. A former slave who served as a probate judge there during Reconstruction cursed the place, calling it "The miserable county of Edgefield." He helped charter a steamship to take some freedmen to Liberia. Another large disenchanted group of five thousand African-Americans left Edgefield for Arkansas. For years, they told a reporter for the Charleston *News and Courier*, "we have tried to make money and have not been able to do so. We are poorer now than when we began, we have less, in fact we have nothing. . . . We have exercised all the economy we knew how to use and we are going further down hill every day. There is no help for us here."

Pud would take a different course. He would not be meek and humble like his father; he would not emigrate. As he was growing up in the 1890s, the most turbulent, dangerous decade yet for blacks in Edgefield, his quest for self-respect would lead him into violence.

CHAPTER 4

PUD

"Don't Step on My Reputation"

Negroes came to look upon courts as instruments of injustice and oppression, and upon those convicted in them as martyrs and victims.

W. E. B. Du Bois, *The Souls of Black Folk*

THEY ALL CAME to the hanging.

There were men in their Sunday-best black suits and hats, women in long, dark dresses sweeping to the ground, and boys with their knickers, white shirts, and ties. Some came in buggies and carriages, some on horseback, others walked for hours under the pale November sun. They all wanted to secure the best positions around the new brick courthouse. The early arrivals clambered up on sawhorses or wooden crates to peer over the jailyard fence at the twelve-foot-high scaffold. Others perched in trees or leaned out the second-floor windows of a nearby bank and general store. It was the first official hanging in Saluda County. Saluda had been carved out of the northern part of Edgefield in 1896 and included the old Mount Willing area.

The man sentenced to be hanged that day, November 27, 1908, was a poor black sharecropper named Will Herrin. He was an in-law of the Boskets, and Pud and his father, Aaron, trudged the three miles into Saluda to be there. Pud was now nineteen, only a few years younger than Herrin. Like the condemned man, Pud had been working in the cotton fields since he was a boy. Aaron needed his labor to help supplement the family's meager earnings, and there was no public school for black children in Saluda anyway. On Saturday nights, Pud and Herrin had often gotten together to drink, sing, and dance. Now Pud was coming to pay his last respects to a relative and fellow sharecropper.

For the county's whites, it was a day of somber celebration and self-congratulation—white supremacy was being forcefully affirmed. "Now that it is settled that they will hang a man at Saluda, we look for better times," proclaimed the new town's newspaper, the Saluda *Standard.* "There was never a time when negroes were more polite in Saluda."

Will Herrin and Pud Bosket aroused deep anxieties in the local white community. They were members of what seemed a frightening new class of troublemakers whites termed the "New Negro." Herrin and Pud had been born after slavery, so they had not been trained as children to obey white masters. They actually believed that emancipation made them free and equal. "Most of the men who were masters and most who were slaves are dead," noted the writer Walter Hines Page. This brought "a grave social danger." The *Standard* quoted with approval a speech by a senator from Mississippi, who declared, "There could never possibly be any social equality between the two races. There is a race prejudice in the south, and I thank God there is." Saluda's white citizens lamented the disappearance of the "old-time darkey" and the rise of the "New Negro." "These younger ebonies of Ethiopian lineage are as different from the old-time darkey as the moon differs from the sun," the *Standard* commented sadly. "Many of them will hardly recognize you when they pass you, and some rarely give you road, even though you may have a lady with you. . . . Give us the old-time darkey every time."

The crime for which Will Herrin was to be hanged appeared to confirm the whites' worst fears: he had killed his landlord, Emanuel Carver. Year after year, Herrin had made what he thought was "a good farm," bringing in twelve or thirteen bales of cotton from the forty acres he was sharecropping. Herrin was "working on halves," meaning that he owed half the crop to Carver, but got to keep the other half, less any money advanced him for "furnishings," for food, fertilizer, and seeds. Yet every year at "settling up" time in the fall, Carver insisted Herrin had no money coming to him. "The man," as Herrin called the white landowner, "just didn't believe in paying," he told his family. Each year, Herrin was left destitute.

Finally, in the autumn of 1908, Herrin was sure he had "made a big farm." He had harvested sixteen bales of cotton, at about five hundred pounds a bale. It was an excellent crop. "Will jest knowed he was going to collect some money," his niece remembered. But when he went to Carver to collect, the landowner said, "You come out even." Carver gave him nothing and kept all the money for which the cotton had been sold.

A quiet, stolid man, Herrin did not argue. But his honor had been much offended, the same sense of honor for which white Southerners had fought for so long. He went to his cropper's cabin behind the landlord's house and got his single-barrel shotgun. On his way back, he found

Carver in a field and shot him, point-blank. Then, as Carver lay dying and Mrs. Carver rushed out to see what the shooting was about, Herrin beat him over the head with his gun.

Herrin knew it was a suicidal attack. He walked the ten miles into Saluda with his gun and turned himself in to the sheriff.

The trial took less than half an hour, "for there was really nothing to try," the *Standard* reported. The court appointed a young lawyer who had just finished law school, Rodney Etheredge, to defend Herrin. It was his first case. "He had not much chance for display of legal acumen," the paper said.

On the day set for execution, the deputy sheriff, Joe Padgett, granted Herrin's last wish; he brought him a bag of apples. As Herrin ate them, a group of white men prepared an elaborate black shroud, complete with cuffs, to cover his head, arms, and chest. They struggled getting this "toggery" on him, the *Standard* reported, but "during all this he never spoke and was perfectly docile." At last, the sheriff announced, "Time's up, Will." Herrin carefully put the cores of all the apples he had eaten back into the bag, and then marched off ahead of the sheriff into the jailyard. A loud cry went up from the spectators assembled outside.

Herrin walked rapidly up the scaffold, "without a moment's hesitation," and again stood by coolly while the hangman fumbled with the noose. Asked if he had something he wished to say, the condemned man replied, "I will meet hereafter with the people who hanged me."

Exactly on the dot of noon, the sheriff pulled the trigger to open the trap. Another "great yell" went up from the crowd. Up on a small hill overlooking the courthouse, Lois Addy, a fifteen-year-old daughter of a Confederate veteran, watched from her second-floor porch. She had "the eerie feeling of taking someone's life." Etheredge, Herrin's young lawyer, was overcome by emotion. Although he continued to practice law the rest of his life, he never took another court case.

The young widow and little son of Carver were "well pleased to see the execution," according to the *Standard*. The paper said Herrin's own relatives "repudiated him entirely" because of his crime and would not come to the hanging. But they were all there, including his widow and the Boskets. "The whole family was angry, but what could you do about it?" a nephew recalled. "The white man had the law, the white man was the law."

THE HANGING OF WILL HERRIN was only one small sign of a crisis that overtook the South in the 1890s and the first decade of the twentieth century, the years in which Pud grew up. In part, the trouble was caused by a severe economic recession brought on as the South joined the world market economy. Farm prices plummeted, businesses failed. In Saluda, conditions got so bad that the editor of the local paper advertised, "In order that everyone may have a chance to pay up . . . we will take any kind of marketable farm products from those who have not got the cash."

Race relations grew dire. After a relatively calm period in the 1880s, when white supremacy had been reestablished by the end of Reconstruction, things deteriorated dramatically in the 1890s. Benjamin J. Brawley, a pioneering South Carolina black intellectual, wrote that the nineties "were in some ways the darkest that the race has experienced since emancipation. . . . It seemed to the rural Southern Negro that the conditions of slavery had all but come again." Suddenly, white Southerners moved to disenfranchise the few remaining black voters; they erected a new system of Jim Crow laws to segregate the races; and they lynched thousands of African-Americans. Why all this happened in the 1890s is a matter of dispute. For some leading Southerners, the now-aging veterans who had fought in the Civil War, it may have seemed their last chance to leave a legacy of white power that would never be breached. The timing was right—the North had withdrawn its interest in reforming the South. In addition, many Southern whites were scared by nightmares of the "New Negro." They worried that blacks were "retrogressing" toward what whites believed was their natural state of bestiality. Not least important, behind these white anxieties, there were often growing economic challenges from African-Americans, like Will Herrin's quarrel with his landlord.

In South Carolina, the campaign against blacks was led by Ben Tillman of Edgefield, who became governor in 1890 and then senator in 1894 on a platform mixing Negrophobia with economic populism. Tillman personified all the traditions of old Edgefield, a county where manhood was measured by readiness for violence. He was a man of commanding stature, intellectual brilliance, and magnetic personality; but his very appearance suggested a certain savagery. He wore a patch over one eye, and he had an enormous shock of unkempt black hair, a scraggly beard, and grim, rugged features. His father and one of his older brothers had both killed men in card games. During the crucial election of 1876 that ended Reconstruction, he had been a leader in terrorizing African-Americans through murder. He once declared, "Governor as I am, I'd lead a mob to lynch a man who had ravished a white woman. . . . I justify lynching for rape and, before Almighty God, I'm not ashamed of it." During his senatorial campaign in 1894, he jested that he would go to Washington and stick President Cleveland with a pitchfork "in his fat old ribs," thus earning the sobriquet of "Pitchfork Ben." To the end of his days, Tillman liked to boast, "I am from Edgefield."

In 1895, with white hysteria about blacks at fever pitch, Tillman convened a convention to rewrite South Carolina's constitution. His triumph was to come up with a law that would disenfranchise blacks without contravening the Fifteenth Amendment and invite federal intervention. He found the answer in a complex set of residency requirements and a provision that forced black voters to answer questions from white officials about the Constitution. One white delegate to the convention, exasperated by his colleagues' worries about the niceties of the new law, said, "We don't propose to have any fair elections. . . . I tell you gentlemen, if we have fair elections, we can't carry it." Soon afterward, the Saluda newspaper reported with satisfaction that when voter registrars showed up for three days in the new county, "They issued registration certificates to nobody whatsoever." Pud Bosket, unlike his father, would never vote.

Jim Crow laws also soon appeared, starting with the railroads. The Saluda newspaper felt they were an urgent necessity. "Give the negro justice, but for decency's sake protect delicately constituted white ladies from contamination by being thrown in company with an inferior race," it said. "Keep the air of our palace cars . . . from being polluted by the *odor africanus*—an element inseparable from a negro's presence."

Benjamin Mays, born five years after Pud Bosket in the hamlet of Rambo, fifteen miles away, recalled of this period:

> There wasn't much going for the Negro in the world in which I was born. The shades of darkness were falling fast upon and around him . . . The ballot was being taken away. Segregation was being enacted into law. . . . Injustice in the courts was taken for granted. . . . Books and articles were being published, sermons preached, and anti-Negro speeches made, all saying in substance: The Negro is a different breed. He is inferior to the white man. At any cost he must be kept down.

AT DUSK ON A spring afternoon in 1897, J. William Thurmond, the state prosecutor and political boss of the Edgefield region, was in his office near the Edgefield courthouse. Thurmond was also Senator Pitchfork Ben Tillman's personal lawyer. As he sat near the open door, Thurmond was accosted by a traveling salesman for a drug company, Willie Harris. Harris had been drinking, and he berated Thurmond for backing Tillman. An argument quickly followed. Harris called Thurmond "a G-d damn dog and scoundrel." At that affront to his honor, Thurmond pulled his pistol and mortally wounded Harris.

Eyewitnesses said Harris had no gun and made no threatening gesture, and no weapon was found on his body. Nevertheless, Thurmond filed an affidavit swearing that Harris had boasted he was armed with "a d—— good knife and a Colt's pistol." Harris had lunged at him with the knife, Thurmond insisted, and when Thurmond then kicked him backward out the door, Harris reached for his gun. It was a simple case of self-defense, Thurmond asserted. A jury took only thirty-five minutes to acquit Thurmond of murder charges. He was also restored to his post as prosecutor, or solicitor, as the job was called in South Carolina. Later, Senator Tillman rewarded his faithful ally by having him appointed United States attorney for South Carolina. Thurmond's son, Strom Thurmond, would emulate Tillman, being elected governor and senator.

Thurmond's killing of the salesman occasioned only a little gossip. It was merely a sign of a rising tide of violence in the 1890s. This increase in violence, among both whites and blacks, was another part of the broad crisis of the period in which Pud was born and came of age. Murder rates had long been high in South Carolina, but in the 1890s and the first decade of the twentieth century, they escalated dramatically. The number of murders reported by the state's prosecutors rose from 79 in 1887 to 151 in 1891, and then to 210 in 1895. The spasm of violence reached its apogee in 1907, when 280 murders were reported. That is an increase of three and a half times in twenty years. By comparison, the national homicide rate only doubled in the thirty years between 1960 and 1990, the period when Americans felt besieged by what they believed was the worst crime wave in history.

In the newly formed county of Saluda, many citizens were appalled by the number of murders. During Saluda's first decade, from 1896 to 1905, there were sixty-six reported homicides, giving it a murder rate of 35 per 100,000. That is higher than the 1992 homicide rate in New York City.

"Saluda county has made and is making a shameful record," wrote A. B. Cargile, the editor of the local newspaper. Quoting another South Carolina paper, Cargile suggested that the explanation for Saluda's high murder rate lay in its past—"a large amount of the old Edgefield spirit has been cut off and included in the new county." He worried that this propensity for violence was making Saluda "the wild west of South Carolina."

Cargile himself witnessed one of the first killings in the newly formed county from his second-floor office window. At noon on December 28,

1896, he heard gunshots ring out from the street below, and when he looked, he saw Tom Henderson, a farmer, level a shotgun at a neighbor, John Buzhard. The blast tore away Buzhard's shoulder, "making it impossible for him to get his revolver." Buzhard tried to make it to a nearby livery stable where a horse auction was under way, but Henderson and one of his brothers kept pumping Buzhard full of buckshot.

By now, the badly wounded man was lying in the entrance to the stable, but even the intervention of the sergeant of the local militia could not make the Hendersons stop. They began stabbing the fallen man with a knife, and then "the father of the Hendersons struck him on the head with two or three rocks." The whole incident grew out of "bad blood" between the two families, Cargile reported.

Cargile's successor as editor was Eugene S. Blease, a rising young lawyer with political ambitions. On September 8, 1905, Blease killed his brother-in-law, Joe Ben Coleman, on Saluda's main street after accusing Coleman of having an affair with his wife. Blease had offered Coleman a pistol before he shot, yelling later to a crowd of fifty bystanders, "I shot him about my wife." Blease pleaded self-defense and was found not guilty. He was later chosen chief justice of South Carolina's supreme court. As was true before the Civil War, murder was no bar to high office or social standing in the up-country area of old Edgefield.

Even the lieutenant governor of South Carolina, Jim Tillman, a nephew of Senator Ben Tillman, killed a man in downtown Columbia in 1903. His victim was Narcisco Gonzales, the editor of Columbia's newspaper *The State* and South Carolina's most distinguished journalist. Jim Tillman was a son of George Dionysius Tillman, the congressman who had once killed a man during a faro game in Edgefield. The younger Tillman and Gonzales had been feuding for years, exchanging insults in print, with Tillman issuing invitations to duel. Tillman, like his father, was brilliant but erratic, a rogue, a gambler, and a drinker. Gonzales looked down on him and opposed his politics, which included a call for closing all of South Carolina's limited number of public schools for blacks.

When Tillman sought to run for governor in 1902, Gonzales intensified his editorial attacks, charging that Tillman was "a proven liar, defaulter, gambler and drunkard," and, finally, "the criminal candidate." When Tillman lost, he blamed Gonzales.

A few months later, at the opening of the new session of the legislature, the two men encountered each other in front of the statehouse. "Good morning," Tillman greeted his adversary. He then took out his German Luger pistol and fired.

The courthouse was packed with celebrities for the murder trial—

even Senator Ben Tillman came to show his support—and the atmosphere was tense. "Practically everyone here connected with either side of the case is armed," wrote a reporter for the New York *World*. "Some of the men carry two pistols, while others are content with but one. These guns are of large calibre, and make the witnesses look as if they had an umbrella under their coats."

Tillman made the usual plea of self-defense and was acquitted.

The causes for this rampage of violence in the 1890s in Saluda and the rest of the old Edgefield area were much the same as in earlier periods. The dictates of honor still bred a fatal sensitivity to the opinion of others. Juries remained reluctant to convict a defendant who acted in a "manly" fashion. The old strain of violence had been perpetuated in families like the Tillmans, who traced their ancestry to settlers in the Cloud's Creek period. Heavy drinking of whiskey abounded, despite the rise of the temperance movement in the late nineteenth century. And guns were more lethal than ever, thanks to the development of modern repeating pistols and rifles.

Some South Carolinians became openly critical of the easy access to firearms. A state judge in 1900 blamed the high murder rate on the "deplorable custom of carrying pistols, a custom carried to such an extent, that our State may be regarded as an armed camp in times of peace. Our young men and boys, black and white, rich and poor, seem to think that their outfit is not complete without a pistol." South Carolina did pass several laws against the carrying of concealed weapons, but they were not enforced. Many young men still had their suit coats tailored with a "revolver" pocket. In 1892, a pistol dropped from the pocket of the state attorney general, J. L. McLaurin, and crashed onto a courtroom floor. Another attorney general, Thomas H. Peeples, accidentally shot and killed the black chef at the Columbia Elks Club in 1913 after Peeples stepped to the bar and asked for a glass of milk. Peeples was acquitted following a brief trial. He claimed he had been carrying the gun because he had been for a drive with his mother in rural Lexington County adjacent to Columbia, and the countryside, as everyone knew, was a dangerous place.

LATE IN THE EVENING of December 22, 1896, J. Oliver Berry, a white farmer and veteran of the Second South Carolina Artillery, was driving home in his buggy. He had gone to do some Christmas shopping in the town of Newberry, across the Saluda River, and had just crossed Bouknight's Ferry on his way back. The river here was a sluggish green-brown, one hundred yards wide and five to ten feet deep. From the ferry landing, the red clay road ran up a bluff and through dense stands of pine woods before emerging onto rolling fields covered with cotton during much of the year. Berry's eleven-year-old son, Robert, was riding in the back. On the front seat, next to Berry on his left, was Cal Smith, a ten-year-old black boy who worked for him. Berry had been drinking from a jar of corn whiskey; Cal was telling a joke and laughing.

Suddenly, Berry's pistol, which he carried in his pants pocket, fired, hitting Cal in the center of the chest. He died instantly, without uttering a sound.

That is what Berry told the coroner's jury the next day. He said he had no idea how his gun fired. It was just barrel up in his pants pocket, as he always carried it. "I had no hard feelings against the boy," he testified. In fact, Berry said, as proof of his goodwill, he had "been keeping Cal around me feeding him and thought a great deal of him."

The coroner's jury, headed by another Confederate veteran, expressed no skepticism of Berry's account. It was found that Cal Smith "came to his death by misfortune or accident." It was the first recorded killing in Saluda County.

In reporting the death, the Saluda newspaper said that "the negro family are satisfied" with the outcome of the coroner's investigation. That was untrue. They dared not protest openly, and therefore kept their feelings to themselves.

The Boskets and the Smiths were neighbors and friends. Pud was almost the same age as Cal and went to Sunday school at Pleasant Hill church with him. Later, Pud would marry Cal's younger sister, Frances Smith, who would be the mother of his children, and the great-grandmother of Willie Bosket. Cal Smith's killing and the indifferent response of the white community left a deep impression on Pud. "Every black man in Saluda is born under a sentence of death," Pud told his friends in later years.

It was in incidents like the shooting of Cal Smith that the violence of everyday life was at its worst in the 1890s and the first decade of the twentieth century. These episodes added the explosive element of race into the already potent mixture of honor, guns, and whiskey. Whites' desire to assert their supremacy created a poisoned atmosphere, and African-Americans were often the targets of senseless assaults that received little or no publicity.

One day, Davenport Padgett, the eight-year-old son of the Saluda postmaster, was standing near the main street. A white man emerged from the post office with a new pistol he had ordered through the mail.

Just then, three black men came walking along. The man with the gun said, "I think I'll see if it works," and he fired his new pistol, killing one of the African-Americans. The other two fled. There was not even a coroner's inquest, Padgett remembered years later, because the two black witnesses were afraid to testify.

At a nearby railway station, three young black boys fell asleep while waiting on the platform for noontime, when their friend, the baggage porter, would finish his work and join them. A white police constable, Officer Rivers, spotted them there, and "assayed to wake them up and send them on home," the Saluda newspaper reported. Rivers punched one, who jumped to his feet. Then the constable leaned over the second boy and nudged him with his double-barreled shotgun. "As he did so, in some unaccountable way, the gun was discharged and the double load of buckshot tore through the little fellow's abdomen, completely disemboweling him and almost cutting him in two. He died instantly." The death was ruled accidental.

In the small railroad town of Johnston, just across the Edgefield line from Saluda County, twelve-year-old Charles Gomillion was walking home from church one day in 1912 with his two cousins, Hazard and Hugh Gomillion, all of them African-American. As they walked down the sidewalk, three white girls came toward them. The sidewalk was narrow, and racial etiquette demanded the black boys step off into the muddy street. Charles Gomillion, raised by his parents to be exceedingly cautious around whites, yielded to the white girls. But Hazard refused and rubbed shoulders with one of them.

Word soon spread around town about his effrontery. There was talk of a lynching, and a group of white men set off for the cabin where Hazard lived in the countryside. Luckily, Charles's father was able to get a message there first, and Hazard and his father fled, all the way to Philadelphia, never to return.

They had run because lynching was a terrifyingly real possibility in turn-of-the-century South Carolina, the world in which Pud grew up. By the calculus of Southern racism and violence, lynching was merely the logical conclusion to enforcing white supremacy. Pud, in his own way, agreed. To him, there was not much difference between the "accidental" shooting of little Cal Smith, the legalized hanging of Will Herrin, and the lynchings he had heard about, with their mob actions. Still, lynching made a black man think.

The word "lynching" probably took its name from Captain William Lynch, a backcountry settler of Scotch-Irish descent who lived first in Virginia and later in South Carolina. In the 1760s, he and his neighbors developed the custom of handing out swift and violent justice to "lawless men" by flogging or killing them. Due process and evidence were not always necessary. One backcountry gravestone read: "George Johnson, Hanged by Mistake."

Vigilante justice soon became a quasi-official institution in the South, where the law and the court system were weak. After the Civil War, it provided much of the rationale for the policy of intimidating and killing freedmen to undermine Reconstruction. Things quieted in the 1880s, but beginning in 1889, the year Pud was born, the lynching of African-Americans increased with dramatic suddenness, bringing an outbreak of terror. In the nation as a whole, one person was lynched every other day, on the average, between 1889 and 1899, and two out of three were black. The great majority of these lynchings were in the South.

In 1898 alone, as many as seventeen African-Americans were lynched in South Carolina, most of them in the area that had formed the old Edgefield district before the Civil War. In one incident near Edgefield village, a mob of 250 armed white men seized three blacks in a church and accused them of murdering the wife of a white planter. Among the prisoners was Wash Mackey, the most prosperous African-American farmer in the area. Some poor white farmers regarded Mackey as "uppity" for being so successful, and this may have contributed to his being charged with the crime. The mob included some of Edgefield's "best citizens, young and old, plain farmers, rich planters, and even the country plough boy," all gathered in anticipation of a lynching, reported a correspondent from the Charleston *News and Courier*.

Inside the church, Mackey, his son, and his son-in-law were put through a seven-hour interrogation, but little hard evidence was obtained. A series of "ministers, physicians, officers and respected citizens" then appealed to the crowd not to lynch the men, rather to turn them over for trial. Some members of the mob countered that a lynching was needed from time to time "to impress the negro with his position and make him more careful." Their arguments were not really needed, for most of those present had come to kill. "They had seen too much of negroes proving alibis," the *News and Courier* reporter found, "and it was too far for them to go to Court to see that things went right, and meanwhile it was dangerous not to act for the sake of an example."

About 10 p.m., the three prisoners were taken out of the church by a guard of fifteen or twenty men. When they had gone a few hundred yards from the church, the mob attacked. "In a flash the deadly volley followed," killing the men. "A souvenir or two" was then carved from the victims' bodies, and they were riddled with more bullets. A grand jury condemned the lynching, but concluded that the killings had been carried out "at the hands of parties unknown."

In Saluda, a young black man was accused of writing an insulting letter to a white lady. There was talk of a lynching. His action was the ultimate crime to white Southerners, simultaneously violating female honor and the racial code. The thought of black men raping white women sent a chill down the spines of all Southerners and often provided the pretext for the spree of lynching. "Lynched for the Usual" was a frequent headline in the Saluda newspaper. "The lynchings will not stop until the outrages do," it trumpeted to its readers in an editorial. "When a negro dehumanizes himself and becomes a beast, he ought to be lynched."

In this case, the father of the suspect sought help from B. W. Crouch, a lawyer and the founder of Saluda, who had gotten the new county created by working with Ben Tillman. Crouch was a tall, slim, courtly man, energetic and fiercely principled; he taught Sunday school at the local Methodist church from 1894 until 1960, when he was ninety years old. Crouch agreed to take the case, despite opposition from other whites, and discovered that the youth could not have written the letter—he was illiterate.

The night before the trial, a mob gathered on the edge of town, but Crouch got his shotgun and sat on his porch, waiting. The crowd decided not to take on the "father" of Saluda.

In court, Crouch approached the judge and described what he had learned. They reached an agreement. The jury found the black man guilty, and gave him a light sentence in the state penitentiary to get him away from Saluda. "We knew if we found him innocent, he might get lynched even though he was innocent," the head of the jury said afterward. "We had to find him guilty to save his life."

Despite Southerners' claims, most lynchings did not involve rape. Much more often, they were directed against black sharecroppers or farmers because of disputes over land and payments. In the old Edgefield district, the area in South Carolina with the greatest number of lynchings, almost half of the incidents began when a black was accused of killing or assaulting a white man, usually a landlord or overseer. Only 19 percent were traceable to rape. At bottom, lynching was another tool to ensure white control, and it grew in the 1890s as blacks increasingly refused to accept their subordinate, oppressed status.

Lynchings left an indelible mark on Benjamin Mays, who grew up in a community where twelve blacks were lynched in the worst single episode in 1898. His first childhood memory was of a group of white horsemen with rifles who rode up to his house during the incident. They cursed his father, made him take off his hat and then bow down several times. Mays was only five years old at the time, but from then on, he recalled, "I never felt at home in my native county."

> Negroes lived under constant pressure and tensions all the time in my community. They knew they were not free. They knew that if attacked they dare not strike back—if they wanted to live. . . . I believe to this day that Negroes in my county fought among themselves because they were taking out on other Negroes what they really wanted but feared to take out on whites. It was difficult, virtually impossible, to combine manhood and blackness under one skin in the days of my youth. To exercise manhood, as white men displayed it, was to invite disaster.

IN 1910, PUD was twenty-one years old. From his mother, whose father was a white man, he had inherited a light complexion, and he had a husky, muscular build, though at five feet nine inches, he was of average height. Pud was gregarious and had a way with people. "If he'd been a minister, he'd have had the biggest church around," said Roy Holloway, then a young sharecropper who idolized Pud and became his protégé. "He had the power of persuasion." But what people noticed most about Pud was how different he seemed from his father. Where Aaron was innately cautious, Pud was bold and tough, a man you did not cross. In a way, he personified the younger, more assertive generation of African-Americans born after the end of slavery. He was also very active, with a great intensity, and radiated a kind of nervous energy. He had a hard time sitting still, his friends remembered. "Anytime Pud wasn't doing anything, he'd be sharpening his knife with a rock he had in his pocket," recalled Holloway.

One Monday morning in the spring of 1910, Pud reported for work in the cotton fields where he was a sharecropper that year. The white landlord was sitting on a wagon, and to demonstrate his authority he gave each of the black croppers who worked for him a few lashes with a whip. The practice was a vestige of slavery, still permitted under South Carolina law. Pud was the last in line that day, and as he came up to the wagon, the landlord said, "I'm going to whip you real bad, 'cause you're a bad nigger."

Pud reacted instinctively. His honor, his manhood, had been challenged. Just like his in-law, Will Herrin, he refused to accept being insulted any longer. When the farmer flicked the whip toward him, he grabbed it and snatched it away from the man, pulling him right off the wagon.

"This is the last nigger you're going to whip," Pud said, as the other sharecroppers stared in amazement. Then, knowing he was risking his life if he went any further, Pud walked away, not turning the whip on the white man.

An important line had been crossed. Pud had begun to develop a name for himself. After the incident, he had a hard time getting another job as a sharecropper; he was regarded as too dangerous, which was okay with Pud because he had come to hate farming. "There is no advantage to life, standing behind some animal's ass every day, and nothing to show for it at the end of the year," was his philosophy.

Short of money, with no prospect of employment soon, Pud broke into two stores in Saluda on the evening of April 22, 1910. He climbed in through windows in the rear of the stores and got away with twelve dollars and "three hundred coppers." Under slavery, this kind of petty thievery had been widespread and looked upon by masters and slaves alike as part of the price of the peculiar institution. But with emancipation, whites moved to toughen the laws against all forms of stealing by African-Americans. Blacks were no longer punished informally on their plantations; they were now subject to the courts.

Ten days after the burglary, Pud was arrested and put in jail. He had boasted about his exploits and had been easy to catch. But Pud did not submit meekly. In June, while awaiting trial, he tricked the jailer into opening his cell door, then knocked him down and escaped. It took the sheriff three weeks to recapture him.

The semiannual court week was a festal season in Saluda. Horse traders from miles around showed up. On one side of the courthouse was a white man in blackface holding a snake above his head, hawking the world-famous cure-all "P.P.P.," Prickly Ash, Poke Root and Potassium. Nearby sat another patent-medicine man proclaiming the marvelous power of his herb concoction to remove warts, restore hair growth, and banish headaches. Stores around the courthouse were busy selling that new drink from Atlanta, Coca-Cola. An ad for it in one window boasted: "The satisfying beverage—in field or forest; at home or in town."

But the real excitement was inside the courthouse. The selection of juries required large numbers of white men to hang around while court was in session. Rural people, like those in Saluda, had few sources of news or diversion, and trials, especially if they were for murder, were the biggest event of the year.

For Pud's trial, it was a "white folks' court." The judge, the prosecutor, the jury, the clerk, the sheriff, the jailer, and the lawyers were all white. Blacks attending the proceedings had to sit in the Jim Crow corner. A popular African-American rhyme put it simply:

White folks and nigger in great Co't house
Like cat down celler wit' no-hole mouse.

In the case of the State v. Pud Bosket, Pud pleaded guilty as charged. He signed with an X. The judge wrote out the sentence in longhand on his indictment. "The sentence of the Court is that you, Pud Bosket, be confined at hard labor upon the public works of Saluda County for a term of one year."

This meant the county chain gang. Before the Civil War, there were no prisons for blacks in the South; slavery had precluded the need for them. Emancipation thus created a new dilemma: what to do with African-Americans found guilty in court. When whites regained control of South Carolina in 1877, they devised what they thought was a clever solution— have the state lease out convicts. This system would keep miscreant blacks in slavelike conditions and pay for itself, too. George Tillman, Ben Tillman's older brother, explained the rationale: "The negro has a constitutional propensity to steal, and in short to violate most of the ten commandments. The State should farm out such convicts even for only their subsistence, rather than compel taxpayers to support them in idleness" in a penitentiary. The first 285 convicts, almost all African-Americans, were quickly leased out and put to work building a new railroad through Edgefield County to Augusta. The work was so brutal, and the food and sanitation so bad, that half the prisoners died within the first year. After this, South Carolina opted for a system of county chain gangs in which the abuse was less blatant.

In Saluda, the members of the chain gang wore "stripes," black-and-white striped uniforms, with shackles welded on their legs. From sunup to sundown, they worked with picks and shovels repairing the county roads or building new ones. The guards carried shotguns and whips, and sometimes, in neighboring Edgefield and Aiken Counties, convicts were whipped to death. At night, the prisoners slept in a tent with a heavy iron chain running through the middle, to which each prisoner's leg irons were attached.

When Pud was on the chain gang in 1910, the sergeant in charge was Warren Henderson, a stern but fair man who also kept a farm. His sharecropper was Pud's younger brother, Dandy Bosket, and he knew Pud well. "The Negroes on the chain gang was sort of afraid of him, they didn't want to fool with him," Henderson noted. "Pud had that sort of reputation. He was the kind of a man who would cut you. He wouldn't use his hands, he'd just get his knife." Pud's name was spreading.

Henderson, like other whites, originally reckoned that the chain gang was an effective deterrent to crime. "When you been on a chain gang, you're not too anxious to do it again," he said. But gradually, some observant Southerners came to recognize that the opposite was happening, that with the legal system in the hands of whites, the distinction between law and lawlessness became so fuzzy as to be meaningless to many African-Americans. B. O. Townsend noticed this as early as 1877. "So often were the slaves whipped and humiliated before each other, often for no cause, that punishment came to be looked on as no disgrace. This sentiment, I am sorry to perceive, has survived the fall of slavery." The editor of the Saluda *Standard* saw it, too. "It is no unusual thing, indeed it is almost always the case, that when a negro is accused of a crime the whole race immediately sides with him. And after a negro has served his time in the penitentiary and returned to his old haunts, he is received on a footing of equality by his former associates and regarded by some of them as a sort of martyr."

W. E. B. Du Bois detected the process from the black perspective. "There can be no doubt that crime among Negroes has sensibly increased in the last thirty years," Du Bois acknowledged in 1903. But black criminality was not the result of black bestiality and poverty, he insisted. It was the outcome of a history in which whites had made critical errors. The Southern police system had developed in slave times "to deal with blacks alone, and tacitly assumed that every white man was ipso facto a member of that police. Thus grew up a double system of justice which erred on the white side by undue leniency . . . and erred on the black side by undue severity, and injustice." After the Civil War, whites had tried to use the legal system to reenslave blacks, Du Bois added. "It was not then a question of crime, but rather one of color, that settled a man's conviction. . . . Thus Negroes came to look upon courts as instruments of injustice and oppression, and upon those convicted in them as martyrs and victims."

WHEN PUD COMPLETED his time on the chain gang, he returned a kind of hero. Other young black men in the countryside, like Roy Holloway and Pud's cousin Mamon Bosket, began to follow him around. For Pud now was seen as what was called a bad man. To whites, that meant a criminal. But to African-Americans, the term was ambiguous. He was revered by many of his friends, looked down on by some of the better-off members of Saluda's black community. The ambivalence was reflected in the very way blacks pronounced the word: bad could be spoken as "ba-ad," meaning good.

Pud got a job at a sawmill, but his interests lay elsewhere. It was Prohibition time, and there was good money to be made running moonshine liquor. On Saturdays, Pud often bought a supply of home-brewed corn whiskey from a still run by a white man and sold it at hot suppers attended by blacks. Hot suppers had become a black institution, one of the few forms of recreation open to poor African-American sharecroppers free from the eyes of whites. They were a respite from the burdens of everyday life. The participants walked miles to attend them, out in a farmer's field or in the woods. There was fried fish, or hash made in an iron wash pot, and corn bread and corn whiskey. Someone would have a banjo or guitar, and people would sing and dance by the firelight until the early hours of Sunday morning. There was also gambling, usually games of Georgia skin, a card game in which each player was dealt one card, facedown, and the players bet whose number would be matched first as more cards were peeled from the deck. Often, there would be thirty or forty people in attendance.

At these hot suppers, Pud would sing a parody of an old African-American spiritual:

> I went down to the valley to pray
> I got drunk and stayed all day.

Sometimes, Roy Holloway remembered, "when people had been drinking, and there were women around, there'd be fussing and they'd start up a fight."

Pud's uncle, William Bosket, was shot and killed over a quarter bet during a game of Georgia skin at a hot supper. Later, William Bosket's son, Mamon, killed a man named George Dozier over a bet of ten cents in a game of skin at another hot supper. Dozier had refused to pay up and then challenged Mamon, saying, "I'm not scared of you." Mamon pulled his pistol and shot him.

Often the drinking, gambling, and fighting continued on Sunday at church. Pud's church, Pleasant Hill Baptist, sat on a hill on the edge of a forest, just above a cool spring. The spring was a good place to drink whiskey and play cards, remembered another parishioner, Mabel Gibson: "They said Pud was the king of Pleasant Hill. He was always drinking and fighting there, outside by the spring, or inside the church. Didn't matter which. Even some of the deacons got drunk. And the men all brought their guns. It got so people couldn't have a meeting. There would be shooting, or someone would get cut, and that would break up the meeting. People would run and yell, 'get the law.' The Lord had to put up with it."

Under South Carolina law, gambling was illegal, and in February 1913, Pud was arrested for "indulging in the great negro national game of skin" at a hot supper four miles outside of Saluda town. He was fined ten dollars, a large sum for a poor rural black man, but Pud paid it with a show of bravado.

Pud lived by a code. "He didn't bother nobody, but if you pushed him, you had to beat him," his brother Dandy said. "Step on his foot, at a dance or walking by, just brush him, and there'd be a fight. He wasn't never scared."

Once, soon after Dandy had married a woman named Bennett, he fell to quarreling with her, and her brother, John Bennett, arrived to beat Dandy up, heaping curses on the Bosket family. Pud heard what was happening and showed up, too. "Pud just threw John Bennett upside of a barn, threw him so hard the barn fell right down."

Afterward, Pud said to Bennett, "Don't step on my reputation. My name is all I got, so I got to keep it. I'm a man of respect."

All this violence was not simply pathology. It grew out of the old white Southern code of honor, an extreme sensitivity to insult and the opinion of others. But where antebellum whites believed they were above the law, blacks at the turn of the century realized they were outside the law. The law was in the hands of the white man, the oppressor, and consequently, violence was the only alternative for resolving quarrels.

Pud, slightly changing the white man's terminology, spoke of his reputation and demanded respect, rather than using the word "honor." Respect was vitally important to him, because everything else had been taken away: his right to vote, his opportunity to get an education, his chance for a good job, the possibility of a fair trial. Over the years, "respect" was a word more and more African-Americans would use. But the dynamic that produced violence was much the same as it had been for whites. The historian Edward L. Ayers has observed:

> Ironically, honor may have been even more lethal in the postwar black community than among antebellum whites. Poverty and degradation often raise the stakes of honor. A wealthy man could afford to ignore the opinions of all but the few he considered his equals, but a poor man had to worry about the opinions of a vastly larger group of peers.

PUD WAS NOT ALONE as a bad man. At the turn of the century, as life worsened for blacks, a new breed of African-American folk hero arose across the South—the black bad man.

Celebrated in songs and stories, men like John Henry, Railroad Bill, and Stagolee were often hard, pitiless toughs who dispatched their oppo-

nents without remorse. Many were based on real-life characters. Railroad
Bill was modeled on the life of Morris Slater, a black turpentine worker
in the pine woods of Alabama, who in 1893 killed a policeman during
an argument and escaped on a freight train. For the next five years,
he lived off the railroad, robbing trains and threatening poor African-
Americans who lived along the tracks. At one point, Slater shot and killed
a sheriff who had been pursuing him. He was finally killed in an ambush.

> Railroad Bill, he went down Souf,
> Shot all de teef, out o' de constable's mouf,
> Wa'n't he bad, wa'n't he bad, wa'n't he bad.

Throughout the black South, there were also local bad men who were
commemorated in song, often in the blues, which came into being at the
end of the nineteenth century. The blues provided a realistic way of
expressing forbidden thoughts in a dangerous world dominated by whites.
Some things could not be spoken, but they could be sung. "The blues
is mostly revenge," one black suggested.

What set black bad men apart, what made them different from, say,
the white Robin Hood figure, was that they were not romanticized as
noble outlaws. They did not steal from the rich and give to the poor.
They killed blacks as readily as whites, unfaithful women as well as men.

> I went down town de yudder night,
> A-raisin' sand an' a-wantin' a fight.
> Had a forty-dollar razzer, an' a gatlin' gun,
> Fer to shoot dem niggers down one by one.

Black bad men appeared as folk heroes at a time when the world
looked desperate to most African-Americans, the time of disenfranchise-
ment, Jim Crow laws, and lynching. The only law blacks knew was in
the hands of whites, represented by the local sheriff or policeman. Most
Southern blacks were still poor sharecroppers, mine workers, or sawmill
hands. The tales and songs of the bad men mirrored the daily experiences
of this downtrodden proletariat and provided psychological release. As
Lawrence Levine, a historian of black culture, has written, "They were
pure force, pure vengeance; explosions of fury and futility. They were
not given any socially redeeming characteristics simply because in them
there was no hope of social redemption."

Pud fit the model well. He was becoming more violent, and his clashes
with the law were getting worse. On May 6, 1916, he was playing skin

at Red Hill Schoolhouse with a group of friends. Coleman Bryant, a sharecropper and one of the other players, called Pud a liar when Pud said Bryant owed him money. Pud whipped out his knife and slashed Bryant across the chest repeatedly; Bryant almost bled to death.

Pud was convicted of "assault and battery of a high and aggravated nature." He was sentenced to three months on the chain gang. That was less than the year he had received for stealing twelve dollars from two white merchants' stores. It was part of the double standard of justice. Black life was less valuable than white property.

Looking back on it, Pud's family wondered if he had been influenced by his mother's death when he was only about twelve. Even as a boy, he was always a bit wild, and after his mother's death, he went to live with his cousin, Carrie Harris. She was the daughter of Aaron Bosket's sister, Rosa, who had been sold with him about 1858. Carrie had done the best of any of the Boskets, having married Guy Harris, a former slave who had learned to read and write and during Reconstruction had managed to buy some land not far from Pleasant Hill church. He grew his own cotton and was not a sharecropper.

Over the years, the Bosket family had gradually, and with difficulty, reconstituted itself around Carrie and her husband, an affluent man by their standards. Aaron's three brothers had moved from the old Bauskett plantation along the Savannah River, forty miles to the south, and by 1900, Aaron, his brothers, and the Harrises were living almost as neighbors. Despite slavery, they had forged strong links as a family. But because of slavery and its aftermath, these bonds sometimes had to be fluid and flexible. Pud knew that his mother had a white father, and that she herself had lived for years with a white man and had borne him three children. As a boy, Pud had been raised under the same roof with them. He also knew that his father had been married before and probably had other children.

Pud married his own first wife in 1910 when he was twenty-one. Her name was Lizzie, and to make ends meet, they moved in with his father. Their union did not last long. "Pud never stayed home on weekends, he just went looking for gals, roaming around, drinking and partying with gals," Roy Holloway explained.

In 1913, Pud decided to settle down and married Frances Smith, the sister of Cal Smith, who had been shot. The killing was her earliest childhood memory. She was a good-natured, plump young woman who, like Pud, had never been to school.

Their first child, William, was born the following year. In 1915 they had another boy, named Clifton, after Pud's real name. He lived only three hours. The doctor who signed his death certificate said he had died of "hereditary syphilis." How the physician determined the diagnosis is not known, but syphilis was a frequent affliction for poor Southerners at the time, and in the age before penicillin, there was no cure. If the diagnosis was correct, it meant that the mother had passed on the spirochetes through the placenta to her unborn child. It probably also meant Pud had syphilis; and it raised the danger that any further offspring they had could be infected.

Two more boys were born. Freddie Lee, in 1918, and James, in 1922. James was Willie Bosket's grandfather.

ON SATURDAY AFTERNOON, November 8, 1924, Pud finished work at his new job as a section hand on the Southern Railway and headed for a sharecropper's cabin just outside Saluda. "There was a man there running a house, and a lot of good-looking gals, yellow gals with big legs," recalled Roy Holloway, who had been present. They had a big party that night, with a lot of drinking, and Pud cut a man badly with his knife. "I'm going to kill him," Pud said, but some people intervened and dragged the man away.

The next morning, Sunday, Pud went to the house of his section boss on the railroad, H. M. Nimmons, a white man. Nimmons had a new Dodge touring car, and a taste for drinking and selling moonshine. They drove north up a red clay road toward the Saluda River, with Pud hanging on to the running board, to where some bootleggers operated a big still in the woods. There, after a few drinks, they bought several gallon jugs of corn liquor to resell for profit in Saluda town.

Early in the afternoon, they started back. They were going fast, and Nimmons was trying to show Pud how to drive. The Dodge began to careen back and forth across the narrow dirt track. Suddenly, the front wheels ran into a ditch on the left side, and as Nimmons sought to steer it back onto the road, the running board struck the ground and flipped the car over. Nimmons and Pud were thrown into the ditch. Nimmons's head had been crushed, Pud's neck was broken. As they lay bleeding and dying, one of them reached back into the car and pulled out a flask of whiskey. They began drinking. By the time help came, the two men were dead. The flask lay empty between them.

It had been a lovely, sunny autumn day, Pud's family remembered. But when the accident happened, the sky grew dark. That night, Holloway and some of Pud's other friends got together to commemorate him. One of the ballads they sang, Holloway recalled years later, went something like this:

Went up town with my hat in my hand this morning,
Went up town with my hat in my hand.
"Good morning, judge, done killed my man,"
This morning, this evening, so soon.

"I didn't quite kill him, but I fixed him so, this morning,
I didn't quite kill him but I fixed him so
He wouldn't bother with me no more."
This morning, this evening, so soon.

Sitting around a fire, one of the men said to Holloway, "The legend is gone. The baddest man in Saluda is gone." It was something blacks in Saluda said over and over in the coming years. Pud had been as bold, as reckless, and as self-destructive as the cavaliers of the antebellum South. Now the men in the Bosket family would try to live up to his standard.

PART II

CHAPTER 5

JAMES AND BUTCH

Coming Up in the Terry

Augusta was sin city: plenty of gambling, illegal liquor, and a lot of houses like the one I grew up in . . . a roadhouse.

James Brown, *James Brown: The Godfather of Soul*

THE COUNTRY BUS rattled down the last of the red Carolina hills and eased onto the bridge over the Savannah River. Across the sluggish stream on the Georgia side, beyond a line of willow trees trailing their branches in the water, was the biggest city Frances Bosket had ever seen—Augusta. It was April 1930, and the dogwoods were in full bloom, a blaze of white and pink. Four centuries earlier, when the Spanish explorer Hernando de Soto visited the region, he found along the banks of the river a thriving Indian village called Cufitachiqui, meaning Dogwood Town. Each spring, the blossoms of Augusta recalled its earliest name.

Augusta was really two cities, tenuously linked. The big part, with the bulk of the city's sixty thousand people, lay on the hot, flat land along the Savannah. It had a large railroad station, rows of cotton warehouses, and hulking brick textile mills. Farmers brought their cotton here to sell from all over up-country South Carolina and Georgia. On Broad Street, a statue portrayed a Confederate private resting on his musket, his eyes cast back forever at the South's lost cause.

The flat section included "the Terry," an abbreviation for Negro Territory, Augusta's crowded black quarter. Mamie Smith, "the world's greatest blues singer," according to an advertisement, was featuring the "Jail House Blues" at the black-owned Lenox Theater the week Frances arrived.

The other part of Augusta was far off, up a sand hill high above the miasma and poverty along the river. It was known as Summerville and contained the spacious neoclassical mansions and gardens of the wealthy, a mix of local businessmen and expatriate Northerners who wintered in Augusta, men like John D. Rockefeller, President William Howard Taft, and later President Eisenhower. Bobby Jones had won the Southeastern golf tournament that week, and he had his eye on some land that he would soon fashion into the Augusta National Golf Club, which would become the site of the Masters Tournament.

The golfing fans were all white, for Augusta was intensely segregated. It was presided over by the Cracker Party, a somnolent, corrupt political machine. The Crackers' power was based on the whites-only Democratic primary, the spoils of patronage, and bribes from the owners of Augusta's many illegal bars. Public education for blacks stopped at the seventh grade, as it had ever since 1897, when the city's board of education shut the only high school for African-Americans. The United States Supreme Court upheld their action, finding no "desire or purpose to discriminate" in the school's closure.

Frances had come to Augusta in search of work. It had been six years since Pud was killed, and her economic situation was perilous. Pud had left no bank account or land to support her and the three boys, Willie, Fred, and James. Her only inheritance was $33.12 owed Pud in back wages by the Southern Railroad, and she had to go to court to collect that. It did not last long. There were few jobs for black women in rural Saluda County in the 1920s. Farmers did not believe women were strong enough to work as sharecroppers, plowing behind a mule. Besides, the arrival of the boll weevil had devastated South Carolina's cotton industry in 1919 and 1920, dealing it a blow from which it never recovered.

So Frances got by as best she could, living with relatives and hiring the boys out to work as young as seven. James, Willie Bosket's grandfather, was only two when Pud died, and he never got to school. He went barefoot, even in the winter, his only clothing a kind of shift made of flour sacks sewn together.

In 1929, the Depression made things worse, if that was possible. Frances made up her mind to leave the countryside and head for the city, as blacks throughout the South had begun doing in sizable numbers since World War I. This migration speeded up in South Carolina in the 1920s, fueled by poverty, the boll weevil, racism, and continued violence against African-Americans. Between 1920 and 1930, South Carolina lost 10 percent of its black population, the biggest drop ever recorded in the state. In Saluda, the figure was close to 20 percent. Frances had a distant cousin in Augusta, and she heard that things were better there for a black woman without a husband. She might find a job as a laundress, cook, or maid for a white family.

Frances rented a small one-room cabin on the Terry's Cartledge Alley, one of a number of narrow unpaved streets in the area, with names like Thank God Alley, Glass Factory Alley, and Slopjar Alley. The house was much like the sharecropper shacks in which the Boskets had lived since slave times, a one-story, unpainted wooden structure without electricity or running water. It was set flush with the dirt alley and had a tiny porch in front and a low chimney in the back where the cooking was done. The only decorative touch was on the porch—bright red and yellow lard cans filled with a profusion of geraniums, ferns, and verbena. Morning glories and white clouds of clematis climbed over the weathered clapboards. Out in the backyard was a large black cast-iron wash pot, set over a wood fire, in which Frances did the laundry of three white families. She balanced the bundles of laundry on her head to carry them back and forth to her customers, as the other black women in Augusta still did, a reminder of their African origins.

The rent for the house was only five dollars a month, but Frances often did not have enough money to make the payment. She was evicted and forced to move ten times between 1930 and 1941, several times after the landlord took her to court. It became a humiliating ritual. Frances was what was known as "po," which was even worse than being poor. There was no such thing as three meals a day; the question was whether she ate once or twice.

Frances arrived that first spring with only her oldest boy, Willie, then sixteen. The other two children were left with relatives in Saluda. Frances, not sure what to expect, was being prudent. Luckily, Willie soon found work as a day laborer, and in 1932, her next oldest, Fred, joined them, getting a job as a deliveryman. She sent for James, the youngest, in 1935 when he was only eleven, but Frances immediately put him, too, to work, as a laborer.

James had grown up without a father, and he found that wasn't so unusual in Augusta. On the ten blocks where Frances lived between 1930 and 1941, on average at least half the black households—sometimes as high as two-thirds—were headed by women. The women worked hard as laundresses, cooks, and maids for white families, and a few earned money as prostitutes in the bars, jukes, and dance halls in the Terry. There was no welfare yet, and the women did not have time to debate how this new society with so few men had come into being, as scholars did later.

"It's just the way it was, womens without mens," recalled one of Frances's neighbors, Annie Diggs. The important thing was to survive.

As he grew older, James reminded people of his father. Like Pud, he stood five feet nine inches tall, with a muscular physique and light brown skin. And like his father, he had an intelligent mind and a hyperactive disposition. Everything he did, he did quickly, as if he had an internal metronome that was set too fast. "He just had to be moving all the time," was the way one of his cousins, Ida Bosket, remembered it.

From time to time, Frances brought the boys from Augusta back to Saluda to visit their relatives. On one such visit, James grabbed the mules to help his Uncle Dandy on the farm, despite Dandy's warnings that he did not know how to handle the animals. "I can do it, Uncle Dandy," James replied, holding the chains. Watching him, Dandy muttered, "He's just like my dead brother, Pud."

Although Frances did her best, James missed the warmth and love and discipline of having a father. He often ran away from the small rented houses in Augusta and showed up back in Saluda at Dandy's sharecropper cabin late at night, walking down the long country road by himself. He needed a father, a strong man around the house, thought Clyde Bosket, one of Dandy's sons. It was something you could sense.

Each time he ran away, Frances came up to Saluda to fetch him. Frances was a jolly woman, and she liked to regale her in-laws with stories about James. Her favorite tale described the day she came home from work as a maid and prepared to cook dinner. It was wintertime, and she had left the three boys at home during the day with instructions to keep the fire going in the oven to keep the house warm. They forgot, and as the heat died down, the cat had crept into the open stove to stay warm. James saw the cat's movements. When it was time for their mother to return, they built a fire, leaving the cat inside. Frances mixed up some flour and water to make cornmeal biscuits, but when she opened the oven door, the dead cat fell out.

Frances screamed, "Who baked the cat?"

"James," the boys answered.

Frances cackled with laughter as she told the story. After all the violence she had seen, all the hardship she had endured, this was funny.

What Frances always told the family was, "He's got the devil in him, same as his dad."

In these family gatherings, with everyone seated around and James listening, the Boskets often recounted Pud's exploits: how he seized the whip from the white farmer, how he robbed the white merchants' stores, his time on the chain gang, and his knifing of those who insulted him. Pud had established the Bosket name, they agreed; he had built a big reputation. James noticed that when he mentioned he was a Bosket in Saluda, people backed away from him. They were afraid of him, and it made him feel powerful. His father was dead, but he was attracted by the legend, and something inside him made him want to emulate his father.

It was an all-American story, with a twist. Americans take pride that if they are doctors or lawyers, farmers or policemen, their sons will follow in their footsteps. James was pursuing the old dream. It was just that his father had beaten and robbed people. He told his relatives, "When I grow up, I'm going to be a bad man, just like my father."

Soon, like Pud, James began carrying a knife, and whenever he had a spare moment, he took it out and sharpened it, in front of whoever happened to be around. It didn't matter much to him whether they were friends or strangers.

Like his father, he treated life as a series of adventures. In 1940, he got a job as a chauffeur for a white man in Augusta. His employer outfitted James in a proper black cap and uniform. One day, after driving him to an appointment at the hospital, James decided on impulse to joyride up to Saluda. It was more than a two-hour journey, even going as fast as James normally did, which was well beyond the speed limit. When he arrived, Dandy was butchering a hog. The car was a big black Chrysler, brand-new and very impressive to the Boskets in Saluda.

The family talked for an hour, then James acted as if he had just remembered something, slapping his hand against his forehead. "I got to go," he said. "I told the man I'm going downtown, and I was supposed to be back three hours ago. He's sitting in the doctor's office waiting."

James laughed at the thought of the white man stranded without his vehicle, wondering if it had been stolen. Then he jumped in the car and sped off. When he got back to Augusta, he was fired. But it made a good story to tell, and James was happy that day.

NINTH STREET WAS the heart of the Terry and the center of black life in Augusta. In the 1930s and 1940s, it was known as the Golden Blocks. It stretched twelve blocks south from where the railroad tracks entered Union Station to Twiggs Street, where the new Federal Highway 1 ran through Augusta, going all the way from Miami to New York. At the southern end of Ninth Street were the city's biggest black-owned businesses, the Lenox Theater, the Pilgrim Life Insurance Company, a savings bank, a butcher shop, a bakery, and doctors' offices and drugstores. At the northern end were a series of cheap restaurants for the men working on the railroad, a smattering of liquor stores, still illegal in a dry state, and the Del Mar casino, a dance hall where Ella Fitzgerald and Count Basie sometimes appeared. The dance hall was made of white-washed brick, and on Saturday nights the music was very loud, remembered Helen Callahan, who lived across the street. She used to watch from her second-floor balcony as some of the patrons spilled into the street drunk and started fights, cutting each other, until someone called the police and the black mariah drove up.

The paddy wagon was the gift of a black man named John S who openly operated a string of gambling joints up and down Ninth Street. Every year, he bought the police a brand-new car to make sure his businesses were not shut down. When he died, the police carried trunks full of money out of his house.

Augusta had a saying: There is a church for every liquor store. It certainly was true on the blocks around Ninth Street. There was the Bethel AME Church, started right after the Civil War; the huge Tabernacle Baptist Church, where John D. Rockefeller would sometimes come to hear the splendid preacher; the Union and Mount Calvary Baptist Churches; a Muslim mosque where the women wore turbans; and Bishop Grace's House of Prayer.

"Daddy" Grace, as he was called, had similar churches in more than thirty cities in the East and South. To the future singing star James Brown, growing up in his aunt's brothel on Twiggs Street, Daddy Grace was like a god on earth. Each year when he came to Augusta, there was a large parade for him, with decorated floats and brass bands, and everyone in the Terry came out to watch. Daddy Grace wore a cape and sat on a throne with people fanning him while he threw candy to the children. He had long, curly hair, and long fingernails, and suits made out of money.

His House of Prayer resembled a warehouse, with a dirt floor covered with sawdust and plank benches. When Daddy Grace got to preaching, the people got into a ring and went around and around, shouting. As James Brown remembered it, "Sometimes they'd fall out right there in the sawdust, shaking and jerking and having convulsions." The pillars were padded so the worshippers would not injure themselves. It was a great show, some of which James Brown would later incorporate into his own act.

Most of Augusta's black churches had their main Sunday services at 2 o'clock in the afternoon. That gave the parishioners time to attend to their human masters—cooking and serving their Sunday dinner—before going to church.

In 1940, Frances and James moved into a tiny, unpainted wooden house at 814 Ninth Street with a chinaberry tree in the backyard. James began stopping by one of the eateries on the street, JK's, because there was a stunning young waitress working there, Marie Hickson.

Marie was only fifteen years old but had the glamorous appearance of a movie star, with high cheekbones, coquettish dancing eyes, a finely formed nose, and a well-shaped figure. She had extremely fair skin, virtually white, which she had inherited from her mother. Her grandmother, a slave, had been taken by a white man named Bush and bore him twenty-six children. Marie's hair was naturally straight, but she had it permed and wore it in short marcelled waves, according to the fashion of the time. She kept her full lips painted a dark red.

Marie liked to go dancing at the Del Mar casino, run by a black woman named Del Crim. Thursday was girls' night, and Marie and one of her girlfriends always won the dance contest, doing the jitterbug. Her feet flew and her hips swiveled, and the men crowding around shouted and clapped and stamped their feet in approbation. She knew men liked watching her.

Marie had grown up as poor as James. Her father, John Hickson, was a brick mason from South Carolina who had left her mother and gone to look for work in New York after getting her pregnant with Marie. Marie's mother, Cora Mae Jones, had to fend for herself, so—like Frances Bosket—she worked as a laundress for white families. Young Marie managed to attend public schools through sixth grade. They lived on the poorest streets of the Terry, next to the sooty railroad tracks and close to the noxious fumes of the Virginia-Carolina Chemical Corporation factory and the Southern States Phosphate and Fertilizer Company plant. When Marie was nine, her mother put an ironing board between two chairs and set her to work ironing shirts, standing there twelve hours a day. Marie's mother needed her help because by then she had four other children, from other fathers. One of Marie's younger brothers was in a gang with James Brown, the toughest boy in the neighborhood, and sometimes the future star of soul music slept on their floor.

Marie and James Bosket decided to elope; they went before a justice of the peace across the Savannah River in South Carolina, because Marie's mother opposed the union. Marie was beautiful and bright, and her mother had social aspirations for her daughter, despite their poverty. She particularly did not want Marie to marry a Bosket, a family with a bad reputation. James, who was eighteen, was working repairing old typewriters at Tyson's Typewriter Exchange, a job in which he exhibited considerable mechanical skill, but his prospects were not good.

Still, to Marie, who was only fifteen herself, marriage represented a giant step forward. It meant she was an adult, and she relished the freedom from the demands of helping out at home. She had older friends who had gotten married, and they told her she would be able to stay out late and do whatever she wanted. If things didn't work out, she could get a divorce, just like they did.

After the wedding, Marie moved in with James, his mother and older brother Fred, and Fred's wife in their one-room house. It was all the newlyweds could afford. Frances was a good cook, and Marie loved her orange sponge cake. "It was some bad cakes, baby," Marie remembered years later.

But there was trouble almost from the beginning. Frances was strict about making everyone contribute a share of the household expenses. On payday, she stood on the porch, waiting for James and Marie to come home, and always took half their wages. It made Marie mad, because she was now working as a waitress at two restaurants, from 10 in the morning until midnight, making fifteen dollars a week. In addition to the half she had to donate to Frances, she gave some to her own mother, leaving little for herself. And she liked fancy new clothes.

Marie quickly tired of Frances's monetary demands. "I said to my husband, you're married to your mother, darling, not me." She also discovered that James liked to drink. "It was serious drinking: he drank, drank, drank, and stayed drunk all the time, just like the stories about his father. He drank 'til he couldn't stand up, and his tongue got so tied up he would stutter." This was the first sign of the fits, or seizures, that would mar James's later life.

Alcohol also made James violent. "He would beat me, with his fists, 'til I was black and blue," Marie recalled. Once when he was drunk, James took out his pistol and shot at Marie five times. But he was so intoxicated that he missed, even at close range. Marie ran out of the house.

By now, Marie was pregnant, and on March 6, 1941, she gave birth to a son, Willie James Bosket. The family called him Butch. He was Willie Bosket's father.

Three weeks after Butch was born, Marie went to Augusta's Juvenile Court to complain that James was "excessively cruel and abusive" and would not let her take the baby to her own mother's house.

In the clinical language of the court report, "The parents were temporarily reconciled, but within a few weeks the mother again appeared requesting support. When a two-dollar weekly order was imposed, the father deserted and left the state."

From James's point of view, it was the worst nightmare. The court, the white man's court, was now interfering in his private life. After all the stories he had heard about his father being arrested, tried, and put on the chain gang, he was determined to avoid the clutches of the law. And, in truth, the Augusta courts were controlled exclusively by whites. The judge of the Juvenile Court, Harry Alphonso Woodward, was a member of the Cracker Party, dedicated to preserving segregation. Judge

Woodward himself was a likable enough man, a short, rotund figure with a bald pate and four chins. It was just that Augusta's African-Americans felt they never had a chance in court.

That was the experience of Charles Gomillion, a native of Edgefield, who came to Augusta on scholarship to attend high school at Paine College, a private institution run by the Methodist church. In his spare time, Gomillion worked as a volunteer at the Bethlehem Center, a settlement house for poor African-Americans. One night when he was trying to break up a fight between two boys, one of them hit him in the back of the head with a brick. The next thing he knew, he woke up in the hospital with a large bandage on his scalp. When he was released a week later, he happened to walk by two policemen who asked him why his head was bandaged. Gomillion explained that he had been hit while trying to break up a fight at the Bethlehem Center. They wrote out a ticket and told him to appear in court on Monday morning.

Gomillion went to court accompanied by Paine College's president. When his case was called, the judge said, almost automatically, "That will be a five-dollar fine for disturbing the peace." The college president tried to explain to the judge that Gomillion was actually trying to stop a fight. After listening impatiently, the judge declared, "I said that is a five-dollar fine. Next case."

So strong was the perception that the white man's court was bound to be unfair that James Bosket calculated he was truly outside the law, just as white Southern cavaliers reckoned they were above the law in the antebellum period. James felt he was trapped, and now he did the only thing he figured a man could do, unless he was willing to go to jail—he left town. James boarded the Atlantic Coast Line train, riding in the single coach reserved for "colored," and got off in Washington.

There James stayed with some relatives from Saluda, but he soon exhausted the few dollars he had borrowed from his mother for the trip. To solve the crisis, he followed his father's example. One day, he spotted a hardware store with only a single clerk. He strolled inside, pulled his knife, and made off with thirty-four dollars. It was the first of a series of petty armed robberies he committed along the East Coast over the next few months, until he was finally arrested on October 19, 1942, in Perth Amboy, New Jersey.

After James took off, Marie did not see much point in staying in Augusta, either. "I have to get away from the Boskets," she said to herself. "I'm out of here. I ain't got no time to waste." She was still a young girl, just seventeen, attractive, smart, and ambitious. "You got to try to get away and make a life for yourself," was her reasoning.

One day, she left the baby with Frances and said she would be back in time to fix supper. She went to Chicago instead. She would not see Butch again for several years.

BUTCH GREW UP an orphan of Ninth Street. Frances was out most days, working as a maid, a job she had graduated to from laundress. It brought in a little more income, but there was no one to watch the little boy. He sat on the porch during the day, waiting for his grandmother to come home. As far as the neighbors could tell, he was always alone. His clothes were odds and ends of apparel, hand-me-downs from the white families for whom Frances worked, often ragged and patched. He went barefoot in the summer. And he was hungry all the time. Whenever Butch spotted Annie Diggs's husband coming home from work on the railroad, he said, "Mister, you got a quarter?" If he got one, he would go to the A & P up the street and buy some bread and milk.

He was always begging, remembered Annie Diggs, a zesty, shrewd woman whose mother had been a chorus girl in the circus. Butch was very polite, so she gave him cakes and pies and cookies she had baked. On Sundays, she made banana pudding.

"I'd say to him, 'You want some pudding?' And he'd say, 'Yes, ma'am.' Then I'd tell him, 'Go wash your hands, the towel is in the bathroom.'" Afterward, Butch often asked, "Can I carry some home to my grandmother?"

Annie Diggs noticed that Butch always seemed to have a brown paper bag that he kept with him. "One day I said, 'Butch, what you got in that bag?' He opened it up and it was full of sweet rolls and cinnamon buns."

A black-and-white picture of Butch as a two-year-old shows a husky, rugged, strong-looking boy. His face was square, his expression tense and unsmiling. There is hurt and anger blazing in his eyes.

Butch was learning early to be a hustler. By age five, he was coupling his begging with offers of work in exchange for money. "He was so small, he wasn't hardly able to do anything, but he was always asking 'cause he was so hungry," Annie Diggs said. To her husband, Butch would say, "Can I shine your shoes for a nickel?" For Mrs. Diggs, he would propose sweeping their backyard or going to the market to buy her groceries. The Diggses were too poor to afford an icebox or electric refrigerator and had to shop daily. At Nick Gavalos's small restaurant up the street, Butch swept and mopped the floor in return for a hot dog.

Another neighbor, a woman named Lucy Wright, thought Butch was going to be a genius. He was so smart, even as a five-year-old, that he could calculate sums of money in his head. She took heavy bundles of laundry to a lady who had a kind of washing machine, and Butch pushed the bundles over in a little wagon. As they walked, he figured out just how much food he could buy for the money she gave him.

"He'd say, 'For two quarters, I can get a fish sandwich for twenty-five cents, a soda for a nickel, and a loaf of bread for twenty cents.' "

The trouble began when Butch was six and it was time to go to school. Frances enrolled him in the Silas X. Floyd School, a segregated elementary school for African-Americans, only eight blocks south on the corner of Ninth and Florence Streets. It was a handsome, new red-brick structure, with white pillars and a wrought-iron gate at the front entrance. The white-run school board would not have built it, except that the Roosevelt administration had offered Augusta money through the National Recovery Act to build new schools for blacks. Still, the school board kept its appropriations for running the Floyd School low.

"They didn't encourage blacks to go to school, because they were afraid of us getting an education and getting organized," said Dr. Isaiah E. Washington, the principal of Augusta's other black elementary school at the time. In the 1940s, Augusta spent twenty times more per pupil for whites than it did for blacks.

The Floyd School had sixteen hundred students and only thirty teachers for its seven grades, an average of more than fifty students per teacher. Louise Jackson had sixty-three students in her first-grade class. But there were only forty desks and chairs, so the pupils had to sit together.

"By the time I got them organized, and stopped them from crying and fighting, there wasn't much time for teaching," she said.

The dropout rate was astounding, for an elementary school. There were four hundred pupils in first grade, but only one hundred by seventh grade, as the parents needed their children to go to work to help support the family.

The small budget for the education of African-Americans also meant that there was enough money for only one truant officer for both black elementary schools combined. Every teacher had to be her own truant officer. "If you had a child absent, you had to go to their home and talk to the parents yourself," Mrs. Jackson explained. "I don't know how they thought we would have the time to do it."

Between Frances working during the day and the teachers being overburdened, no one was fully aware at first that Butch was playing hooky. It started as a prank, to see what he could get away with and because he didn't like the classroom discipline. But it soon became a regular habit, as he fell further and further behind the other students in their lessons.

It wasn't that Butch was dumb. In fact, he might have been the smartest pupil in his class. But he felt a compulsion to show off by breaking the rules. He had been neglected and rejected by his father and mother, and he burned with an inner rage. Skipping school was a way to demonstrate his anger.

One teacher who did finally go look for Butch found him hiding under the steps of his house. That night, when Frances came home, he was still there. "Git up here, git up," she yelled at him. "What you doing sitting there?"

She made a switch out of a big branch of the tree in the backyard and beat him. Being close by, Annie Diggs could not help witnessing it. She could also hear his grandmother shouting at him. "Boy, why you so bad? You ain't going to school."

"Yes, I am," Butch replied.

"No you ain't. You got the devil in you, just like your granddaddy and your daddy," Frances told him. Then she hit him again.

The next day, she dressed Butch and walked him down the street to school. But as soon as his grandmother left, he fled the building.

By now, the Diggses and other neighbors noticed that Butch was getting into more trouble than truancy. He had begun to steal things. "He'd take anything that wasn't nailed down," Annie Diggs said.

Sometimes he stole food from the A & P, sometimes from a general store run by Angiolina Damiano, next to the Blue Moon Cafe on Ninth Street. She had big glass jars with candy, peanuts, and bubble gum on the counter near the cash register by the front door. If she had to walk to the back of the store to help a customer, Butch would run in and grab a handful of sweets. Other times, he would sneak into the house of Miss Cater, who lived by herself around the corner on Calhoun Street, and eat all the food in her refrigerator and drain her milk.

Once, when Miss Cater realized he was stealing from her home, she yelled out for the neighbors to hear: "I'm going to get that little devil. I'm going to get the police and put him away. I hate to do it, but his mommy and daddy aren't around to care, and his grandmother can't do anything with him, so let him stay in jail."

Soon the police were coming by Frances's house all the time to look for Butch, and sometimes they put him in jail overnight, to scare him. When they brought him back, Frances would beat him again, "with anything she could get her hand on that wasn't too big," Annie Diggs said. "She'd lay into him, and then you'd see him come flying out of the house. She was awfully mean to that boy."

One time after the police had taken Butch away, Frances told Annie Diggs, "Lawd, have mercy. I got plenty of trouble trying to get that boy right. I got to beat him all the time, but it don't seem to do no good." Frances retained an old black folk belief, dating back to their African ancestors, in the evil power of conjurers, and she thought she saw signs of Satan in her grandson. "Maybe somebody worked roots in him."

To the neighbors, Frances seemed a simple, stout, old-fashioned country woman. "She looked like she was living in slavery times," Annie Diggs remembered. She had lace-up shoes, like men's shoes, wore long dresses with an apron and an old bonnet, and often covered her head with a red bandanna. In the evenings, she sat on her porch and smoked a clay pipe, listening to the moan of the train whistles. She spoke very slowly. Once, she confided to Annie Diggs, "I wish I'd never seen that boy. I don't see why I'm punished to have to raise my grandchild. He's too much like his bad old granddaddy."

Frances sensed she was powerless to stop Butch from playing hooky and stealing; even her regular whippings, administered with the best of intentions, failed to produce the desired conversion. Instead, they only seemed to harden Butch and prepare him for life on the street. If he could tolerate the pain of the beatings with sticks and belts, he could face the danger of fights with older boys in the neighborhood.

THE CYCLE OF Butch's life got worse. Although he was not yet eight years old, he started staying out late so his grandmother would not whip him, hiding in an abandoned house around the corner. Sometimes he was gone for days at a time.

He also hung out with a neighbor's boy, Richard Lockett, who was two years older than he was, and part of a gang that ruled Ninth Street. Lockett's older brother was a big-time hustler and gambler and had recently shot and killed a man in a card game, "put his lights out," as another brother described it. To avoid the law, the family put him on a train north, and he ended up in New Jersey. The story was much like that of Butch's own father and created a bond between the two boys.

Ninth Street had changed during World War II, while Butch was still very young: it had become more rowdy, with a huge influx of GIs beginning to pour into Augusta in late 1940 with the buildup of Camp Gordon on Tobacco Road south of town, the scene of Erskine Caldwell's novel. Three army divisions trained there for the invasion of Nazi Europe. Jimmy Doolittle's fliers practiced for their bomb run on Tokyo at Daniel Field, an airstrip on another edge of town. The old Augusta Arsenal was greatly expanded, at first to make bombsights and later to house German prisoners of war. Many of the GIs were African-Americans, and they made their way to Ninth Street, which had a segregated USO.

"Ninth Street was wide open, jumping, like Bourbon Street in New Orleans," said Jeffrey Lockett, who headed the teenage gang in the area.

"Anything you wanted, you got when you hit Ninth Street." The soldiers arrived at the train station and came down the street, which was filled with clubs—the Del Mar casino, the Top Hat, and John Strothers—and liquor stores. The liquor flowed twenty-four hours a day, there was gambling, the prostitutes hung out on Ninth Street or in the clubs, and people rented their rooms to GIs on weekend leave.

Ninth Street also had its pimps. Percy and Jesse were the two top dogs with every good prostitute on the block. "They walked around like kings, strutting, with big brim hats," Jeffrey Lockett recalled. "When they opened their coats, you could see a bulge in their pants where they carried their .38s." Day and night, they cruised Ninth Street in their Cadillacs.

"When Ninth Street was in bloom, there would be plenty of fighting too," Lockett said. "There were some bad cats there."

Butch began running errands for Percy and Jesse, getting them food from Joy Young's chop suey restaurant, or carrying a message to one of their prostitutes, sometimes even holding the money, in case the white police staged a raid. He was so small and cute, in those days, that the prostitutes called him their mascot.

The Ninth Street youth gang was called the Bells, from bells they wore on their shoes, and they had the best territory in Augusta. The gang members hung out at the Lenox or Palace theater, waiting for boys who came from other streets. "If they didn't pay us, we would whup their asses and take their ticket money," Lockett related. "Then they had to walk all the way home." Butch joined in when the older boys would let him.

One day, Butch saw two men get in a fight, after an exchange of insults. Each with one hand locked to the other's and a knife in the free hand, they fought it out. They kept cutting each other until one fell down dead in a pool of blood. Butch was not learning reading, writing, and arithmetic in school, but he was carefully absorbing the lessons of the street. Nothing was more strongly impressed on him than the need for a boy to fight, and that fighting was socially approved. It was the way the adults he knew lived, and they encouraged the little boys to fight, too.

One time, Percy said to Butch, "There's a boy from King Street, and I know you can kick his ass. Here's a dollar if you do it."

Butch was afraid at first. The other boy was bigger than he was, two years older, and everyone knew he was mean. Percy sensed Butch's reluctance and gave him a pep talk. "If you want to be a man, you got to fight to get respect. Now people know me, and they know I don't take no shit from nobody. But if anyone bothers me, I'd shoot them in a heartbeat."

To demonstrate, Percy snapped his fingers. "Just like that, bam. Better them dead than me."

Even Butch's grandmother supported his fighting when challenged. "I tell my children to fight it out," she told her neighbors. "If Butch don't fight, I'm gonna beat him myself."

So Butch, more afraid not to fight, fought the other boy. His eye was blackened and his nose was bloodied, but in the end he grabbed a brick off the sidewalk and bashed the older boy in the head. His opponent fell unconscious, to the cheers of a large crowd of spectators who had gathered from a pool hall and the beer joints. The fight made Butch's reputation. He was a boy who didn't let anyone mess with him.

It was a reputation he had to keep living up to every day. Before he was nine, Butch had a long scar on his left cheek, a proud souvenir of a battle on Ninth Street. Both his hands had been broken from punches thrown in fights, and he had a gunshot wound in his right leg. It was in this world of violence that Butch was coming of age. Instead of a normal childhood, he had been trained to be sensitive to insult and to fight whenever necessary to make sure he was respected.

This was where the old white Southern code of honor merged with and became the code of the city street. Honor had begun on the frontier, among whites, and now in the mid-twentieth century, it was moving into the new frontier of American life, the poor inner city, among African-Americans. In neither place was the rule of law trusted. Honor, or, as Butch called it, respect, remained a creed for a dangerous world, where the man with the most courage survived and dominated. But for Butch, without a father or mother, the code was even more lethal. It was a steamroller coming right at him. He had no human attachments to buffer the call of violence that lived in honor. With all his troubles, the one thing he could take pride in was being the toughest boy on Ninth Street.

IN 1943, JAMES BOSKET returned from Washington. Butch was never told exactly what had happened to his father, except that he had been in jail.

That Christmas, James was drafted into the army in Augusta, even though he had been in jail in Washington. Apparently, he did not tell the draft board about his criminal record, and it was a time long before computers kept better track of such things. For basic training, the army sent James to Camp Claiborne, Louisiana, a huge base in the central part of the state, in the Kisatchie National Forest. There were hundreds of barracks on flat, sandy soil. Among the other soldiers in training there at the time was a young German-born member of the Eighty-fourth Infantry Division named Henry Kissinger.

At the end of James's two-month training program, on his first overnight pass, he went AWOL. He went to town, in Alexandria, got drunk, and stayed away from the base for three weeks before turning himself in. James was confined in the stockade from May 24 to June 17, 1944, and then was given a choice of being court-martialed or mustered out of the service on a "discharge without honor." James took the discharge, later to be called an undesirable discharge, and was fined twenty-seven dollars for drinking. Afterward, his lieutenant gave him bus fare to return to Augusta.

Back at home, James tried staying with his mother and son for a time, but he was frustrated by his life and more restless and impulsive than ever. A few nights when he had been drinking, he beat Butch savagely with a belt, leaving scars on his back. It was like the mark of slavery. The Boskets had been whipped for so many years as slaves, it seemed as if now they couldn't stop repeating the cruelty.

About that same year, 1944, Marie returned briefly from Chicago because her mother was ill. Marie and Frances hated each other so much that when Marie showed up to see her son, Frances told Butch to spit on her. Marie soon took off again, this time for New York. A few months later, James brought three-year-old Butch up to Saluda to visit his relatives. Emmie Bosket, a cousin of his father's with whom he stayed, thought he was a very pretty little boy and asked him what his mother was called.

Butch said, "I don't have no momma."

In December 1949, at the age of eight, Butch, along with his friend Richard Lockett, was arrested for robbing a woman of five dollars at knifepoint—a much more serious offense than the truancy, habitual runaways, and stealing that Butch usually was picked up for. The police took them both before the Juvenile Court, which met on Saturday mornings to accommodate the working parents whose children formed the bulk of its cases. The Richmond County Courthouse was a big, gray legal temple, with a Confederate flag out front, just to make sure everyone knew what kind of justice was being dispensed. Juvenile Court met in a small side chamber, hardly like a courtroom at all, since Judge Woodward did not wear a black robe and sat at a regular table on a level with everyone else.

According to the court's report, Butch had become "completely uncontrollable." He alternated between staying at Frances's house; staying at the home of his other grandmother, Cora Mae Jones; and sleeping on the street. "He left at will whenever he became dissatisfied at either home," the probation officer found. "Both sets of grandparents work during the day, and, apart from not being able to physically look after the defendant, they also felt they could not control him."

The probation officer was a bright, caring young woman, Louise Laney, a member of one of Augusta's leading African-American families. In the past few years, she had spent long hours at the Bosket home, talking with Frances and Butch. All her efforts had failed. Now, she warned them, Butch was likely to be sent to the county reformatory, on a farm outside Augusta. Discipline was harsh there, and the boys had to pick cotton.

Cora Mae Jones had a better idea. Just before Butch was scheduled to appear in court again to hear the judge's verdict, she decided to take him to New York, to his mother's apartment.

Richard Lockett was sent to the reformatory for six months. Later, he would be convicted of theft, and then of rape, and finally of murder. He is currently serving a life sentence in a prison in Valdosta, Georgia. Ninth Street was a hard training ground.

CHAPTER 6

BUTCH

The Promised Land

They came from all parts of the South, like all the black chillun o' God following the sound of Gabriel's horn on that long-overdue Judgment Day. But it seems that Cousin Willie, in his lying haste, had neglected to tell the folks down home about one of the most important aspects of the promised land; it was a slum ghetto.

Claude Brown, *Manchild in the Promised Land*

SIX YEARS HAD PASSED since Butch had seen his mother, but Marie was hardly joyous when her eight-year-old son showed up in Harlem in February 1950. She had been living with a construction worker named Arthur Jackson and had borne him four children in rapid succession. Jackson was an alcoholic who beat her regularly, so life was difficult enough. She hardly needed another child, especially one from an earlier, unhappy life that she had fled. To her, Butch was an unwanted imposition.

She bought him a new suit and enrolled him in Public School 170 in the neighborhood. In their apartment, Butch was relegated to being a watchdog for his younger half-brothers and half-sisters. Jackson was drunk most of the time and now beat Butch, too. After one savage assault, Butch set fire to the house to get even.

His troubles at home affected his performance in school. There he teased the other children, was restless, and frequently lied to his teacher, so the school reported. He also resumed his familiar practice of playing hooky. It was even easier than in Augusta, because he rode the subway all day to escape detection by the truant officer. He showed up for school only for lunch. Some nights, to avoid being beaten, he slept in the subway, where he was picked up by the police. Other nights, he took himself to a shelter run by the city welfare department, claiming he was lost. At least there he was given three meals a day.

Marie was growing increasingly restive over his presence and his behavior. So one day, she dressed him in his good suit, gave him a quarter, and told him never to come back. He rode the subway for several days, until he was found by the police asleep in a subway car. He told them his mother had said, "Never darken this door again."

This time the police took him to the Manhattan Children's Court. It was June 11, 1950, five months after he had been brought to New York to escape the law in Augusta. As a preliminary solution, the judge ordered Butch sent to a shelter set up by the Society for the Prevention of Cruelty to Children. The Children's Court also ordered Marie to appear, but she refused, until a warrant was issued for her arrest.

In court, a social worker assigned to the case testified that Marie "doesn't want her own son." Marie shot back in front of the judge: "Miss, you don't know a darn thing about me. You-all can do more with him than I can. You can keep him. He's too far gone already. His grandmother spoiled him. He didn't have his mother or father to discipline him. Now I can't take him. I've got four kids of my own, and they've got measles. I just don't have time for him."

Marie complained that it was impossible for her to keep track of Butch. One time, she said, the police had picked him up for sleeping in the subway at the Far Rockaway station, at the opposite end of the city, and told her to come get him. It took her over an hour's ride on the subway to get there, but when she arrived, she found that "he had sweet-talked the police into letting him leave before I got there." That made her furious, wasting her time on a boy who just kept running away.

The judge concluded that Marie had legally neglected her son and on August 21, 1950, ordered him sent to the Children's Center of the city welfare department on 104th Street in Harlem. It seemed like a benevolent decision. But it was a critical step for Butch, the beginning of a lifetime of being committed to institutions.

LIKE SO MANY Southern blacks, Butch had heard that New York was the "promised land." On the long bus ride from Augusta, his grandmother had told him wonderful stories about how everyone in Harlem lived in houses with indoor bathrooms, electricity, and running water, how most folks drove around in big new cars, and how he would never be hungry again. "Going to New York," Claude Brown wrote in his memoir of growing up in Harlem, "was goodbye to the cotton fields, goodbye to 'Massa Charlie,' goodbye to the chain gang, and most of all, goodbye to those sunup-to-sundown working hours. One no longer had to wait to get to heaven to lay his burden down; burdens could be laid down in New York."

Butch, of course, knew nothing about the development of Harlem when he arrived: that it had originally been settled in the 1600s by people from Holland who called it Nieuw Haarlem, or that for most of its three centuries it had been a rustic outpost of New York, the seat of prosperous white farmers and the country estates of some of America's most illustrious early families. Or that the first Africans brought to the Dutch settlement of New Amsterdam arrived in 1626 to work as indentured servants. After 1664, when the Dutch surrendered to the English and New Amsterdam became New York, the servants became slaves.

Most of Manhattan's early black population lived near the southern tip of the island until 1827, when slavery was abolished in New York. Thereafter, the city's small African-American colony gradually began moving or being pushed northward as New York grew rapidly. By the 1890s, the majority of blacks lived in an area known as the Tenderloin between Twentieth and Sixty-third Streets on the West Side. They were still few in number, about one percent of the city's population, and they were confined to low-paying work as domestics or manual laborers. There was little more opportunity for upward mobility than in the South. The Tenderloin was the home of New York's red-light district and a center of vice, gambling, and corruption. The Reverend Adam Clayton Powell Sr., minister of the Abyssinian Baptist Church, which at the time was located in the Tenderloin, lived in a coldwater flat "with prostitutes living over me and all around me." He preached to the "pimps, prostitutes, keepers of dives and gambling dens" who sometimes came to his prayer meetings.

Beginning in the 1890s, driven by the desperate plight of blacks in the South during that decade, there was an upsurge in migration to New York, principally from Virginia, North Carolina, and South Carolina, with some from Georgia. Between 1890 and 1910, the black population of New York almost tripled to 60,534, of whom almost two-thirds were born outside New York State. This flow of people increased further with the advent of World War I in 1914, as new jobs for African-Americans opened up in what came to be called the Great Migration. The new settlers gave the black community of New York a Southern flavor that it had not previously had.

Coinciding with this migration, there was a phenomenal boom in the old village of Harlem, as elevated railroad lines were extended north to it and rows of brownstones and exclusive town houses were erected overnight. Speculators and builders like Oscar Hammerstein and Henry Morgenthau made quick fortunes in Harlem land. The new neighborhood at first was a genteel upper- and upper-middle-class community, with elevator apartment houses equipped with servants' quarters, affordable only to the wealthy.

The construction of subway lines up to Harlem in the late 1890s triggered a second wave of speculation, with developers betting that the completion of the new "tunnel roads" would double or triple their investments. But the Harlem bubble burst in 1904–05, leaving a glut of unoccupied and expensive new buildings. When the boom collapsed, landlords vied with one another for tenants by slashing rents, and some desperate businessmen began opening their buildings to African-Americans. As blacks moved in, white residents panicked and moved out, lowering property values still further and opening the path for more African-Americans. Suddenly, Harlem became the new mecca for blacks in New York. For the first time, they were being offered decent accommodations in a respectable neighborhood, and there was a vast new influx of migrants to house.

Harlem was an unusual ghetto. Its name had initially connoted elegance. "Harlem was originally not a slum, but an ideal place in which to live," observed the historian Gilbert Osofsky. But in the 1920s, Harlem was transformed into a slum under the pressure of another even larger surge of immigrants from the South. Between 1920 and 1930, New York's black population jumped 115 percent, rising to 327,706. The situation was exacerbated as African-Americans were trapped by racial prejudice; they were stuck with the lowest-paying jobs while being charged exorbitant rents. To cope, Harlemites broke up the large five- and six-room apartments that had been designed for affluent white families, taking in whatever lodgers they could find. Overcrowding, poverty, squalor, gambling, prostitution, and juvenile delinquency appeared.

It was in the 1920s that the dominant patterns of Harlem were set, and then fixed. The early Southern migrants had arrived full of hope, but by 1950, when Butch was brought to New York, they had grown disillusioned. Now their children, as Claude Brown wrote, "inherited the total lot of their parents—the disappointments, the anger. To add to their misery, they had little hope of deliverance. For where does one run to when he's already in the promised land?"

B UTCH TREATED HIS NEW HOME at the Children's Center as just another challenge. The building was not locked, and he often ran away and stayed out all night, just as he had while living at his mother's apartment. It was like being out on the street, only better. He could do whatever he wanted, and nobody punished him.

Many of the other boys in the center were also troubled youngsters from broken families, picked up for truancy, running away, or petty theft, and Butch fought constantly with them. He felt he had to fight to keep his respect, his youthful, precarious masculinity; this was the old code, translated for life in the streets. He had learned, too, that a willingness to fight was essential for survival.

Once, a bigger boy threatened Butch with a knife that he had smuggled into the center. Butch reacted instinctively. There was no time to think; thinking could be dangerous. He grabbed a chair and hit Johnny over the head, knocking him unconscious.

The victory earned Butch his reputation as the toughest boy in the center, but each triumph like this came at a price for a nine-year-old. He was developing a truculent, belligerent exterior to cover his inner fears. He hid his rage at his family and his terror at always having to fight for his life on the street behind a front of hostility and aggression. In the places he lived, anger and impulsiveness became assets, and he had little reason to learn other, more mature methods to resolve conflict.

Slowly, unconsciously, Butch was also creating a hard shell around himself, an invulnerable defense—almost another self that could take the pain away from his child's psyche. It was at the Children's Center that he began to hear voices, to hallucinate. He told the counselors it was the voice of his grandmother, which he heard when he got headaches.

To keep his reputation, Butch frequently bullied the younger boys. Some of these smaller boys reported that he forced himself on them sexually, making them engage in homosexual activity. He called it taking their buns.

After four months, the authorities who ran the Children's Center concluded they could not handle Butch and shipped him back to the Children's Court. The judge listened to a social worker present the facts, then warned Butch that his behavior was only going to get him into more trouble and that he faced the prospect of a prolonged stay in a more disciplined institution.

"It don't mean nothing, man," Butch responded. He had locked himself inside his shell, protecting himself by rejecting the world before it could reject him. "I don't care what you do with me, because there's nothing I can do about it anyway." At the age of nine, Butch was already a fatalist.

On January 1, 1951, the judge ordered Butch committed to the Wilt-wyck School for Boys, what was known as a reform school. If this bothered

Butch, he did not show it. His mother had abandoned him, and he had come to hate her for it; his father was far away someplace, and besides, being sent to Wiltwyck was a kind of promotion. It made him feel big. He had outgrown the Children's Center.

Butch traveled to Wiltwyck by train, eighty miles up the Hudson River. The school was located on a bucolic 350-acre estate of woods, fields, and streams just south of the small city of Kingston. Kingston had originally been called Wiltwyck by the early Dutch settlers; its name meant "home of the wild ones."

Later, the site had become the country home of Colonel John Jacob Astor, the richest man in America, and after that the mansion of Colonel Oliver Hazard Payne, an oil magnate who had been treasurer of John D. Rockefeller's Standard Oil Company. Payne never married, and in 1933, his nephew, who inherited the property, turned it over to the Protestant Episcopal Mission Society of New York City. The church decided to convert the elaborate barn and the fieldstone farm workers' cottages into a school for neglected and abandoned African-American boys from eight to twelve years old. It was a noble experiment, because at the time, under New York law, youngsters placed by the court were sent to private agencies and schools according to their religion, and the bulk of these were run by Catholic and Jewish organizations that did not accept blacks. Most blacks, after all, were Protestant. Even the few existing Protestant institutions also discriminated.

The Episcopal mission ran out of money a few years later, but the school was saved and reorganized in 1942 by a small group of wealthy, progressive patrons. They included Marshall Field, the department store magnate; Justine Wise Polier, a judge on the Children's Court; Louis Weiss, a founder of the prestigious New York law firm of Paul, Weiss, Rifkind, Wharton and Garrison; and Eleanor Roosevelt. Wiltwyck was almost directly across the Hudson River from the Roosevelts' home at Hyde Park, and the school became her favorite charity. Every year, on the Fourth of July, Mrs. Roosevelt had the one hundred or so boys from Wiltwyck brought to her cottage by bus; fed them hot dogs, baked beans, cole slaw, and ice cream; and then read them "How the Elephant Got His Trunk" from Rudyard Kipling's *Just So Stories*. "Those poor little boys make your heart ache," she wrote to her friend and later biographer, Joseph P. Lash.

By the time Butch arrived on a wintry day in 1951, Wiltwyck had become a nationally renowned school, officially called a "residential treatment center" for emotionally disturbed boys, most of them black or Hispanic. In place of the punitive approach employed until then in virtually all other juvenile detention centers, where the children were kept behind walls and were subject to frequent physical punishment, Wiltwyck was dedicated to rehabilitation. There were no walls or locked gates, corporal punishment was banned, and the boys lived in four cottages that were divided into groups of ten or twelve, each with a counselor and a professionally trained social worker. If any place could help Butch, this seemed to be it.

There was also a school administered by the New York City Board of Education that all the residents were required to attend. Butch went grudgingly at first. The anger and suspicion he felt made it hard for him to sit still in class or learn anything. But he soon found himself attracted to a special art class run by a small, dark-haired woman with a gentle face, soft brown eyes, and a strange foreign accent. Her name was Edith Kramer. She had been born in Vienna thirty-four years earlier and was trained as a painter. She was also a friend of some of the early psychoanalysts, having undergone analysis herself. In the late 1930s, while conducting art classes in Prague for the offspring of Jewish and Communist refugees from Nazi Germany, she helped pioneer the idea of art therapy for traumatized children. Eventually, she, too, fled Hitler's persecution, and, by a circuitous route, was offered a job developing an art therapy class at Wiltwyck.

Miss Kramer, as the boys addressed her, felt an instant sympathy for Butch, for she had heard about his mother turning him out. The sympathy was important, because Butch "was hell on wheels when he first came. He spent most of the time suspecting persecution and going after people with a bottle," which she had to keep taking away from him.

He immediately displayed an innate gift for art, in his choice of colors and his drawing. But he was always in fights, one time getting so angry he grabbed the table in the art room and knocked it over, spilling the paints, brushes, and unfinished pictures on the floor. Kramer, for the only time in her seven years at Wiltwyck, had to get a male counselor to restrain a student. Wiltwyck was a violent place, and Butch was one of the most violent, she observed. The other boys were all afraid of him.

Fights, she learned, were an ordinary part of class at Wiltwyck. Street life had created a pattern of aggression and brutality that made group activity difficult. The boys approached art, like everything else, in a spirit of mutual distrust and hate, Kramer came to realize. Each painter saw the others as potential enemies and rivals, vying for art materials, space to paint, and the teacher's attention. Even when the boys were playing happily, much of what they did involved insults, threats, curses, and belligerent acts.

Butch, in particular, had another troublesome habit—he rarely finished a painting without reaching an impasse and becoming frustrated and violent, his emotions surging to the surface. Often, he tore up the work, and sometimes he threatened to destroy all his previous paintings, which Kramer kept in a folder. One time, when she had locked up his portfolio in a closet, he nearly kicked down the door, wildly shouting for the key.

Another time, when he was painting an Indian with a raised toma-hawk, he suddenly began to attack the painting. He had come to believe that the menacing figure he had created, and with whom he had identified, had turned against him.

Kramer tried to tell him, "Look, this is only a painting." But as she watched him, she thought, "He thinks this thing has come to life."

She had seen other children vent their anger on their own pictures, but usually they chose discarded paintings and kept fantasy and reality separated. Here, Butch had lost touch with reality; it was a moment of psychosis.

To Kramer, Butch was "very similar to most of the children at Wilt-wyck, except he was a little more extreme. He was extreme in both being brighter and more gifted than most of the children, and he was a little madder, a little more quite at the edge." When he did destroy a painting, his fury knew no bounds. "He then was dominated by a need to revenge himself for his failure. He needed to punish the brush, the paint, his pictures, the art room, and everybody around him." It was not Butch who had made the mistake: it was the "table that had bewitched him, some hostile force against which he had to defend himself by indiscriminate counterattack."

In Kramer's view, Butch was projecting his own suspicions, his con-stant preparedness for counterattack, and his exaggerated sense of himself as a tough guy onto the outside world. In art, this was acceptable; it furnished a creative impulse. But in daily life, it made him hostile and paranoid. "He was sure that everybody was against him, before anybody was yet against him. He then made sure it would happen because he behaved in such a way he turned people against him."

What saved him, at Wiltwyck, was his ability to learn to anticipate an outburst plus his capacity for friendship. Gradually, he came to realize when he was about to attack a picture or another boy. Sometimes when he felt restless, he would stop, play a game of marbles, or run around the school. On other occasions, he would visit Mrs. Haggerty, an older white woman who worked in the attic, mending the boys' clothes. Mrs. Haggerty was too poor to have anything to give Butch—not even candy— except for sympathy. But she and Butch liked each other.

As Kramer remembered Butch, "He had lots of charm, and also some kindness and goodness, which made it hard to stay angry at him."

After a year at Wiltwyck, Butch began making pets of the smaller boys, whom he protected and spoiled.

Kramer noted with quiet satisfaction when Butch completed a painting of two sailors coming ashore on a brown beach from a large red and white warship. The sailors' hands were reaching for each other. To an outsider, there was little to distinguish it from other children's art. But at Wiltwyck, the boys were so isolated, so emotionally neglected, and so defensive that they almost never depicted more than one person in a picture, and that figure was somehow themselves. They had a saying, Kramer had noticed: "I trust three people: I, myself, and me."

But although Butch gradually learned to anticipate his outbursts, and was willing afterward to try to reconstruct what had happened, when he did fly into a rage, no one could reason with him. He was so paranoid and had such an uncontrollable temper, Kramer thought, that he was like a volcano in your kitchen.

When the boys agreed not to fight, Kramer would often tell them fairy tales while they worked on their pictures in the art room. Of Grimm's fairy tales, Butch's favorite was "The Master Thief." It is the story of a mischievous boy who ran away from his poor peasant parents and became a skilled and wealthy robber, finally returning one day to visit his aging mother and father. But the father is not pleased to learn of his exploits, warning him, "Once a thief always a thief."

Another of Butch's favorites was *The Wonderful Adventures of Nils*, a classic Swedish children's novel that Kramer had read in German as a girl and retold to her students. It is about a naughty boy who is changed into an elf because he cares only for himself; he ends up traveling with a band of geese, led by a wise old female goose named Akka. Nils is the main character in the book, but Butch thought the real hero was Akka, the mother figure he desperately needed. "Talk about Akka, tell us about Akka," he would beg his teacher.

Over time, Butch formed a close relationship with the other best painter in the class, a boy named Smitty. Smitty had done a picture of a prisoner, and Butch followed his example, turning out a large, haunting figure, two feet by three feet, with tempera paint on the cheap brown paper the class used. The prisoner was dressed in the striped uniform of a Southern chain gang. The black stripes of his suit merged with the background, which was also black, suggesting that he emerged out of darkness and belonged to the dark, thought Kramer when she viewed the finished work. The ground was painted in wild red brushstrokes, typical of Butch's flamboyant, dramatic personality. The prisoner's feet and hands were out of the picture, rendering him helpless. His eyes were empty, with no pupils. The whole painting conveyed a feeling of desperation and tragedy.

Butch told the class that the prisoner was his jailed uncle. Kramer and other school authorities knew that Butch's father, James, had been serving a five-year sentence in Ohio for armed robbery. He had been arrested on October 13, 1947, after holding up a delicatessen in Cleveland and getting away with eleven dollars. To the teacher, it was clear that the prisoner in the picture was really Butch's father. He had identified with his father. Kramer had seen it in the other boys, too. For them, there weren't many possibilities of what you could be when you grew up, and being a criminal and a prisoner was one of the few, she thought. Prison was their destiny. In the language of psychoanalysis that she applied to her pupils, Butch had a delinquent ego ideal. It was what he aspired to be when he grew up. Becoming a man meant becoming a criminal.

Butch's last painting at Wiltwyck, which his teacher reckoned to be his best, underscored his fixation with a life of crime. It was painted when he had turned thirteen; it depicted a young man with a switchblade. The delinquent, in his late teens, was a light-skinned black, like Butch, standing against a city street at night. He had a broad, muscular chest but a sad face, suggesting that violence both fascinated and frightened him. Examined carefully, it became clear that the hand holding the switchblade was turned toward the youth's own body. That was not an accident, Kramer believed. Butch was a skilled artist and could draw anything he wanted. The knife pointed at himself, she concluded, was a portent.

Still, Butch seemed to have made progress. He had learned to read and write at Wiltwyck and had risen to his appropriate grade level in school, a significant accomplishment. He now demonstrated a new ability to concentrate, sometimes painting for an entire afternoon until he finished a picture. And his capacity to express his feelings through art appeared to offer a way to maintain his precarious emotional balance.

Under Wiltwyck's self-imposed policy, it did not keep boys after the age of thirteen, when they became adolescents and much more difficult to handle. So Butch would soon have to leave. This was a problem, because there were no alternatives to his returning either to his family or to the streets of New York.

In the early fall of 1954, his father was released from a second prison term in Ohio for robbery and appeared at Wiltwyck, demanding that Butch be released to his custody. After Butch made a trial visit to James's new home in the Bronx, the school complied that October. Butch had been in Wiltwyck three years and ten months. It was the first place in his life where he had been happy, where people cared about him and he felt acknowledged and safe. Three decades later, he still remembered Miss Kramer as the person who had the most positive impact on his life. He later wrote to one of his former counselors at Wiltwyck, "The only real sense of family I've ever had, I had at Wiltwyck. The values and love that I received at Wiltwyck are without a doubt the single most influential source of strength that has kept me going. . . . No matter how bad or hurting anything was, there had been a Wiltwyck, consequently, there could be a happiness somewhere."

In the fall of 1954, when he was not yet fourteen, all this came to an end for Butch. "For me," he would say, "that meant back to a home that was not a home, and streets where the first law is survival."

JAMES HAD RENTED an apartment in a run-down tenement on David-son Avenue in the Bronx and worked, when he could find a job, as a laborer. He enrolled Butch in eighth grade in the local junior high school.

At first, Butch looked up to his father, admiring him for his criminal exploits and his time in prison. But James got drunk much of the time, and when he did, he often broke down and cried, revealing a weak, timid side to his nature that disgusted Butch. His father, he concluded, was nothing more than "a no good bum." Life now degenerated into a "night-mare" and "a series of tragedies," Butch recalled years later.

His father often beat him viciously. One morning when Butch sassed his teacher, the principal called James, who came to school and hit Butch in front of the class. Another day, James informed him that his mother was a prostitute. Butch argued with his father about this, saying he did not believe him. But that night, he went to Marie's apartment without her realizing it. "I saw with my own eyes that my father had been speaking the truth," he later told a psychologist. After this experience, Butch began to wonder whether he was an illegitimate child or not. "My mother," he said to the therapist, "changes men like you do hats."

With these troubles at home, Butch reverted to his old habit of playing hooky. He also had some bigger ideas. A few weeks after leaving Wiltwyck, Butch climbed into a taxi in Queens, took out a knife, and put his arm around the neck of the driver, Joseph Sprotser.

"Give me all your money," he demanded. He got away with twenty-five dollars.

Two days later, Butch turned himself in to the police. He said his name was William Alonzo. He also insisted he was seventeen years old, making him an adult under New York state law and liable to go to prison with a permanent criminal record, rather than merely a juvenile delinquent who would be sent to a reformatory. The robbery was part of his dream to become a real criminal. It was as if going to prison was the only future he could envision.

By coincidence, however, a former staff member from Wiltwyck was serving as a court probation officer the morning Butch was arraigned and recognized him. "His name is not William Alonzo," the man said, "and he's only fourteen." A check of Butch's records confirmed this, so the criminal court sent Butch to the Children's Court, which committed him to Youth House, a grimy old building on the Lower East Side with locked iron gates over the windows. The city used it as a detention center for neglected or delinquent youths awaiting court hearings.

Here all the terrible forces in Butch, his shattered home life, the terror of living by the code of the street, seemed to come together in a tremendous rush, imploding like a thermonuclear explosion. He became violently angry without provocation. The intelligence Kramer had found in him also disappeared. The staff thought he was mentally retarded.

He claimed he was crazy, that he heard voices and that people were pursuing him. He said he felt like killing someone. Finally, he tried to choke another boy, putting a pillow over his head until the other youth broke away.

After this, Butch was transferred on an emergency basis to Bellevue Hospital for psychiatric evaluation. The psychiatrist assigned to Butch found him "seething with anger, sullen and hostile—ready to fight or explode at any moment. But one also sensed an overwhelming loneliness and a great need to be loved and have someone to love." The doctor warned that Butch "was capable of explosive, possibly homicidal behavior."

After Butch's two-week stay, the psychiatrists at Bellevue gave him the most serious diagnosis possible—they concluded he had childhood schizophrenia. At the time, American psychiatrists tended to overuse the diagnosis of schizophrenia, assigning it to almost anyone who was hallucinating or hearing voices, as Butch said he was. It was not yet recognized that young people with Butch's symptoms might be suffering from some other disorder, such as manic depression.

But the Bellevue doctors had also taken a bold stand, considering the way Butch and other members of his family would be treated in the following years. Psychiatrists are often reluctant to deal with violent children. They are dangerous, not very likable, and they are considered hard, if not impossible, to treat. It is easier to find that they have no emotional disorder and send them into the juvenile justice system, to a reformatory instead of a mental hospital. Now, because Bellevue diagnosed Butch as schizophrenic, he was transferred to Rockland State Hospital, ninety-five miles northwest of Manhattan. He arrived there on Christmas Eve.

"On admission this was a 14-year-old colored boy, fairly well developed for his age," said Dr. Simon L. Victor, assistant director of Rockland, in his initial examination. "He was in good contact, cooperative, however, he was rather hostile and on his defensive. He stated that after he was discharged from Wiltwyck he had a great many difficulties at home and that neither his father or mother wanted to have anything to do with him. He continually stated in a defiant manner that he didn't care what happened to him. No definite hallucinations expressed. But the patient appears to have a mild persecutory trend."

Because of his "aggressive tendencies," the doctors initially put Butch in a ward for psychotic patients, and he was injured several times when some of them attacked him. But he was suddenly calmer and showed a "remarkable understanding of the situation." In fact, under the sympathetic care of the hospital's therapists, he became helpful in working on the ward and "did a great deal of good." He even "displayed an intellectual grasp and judgment far beyond that of his stated age," Dr. Victor reported. Butch came to recognize that his father beat him because of his own unhappiness. By March 1955, only three months later, the hospital said Butch's progress "has been very excellent and most gratifying."

The key to Butch's abrupt turnabout was that he had been removed from the maelstrom of his parents' troubles, and for the first time, someone made the effort to investigate his plight. A social worker Rockland sent to check on his parents could not find Marie. But Marie's mother, Cora Mae Jones, told her that Marie "was no angel." The social worker did locate James, who reeked of alcohol. He struck Rockland's emissary as "an overtly hostile and belligerent man who shows clear evidence of a present acute mental disturbance of his own."

There was also evidence that James was in the advanced stages of syphilis. Whether this was syphilis James had contracted himself or was congenital syphilis he had inherited from his mother, Frances, is unclear. One of James's older brothers had died shortly after birth from hereditary syphilis in Saluda, and another of his older brothers, Fred, went blind in his thirties, a common symptom in someone born with congenital syphilis. Not all children born to mothers with syphilis will have it. But in a family in which an older sibling has died of congenital syphilis, the younger siblings may well be at risk, as in James's case.

Many children born with congenital syphilis have only a mild form of the disease and live for decades. Some of these offspring eventually develop what is known as neurosyphilis, in which the disease attacks the brain, causing problems such as seizures. James began in his twenties to suffer from seizures that grew progressively worse, leading him to collapse on the floor for periods of time. His personality also changed in these years, transforming him from an energetic, exuberant, and outgoing young man into a moody, ill-tempered person in middle age. Personality changes are another symptom of neurosyphilis. Without blood tests, it is impossible to determine whether syphilis lay behind James's condition. But the disease may have contributed to the family's troubles.

Examining Butch's background, the doctors at Rockland found a terrible plenitude of reasons for his behavior. Under the heading "Developmental Factors," Dr. S. Vaisberg wrote:

> The parents were separated when the child was three months of age. There is evidence that the father beat him unmercifully on many occasions. It is very evident that the father represents to this patient a tremendous fear problem. . . . This boy was practically devoid of any affection from either his mother or from his father. He was traumatized by their quarreling and separation. The boy is of a highly intelligent status and it is indeed remarkable that he did not crack under the traumatizing influence of his father long before he did.

Under "Precipitating Factors," Dr. Vaisberg added: "It was his last residence with his overwhelmingly punitive father that apparently caused his condition to be precipitated."

The diagnosis was "Primary behavior disorder in children, conduct disturbance."

Butch was not schizophrenic, after all, the Rockland staff concluded. Instead, he was suffering from what is today called "conduct disorder," or childhood antisocial behavior. Modern research shows that the condition appears as early as age two or three, and certainly by six or seven, the time when a child enters first or second grade. Irritability, inattentiveness, and impulsivity are early warning signs. Many adolescents outgrow it, but researchers now believe that virtually all young people who become violent juvenile delinquents and adult criminals have started off with symptoms of antisocial behavior at an early age. It is a strong predictor of later violence. In adults, the syndrome is termed psychopathy, or antisocial personality disorder.

In its earliest formulation, in the nineteenth century, psychopathy was thought of as moral insanity. That was a pretty good description: a malfunction in one's moral machinery. Psychopaths tend to be deceitful,

impulsive, enormously self-centered, superficially charming, highly manipulative, thrillseeking, and utterly lacking in conscience. Antisocial personality disorder is the most common mental diagnosis given inmates in
prison. The more violent a criminal is, the more likely he is to display
the most serious psychopathic traits, like callousness.

But there are drawbacks to the diagnosis. One is that many people
who tell lies and are egotistical don't break the law. And saying a person
is a criminal because he is a psychopath is a little like saying fat people
tend to overeat, or alcoholics have a problem with drinking. It begs the
question why. Is psychopathy an actual mental disorder, or just the product of a troubled childhood?

In young people, the diagnosis of childhood antisocial behavior is
often a catchall. To receive it, a child or adolescent need exhibit only
three problem behaviors from a list of fifteen, including telling lies, bullying, running away from home, setting fires, showing cruelty to animals,
stealing, and fighting with a weapon. A finding of childhood antisocial
behavior therefore reads more like a juvenile court docket than a psychiatric analysis. It is easy to make and hard to avoid. Such a broad definition
also makes it difficult to distinguish between boys who are merely truants
and those who are likely to commit violence in the future. Most other
childhood psychiatric conditions, from mental retardation to schizophrenia, may evince the same symptoms as antisocial behavior and are therefore overlooked.

But the more the doctors at Rockland examined Butch, the more
they came to believe he was a textbook model of what made children
into little psychopaths. To begin with, there was his social and economic
background. He had grown up poor, in a high-crime neighborhood, with
little opportunity for education or employment. There was also his life
on the street, where he had absorbed fully the code of honor and violence.
Many minority youngsters raised in the inner city are labeled antisocial
simply because that is the way they have learned to act, though they are
not psychopaths. Then there was the abuse and neglect he had suffered
as a child. Butch's parents had physically fought in his presence; both
his father and his mother had abandoned him as an infant; and his father
as well as his grandmother had savagely beaten him. Psychiatrists were
just beginning to understand that this kind of abuse has lasting effects
on its victims, filling them with rage and giving them a model for their
own later behavior, thus creating a cycle of violence.

Equally important, the doctors thought, was the fact that Butch's
father had a criminal record. Children of criminal parents turn out to be
juvenile delinquents in disproportionate numbers, regardless of race. One
of the most comprehensive studies ever conducted about delinquent boys

in reformatories found that two-thirds had a father with a criminal record. Of these, 40 percent had a grandfather with a criminal record. The subjects of this study, done in Massachusetts in the 1930s and 1940s, were all white boys.

One reason for this striking continuity might be that the boys, like Butch, dreamed of copying their fathers. Or perhaps the fathers and children in these criminal families shared an underlying vulnerability, like impulsiveness, that predisposed them to antisocial lives if they grew up in a certain environment. Impulsiveness is a trait of temperament, and such traits are to some degree inheritable. Pud, James, and Butch were all impulsive.

The doctors were not suggesting genetic determinism; far from it. Even if Butch's impulsiveness had been passed on by his family, it was still only one of the many causes that put him in jeopardy. And there is no crime gene. Crime—everything from forgery and income tax evasion to armed robbery and murder—is too complex a behavior to be the product of a single gene.

So what the doctors saw in Butch was not one simple explanation for his violent behavior. Instead, it was the sum of all the troubles in his childhood that made him delinquent. Anything that impaired his thinking, subverted his capacity for empathy, made him overly suspicious, or diminished his control over his impulses played a role. Criminologists like to talk about "risk factors" as predictors of violence. The more risk factors you have, the greater the likelihood of a bad outcome. Unhappily, Butch seemed to have almost all of them.

Still, after Butch had been at Rockland for two and a half years, the doctors were convinced that he had made an "excellent recovery" and that his "prognosis for future normal conduct is excellent." So, in September 1956, they decided to release him. Despite everything they had learned about the relationship between him and his family, they sent him back to live with James. Rockland had no choice. James was his father.

THE DOWNWARD SPIRAL began all over. On November 17, James beat Butch again, punching him in the face with the full force of his fists. But by now Butch was taller than his father; he had reached six feet two inches, with powerful muscles, and he decided to fight back. The sound of the two men's blows, their curses and screams, aroused a neighbor on Davidson Avenue, who called the police. When the police arrived, they found a loaded .38 caliber revolver on the floor between father and son. James was arrested for possession of a dangerous weapon, and both James and Butch were sent to Bellevue for psychiatric observation.

On admission, James smelled of alcohol. He told the psychiatrists: "I'm sick. I see things. I hear things. I need to be put away for awhile."

Hallucinations and delusions are classic signs of psychosis, of being out of touch with reality, and the doctors initially contemplated diagnosing James as schizophrenic. Being labeled psychotic would have made him legally insane and kept him out of prison. The law recognizes psychosis. But the doctors eventually dismissed James's voices and visions, concluding he was only a psychopath, or in the then-current language of the official *Diagnostic and Statistical Manual of Mental Disorders* of the American Psychiatric Association, a "sociopathic personality with aggressive trends." It was the adult equivalent of the antisocial diagnosis given Butch at Rockland. Because James was only antisocial, Bellevue returned him to the court, and he was sentenced to two months in the city prison on Rikers Island on the gun charge.

Butch's case, however, was more serious, the Bellevue psychiatrists concluded. They still thought he was schizophrenic, and they sent him back to Rockland.

The doctors there were not pleased to have him back. When they examined him, they concluded again that he was not psychotic. Perhaps he hallucinated or got into explosive rages only from time to time, as when his father beat him.

The doctors at Rockland could see Butch was going to be a trouble-maker. He already knew a lot of the other boys, from Wiltwyck or Bellevue, or from his earlier stay in Rockland, and now he was older and bigger. Some of them had stolen cars or used guns in robberies; they had useful lessons to teach. For Butch, it was like graduating from high school to college. "I believed I was a big man," he later wrote. "Rockland was just a playpen. I was a big kid for my age, so the staff left me alone. So instead of learning anything, I ran wild."

One Saturday in September 1957, a doctor restricted Butch to his room for the weekend. He had been caught bullying a younger boy, perhaps as a way to prove himself. The next day, when a ward check was made, he was missing. Butch had "eloped," the hospital called it. Rockland notified the police and sent a telegram to James, which was returned. His old apartment building had been razed for urban renewal. Rockland made no further attempt to locate Butch, nor did any other agency. He had slipped through the cracks of normal society.

With no one looking for him, Butch happily returned to Harlem.

"I went back to the street and was treated by the rest of the kids as a homecoming hero," he wrote later.

He was now sixteen, legally an adult under New York law, and he wanted to live the part he had long envisioned for himself. He would be a hustler. "This was my way of life, all that I knew." Butch began by running numbers, then tried delivering drugs, and eventually turned to pimping for a prostitute he knew.

"I was very proud of doing these things," he recalled. "I was big time, the slickest cat around."

He lived for a time with his grandmother, Frances, who had moved north from Augusta in 1954, and spent a few days with his mother, Marie. But that ended when they quarreled over his demands for money, Marie told the police. When she didn't give him as much as he wanted, he pulled a knife and threatened to kill her, Marie claimed.

Butch had a different memory of the encounter. As he recalled it, he was "extremely disgusted" to find that his mother was still a prostitute. It hurt him. Marie was working at the Dreamland Cafe at the corner of Lenox Avenue and 111th Street, an establishment "frequented by prostitutes, pimps, and drug addicts," according to a parole officer who investigated Butch's background.

Life was now moving fast for Butch. He found a girlfriend, Bertha Price, and a few weeks later, she was pregnant. He also began hanging around with two other teenagers who had been in Wiltwyck or Rockland with him, Russell Williams and Arnold James. Williams, like Butch, was an escapee from the mental hospital. They all smoked marijuana together and mugged a few people on the street. Butch was the tallest, strongest, and smartest, and he became their leader.

On December 19, 1957, a little more than two months after he ran away from Rockland, Butch suggested doing something bigger. They were short of cash, and the others favored another mugging. But Butch said, "If you do something, you should do something big, because if you get caught, you get the same time."

What Butch had in mind was robbing a liquor store. At 11 o'clock that evening, he strapped a hunting knife to his back and the three of them walked to the Jade Liquor Store at the corner of Broadway and West 109th Street. They checked first to make sure there were no policemen around, then Butch and Williams sauntered in, leaving James outside as a sentry, and Butch ordered a bottle of wine. When the clerk, John Gabriel, bent down to get it, Butch drew his knife over his shoulder and pointed it at Gabriel.

"Give me the money from the cash register," Butch demanded. "If you make a move you're a dead man."

As the clerk moved to comply, Butch called James to come in and take the money, $82.75, as well as strip the clerk's wristwatch from his arm. Butch helped himself to a bottle of Calverts Reserve Whiskey from behind the counter.

"Don't move, or you're dead," Butch repeated as the three ran out the door.

Butch's winning streak now ran out. They had gone only a few blocks when patrolmen Don Balancia and Martin O'Halloran spotted them from their squad car and chased after them. Balancia pulled his gun and ordered them to stop. Butch heard the command. "I saw the gun and decided not to outrun no bullet," he said in a handwritten confession made less than an hour later. He was still laughing about the robbery in the station house, but he agreed to plead guilty. In his own way, he had reached manhood.

Before sentencing, a judge ordered Butch to Bellevue one more time to determine whether he was mentally competent. When asked why he had escaped from Rockland, Butch replied: "I was crazy." That satisfied the two psychiatrists who examined him. This time they found no evidence he was psychotic; in their estimation, he was merely antisocial.

His father came to his sentencing on April 22, 1958. James asked the judge, George M. Carney, to release Butch to his custody and said he would take him to Ohio, where he had foster parents. It was a tale concocted for the court. James himself had been arrested on a burglary charge shortly after Butch had been picked up, and he was out on bail awaiting trial. A few days after Butch was sentenced, James would be sentenced, too, to a year on Rikers Island.

At Butch's sentencing, his attorney from the Legal Aid Society, Jean Cox, asked Judge Carney to be merciful "in view of the defendant's unhappy history of mental disturbance and certainly unhappy circumstances in his home."

Judge Carney ignored her appeal. He gave Butch five years in prison. "I hope," he said as he passed sentence, "that when you come out you learn to live a normal life."

Butch had to laugh at that. To him, prison and reformatories were normal.

"I never had what good people call a home, so when they kept putting me in institutions, I had to make my own home," he told prison officials. "After awhile, it was okay in a way, because wherever I went, I had friends. They became my family."

Butch was sent first to Elmira, a prison that was used as a "reception center" to test and classify inmates for assignment to more permanent quarters in other prisons around New York State.

"I have been a wild animal all my life," Butch told a prison psychologist, one of a battery of social workers, doctors, mental health counselors, and chaplains who tested him. "I spent my entire life taking whatever I wanted, in any way I could get it, and violence was the usual method."

There was an element of boastfulness, of grandiosity, in what he said that was becoming characteristic of him. But there was also more than an element of truth.

"It's fortunate I was arrested when I was," he added. "Otherwise it was only a matter of time till I ended up killing someone."

Butch scored well above average on a series of psychological tests, with an IQ of 130—a surprise to the authorities. If he had had a different upbringing and education, his score might have been even higher. The "Psychologist's Examination Report," by Howard Pashens, Ph.D., read: "Figure drawings suggest above average ability. Bosket has probably a strong need to appear as a virile, adequate male which might conceal underlying feeling of inadequacy. His drawing of the female suggests much anxiety in that area."

A medical exam revealed clues to his life story, like the rings of a tree. He had a gunshot wound in his right leg from boyhood, a two-inch knife-wound scar on his left cheek, and traces of a fracture in his right leg suffered when he was hit by a car during a failed escape from Wiltwyck at age twelve. Three teeth were missing, casualties of street fights. He had once been thrown out of a building and fell twenty feet, landing on his head. At fourteen, he had been treated for gonorrhea.

The prison psychiatrist, Dr. Leonard J. Bolton, reported the now-familiar findings:

> Subject here reveals a youth who has been subject to rejection. He has been subjected to a pathologic environment, an indifferent father who is an alcoholic and mentally disturbed. . . . It is clear this youth, resentful and hostile, has turned his resentfulness and hostility against the world. His behavior is a dramatization of his feelings.

Dr. Bolton's diagnosis was "sociopathic personality, antisocial type."

It was just the latest term for a psychopath, and Dr. Bolton held out little hope for Butch. "There is no need for any psychiatric attention, nor can psychiatric treatment change his personality," Dr. Bolton wrote. "Prognosis, poor."

The doctor was following the conventional wisdom that psychopaths are essentially irredeemable. There are no drugs to treat the condition, as there are now for schizophrenia and depression. The only possible hope for rehabilitation, most psychiatrists believe, is to confine antisocial patients for a prolonged period in a special secure institution, with strict controls over them, and to totally eradicate their old ways of thinking. The Chinese had a word for it—brainwashing.

This was a grim finding for Butch. He was being permanently written off despite an early background that was not his fault and the potential his IQ test showed.

After three months at Elmira, he was assigned to Great Meadow Correctional Institution, where he tried to prove all the worst analyses of him correct. He was constantly in fights with other inmates and once, in the exercise yard, knocked a prisoner named Anderson unconscious by hitting him in the head with a crowbar. A guard tried to intervene, but Butch threw a rock at him and screamed, "Fuck you. I don't give a fuck what you do." He was rewarded by being kept in solitary confinement for nearly a year.

His conduct earned him the reputation he sought—he was labeled "a strong arm type and a real troublemaker."

The code for survival in prison, Butch had learned, was an extension of the code of the streets. Maintain a truculent exterior, beware of insults, and always be ready to fight. The only law in prison was the law of self-defense, the same as on the streets of Harlem and Augusta and much the same as it had been in Saluda and Edgefield in the nineteenth century. A man of respect did not depend on the law to protect him.

BUTCH WAS PAROLED in June 1961, after serving a little more than three years of his sentence. He moved in with his uncle, Johnnie Miller, his mother's younger brother. Miller lived at 114 West 114th Street, just north of Central Park. When Butch's parole officer, John A. Taylor, first visited there, Miller was drunk and "his speech was hazy and incoherent." But Miller assured Taylor that he would give Butch a good home.

Butch was soon spending most of his time in an apartment on the ground floor of the building with Laura Roane, a short, outgoing twenty-year-old who lived there with her mother. Laura had dropped out of high school three years earlier, when she gave birth to a daughter named Cheryl, and she was now working in a ballpoint pen factory in the Bronx as an assembly-line worker.

Butch was a very handsome man, Laura thought when she first glimpsed him from her window going in and out of the building. "He was a chunk, a real chunk," she said to herself. Miller had introduced them, and in no time, Butch and Laura were going to the movies and walking in the park.

"He was very intelligent," Laura quickly sensed. "And very manly. He wasn't like those other ones out there, who, as soon as they see a woman, think she'll go to bed with them. He wasn't that type of man. He was very nice. He had respect for women."

Laura was also impressed that Butch always seemed to have money. "He was never out of cash," she observed. She didn't ask where he got it.

A few weeks later, Butch proposed to her. Laura said yes immediately. "He didn't have to ask twice."

They had to tell Butch's parole officer and get permission from the parole board; that was still the law in New York at the time. Laura was also supposed to be informed about Butch's criminal record. It didn't bother her. "That didn't make no difference to me, no difference at all. He said he had murdered a man, but he was very charming and very intelligent."

After the parole board gave its approval, Butch and Laura were married in Municipal Court in lower Manhattan on October 24, 1961. It was a festive occasion, the past forgotten for the day. They even invited Marie.

Things were looking up for Butch. After a series of manual jobs, which he quit or was fired from after a few days each, he had started working steadily as a laboratory technician trainee at Evans Color Lab in Long Island City. He was learning to process color photographs, making fifty-five dollars a week, and the owner thought highly of him. The lab had a government contract, which gave Butch "a feeling of immense significance," Taylor reported.

Early in June 1962, Butch confided to Taylor, a conscientious though sympathetic fellow African-American, that Laura was pregnant. The baby, scheduled to be born the following December, would be named Willie Bosket.

A big smile came over Butch's face. "The wildness," he insisted, "is all gone."

CHAPTER 7

BUTCH

The Pawnshop

Murder is a hard pillow to sleep on.

Butch Bosket

H IS EARLIEST MEMORY, David Hurwitz used to say, was of a
pogrom in czarist Russia. He was born there in 1898, the same
year as Golda Meir, and like her, he moved with his family to Milwaukee
early in the next century.

Milwaukee was a proud, clean, prosperous city made up heavily of
German and Eastern European immigrants, with an improbably conservative Socialist municipal government. It had been founded by fur traders
on propitious land where three rivers flowed into the western edge of
Lake Michigan. The Potawatomi Indians, who originally inhabited the
site, called it Mah-au-wauk-seepe—"gathering place by the river." Beginning in the 1840s, the German settlers made Milwaukee the brewing
capital of America, some of them lending their names to its beers: Frederick Pabst, Joseph Schlitz, and Frederick Miller. By 1900, Milwaukee had
more than three hundred breweries. There were good jobs in the breweries
and in the heavy machine foundries, like Bucyrus-Erie, and there were
taverns on every corner where the workers went in the afternoons to have
their beer. On the lake, you could take a steamer with a dance band at
9 o'clock Saturday night and float down to Chicago, stay fifteen minutes,
and be back home in bed by 3 o'clock Sunday morning.

But Milwaukee was also a serious city, with good museums, libraries,
and hospitals reflecting its Germanic heritage. Few people worried about
crime. Milwaukee liked to boast that it had the lowest crime rate of any
city in the country. In the spring of 1962, when Butch told his parole
officer that Laura was pregnant, the students at Marquette University felt

perfectly safe walking downtown along Wisconsin Avenue, Milwaukee's grand boulevard. They walked from the campus to basketball games, or to a restaurant and the movies. On weekends, if they were broke, they took their stereos to a row of pawnshops on West Wells Street, around the corner from Wisconsin Avenue. It was a run-down block of shabby one-story brick buildings, with an X-rated movie theater and an all-night coffee shop in the old Belmont Hotel, advertised by a big red art deco neon sign. Coming out of the larger, more respectable movie theaters nearby, the students often stopped in the coffee shop for a late-evening snack and were surprised to see paunchy older men talking to heavily made-up young women who hung around the area. Prostitution was not something students at a good Catholic school in Milwaukee in the early 1960s knew a lot about.

David Hurwitz operated one of the pawnshops, called Dave's Tailor Shop, at 330 West Wells Street. It was a small business, just one long room that ran back deep and narrow from the front display window. There were racks with men's suits and pants along both sides of the shop, and toward the back, a big worktable held the cash register. Hurwitz was a short, stocky man, only five feet five inches tall and one hundred forty pounds. His neighbors and the waitresses in the Belmont Hotel coffee shop, where he stopped every morning for a cup of coffee before work, thought he was a nice enough man, friendly and talkative. But you couldn't run a pawnshop for twenty years, as Hurwitz had, without developing a little crust. And some people said he supplemented his store's income by dealing in pornography.

At 1 o'clock in the afternoon of Thursday, July 19, 1962, a tall, well-built black man with a hairline mustache walked into Dave's Tailor Shop. He was dressed in a short-sleeved light blue sport shirt and dark pants. "Who's Dave?" he asked. "Where can I find Dave?"

It was Butch. He explained politely to the man who identified himself as Dave that he was a stranger in town, that he was from New York, and that he was getting desperate for money. He had not been able to find a job, he said, and his wife was pregnant. They had arrived in Milwaukee two days earlier with only fourteen dollars, and he had spent ten of that the first day getting a room in a boardinghouse. He was worried that he wouldn't be able to buy dinner that evening for Laura.

But he had something to sell, Butch said: 150 pictures and their negatives.

"What kind of pictures?" Hurwitz asked.

"Pornographic pictures," Butch replied.

"Let me see them," Hurwitz said, moving closer.

So Butch pulled the photographs out of an envelope he was carrying.

There was one with a caption entitled "Show Auntie How Big," another bearing the inscription "What's Your Position in Life," a photograph showing a small boy and a goose, and lots of nudes of both sexes.

Butch did not say how he had gotten the pictures, that he had stolen them from his employer in New York, the Evans Color Lab. Nor did he say that he had also taken a bunch of blank checks from the office and had been cashing them around the Midwest over the past month, after violating his parole in New York. Of course, the owner had not reported any of this to the police, for it might have raised questions about what he was doing with the pictures in the first place.

Hurwitz liked what he saw. "Yes, they're real nice," he said. "I think I'll be able to do something with them." But Hurwitz insisted he did not have the cash to pay for them today. "I have to see somebody about this," he told Butch. "Come back tomorrow. I'll give you fifty dollars."

Butch, needing money immediately, wasn't too happy about the arrangement. Patience had never been one of his virtues anyhow, and his agitation was beginning to show. His eyes grew wide, bulging out, his neck muscles tensed, and his jaw started working. He looked like somebody who had just been given some disastrous news and was on the edge of a breakdown.

He asked Hurwitz for a small advance payment, a dollar or two. Hurwitz refused, saying the only money he had in the cash register was for making change.

Butch walked across the street to Lubin's Pawnshop, where he tried to hock his black corduroy coat. But Mary Lubin, the proprietor, did not want it. He finally found a taker at Kahn's Second-Hand Store, just up the block, where Gertrude Kahn paid him ten dollars for it. He signed the pawn ticket Butch Bosket, giving the address where he was staying, 2619 North Palmer Street.

With the cash, Butch continued his search for work. He registered at the Wisconsin state employment office and checked a lead at the Krause Milling Company, which was looking for a maintenance man. That evening, he stopped by the office of the Milwaukee *Star*, having heard they might need a darkroom technician.

Naturally, he embroidered his resumé a little. It was pretty hard to come right out and say you were a convicted felon who had spent practically your entire life incarcerated in one institution or another. Besides, Butch had become a smooth talker. As an orphan of the streets, you learned to talk fast and convincingly. So at one place, he said he was a wounded marine veteran, that he had just been discharged from the Second Marine Division in Japan. Elsewhere, he let it be known that he had attended City College in New York, or alternatively, that he was an experienced machinist. But everywhere he applied for work, he gave his real name, address, place of birth, and social security number.

Butch didn't get back to the boardinghouse until 11 p.m. Laura was upstairs in their room, reading a magazine. He had bought her a supply of reading matter, since he was going to be out all day. She had copies of *Modern Romance, Confidential Confessions,* and *Official Detective.* At four and a half months, Laura was beginning to show the baby she was carrying. Her belly was bulging, and her breasts were getting larger by the day. She was always after Butch to buy more food. It takes a lot to satisfy an appetite when you are eating for two.

That night, Laura complained that her feet were becoming swollen, a side effect of pregnancy. But he told her that he was going to be paid the following day, and they went to bed happy. With Butch, things were never exactly normal, yet they seemed to work out.

The next morning, Butch was up early. He had the energy of a maniac. He was out of the house before 7, even before the landlady, Bertha Fields, was awake. He took the bus downtown and walked by Dave's Tailor Shop to see if it was open.

About the same time, David Hurwitz was entering the Belmont Hotel coffee shop for his usual morning refreshment. He left at 8 o'clock and stopped to talk with his neighbor on West Wells Street, Frank Browender, the owner of Midwest Stores, a cheap clothing shop. It was a muggy summer morning, with the temperature in the mid-seventies already, so they stood outside on the sidewalk, which was cooler than the interior of the stuffy, non-air-conditioned store. Just before 8:30, Hurwitz noticed a regular customer, William Locke, walk up to his shop, so he left Browender and unlocked his front door.

A minute later, Butch walked in. Hurwitz was in the back, hanging up his dark green plaid jacket.

"Good morning, Dave," Butch exclaimed cheerily.

Hurwitz looked at him as if he had never seen Butch before—a real unfriendly greeting, Butch thought.

Still, undaunted, Butch asked, "Do you have the money for my pictures?"

"What pictures, what are you talking about?" Hurwitz said sharply.

"The pictures I left with you last night," Butch replied, puzzled.

Hurwitz got a big grin on his face. "You didn't leave any pictures with me last night; I don't have any money for you."

"But I did leave the pictures with you last night, I know I did," Butch said, his eyes protuberating and his jaw clenching. He took a step closer to Hurwitz. The anger was starting to emanate from him, like the heat from the backwash of a jet engine. "Look, all I want is my money, or the pictures back, either one."

Butch towered over the diminutive pawnbroker, but Hurwitz seemed to think Butch was in the weaker position, being from out of town and down on his luck. Maybe he didn't think much of Negroes, as they were then called. For a big city, Milwaukee still had a very small African-American community, nothing like Chicago's or Detroit's. Whatever the case, Hurwitz was defiant. "I got no pictures for you," he yelled at Butch. "I don't deal with filth like you. Now get the hell out of my store, you son of a bitch, or I'll call the cops."

Just at that moment, Butch happened to glimpse his photographs behind the cash register. He reached around to reclaim them, and Hurwitz started pushing and grabbing him, to get him out of the shop.

Now everything in Butch's life came together at once. Here was a man calling him a liar, and trying to hustle him, of all people, and flinging insults at him. From the time he was a small boy, he had learned that disrespect was the worst thing a man could do to you. He had been taught to fight, to use physical violence to meet a threat. It was a tradition as old as the county his family came from, as old as Edgefield.

"The man is just trying to take advantage of me," was the thought racing through Butch's mind. "He is disrespecting me."

He felt the blood rush to his head, and a pounding welled up in his ears. He had the feeling that everything was going wrong at once. He needed to take instant action, to get his hands on something and smash it. Just as at Wiltwyck, when he attacked the painting he was drawing of the Indian with the raised tomahawk, Butch went wild with rage and lost control. Afterward, he could never remember exactly what happened. It was all very hazy.

He must have grabbed the long hunting knife from the sheath strapped to his back, though afterward he claimed it was a knife he happened to find on the pawnshop table. His first thrust hit Hurwitz on the right side of his chest, just above the nipple area. The knife cut through the skin, through the rib cage, and on through the lung, and pierced Hurwitz's aorta. Blood spurted out of the wound; the knife had caused a massive hemorrhage in the pericardial sac around the heart.

Hurwitz staggered, trying to clutch at Butch. As he slid down, his body twisted, and Butch stabbed him five more times, in the back.

Until now, Butch had not paid much attention to the other man in the shop, William Locke. Locke was a small man, five feet six inches tall, and weighed only one hundred and one pounds. He was fifty-eight years old, and for the last twenty-five years, he had worked as a stereotyper at the nearby Milwaukee *Sentinel.* He had come to pawn a pair of pants, which he was holding in his hands.

When he saw Hurwitz shouting at Butch and trying to push him out of the shop, Locke had come over to help. He was grabbing at Butch's arm. Butch stabbed him, too. He drove his knife into Locke's chest six times in rapid succession, like a machine gun firing. One of the blows— it was impossible later to tell which one—went right into the center of Locke's chest and punctured his heart.

Blood from the fatal wound spurted in Butch's face. It was like a cold shower that awoke Butch from a trance. He looked down and saw the knife in his hand. "Oh, my God," he said out loud to himself.

He noticed that his shirt was soaked with blood. He couldn't go outside that way, so he walked over and picked up Hurwitz's jacket, which the dead man had taken off only a few minutes before. He could feel Hurwitz's wallet in the coat, which was very tight on him, and he stopped to take Locke's wallet out of his jacket. Butch did not touch the cash register.

He rushed to the door, to get outside and run home. But just as Butch turned the doorknob from the inside, another customer was opening the door from the outside.

Wenzel Stenowski had been standing in front of the display window watching when the argument started. He had seen Hurwitz gesticulate angrily at Butch and try to shove him, and he had seen the look of rage on Butch's face. He had decided to leave, however, just before the stabbings occurred. Then he abruptly changed his mind and came back. It was his day off, and he wanted to buy a suit.

As Butch came out the door, Stenowski could see blood everywhere on him: on his shirt, on his hands, and on his face. He thought maybe Butch had been the one attacked and was concerned for him.

"Pardon me, mister, I know one of you are [sic] hurt," Stenowski said with the heavy German accent of his native Munich. "You look like a butcher."

Butch walked rapidly down the sidewalk, turning into an alley to get out of sight. He had learned enough about Milwaukee's geography in his three days there to know the rooming house was to the north and a little west of where he was, and he headed up Third Street. When he reached the Schlitz brewery, a hulking compound of antiquated red-brick structures almost four blocks square, he threw away the knife.

About 9:30, Butch got back to 2619 North Palmer Street. It was a three-story, wooden, Victorian-era house with a steeply pitched roof and craftsman's details typical of Milwaukee. The neighborhood had once been solidly German. But in recent years blacks had begun moving in, and the landlady, Bertha Fields, was African-American.

After he returned, Butch just said to Laura, "Come on, we're gone."

He didn't say anything about the killings, though he told her to pack and gave her fifty dollars to hold. It was all the money he had taken from the two dead men's wallets; it also happened to be precisely the amount Hurwitz had agreed to pay him for the photographs.

Butch washed off the blood and changed his clothes. Then he went down to the basement where Mrs. Fields was cleaning up her rumpus room and watching television. He wondered if she could call a cab for him, because he had been lucky to find a nice job in Racine, Wisconsin, as a caretaker for some elderly people. He said it was on account of his army record, having been wounded in Korea and having received a medal. That made the people happy to hire him.

"Thank you, ma'am, for being so nice to me," Butch said to Mrs. Fields. He was effusive and polite, and made a good impression on her. The whole time he had stayed in her house, he was always smiling and laughing.

Butch then went outside, where Victoria Fields was playing. She was a bright, vivacious eight-year-old who liked attending Sunday school at St. Mark's AME Church. Butch was carrying a large juice container. He had stuffed Locke's and Hurwitz's wallets into it, along with his bloody shirt and Hurwitz's suit jacket. Victoria saw him throw the container into the big in-ground garbage can. She was watching him closely because Butch had promised her a nickel. Now, as he walked back to the house, he said, "Here, share this with me," and handed her a dime.

When the unlicensed Apex taxi arrived, Butch put Laura and their two suitcases in the cab, and then came back to the front porch, where Mrs. Fields was standing. With great courtesy, he said goodbye, adding, "I want to shake your hand for being so nice to me."

In the cab, Butch asked the driver, L. C. Jamison, "What's the quickest train out of town?" Jamison said it was the North Shore, which left every hour for Chicago, so they headed for the railroad station.

Along the way, they happened to drive right by 330 West Wells Street. By now, the news of the double murder was on the radio, and the driver pointed out the location to Butch.

"I wonder if they've caught the guy yet?" Butch inquired.

LOUIS JANKOWITZ WAS ten minutes late for work Friday morning. He saw the hands reading 8:40 on a barbershop clock at the corner, just before he walked into Dave's Tailor Shop. It made him feel bad. He had been a salesman for Hurwitz as long as either of them could remember, and he was always punctual. Jankowitz was sixty-five years old and about to retire.

He hung his coat by the door and called out, "Good morning." No reply. That seemed kind of funny, but he began to busy himself. It was only a little later that he walked to the back of the shop and saw the two bodies on the floor. Jankowitz was dazed. He didn't see the blood, he was so stunned. He thought maybe they were unconscious. He went next door to Frank Browender's store. "Something's wrong," he said. "Dave is lying back there."

The two of them returned to the shop and took a long look. Hurwitz was flat on his back, with his head resting on the top step of the stairs to the basement. There was blood all over him, and a big pool of blood on the floor of the basement where it had run down the steps. Locke was doubled up in a squatting position, as if in pain. His head and chest were hunched forward, on top of Hurwitz's feet.

The police arrived three minutes after Browender called them. By noontime, forty-seven detectives had been assigned to the investigation, essentially the entire Milwaukee police force.

The murders shocked Milwaukee. A double homicide was rare in the city by the lake, particularly one this vicious. Before it was over, before Butch was found and convicted and put in prison, and then escaped and was recaptured and escaped again, he would become about the most notorious murderer in Milwaukee until Jeffrey Dahmer.

PEOPLE LIKED TO THINK that murder was linked to cities. The commonly accepted wisdom was that as America's cities got bigger and more crowded, traditional social bonds broke down and neighborhoods decayed, replaced by impersonal factories and then by increases in disease, disorder, delinquency, and violent crime. It was a clear, precise thesis— cities bred pathology—and it had been given scholarly backing by an eminent group of sociologists from the University of Chicago. The murders of David Hurwitz and William Locke only seemed to confirm the notion to the people of Milwaukee.

The trouble was, the theory was wrong. From the 1850s to the early 1960s, for a full century, the murder rate in big cities across the northern United States had actually been declining. It was a long, uneven but steady decrease that made a nice, clean, swooping descent when plotted on a graph.

In New York, Philadelphia, and Boston, and, in fact, in the twenty largest metropolises, the homicide rate dropped by 40 to 50 percent in the late nineteenth century. The bigger the cities grew, the lower their level of violent crime. In Philadelphia, the murder rate fell from 4 per 100,000 in the 1850s to 2.2 per 100,000 in the 1890s. In New York, the biggest city in the country, a city whose name became synonymous with violence, the homicide rate dropped from 6.6 per 100,000 in the decade of the 1850s to 4.2 per 100,000 in the 1950s. By contrast, in Saluda, the homicide rate around the turn of the century was about 35 per 100,000. If Samuel Colt had not introduced his repeating pistol after the Civil War, making murder much easier, the reduction in the North's big cities would have been even greater.

The decline in urban violence in the nineteenth century was part of a long-term decrease that began in the sixteenth and seventeenth centuries in much of Western Europe. In earlier years, in the Middle Ages, historians have found, murder rates may have been ten times as high as they are today in Europe. Most homicides started as sudden quarrels among peasants in their fields who were grubbing for existence. Insults to honor were taken very seriously, and violence was the accepted method of settling disputes, since the king's courts were slow, expensive, and corrupt. The weapons of choice in England were the quarter-staff, a stout wooden stick used for herding animals or for walking on the muddy roads, and the knife. Everyone carried a knife, even women, since if you sat down somewhere to eat, you were expected to bring your own. Wounds often proved fatal because of the danger of infection in an era with little sanitation. But after 1500, the growing power of the state gradually exerted a "civilizing process," in the phrase of the German sociologist Norbert Elias. Violence diminished first in urban areas, rather than in villages, as the nobility was transformed from knights into courtiers, and official justice administered by courts replaced private vengeance conducted by feuds, knife fights, and duels. Slowly, individuals had to learn better manners and to control their reckless, impulsive behavior. The resulting decrease in violence was so sharp that the homicide rate in Amsterdam fell from 47 per 100,000 in the mid-fifteenth century to only 1 to 1.5 per 100,000 in 1800.

In American cities, where homicide rates have tended to be higher than in their European counterparts, the civilizing process speeded up after 1850 with the coming of the Industrial Revolution. In the thousands of new factories, people had to answer to the discipline of the bell, clock, and foreman, the historian Roger Lane has written. Factory time replaced individual time, squeezing out the easy workaday drinking, the leisure and unpredictability of life that often led to violence in the countryside or early cities.

For children in late-nineteenth-century urban America, the burgeoning system of public schools taught not only literacy but the self-control to sit still, take turns, and obey the teacher. The growing popularity of Sunday schools, the YMCA, and the temperance movement also inhibited reckless behavior. By the last decade of the nineteenth century, millions of Americans in the nation's big cities went to school, to work, and to baseball games in a more peaceable way than their grandparents did.

The cities of the North were also helped by being bastions of dignity, the polar opposite of honor. Dignity held that every person was born equal—theoretically speaking—and possessed his or her own inner worth. Disciples of dignity did not depend on the opinion of others, as did the exponents of honor. Hence, they could ignore the slights and insults that precipitated fights in the South.

As poor African-Americans began migrating to the northern cities at the end of the nineteenth century and then in bigger and bigger waves during World War I and the 1920s, it might have seemed likely that they would adopt the new ways of the metropolis. But blacks were largely shut out of jobs in the industrial economy, and therefore did not share in its new values. They were isolated by discrimination, high unemployment, bad schools, and unsafe neighborhoods.

In these desperate conditions, Southern-born honor found a new spawning ground. Honor became even more dangerous when combined with poverty, racism, and big-city slums. In a world with so little opportunity for young black men, respect was one thing they could aspire to. "The significance of a jostle, a slightly derogatory remark, or the appearance of a weapon in the hands of an adversary" means something to poor blacks that it does not to the middle and upper classes, wrote the criminologists Marvin Wolfgang and Franco Ferracuti in a study of urban homicide. "A male is usually expected to defend the name and honor of his mother, the virtue of womanhood . . . and to accept no derogation about his race, his age or his masculinity."

It could have been a description of Butch. His sensitivity to insults and threats vibrated like a tuning fork.

THE ONLY CLUE the Milwaukee police had, the morning the two bodies were found, was the description Wenzel Stenowski gave them of the man who had come out of Dave's Tailor Shop covered with blood. It wasn't too good.

Question: "Would you know this colored man if you saw him?"

Stenowski: "When I see him I will know him again. One colored man looks like another man."

That afternoon, however, the investigators got lucky. At 3:30, Harry

Kahn, the proprietor of Kahn's Second-Hand Store on West Wells Street, called to report that he had just seen a television broadcast with a description of the suspect. He thought the man resembled a fellow who had sold a jacket in his store the day before. Yes, Kahn said, he had the sales ticket. The man had signed it Butch Bosket. He had listed his address as 2619 North Palmer.

Butch had not made any effort to disguise his identity or his whereabouts. He had not planned the murders, so he had not taken any precautions. On the contrary, he had left clues scattered everywhere. All the police needed, it turned out, was to find one dangling thread. Then, when they gave it a tug, the whole fabric unraveled in their hands.

As soon as headquarters radioed the name Bosket and the Palmer Street address, Detective Dewey Russ and his partner, Leroy Jones, were on their way. They were quite a pair. Russ and Jones were the first two African-Americans to make the rank of detective in Milwaukee. They were both intelligent, ambitious men who had been born into poverty in Arkansas and had come to Milwaukee as teenagers. Russ was big and rawboned, with a broad, pleasant-looking face and an avuncular manner. He walked into a room, and you felt comfortable.

Having grown up on the street himself, Russ knew something about it, about how to work a suspect. Of course, it didn't hurt that he was often assigned to cases with black suspects, and these men, many with long rap sheets, were not used to seeing a black detective. That helped him get past their natural defensive reflexes.

Bertha Fields was happy to oblige the policemen when they knocked on her door. Butch had indeed stayed in her house, she said. "He was very memorable, always saying, 'Yes, sir,' or 'Yes, ma'am.' Couldn't ask for a nicer fellow." He even cleaned up his room real nice before leaving, she related, and took out the garbage. Maybe Victoria, her eight-year-old daughter, had seen him throw away the garbage. She had been playing outside.

Victoria remembered well. She had watched Butch closely because of the money he had promised her. So she told Detectives Russ and Jones that she had seen him take the juice container and dump it in the concrete garbage bin.

Russ and Jones thought there might be something in it. They climbed down amid the garbage, dirtying their suits, but it was well worth it. By 5:30, they had most of the evidence they needed—everything except the knife. They sent Butch's blue shirt off to the state crime laboratory. Eventually, the lab found that it contained both Hurwitz's and Locke's blood.

That same afternoon, a man from the Krause Milling Company called in after hearing about the murders on the radio. He had Butch's social security number and address in New York.

Some other detectives got in touch with Apex cab. Since Apex was unlicensed, it was easy to put the squeeze on its drivers. Afraid of being arrested, the cabby who drove Butch to the railroad station even remembered that he said he was planning on going to Chicago, then back to New York. Milwaukee had turned out to be a disappointment, Butch explained, too small and dull.

Butch had nearly drawn a map for the police, leaving out only his estimated date of return to Manhattan.

Once they had a name, the FBI called the New York City police and Butch's parole officer, John Taylor. Taylor had been dutifully looking for Butch for a month, since June 20, 1962, the day he failed to show up for work at Evans Color Lab. Well before Butch took off, Taylor had sensed he was growing increasingly agitated. He didn't like sharing an apartment with Laura's meddling mother, Nancy Roane, he told Taylor, and he was beginning to feel attracted to some ladies on the street he had known while pimping.

That was the way ex-cons were, Taylor had learned in studying to be a parole officer. They were used to the criminal life, to taking what they wanted by manipulation or violence, and they did not have much impulse control to slow them down. Prison did not really rehabilitate them. They only learned how to be more predatory to survive. So after they were paroled, there was an 80 percent chance they would slip back into their old ways and be rearrested.

One afternoon, Laura had found Butch in bed with one of his prostitutes. She fled back to her mother. That made Butch feel bad. After all, Laura was pregnant. To win her back, he proposed an adventure. He was leaving for Chicago, he said, on a big business deal. He didn't provide any details. But he would send her the money to join him after he got there.

He was a nice guy who always seemed to have lots of cash, Laura reckoned. She was real impressed by his trip. Why not join him?

When his letter arrived, with the money, she took off. Butch had cautioned her not to tell anybody anything; she just said she was going to the movies. Butch knew he was wanted for stealing the pornographic pictures and checks from Evans Color Lab and didn't want anyone tracing his movements. Of course, he did not realize at the time that his employer was afraid to report the theft. He could have just stayed in New York. That way, he said to himself later, there might not have been any murders.

On the morning of August 22, 1962, a month after the killings, Taylor received a phone call in his office. He recognized Butch's voice.

"What is this I hear about the FBI wanting to see me, man?" Butch asked.

He had just arrived by bus from St. Louis, he said, and had dropped Laura off at her mother's apartment. Her feet were pretty badly swollen, and she was feeling sick, so it seemed like a good idea to take her home. But when he got there, her mother reported that the FBI was all over the place hunting for him; something about two men murdered in Milwaukee.

Butch told his parole officer that he had been in Milwaukee, sure enough. But he wasn't involved in any murders. That disturbed him deeply, he said. He asked Taylor for advice.

"If you are innocent, you should turn yourself in to the FBI immediately," Taylor counseled.

Over the phone, it was hard for Taylor to gauge Butch's mind. One moment, he insisted on his innocence, with a display of bravado; the next he sounded frantic, as if he might be about to confess. Taylor guessed that whenever something bothered Butch, he got very brave. One part of him was boastful and probably thought he could talk his way out of it. Taylor never ceased to be amazed by how felons tripped themselves up by talking too much through sheer braggadocio. But the other part of Butch was in that advanced stage of frenzy where he couldn't keep a thought to himself.

Turn yourself in to the FBI, Taylor kept repeating, until Butch hung up.

Fifteen minutes later, Butch appeared at 209 East Sixty-ninth Street in Manhattan, FBI headquarters. In surrendering, he said, "I'd like to correct this gross error."

THE NEXT MORNING, Detective Dewey Russ flew to New York.

So far, although it had been a really heinous crime, the police had done an excellent job, Russ thought as he flew eastward. Or rather, Butch had done a good job for them. But Russ still felt he needed a confession to get a conviction. The police had a witness who could put Butch at the scene of the crime, but they didn't have the murder weapon, nor did they have a motive. A confession would be real handy. It would also raise morale back at the Safety Building, Milwaukee's combination police headquarters, jail, and criminal courthouse.

Right from the start, things went well for Russ in New York. Butch told the judge hearing his case that he would waive extradition to Wisconsin. He didn't even want a lawyer. He just wanted to get back to Milwaukee and clear up the misunderstanding.

Butch was surprised to see Russ was a black man. Russ told him,

"I'm your kind, and I will do what I can to help you." The detective also bought Butch some sandwiches, and asked if Butch wanted him to get Laura in for a visit before he was taken back to Milwaukee. Yes, Butch said, thanks, and he gave Russ his wife's address.

Of course, that made it easier for Russ to question Laura and get her to write out a statement. Russ didn't mention that to Butch in New York.

He called Laura and told her to come to his room at the Taft Hotel, Room 2029. She arrived with her mother, Nancy Roane. They had assumed Russ intended to make Laura go back to Milwaukee and face a police investigation, and possibly a trial. They didn't have a lawyer and didn't know that a wife cannot be forced to testify against her husband.

Laura was very scared. She kept thinking, "Here I am with my big belly and I don't even know what's going on." So she was enormously relieved when Russ said, "I know you didn't do it." All you have to do, Russ told her, is write out what happened in Milwaukee. "It would be a shame to make a pregnant lady like yourself go all the way back to Wisconsin and get involved in a trial," Russ said courteously. "Just write everything down and you'll be free and clear."

For forty-five minutes, Laura labored over the long yellow pad Russ handed her, finally filling out two pages in her schoolgirl's hand. She tried hard to tell the truth, while not implicating Butch. However, she wasn't a pro at this sort of thing.

> On Friday July 20, My husband, Butch Bosket went out, and when he returned he told me to start packing, and said that we were leaving. When my husband came home that Friday morning, he give me some money to hold. He had about $50. He took the garbage out while I was packing. Later on Butch told me that a second man came at him with a pair of sissors [sic] from in back of him. When we took a cab to the train station, we past [sic] the store where two men got killed. The knife the F.B.I. took from my home belong [sic] in my kitchen and was not used by my husband because it never left my room.
>
> Mrs. Laura Bosket
> August 26, 1962

Legally, it wasn't much of a statement and did not directly incriminate Butch. But read another way, it suggested that Laura knew something and that Butch was involved. For Dewey Russ, the trick would be in how he used it.

Still, he was feeling good after talking with Laura. He sent a telegram back to his commander in Milwaukee: "Confident will get confession from Bosket as soon as return. Have car waiting. Subject is a wild one and a mental case."

Northwest Airlines Flight 229 left Idlewild Airport at 6:10 p.m. for the flight to Milwaukee. A New York squad car drove Butch, Russ, and his new partner, Sergeant Henry Zwick, right onto the tarmac. The three men boarded the plane before the other passengers. Butch was seated in the front row of first class, next to the window, with Russ beside him in the aisle seat and Zwick just behind them. Airline rules forbade prisoners from being handcuffed while on board, so as not to alarm the regular travelers. Russ figured it didn't matter anyway, because where would Butch escape to with the plane in the air?

When the stewardess came by and asked Butch if he wanted a pillow, he got a big smile on his face and said, "Yes, ma'am. Thank you very much." She served him shrimp cocktail and a filet of turkey dinner, with a baked potato, green beans, and a choice of two kinds of ice cream for dessert.

Butch was having fun, like a kid in a toy store. It was his first plane ride, and it made him think of all the things he had never been able to do in his life: drive a car, make out in a drive-in movie theater, live in a house with a lawn, swim at the beach. He lived in America, but he was not part of it.

All the time he was eating, Butch was pestering Russ with questions. Why are you taking me to Milwaukee? he asked. Did the police have a witness to the killings? Who was it? Would he be able to see the witnesses? How would the witnesses be able to identify him? How did they find him in New York?

Butch kept denying he had anything to do with the murders. But then he said, "Dewey, when I get ready to tell, you will be the first one I tell."

From prior experience, Russ felt that Butch was like a bottle. Pull out the cork, and everything would come pouring out. He was at that extreme stage of agitation where he needed to confess. There was a vulnerable, human side to him, after all. But to keep things legal, Russ didn't want to talk about the killings until they got back to Milwaukee.

They landed at 7:10 at Milwaukee's General Billy Mitchell Field. Two squad cars were there to meet them. Butch was seated in the back of the lead car, next to Russ. Photographers were standing right next to the vehicle, snapping pictures with flashbulbs and blinding Butch.

"These are your rights, Butch," Russ advised him after the car started to move. "If you don't want to tell me anything, you don't have to."

Butch nodded.

"Do you know your wife's handwriting?" Russ asked him.

When Butch nodded again, Russ took out the yellow sheet with Laura's statement on it, covering the front and back.

"Yes, that's my wife's handwriting," Butch said.

Russ folded it carefully and put it back in his breast pocket.

"Can I read it?" Butch asked.

Russ took it out again, and Butch read it slowly.

Then Butch shouted, "My wife, my own wife. I love the girl. I have done everything for her, and she's trying to get me hanged."

After that, Russ said, "Well, son, this is what she wrote, and she gave it to me." He was implying Laura may have said more. He certainly wasn't going to point out that her statement did not tie Butch unequivocally to the murders. The car had gone less than a mile from the airport.

"Dewey," Butch said at last, putting his face in his hands, "I'm no good. I killed two guys for a lousy fifty bucks." He was talking very loud, screaming, really.

"Son," Russ said, patting Butch on the shoulder, "take it easy. Just settle yourself down. You'll feel better now."

"Yes, but you don't know, Dewey, what it's like to kill two men. I have committed the most horrible crime a man can."

Now Russ had some questions about the murders. "We don't know why you did it," he said to Butch. Was it a robbery? Russ wondered. What happened to the knife?

Butch told them the whole story, except for the part he could never remember, actually stabbing the two men. He also told them about his childhood, about growing up without a father or a mother, about being left on the street to fend for himself, about discovering his mother was a prostitute and his father a drunk and convicted felon. Butch was crying now.

Russ listened and said how sorry he was to hear such a story, and did not ask any more questions. The car drove on in silence.

When they reached the Safety Building, the officers took Butch up to one of the detectives' rooms and asked him to sign a written confession. In nervous, uneven letters, Butch wrote:

On July 20th I killed two men at dave's tailor shop at 330 W. Wells st. because one tried to take advantage of me by not paying me for pictures I gave him.

When he finished, he wanted to tear up the confession. He had started to misspell the word "advantage" and was embarrassed at having to cross it out.

Butch never asked for a lawyer, and the police never advised him he had the right to have an attorney present. It was in the years before the Supreme Court, in the *Miranda* case, required that suspects be told of this constitutional right before questioning. Later, Butch would come to think he had been almost as much out of his head that evening talking to the police as he had been in killing Hurwitz and Locke.

When Butch came out of the detectives' office, Dewey Russ introduced him to his wife, who was waiting there.

"You have a real nice husband," Butch said to her. "If I had been around a man like that while growing up, I wouldn't be in this trouble today."

THE TRIAL BEGAN on February 26, 1963, in a big, old-fashioned courtroom in the Safety Building that was the size of a theater. The ceiling was fifty feet high, with dark wood cross beams and large glass lamps that hung down on long wrought-iron chains. The walls were finished in dark mahogany paneling, except for a bank of windows on one side that ran from floor to roof. The room itself was a third the length of a football field, giving it gravity, as if great events transpired there.

The Honorable Herbert J. Steffes presided on the bench. He was the embodiment of an upstanding Milwaukee burgher: tall, with watery blue eyes, pale skin, and an open Midwestern face. He had grown up in Milwaukee in a German Catholic family and wore his Marquette University class ring with pride. Outside the courtroom, he worked hard as a booster to make Marquette's basketball team one of the best in the country. Inside, he was everything a felony judge is supposed to be— fair, consistent, intelligent, and tough. He had an ashtray in his office, a gift from his fellow judges, that recognized a judicial milestone: he had handed down 100,000 hours' worth of sentences. It was his proudest possession.

Judge Steffes was a quick wit. Once a man he had just sentenced shouted at him, "You're a bald-headed cock-sucker." The judge replied, without missing a beat, "I'll stipulate to the former, but I'll deny the latter to my death."

The day Butch's trial began, it was eight degrees below zero in Milwaukee, making it the thirty-second day of below-zero temperatures for the winter—a record. Butch was charged with two counts of first-degree murder. Wisconsin did not have capital punishment, so the longest sentence he could receive was life in prison.

At first, he tried to plead insanity. Judge Steffes appointed a panel of three psychiatrists to examine him. Despite his earlier record in New York, the Wisconsin doctors found no evidence of psychosis.

To Butch's court-appointed lawyer, Louis Wiener, one of Milwaukee's flashiest criminal attorneys, his prospects weren't good. Normally, if there is no arrest at the scene of a crime, the critical issue is identification of the suspect. But this was not a whodunit. Butch had confessed. The heart of Butch's case, therefore, was intent. Did he really go into the shop intending to stab the two men? Or did he just react to Hurwitz's arguing with him and pushing him, making it a crime committed in the heat of passion? Butch insisted he had never intended to kill the men, and he felt he had been improperly charged. Wiener tried for this defense, which would have reduced the crime to manslaughter.

Judge Steffes did not buy it.

"Merely because a person gets into a violent frenzy doesn't get him into a lower degree of homicide," the judge pronounced. "Here this defendant, by his own testimony, was attempting to retrieve something. He himself got into a very violent argument. The actions on the part of the deceased were not such as to justify him generating heat of passion from the objective viewpoint."

There was still another possibility. If Butch had not intended to kill Hurwitz and Locke, Wiener could argue that it was murder in the second degree, homicide without an intent to kill. But there were the six stab wounds in each victim. That made it hard to claim there was no intent to kill.

The jury of ten men and two women retired at 3:40 p.m. on March 1, 1963. With a break for dinner, they were back at 10 o'clock that evening. Jerome J. Sikorski, the foreman, read the verdicts: "We, the jury, find the defendant, Butch Bosket, guilty of murder in the first degree."

Judge Steffes then excused the jurors, thanking them for performing "a transcendent kind of civic service." Turning to Butch, the judge asked, "Have you anything to say as to why sentence should not be pronounced upon you?"

Butch stood up, looking Judge Steffes in the eye. "Your honor, murder is a hard pillow to sleep on, but the verdict that was brought back, I think, was an unjust one. For I know I never had the intention of hurting anyone. It is going to cost me many years in prison and maybe the loss of my wife and children. But I am not going to let myself become embittered. That would just prove what the District Attorney tried so wholeheartedly to prove, that I am an animal. I can sincerely say that I am no animal, and I will spend every day educating myself to prove otherwise. I will become the best educated prisoner you have ever had."

Judge Steffes was not moved. He thought it was just another last-minute, self-serving plea. "There is only one sentence the Court can pronounce and that is life imprisonment," the judge read from a prepared statement. "This defendant displayed, in my view, a homicidal temper, which demonstrated a lethal quality, a lethal luxury, which this community cannot tolerate."

Judge Steffes was staring at Butch now, looking at him in a way he had of boring right into your every thought that you might want to keep to yourself.

"I do hope," the judge added, "that in the passage of time the parole board will remember very clearly that this was not just one cold-blooded murder, but two cold-blooded murders."

Here he paused for a moment, as if he were thinking of something very far away. Then he regained his train of thought.

"The sentence commences at twelve noon today. The Sheriff will transport you to prison, I presume, with alacrity."

PART III

CHAPTER 8

WILLIE

Bad Little Booby

They don't have any kids in Harlem, because nobody has time for a childhood.

Claude Brown, *Manchild in the Promised Land*

S HE WAS JOBLESS and five months pregnant, so after Butch was arrested in August 1962, Laura followed the path of generations of women before her. She went home to mother. Nancy Roane was already caring for Laura's five-year-old daughter, Cheryl, whose father had long since disappeared. Nancy worked long hours as a maid for a white family in Manhattan, the only job available to her when she came up to New York in 1922—poor, sixteen years old, and, like so many other Southern blacks, looking for the promised land. Her family lived in Erica, a hamlet of a few houses, a store, and a post office in Virginia's Northern Neck, a mile down a dirt track and through the pine woods from the Potomac River. Nancy's father, John Roane, was a proud, churchgoing man who worked as a laborer for a white farmer. In the slack season, he supplemented the family's meager income by fishing in the muddy gray Potomac for crabs and oysters. In the 1920s, when Nancy left home, Erica and the surrounding county, Westmoreland, were remote, slumberous, and impoverished. There were few signs of Westmoreland's rich heritage.

But one of the area's earliest settlers was John Washington, who acquired land along the Potomac in 1657. His great-grandson, George Washington, was born in the family house on Pope's Creek in 1732, about a dozen miles from Erica. Washington grew up in the brick manor house there, learning to cultivate the "noxious weed"—tobacco—that provided the young Virginia colony's wealth, and how to work the slaves. James Madison and James Monroe were also born in Westmoreland, making

it the only county in the United States to give birth to three presidents.
Thomas Lee, another of the great Virginia planters, built his magnificent
Georgian plantation house, Stratford Hall, on a high bluff above the
Potomac only eight miles from Erica. Two of his children, Richard Henry
Lee and Francis Lightfoot Lee, were the only brothers to sign the Declara-
tion of Independence. Their cousin, Henry "Light-Horse Harry" Lee, a
dashing cavalry leader in the American Revolution, also made his home
at Stratford Hall. Upstairs, in the big sunlit bedroom, his son, Robert E.
Lee, was born, destined to be the Confederate commander of the Army
of Northern Virginia and the most beloved son of all the South.

Nancy Roane grew up in humbler circumstances, an unpainted frame
dwelling set in a clearing in the woods, with apple trees, a vegetable
garden, and a pasture for horses and cows outside. The Roanes had their
own history, too. They had never been slaves. And they traced their
ancestry to another prominent Virginia gentry family.

The first member of the Roane family to settle in America, Charles
Roane, came to Virginia in 1664 from Surrey, England. With money from
his father, he soon acquired several large plantations and a goodly quantity
of slaves, planted tobacco, and became a member of Virginia's fledgling
aristocracy. His grandson, Thomas Roane, was noted for his generous
hospitality, holding court from his plantation house furnished with fifty-
four beds, which were frequently filled with guests. In February 1766,
Thomas Roane took part in the first meeting in Virginia to protest the
hated Stamp Act passed by the British Parliament, a precursor to the
Revolution. The meeting was called by his neighbor Richard Henry Lee;
four of George Washington's brothers also participated. They signed a
resolution pledging not to pay the new stamp tax even at the risk of
"Danger or Death." Then they marched on a local merchant who had
announced he would use the tax stamps, forcing him to recant on pain
of being tarred and feathered. Roane later became a member of his
county's Committee of Safety, the local revolutionary organization, and
fought as a colonel of militia at the climactic battle of Yorktown. He
seems to have thought as little of Tories as he did of slaves. A family
ditty went:

> Side by side, Colonel Roane tied
> A negro and a Tory.

After the Revolution, one of his nephews married a daughter of Patrick
Henry's; another became a United States senator from Virginia.

But one of his own sons, John, "came to a very unfortunate end,"
according to a family history compiled by a friend. The written account

offers no further information. The story, however, passed down by word of mouth from one generation to another in the family, is that John Roane married a black woman, apparently a free black woman. In turn, they had a child named John, born about 1805. By Virginia law, he was entered in the county's registry of free blacks. His entry read: "John Roane, negro man of light Complexion, Straight hair, five feet eight inches high, with no particular mark or scar about his person, born free in Westmoreland County." This younger John Roane later married another free black, Lucy Lee, and was a man of some substance. In the federal Census of 1860, he proudly reported that he owned $1,300 in farmland and $250 worth of personal property, probably animals like horses, mules, and cows.

As free blacks in Westmoreland, the Roanes were not alone. In 1860, almost one-quarter of the county's thirty-one hundred African-Americans were listed as free, making Westmoreland something of an anomaly. Many of them were emancipated by Robert Carter 3d, one of the wealthiest men in Virginia, who owned sixty thousand acres on eighteen plantations. On August 1, 1791, he stunned his family, friends, and neighbors by filing a deed of manumission granting liberty to the more than five hundred "negroes and mulatto slaves" who were his "absolute property."

"I have for some time past been convinced," Carter wrote, "that to retain them in Slavery is contrary to the true principles of Religion & Justice & therefore it is my duty to manumit them." It was the largest individual act of emancipation in American history. Still, it was an unpopular move with other whites, and while for decades Southern pilgrims made their way to Robert E. Lee's ancestral shrine and George Washington's birthplace, no one put up a monument to Carter. So the Roanes kept their family history to themselves, a safe strategy in a region where William Faulkner once observed, "The past is not dead. It isn't even past."

Laura was born in the Roane family farmhouse on November 17, 1940. Nancy had come home from New York to take care of her own mother, who was ill, and seventeen days after Laura was born, they returned to Harlem. Laura had what she thought of as a happy, uneventful childhood. She loved to jump rope, roller skate, and ride her bicycle. When she grew up, she dreamed of becoming a nurse. There were a few winos on the street in those days, but no drugs and little violent crime, at least as Laura remembers it, and Harlem was an exciting place for a child. With her mother, she went to hear the Reverend Adam Clayton Powell Jr. preach at the Abyssinian Baptist Church, a few blocks from their apartment, and Sundays she sang in the choir. Sometimes, dressed in her best blue skirt, white blouse, black shoes, and a little red tie, she took part in competitions with other church choirs, singing gospel music, and singing well enough to win many of the contests. She was developing into a short, round-faced young woman with dark auburn hair and a lively manner. Her mother still had the slow cultivated strains of upper-class Virginia in her voice, the product of her unusual heritage; Laura spoke in the fast, streetwise cadence of Harlem.

If there was something missing in Laura's childhood, she did not seem aware of it. She was the youngest of six children, and her mother at some point had taken the married name Spates, which she used along with Roane. But Laura never knew her own father, so she just kept Roane. All her mother ever told her was that her father's name was Benjamin and that he had died in a car accident when she was about two years old.

This did not seem strange to young Laura. Many of her girlfriends had no fathers, either. "You can't miss something that you don't never have," was her view of it. "I didn't know nothing about my father. I didn't remember him. Just some other man gone, that's all. My mother took the place of him. She was a good mother."

But the lack of a father left its mark. The limited, crimped notion of men that Laura grew up with seemed to stunt her emotional life. It left her defensive and reluctant to express her feelings. Men used women for sex, to make babies, then they took off, Laura thought. "They put it in, then they're gone," she often said. "Shame on them." That was as much as she allowed herself to feel.

And so Laura got herself pregnant in the eleventh grade at Jane Addams Vocational High School, a school named after the great nineteenth-century pioneer of social work among Chicago's poor. "There was a man," is the way Laura remembered it later. "I got what you would call expecting a baby." But the father didn't stick around, and Laura had to drop out of school. Instead of becoming a nurse, as she had dreamed, she got a job working in a hospital pantry. Laura had stopped going to church, too; it no longer held any interest, or hope, for her or her friends. She registered to vote when she turned twenty-one, but only to get the identification card so she could buy liquor. It never occurred to her to vote, even for the Reverend Powell, the enormously popular congressman in her district. She was starting a long journey into a kind of social void, a world where the everyday institutions of middle-class America did not reach, though geographically she lived only a few blocks from the elegant apartment buildings and the well-stocked shops of white Manhattan. Her apartment at the time was on West 111th Street, perched on the northern edge of Central Park, with a panoramic view of New York spread out before her. To Laura, the rest of the city could have been on another planet.

When Laura met Butch, about the time she got her first voter registration card, he brought a sense of exhilaration back into her life. Then the murders in Milwaukee dampened it. She was frightened, on the run, and pregnant, and she lost a lot of weight when she should have been gaining it. For a while, she was scared she herself would be put on trial in Wisconsin, and she didn't know what to say when Butch called her collect from jail. She had gone on welfare, and she didn't have the money to visit Butch in Wisconsin or attend his trial. Her friends and social workers later felt that she was angry at being abandoned just when she was going to have a baby. It was hard for her to put into words, but Butch was repeating the pattern of her own father deserting her. After the murders, something in Laura changed. It was as if an icicle formed inside her, freezing her fragile emotional system.

Her best friend and neighbor, Gloria Reddick, found Laura sitting alone in her room for long periods of time. Gloria had lived with Laura and her mother, Nancy, since she came to Harlem as a poor, illiterate country girl from North Carolina in 1957, and she and Laura had grown to call each other sister. Now she and Nancy worried that Laura might try to harm herself, so they hid the kitchen knives.

Slowly, during the fall of 1962, Laura seemed to recover. But she never came back to herself, Gloria thought. Laura was more reserved, more reticent, even gruff. When she did talk, much of her conversation was monosyllabic, "yup," or "nope," and her language grew coarser. When she was younger and had a dream and felt lucky, she had liked to play the numbers, with the neighborhood numbers runner. But now she stopped. "My dreams don't count no more," Laura explained. She also became forgetful about the past, her family noticed. They figured it was her way of protecting herself. Her emotions were constricting just as she was about to give birth to Butch's child, when her baby would need all the love she had. The terrible consequences of murder were starting to pile up, even on the family of the criminal.

WILLIE JAMES BOSKET JR. was born on December 9, 1962, shortly after 2 o'clock in the afternoon at Metropolitan Hospital. As a mark of honor, Laura gave him his father's formal name, even though Butch was in jail. It was a full-term pregnancy, no complications with the delivery. Gloria helped bring the baby home in a taxi, holding him in a blue blanket. The very next day, it seemed, Willie began turning over and raising his head. Gloria said to Laura, "You better look out. He's going to grow right up."

Sure enough, Willie began walking at nine months, was potty trained at ten months, and started talking at just over a year, all very early. The family thought he was intelligent, just like his father.

From as far back as anyone could remember, Willie was an active child. He was always running, had trouble sitting still, and was mischievous. At first, his family and the neighbors put his actions down to boyhood pranks, like the times when he walked up behind women on the street and slapped their rear ends, or the occasions when he stole old men's canes. Sometimes he was downright funny, and the neighbors hung out their windows or sat on the stoop to watch him, as if he were the local form of entertainment. Once Willie told Gloria's daughter, Debbie, three years his senior, that he was going to rob an elderly lady. He grabbed the woman's pocketbook, but he had not calculated that she had a chain running from under her sleeve connected to the handbag to foil a robbery. As he struggled to steal her possessions, the woman wrapped the chain around Willie with one arm and hit him repeatedly with her cane with the other arm.

"Oh, Lordy," she shouted over and over, "Jesus is going to get you." Willie came home with no money and covered with little red lumps and splotches.

It was after one such incident that his older sister, Cheryl, gave him the nickname Booby, as in booby trap. It stuck.

Willie was not yet six years old, and he was short and slight for his age, with the face of an angel. He had a beatific smile and big dimples in each cheek. His size and looks only made his behavior more comical in those early years. Debbie, who was his best friend and referred to him as cousin, thought he was trying to be a comedian. Often, she believed, he would do things just to make people laugh, and if you did laugh, he would do it again. Like the time on the subway when he spotted a woman with lots of bright red lipstick and a big pretty wig. As he and Debbie got off the train, he said to her, "Debbie, watch what I do." When the doors closed and the subway began moving, Willie reached through an open window and snatched the wig right off. It turned out the woman was completely bald. She screamed as her hairpiece disappeared, and Willie, Debbie, and the passengers on the train all began laughing. From a young age, Willie had a special thing about the subway.

He also displayed his bravado in their own neighborhood. There was usually a dice game on the corner of 114th Street and Lenox Avenue, where Laura had moved after Willie was born, and he often ran up and grabbed the dice from the players. Or if they saw him coming and protected the dice, he grabbed the money they had put down for bets and ran off with it. It was a risky business. Some of the men were drug pushers, others were pimps, and there were always addicts on the corner, looking to make some money for a score. It was a way for a young boy to show he had nerve, that he understood the code of street life. You earn respect by being the baddest, the toughest person on the block, always ready to use violence to assert your superiority. Early on, Debbie concluded, "Booby had no fear in nothing he did." On the street, that was the highest compliment.

Some of his tricks were endearing. One day, he came by and asked Gloria, whom he called Aunt Mick, "What you cooking today?" Gloria was broke and had no food. So she replied, in her blunt way, "I ain't cooking, Booby." An affable smile softened the expression on her face, which was framed by long, straight, dark hair and a hawk nose that reflected the Cherokee Indian in her ancestry.

"Don't worry, Aunt Mick," Willie reassured her. "My mother is cooking."

Then he went around the corner to a grocery store, loaded up a cart, and went to the checkout counter. When the clerk looked quizzically at him, Willie patted his pocket, as if he were fingering his money. The clerk put the groceries in a bag, and Willie took off without paying. The store owner sent someone to get him, but Willie, who was barely four feet tall and weighed about sixty pounds, said, "You're a lying motherfucker. You ain't seen me. I've been sitting right here on the stoop."

His ability to curse was legendary. The first words he ever learned, said Debbie, were "shit" and "motherfucker." On a street where virtually everyone used this vocabulary, he was king of the cussers. His mother had taught it to him. "If a man threatens you or hits you, this is something you can do to keep your respect," she told him. That was fine until one day when he came into the candy store where Laura worked. For some reason, she was mad at him and told him to stand in the corner. He refused, snapping at her, "Fuck you, you black motherfucker."

Willie did not like to play with the other boys in the neighborhood; he didn't shoot baskets or play baseball in the little concrete park across the street in the Stephen Foster Houses project. He didn't have the patience for teamwork. He was happier being a loner.

From early on, he dreamed about being a policeman. He loved to watch cop shows on television. There were "Adam Twelve," "Mod Squad" and "Hawaii Five O," and later "T. J. Hooker" and "Charlie's Angels." More than most kids, Willie played so hard at his fantasy life that it almost turned into reality. Nearly every day, as Gloria remembered it, Willie asked to use her phone to call the police to report an imaginary robbery in progress, then waited on the stoop to watch the squadrons of police cars arrive with sirens wailing and lights flashing. The local drug pushers got even madder at him than the police, because they were always having to scramble up on the rooftops or down an alley. One evening, Gloria had an attack of high blood pressure and passed out. Her family called an ambulance, but it never came, a common indignity in their neighborhood. So Willie called the police. "There's some cops got killed in our house," he told them. Several police cars and an ambulance arrived instantly, and policemen poured in through the door with guns drawn.

When they saw what had happened, they chastised Willie. But he was unrepentant: "We told you my aunt was sick and you didn't come, so that was the only way I could get you here. I love my aunt, and I ain't going to let her just stay here and die."

Another time, Willie used the police box on the street to report a robbery under way at a grocery store on the corner of 113th Street and St. Nicholas Avenue. What he didn't know was that there really was a man with a gun in the store. The police arrived just in time to prevent the owner, a man named Raymond, from being shot. Raymond rewarded Willie with a gift of money for saving his life. A year later, Raymond was killed in another robbery.

Willie, Gloria decided, was never predictable. Like the time she took him to the movies, a gangster picture, with her three daughters, Debbie, Joanne, and Eunice, all older than he. Willie was sitting between Debbie and a big, tall, very dark-skinned man, who started laughing at something in the film and knocked the popcorn out of Willie's hand. Willie was only a tiny figure, hardly as tall as the seatback, but the next thing Gloria knew, Willie had jumped up and grabbed the stranger around the neck.

"Aunt Mick, see how I'm going to choke this fucker to death," Willie shouted.

Then he laughed. "I'm only kidding," Willie said. "I just felt like choking somebody."

But that was enough for the man, who got up, shaken, and left the theater. "Bad little Booby," Gloria scolded Willie. "One of these days all this stuff going to come back to haunt you."

In later years, people would try to figure out why such a young boy—he wasn't even in school yet—did these things. Everyone had an explanation, and each theory probably contained some element of the truth.

Laura blamed the neighborhood. She believed she had been a good mother—she worked hard, she saw that her children had a roof over their heads, food to eat, and clothes to wear. But Harlem had deteriorated since she was a girl, she reckoned—lots more drugs and crime and guns.

"There was people out there doing things, and Willie thought he could do the same thing he saw them doing," Laura said.

In truth, it was a tough neighborhood. In the eighteenth and nineteenth centuries, the area had been bucolic farmland, with the Harlem Creek running nearby, but now the local heroin dealer, Miss Emma, lived in the building next door. She often sat with her children on the stoop and talked to Laura and Willie. He grew up knowing the daily details of the drug business the way other American boys knew the box scores in baseball. There was always a congregation of men on the corner, drinking from brown paper bags, or shooting craps, or playing chuck-a-luck, a game with dice and a cardboard box full of handwritten numbers. They hung out at the corner, Willie learned, because that made it easier to spot the police coming down Lenox Avenue, allowing them to disperse up the side streets to escape. "Bulls on the way," the men shouted when they saw a squad car. Sometimes, Willie played chickie for them, serving as their lookout. Broken pieces of green and brown glass from old liquor bottles covered the sidewalk like ersatz grass. Along the curb, people left piles of discarded furniture, parts of wooden chairs or table legs, as if the street were a garbage dump. Sometimes in the morning, when Willie came outside to play, there would be winos asleep on his stoop, or mounds of stinking vomit, or occasionally, the body of a heroin addict who had overdosed, his hands swollen like basketballs.

There was one wino on the block whom the boys liked to tease. They urinated in a wine bottle, then gave it to him to drink when he woke up. In the highly charged atmosphere of the street, Willie always tried to outdo the other boys, who were bigger than he was. It was a matter of preserving his respect. So he took penny nails and stuck them in the man's bare feet.

The first apartment Willie lived in, at 89 Lenox Avenue, by the corner of 114th Street, had only one small bedroom, a radiator that was always exploding in the winter, and holes in the floor where the rats had eaten through. One time the toilet fell through the floor. The Christmas he was five years old, Laura had only enough money for one gift and gave him a toy race car as a present; Willie treasured it. That night, though, a fire struck the building next door. The fire engines arrived too late to put out the flames, but water from their hoses flooded the Boskets' apartment, forcing them out of the building. They moved in with Laura's mother, Nancy, around the corner at 114 West 114th Street. Willie remembered afterward that the race car got lost in the confusion. He could never recall a happy Christmas after that one.

Conditions weren't much better in the new apartment, on the ground floor of a typical turn-of-the-century dumbbell tenement, narrow in width and running back deep through the building. Only a small airshaft separated it from the house next door. Inside, the apartment was perpetually dark. The only windows were in the front room, and the family was too poor to afford more than a couple of bare electric bulbs. Outside, the building was a dingy brown brick. They had no telephone. Most of the time, Willie subsisted on peanut butter and jelly sandwiches. Twice a month, he went with his mother to the welfare center to pick up handouts of United States Department of Agriculture surplus butter and cheese.

Money was always a problem. Once a month, when the white landlord from New Jersey came by to collect the rent, Laura would tell Willie, "Say your mother ain't here." So Willie would go to the door and in his most innocent voice say, "My mother ain't here, mister." Of course, being as smart as he was, he couldn't resist turning around and saying to Laura, "Right, Mommy?" He was playing a joke on both of them. Laura would end up grabbing Willie and slapping him hard.

Some nights, when residents were seated on their stoops talking, they would hear shooting down at the corner, at the Royal Flush bar, and people would come running up the block with others chasing them, firing their guns or throwing bottles. Then the police would arrive and someone would be arrested. Over time, it seemed like sooner or later every boy on that stretch of 114th Street went to reform school and then to jail, or got himself killed. It was a natural fact of life.

Coming up in that neighborhood, Willie had learned the code of the street at a very young age, just as his father had in Augusta—that the secret to survival was a willingness to use violence, to be always ready to fight. But Willie was much smarter than the other kids on his block, and also more driven, more highly motivated. He wanted to be the best. So he took the code of the street to the extreme—he would be the most violent. It would be his ticket; it was the only way Willie knew to get ahead.

Early on, people sensed there was something special at work in Willie, something that came from inside him or his relationship with his family. From his youngest years, Laura and both his grandmothers, Nancy and Marie, noticed that Willie looked and acted an awful lot like his father. The older he got, the greater the resemblance. Their faces were so similar, they could have been twins, all the women believed. "When you see Willie, you see Butch," they said to one another. And Willie had that same impulsiveness and lack of patience as Butch; when he wanted something, it had to be right away, otherwise he threw a temper tantrum. When that happened, he jumped up and down, cried, cursed, knocked things off the kitchen table, or broke anything he could get his hands on. What was still more remarkable, when Willie got upset or sensed trouble, his eyes bulged out and his jaw began to work, just like his father.

Science has not advanced far enough to say whether Willie inherited any part of his aggressive tendencies from his father. Willie himself often thought so; he believed he could feel something of his father inside him. But you have to be very careful in drawing such conclusions about biology. The poverty and neglect in which Willie grew up, along with the violence on the streets in his neighborhood, were trouble enough to explain what happened. Still, in later years, researchers would find that some traits of temperament, the qualities of personality a person is born with, are often heritable. In particular, studies found that impulsive-aggressive behavior is roughly 25 to 40 percent heritable. If that happened with Willie, it could have given him a predisposition to impulsiveness, to being ready to explode at the slightest provocation. This alone didn't make him violent, but such a predisposition would have magnified in his mind the threatening nature of street life. And it would have made for a powerful combination at work in Willie, the interaction of nature and nurture.

There were also the difficult circumstances of Laura's pregnancy while she was carrying Willie. She had been in Milwaukee when Butch killed the two men, and she had been on the run with him before he got arrested. Years later, scientific studies would find that mothers subjected to high levels of stress during pregnancy, everything from divorce to poverty or violence, often have babies that are hyperactive or unusually irritable. After the fact, there was no way to prove this was the case with Willie. But it, too, could have affected his behavior.

Laura didn't know about these scientific findings, but the more she watched Willie, the more she said to herself, "Yup, that's Butch's son. That's him." This worried her. She began to wonder if Willie was really her child, or was he just Butch's? Laura already had put a brake on her emotions, rationing them out cautiously so she wouldn't get hurt. Now, with Willie turning out like Butch, she withdrew more, putting a distance between herself and her son, a chasm that Willie intuitively felt as a form of rejection.

From the beginning, Laura came right out and told Willie, "You look just like your father." Sometimes, when he acted up, she would also say, "Boy, you bad, just like your father. You sure got the devil in you. You're going to grow up to be no good." It was a heavy load to put on a bright youngster, especially when both his grandmothers constantly repeated the notion.

At first, Willie didn't know exactly what this meant, because Laura didn't tell him the truth about Butch. Instead, when Willie asked where his father was, his mother replied, "He's in the army." She didn't want to tell a little boy that his father was in prison, and she didn't want the other boys in the neighborhood teasing him about an absent father, so she made up a cover story.

This went on for several years, until Willie began to get curious about who his father really was and why he was so bad. Finally, when he was about seven years old and staying at Marie's house one day, he noticed his grandmother holding a black-and-white photograph of a tall man standing beside some weightlifting equipment. The man was dressed in a T-shirt and fatigue pants, revealing a heavily muscled chest and set of arms.

"Who is that man?" Willie asked.

"Your father," Marie replied.

"Where is he?" Willie persisted, his mind racing.

"He's in prison," his grandmother revealed. "He killed some men in a fight. One day, you'll see him, he'll be home."

This was exciting information. In the pecking order of the street, being in prison for murder was first-class, something you could brag about. But his mother's deception also made Willie angry.

In later years, social workers and therapists who worked with Willie would come back to this episode again and again. "When Mrs. Bosket finally admitted to Willie that his father was in prison, he expressed deep anger at her for not telling him the truth before," a psychologist reported when Willie was eleven years old.

"It is further observed that Mrs. Bosket has rejected Willie from birth," the report added.

After his father was convicted and imprisoned prior to his birth, his mother rejected him and expected him to act out in a violent fashion because of the similarities she had drawn between father and son. The trauma of her husband's violent actions, and her subsequent feelings of rage and abandonment in the face of a newborn child may have caused her to associate these attributes with the expected child. In any case, she has constantly drawn attention to his physical similarity to his father and therefore remarks about their comparison, particularly to Willie. This comparison is usually negative. It is believed she has conveyed to Willie this negative feeling and the image of inadequacy, violence and worthlessness to him. Willie, apparently feeling rejected, incorporated these qualities into his personality in order to gain his mother's love and approval. Unfortunately, it did not.

Willie's anger with his mother, and his simultaneous need for her love, were complicated by Laura's relationships with other men. Soon after he was born, she began bringing a series of men to the house, some of whom spent the night, or stayed for a period of weeks. It was as if she were trying to cheer herself out of her depression following the murders by an overdose of romance.

Years later, Willie still remembered some of them, and the giggling in the bedroom at night. His mother never explained anything to Willie, or prepared him beforehand. The first thing he knew, another man was in the house. There was Tommy Robinson, who became the father of his younger sister, Shirley, born three years after him in 1965. Then there was Jose, a tall, very black man, six feet ten inches in height, who lived with Laura for a period. When they got in a fight one day, Jose held her down on the bed, then shoved her against the scalding hot radiator pipe that ran from floor to ceiling. Laura screamed, and when Jose let her down, a patch of her charred skin was stuck to the metal. "Booby saw it and went crazy," Gloria recalled. He picked up an iron pipe and hit Jose, then slashed him with a knife.

Bert was next. He beat Laura up so badly that Nancy had to come and take her to the hospital, where they kept her overnight. She came home with her head bandaged. Willie got so angry he went to Gloria's apartment and told her, "I'm going to burn that motherfucker up." Then he dragged a can of gasoline back to the Boskets' house, pouring it on the living room couch and setting it on fire. Gloria thought to herself, "He sure loves Laura."

He did. But he hated his mother, too. It was a complex, tumultuous relationship. Laura had a hard time controlling Willie when he did something bad. Sometimes, she slapped him around with her hand until the veins popped out, or she would give him a whipping with a belt. It wasn't that she hated him; it was just the only form of punishment she knew. But he would shake it right off. Worse, it reinforced Willie's belief that the way to settle things was by getting physical. Watching from across the street, Debbie thought, "There isn't nothing she can do." Laura herself despaired. She was trying hard to be a good mother. But she honestly didn't know what else to do.

One time, after she fought with a boyfriend at home, Willie set fire to his own shirtsleeve and threatened to stab himself. Another time, when Laura punished him, he shouted, "I hate you. I can't stand you. I wish you wasn't my mother. I'm going to jump in front of the subway and kill myself." She had to run after him and restrain him from going into the subway station.

Sabrina Gaston, the daughter of the local heroin dealer, watched Willie from her window after episodes like this and saw his face dirty with tears. Once, he went outside, picked up a bottle, and smashed a cat in the head and killed it. She thought he was a very sad and angry boy, lost in his own world.

All this was happening at a time in Willie's young life when children develop their moral emotions, including their sensitivity toward others and their ability to empathize. Willie's feelings for other people were being stunted. His difficulty in dealing with people showed up early in his relationship with his younger sister, Shirley. Although he had been toilet trained by the age of one, he was so jealous after her arrival that he started wetting the bed again. This enuresis persisted, on and off, until he was eleven years old. As Shirley began to grow a little older, Willie was often belligerent with her. Once she told their mother about something bad Willie had done, and he got angry. He grabbed a long-handled kitchen fork and stuck it down her throat. "I'm going to get her goosepipe out of there and make her shut up," he told Debbie, who was in the house. Shirley was choking, but not seriously harmed. At the time, Debbie thought it was funny.

The seeds of Willie's problems were planted early. When he was older, he looked back and felt there had always been an anger in him. It started with his childhood hatred of his mother. Then, as the years passed, he identified it as a hatred of the American system. It might all have been the same rage.

AFTER WILLIE TURNED SIX, Laura enrolled him in first grade at P.S. 207, a few blocks from their house. School was a nightmare from the start. It wasn't that Willie lacked intelligence; in fact, the teachers all agreed he was unusually bright. He just couldn't sit still in class, or follow the teachers' instructions, which made it hard to learn. He was always throwing temper tantrums, and when the teachers tried to discipline him, Willie hit them. He also fought with the other students, ran out of the classroom into the hallway, pulled the fire alarms, and stole supplies like crayons and construction paper. The principal quickly put Willie in a special class for destructive children—that worked for a while. His teacher now was Mrs. House, a soft-spoken, gentle black woman who wasn't afraid of him. She controlled him with a mix of firmness and affection. If he acted up, she hit him on the butt with a long ruler. When he was well-behaved, she said, "Come here, give me an Eskimo kiss." Willie adored her as the mother he had always wanted.

But he soon had another teacher, and his behavior deteriorated again.

Willie began playing hooky, just as his father had. Laura would walk him to school in the morning, and as soon as she dropped him at the front door, he would run out the back door. That was especially embarrassing to Laura, because she had begun to work at the school as a teacher's aide. One day, as he was escaping, he spotted several of his mother's fellow workers walking toward him, so he dashed out into the street to avoid them and was hit in the head by a car. The impact knocked him out and threw him to the far side of the street. He woke up in Lenox Hill Hospital, where he complained of headaches for several days, but X-rays showed no damage. In the future, some psychiatrists wondered if the accident contributed to his behavior; a number of extremely violent criminals have suffered damage to their brains when young.

After the accident, the school recommended that Laura take Willie to a psychiatrist. She did, once, but saw no improvement and thought it was a waste of time. "The stupid public school thinks he's crazy, but he's not," she told Gloria.

By now, Willie was eight years old and in second grade, technically, at least. It got so the teachers often told him he was crazy right to his face, which made Willie laugh. On the street, being called a "crazy nigger" was high praise. A "crazy nigger" was someone who developed a reputation for being unpredictably violent and aggressive. You had to show deference to a person like that. Willie discovered that if he acted crazy, people were afraid of him and he could get what he wanted, like being sent home for bad behavior. Willie was a human nuclear chain reaction—the worse he acted, the more people said bad things about him, and then the more impossible he behaved. One time a teacher Willie called Mr. Sauerkraut, because of his German-sounding name, took him aside and told him he was no good and was going to grow up to be no good. Afterward, Willie and another boy broke into a storeroom on the school's third floor, which was normally kept locked. In the forbidden area, they found stacks of textbooks that were fun to throw around, a mimeograph machine that was asking to be smashed, and a nice big typewriter sitting on a desk. Willie picked it up, carried it to a window, and hurled it out. The typewriter just missed hitting a pregnant teacher who was walking below.

That was the final straw for the school. Willie was expelled, and the city school board ordered Laura to take him for psychiatric observation to Bellevue Hospital, where both his father and his grandfather had been sent, though no one was aware of the fact.

Laura brought Willie to Bellevue on March 8, 1971, a bad day for her. The same morning, the police took her older daughter, Cheryl, now thirteen, to Zarega, one of four juvenile detention centers in New York where children were sent while awaiting the outcome of their cases in Family Court. At Laura's reluctant insistence, Cheryl had been charged with running away from home and consorting with older boys. She was wild in school, sitting in class throwing pumpkin seeds and cursing her teachers. Now she was also playing hooky and disappearing from home for long stretches of time. Her neighbor and schoolmate, Sharon Parker, thought Cheryl was full of anger at her mother for the way she was raised and was trying to get back at Laura. Whatever the reason, many nights Laura and Gloria set out frantically to search for Cheryl, so Laura had finally been persuaded by the Bureau of Child Welfare that the best course was to bring her before the Family Court. To Gloria, Laura seemed. like a tiny raft on the ocean being tossed about by huge waves; she was at the mercy of larger forces. Butch had married her, then set off on a spree that ended in murder and her abandonment while pregnant. Just getting through each day was a trial, like being flooded out of her apartment on Christmas Day. Now nothing she did with Willie or Cheryl worked. She sensed she had lost control of her children.

Laura and Willie took the bus to get from Harlem down to Bellevue, at First Avenue and Thirtieth Street. It was an old green bus, with hard seats, and they sat diagonally across from the driver. The bus ride seemed to take hours for Willie, and he had a premonition that his life was changing forever. His mother had told him the doctors in Bellevue wanted to keep him for thirty days. He hated being controlled, and he didn't understand how he could be separated from his mother and deprived of his freedom. Only grown men got locked up, in jail, he believed. It would be his first taste of a lifetime of institutionalization.

Bellevue had been founded in 1736, making it the oldest public hospital in the country. It had a long, distinguished history of work with children and psychiatry. In 1874, it had been the site of the first children's clinic in the United States, and in 1923, it developed the first child psychiatry inpatient unit in the country. When Willie arrived, the children's psychiatric ward occupied the sixth floor of what had once been an elegant brick building. There were marble floors in the grand entrance hall, a double staircase with bronze railings, and fine metal chandeliers. It was a monument to noble intentions. The children's ward had big windows overlooking the East River, a spectacular view for which many New Yorkers paid high rents. But the windows were covered with heavy wire mesh security screens, making it hard to see out. Over the years, the rooms in Bellevue had grown gloomy; the battered plastic furniture and an old television set that the young patients kept breaking lent little cheer.

The psychiatrist who saw Willie was Dr. Mahin Hassibi, the doctor in charge of the children's unit. Slight and short, with narrow eyes, straight dark hair, and a gentle, self-composed manner, she looked like a figure in a miniature Persian painting from her native Iran. She thought Willie was very handsome but the saddest little boy she had ever seen. It wasn't something she had to interpret. He looked sad and frightened all the time. He talked to no one, and when he walked into the room to meet her, he just straight out said he didn't want to be alive. In fact, Willie told her he was going to jump in front of a subway train and kill himself. He was quite capable of doing it, she thought. Usually, in Dr. Hassibi's experience, kids would be sad when they were admitted to Bellevue, but the sadness would lift after a few days. Willie remained depressed the whole time he was in the hospital.

Willie also told the psychiatrist about his father. "He's in prison for killing two men," Willie said accurately, now that he knew the story. Dr. Hassibi mentally calculated the effect that must have had on him. She believed Willie was an abused child, which was why he was so depressed and suicidal. "Not physically abused necessarily, but an abused, neglected child," she told her colleagues. Dr. Hassibi met Laura, too, and got the impression his mother "did not really care for him. Not only did she not care for him, she had identified him with his father and she was quite sure that he was not going to end up anyplace else. She foresaw only a bad future for her son."

After seeing Laura, Dr. Hassibi was even more upset. She tried to explain her findings, that Willie was very sad and might try to hurt himself.

"I'll beat the craziness out of him," Laura responded.

After consulting with other doctors on the staff, Dr. Hassibi wrote out her conclusion: "Diagnosis—Hyperkinetic reaction of childhood with depressive features."

The first part of the diagnosis was common enough. In current psychiatric terms, it meant Willie was suffering from attention deficit disorder, that he was hyperactive. But the reference to "depressive features" was unusual. At the time, psychiatry did not yet recognize depression in children. The assumption was that a period of depression in a child was an isolated event that the child would soon outgrow, with no lasting effect. But Dr. Hassibi had seen something so deep in Willie that she wanted to call attention to it. In hundreds and thousands of charts of children she saw over the years at Bellevue, he was the only one with that diagnosis.

Despite everything, however, Dr. Hassibi believed there was a softness in Willie, an openness, that a good therapist could work on. He was still only eight. It was important to act quickly, because she had seen children much like Willie, sad and frightened youngsters, who turned into violent, aggressive kids to deal with their fear. Their anxiety was so great that if you touched them, they thought you were going to kill them, and they reacted violently, in self-defense. They had to be defused. So Dr. Hassibi recommended that Willie be kept for further observation after the initial thirty-day commitment and then be sent to a residential facility where he could receive intensive treatment.

But Willie was working on his mother. He cried and screamed when she came to visit and told her a male nurse had attacked him. He accused her of betraying him by leaving him there, playing on her guilt. Finally, his entreaties were too much, and she told the hospital she was signing him out, against the hospital's advice. Dr. Hassibi was concerned. She notified the Bureau of Child Welfare that Laura's action constituted neglect. The bureau opened a file on Willie, but it was swamped with far more serious cases, so there was no follow-up. Willie, though, had learned another lesson about the power of manipulation—he could get what he wanted by staging a fit.

After he was released from Bellevue, things went downhill abruptly. Willie's school refused to take him back, and he figured out ways to play hooky from the new special school he was supposed to be enrolled in. He began spending a lot of time in a neighbor's apartment across the street, with three girls who were twelve, thirteen, and fourteen years old, and also playing hooky. The girls were experimenting with sex, and Willie was the happy guinea pig. They each had a room, and they would take turns with him, calling him in, then showing him how to do it, where to put his penis. It took several tries, but they finally got it right. Some days, Willie got tired and said, "It's the next one's turn." But one of the girls would shout, "I ain't done yet. Just a little bit more." And Willie would plead, "No, no more. I'm getting sore." They called it "doing it." Willie was just shooting dog water, of course. He was only nine years old.

About the same time, his grandfather, James Bosket, who was now fifty years old, began taking Willie for weekends to the apartment he rented in Queens. Willie didn't much like going with James. It was a long, tedious ride on the subway, and then the bus, and it was ten blocks from James's house to the nearest candy store where he could steal things. James drank a lot, and Willie was always afraid he would suffer one of his epileptic fits and fall on the floor. That embarrassed Willie. James had recently been released from the city prison on Rikers Island, where he had served a year for kidnapping and sodomizing a young boy, though no one had told Willie about that. In the evenings, on those weekends at James's apartment, they watched television, and then James had Willie sleep in the bed with him.

"I'm going to teach you about sex," James told his grandson. "Your father loved having sex, and the ladies loved him. He was a regular Casanova."

Then James lay on the bed and told Willie to penetrate him with his penis. He used Vaseline as a lubricant. "This is how you do it with girls," James told him. "It will be our little secret."

The fourth time this happened, James also beat Willie, so he ran out of the house, to the nearest store he knew about, and the store manager called the police. Willie never told any of the psychiatrists who saw him about his adventures with the three girls, or about his experience with his grandfather. But a therapist would have concluded that all this sexual stimulation at the young age of nine was a lot for a young boy to handle. It was another form of abuse, and it might have added to the rage and agitation already burning inside him.

Willie's file with the Bureau of Child Welfare was rapidly growing longer in 1971 and early 1972 when he was eight and nine. The police reported that he snatched a woman's pocketbook, stole a car, set several fires, pointed a knife at a girl one day when he did attend school, and was truant most of the time. But many of the things he did were never reported. Like the hot summer evening he and Debbie and Debbie's boyfriend, Arthur Habersham, and a few other friends were in Central Park. The sun was just going down in a big red ball and they were getting ready to go home when they spotted a black man lying on a bench asleep. Willie gathered up some newspapers and wadded them under the bench, where the man's shirtsleeve was hanging down. Then he set the papers on fire. Pretty soon, the man felt his arm burning, jumped up, and ran straight for a little lake. As he ran, the flames billowed out all over him. He screamed and jumped in the lake. Willie was standing there laughing, a deep laugh for a small boy.

After a few more such episodes, Laura finally gave in to pressure from the Bureau of Child Welfare. She agreed to take Willie to Family Court and seek a petition that would have him committed to an institution. The agency told her it would try to get him sent to Wiltwyck, which hit Laura kind of hard. She remembered how Butch used to tell her that he had been sent to Wiltwyck at nine, the same age Willie was now.

After talking with the agency, Laura sat on her stoop that evening and cried. She told Gloria, "I feel sad and hurt, 'cause I don't want Willie to go. But he don't listen to no one. Maybe he'll learn something there."

Laura's worst fears seemed to be coming true. She was doing the best job she could, given a difficult situation, and it never seemed enough. And now Willie was turning out just like his father.

CHAPTER 9

WILLIE

"Little Man"

Let any of our readers imagine a little fellow given to mischief suddenly put into an "institution" for reform, treated altogether as a machine. . . . The longer he is in the Asylum, the less likely he is to do well in outside life.

Charles Loring Brace, *The Dangerous Classes of New York*, 1872

JUDGE HAROLD A. FELIX was wearing his black robe over his Brooks Brothers suit. He always wore a Brooks Brothers suit. It was a way for a man from a wealthy, patrician family on Manhattan's Upper East Side to maintain his dignity in the face of the daily bedlam that confronted him in the Family Court. Short and mustachioed, he had won appointment to the bench through his political connections to city hall. But it was not a plum job, it turned out, and sometimes Judge Felix seemed aloof from the proceedings before him. His heart was good, those who worked with him believed. It was just that his Silk Stocking background made it hard for him to understand the young people who were brought into court.

On this summer day in 1972, he had fifty-two cases on his calendar, giving him about six minutes for each, the average amount of time allotted him each day to decide a child's fate. Outside his wood-paneled court-room, the hallways were thick with people waiting for their cases to be called, most of them black or Hispanic, and almost all of them mothers or grandmothers with their children. Judge Felix did not see many fathers in the dingy gray stone Manhattan Family Court Building, at the corner of Lexington Avenue and Twenty-second Street. There were mothers bottle-feeding babies, and children asleep on the marble floors of the once-handsome edifice, along with empty soda bottles, candy wrappers, and half-eaten hot dogs. When the courthouse was opened in the 1930s, Mayor Fiorello La Guardia himself spoke at the dedication. "The Little Flower" predicted that the progressive programs of the New Deal, by lifting people out of poverty, would soon end parental negligence and juvenile delinquency, obviating the very need for a Family Court. But in the 1960s, rates of violent crime had doubled, and it was clear that the American family showed signs of breaking down, so the building was vastly overcrowded. Already the city was planning to construct a new, much bigger Manhattan Family Court. By the early 1970s, 100,000 people a year were coming through the city's family courts.

Judge Felix looked up to watch as those involved in the next case were brought in, as fast as the blue-uniformed court officers could manage the flow of human traffic. The tempo was more like that of a factory assembly line than that of a decorous temple of jurisprudence.

"Let's go, let's keep moving," one attendant barked. "Take the chewing gum out of your mouth," another court officer commanded a boy who, along with his mother, had been led to a low table in front of Judge Felix. The judge saw a very small nine-year-old, less than seventy pounds, with a round face, strong white teeth, and sad, frightened eyes. But he had big dimples in each cheek and at times an angelic smile. As Judge Felix examined the papers in front of him and conferred with the probation officer on duty, Seymour Gottfried, he wondered how this tiny boy named Willie Bosket had already caused so much trouble.

The documents said that his mother, Laura Bosket, had filed a petition with the Family Court to have Willie declared a "person in need of supervision," what the judges, lawyers, and social workers around the court called, with Kafkaesque simplicity, a PINS. A PINS was a status offender, an individual whose very state of being rather than any specific criminal act got him hauled before the court. The New York State Family Court Act defined a person in need of supervision as a child under sixteen "who is an habitual truant or who is incorrigible, ungovernable or habitually disobedient and beyond the lawful control of parent or other lawful authority." Of course, it might be the parents who were really to blame, but the court couldn't punish the parents.

In the petition Laura had drawn up, three charges were listed against Willie. He was accused of coming home as late as 11:30 at night, of having not attended school for two weeks, and of stealing a woman's pocketbook. After the petition had been typed up, an earlier judge handling the case had adjourned it for several weeks so a lawyer from the Legal Aid Society, appointed as Willie's defense counsel, could learn more about him. In the interim, the judge had sent Willie to the Children's Center in Manhattan, an unlocked facility. He had immediately walked out and gone home.

A second judge then ordered Willie to Metropolitan Hospital because he had fainted, but when the police arrived at the hospital to take him back to court, he had once again skipped out and gone home, clad only in his pajamas and slippers.

Having scanned the record, Judge Felix declared to no one in particular, "He's a runner." That was a damning indictment in the judge's eyes, an indication of the boy's future behavior.

"Listen fellow, I'll tell you something," Judge Felix said to Willie, who was staring down at his sneakers. "Your mother is worried about you. For nine years old, you're turning out to be quite a problem."

That roused Willie. "You're a lying motherfucker," he told the judge. "You can go fuck yourself. And I don't need no motherfucking white lawyer neither. I want to go home."

With that, Willie spun around, charged past one of the beefy court officers, and ran out of the courtroom. "Go get that kid," Judge Felix commanded. Two uniformed officers gave chase, but Willie was way too fast for them. He was down the five flights of stairs and out of the building and headed for the subway before they could figure out where he had gone.

The Family Court had no police of its own to track down Willie. In fact, it didn't even have a real warrant squad anymore because there wasn't enough money in the city's budget. Judge Felix had to issue a warrant for Willie that he gave to Laura, who in turn was supposed to call her local precinct house when she found him.

That afternoon, Laura went straight from the courtroom to the candy store where she was working. She resented all the time she had to spend in court, fussing about Willie, when she needed to earn money. But she was laughing to herself about Willie's performance. He certainly was smart, and not even the judge could do anything with him. Then some neighbors stopped by the store and told her Willie was holding a knife on a boy at the corner of 114th Street and Lenox Avenue. She ran out and grabbed the knife away from him, brought him back to the store, and called the police at the Twenty-eighth Precinct. That night, they took him to Spofford.

Spofford was New York City's "secure" detention center for boys and girls, ages seven to sixteen, a temporary stopping-off place on their way to the different outposts of the juvenile justice system. It was a bigger, more formidable version of Zarega, where Cheryl had been sent the previous year. From the outside, Spofford resembled a large, white brick fortress, eight stories high, built on a hill in the poor, ravaged Hunt's Point section of the South Bronx. It was surrounded by a high wall, the windows were covered by security screens, and the entrance was guarded by an electrically operated gate. Inside, the three hundred or so youthful inmates were marched in military style between rooms, which were kept locked with heavy three-inch keys. Over the years, state legislators, grand juries, and private groups, such as the Citizens Committee for Children, had investigated Spofford and accused it of condoning brutality by the staff, rampant drug use, homosexuality, and overcrowding. Boys had been found beaten to death. One time, a teenage inmate delivered her own baby on the night of her arrival and carried it to the dining hall at breakfast time, wrapped in a raincoat. The irate investigators called Spofford a children's jail, which in essence it was, and demanded that it be shut. But Spofford kept running; the city needed it.

Taking Willie to Spofford was supposed to frighten him. At least that was what Miss Grayson, a kindly, veteran police officer in the Twenty-eighth Precinct, hoped would happen. She had watched with mounting concern as Willie had gotten in trouble over the past few years, and she knew that most of the boys in Spofford were much bigger than he was, with some having committed murder, rape, or armed robbery. They could put terror in your heart. But not in Willie's. To him, being sent to Spofford was an honor. A boy who had been there came back to the streets with an enhanced reputation. It was like an adult saying, "I've been to Attica," the most notorious of New York State's maximum security prisons, where forty-three people had been killed after a riot in 1971. The night Willie was admitted to Spofford, he saw a plea written under a picture of Frankenstein: "There is a little bit of monster in all of us, but please control yourself while you are here." A monster, he was beginning to think, was what the world expected him to be.

The next morning, at 10 o'clock, the bus from Spofford delivered Willie back to the Manhattan Family Court. Judge Felix resumed the hearing. "Do you know you left court yesterday?" he asked Willie. "Do you know the kind of language you used, what you said the judge could do to himself? Do you remember that?"

Willie stared at the floor, silent.

"You have to answer," Judge Felix commanded.

After a long pause, Willie finally said, "Yes."

"You know, your mother has to go out and work and you went out and bought a knife," the judge continued, trying to make some sense of the situation. "Where did you buy it?"

"A store," Willie said.

"How much did you pay for it?"

"Three dollars."

"Where did you get three dollars?" Judge Felix pressed him.

Willie lapsed into silence again.

Judge Felix tried a new tack. "Why did you need a knife, to clean your fingernails? Your mother said you had the knife up against another boy. Why was that?"

"Because he tried to take my ten dollars," Willie responded.

Now Judge Felix was incredulous. "Where did such a young boy get ten dollars?" he inquired.

"I sold my TV back to the TV man," Willie said.

"Did he sell his own family's television set?" the judge asked Laura. "He might have," she answered with a shrug. "It's not in the house today."

Judge Felix was beginning to get the picture. He had seen it too often before. "I have an ugly choice here," he said to Willie. "You're no angel. I have a petition to declare you a PINS and have you sent away. I can do that. But there's a lot of abdication of responsibility on the part of the mother. She signed you out of Bellevue against medical advice. She doesn't seem to discipline you."

The judge was staring at Laura now, trying to make a point. "There are a lot of parents who feel that by filing a PINS petition they can say to the court, 'It's your problem now.' I take the position that it should be their cross to carry. It's their children. They shouldn't just be able to dump their kid on the court."

That was what was going wrong with the Family Court, Judge Felix thought. It was becoming a dumping ground for dysfunctional families and a dysfunctional society. He was no bleeding-heart liberal, but he hated what was happening to his court. It didn't have the resources to handle the tidal wave of broken kids who were inundating it. The court could only decide to send the kids back to their families, where their troubles had begun, or deliver them to an institution where they would come in contact with other kids with even worse problems. Given that situation, the chances were that a kid like Willie, if he was sent away as a PINS, would return as a full-fledged juvenile delinquent. It was an inexorable process. The system to protect and take care of neglected, abused, and troublesome kids had become a recycling system, feeding on itself. Once, Judge Felix thought, there had been an answer to the problem. It was called the family.

Looking at Willie, who was standing beside his mother, Judge Felix pronounced his decision. He declared Willie a person in need of supervision and ordered what was termed a placement for him at the Wiltwyck School for Boys. His Honor had no idea Willie's father had been there before him.

• • •

THE FAMILY COURT traced its origins to medieval times, to the old English doctrine of *parens patriae*. This was the notion, drawn from chancery courts rather than the common law, that the Crown could step in to take care of orphans, operating as if it were a parent. In England, *parens patriae* was confined to this narrow purpose, for children were usually spared the routine forms of punishment of the time, heavy fines or hanging, since according to common law a child under the age of seven could not be charged with the commission of a crime. Boys between the ages of seven and fourteen were protected by another device—a strong presumption of infancy, a presumption that they lacked criminal intent.

But American reformers in the late eighteenth century unintentionally breached the old protections of the common law when they began building prisons. Prisons, they reasoned, were a more humane form of punishment than forfeiture and hanging. Imprisonment was an invention of the age of enlightenment, predicated on the idea that criminals could be rehabilitated through solitude, reflection, and religious training. And if older malefactors could be rehabilitated, certainly younger miscreants would benefit, too, the prison builders believed, drawing on the idea inherent in *parens patriae* that the state could intervene to protect wayward children. Soon children were showing up in the new prisons, housed indiscriminately with hardened adult criminals. This appalled a new generation of reformers and philanthropists in the 1820s. "The present plan of promiscuous intercourse," John Pintard complained, makes "little Devils into great ones and at the expiration of their terms turns out accomplished Villains." To remedy this evil, the new reformers established special "Houses of Refuge" for a class of people they called juvenile delinquents. The first of these new asylums opened in New York City in 1825.

These reformers' motives were humanitarian and were based on the best social theory of their time. They believed deeply that crime was caused by poverty and by parents who themselves were drunkards, louts, or thieves. Immigrants were looked on as a special source of contagion. Three-quarters of the children in the New York House of Refuge, in fact, were foreign-born, the majority of them Irish. These children could be spared from lives of crime, the reformers were sure, by isolating them from the wickedness of the world and filling their heads with the middle-class values of neatness, diligence, thrift, and punctuality. Achieving this lofty purpose, of course, required stern discipline, and conditions in the new institutions were harsh. In the New York House of Refuge, the authorities kept recalcitrant boys in leg irons or whipped them, and the daily regimen was spartan.

At sunrise, the children are warned, by the ringing of a bell, to rise from their beds. Each child makes his own bed, and steps forth, on

a signal, into the Hall. They then proceed, in perfect order, to the
Wash Room. . . . The morning school then commences where they
are occupied until 7 o'clock. A short intermission is allowed for
breakfast; after which they proceed to their respective workshops.

And so the day continued, with half an hour for supper, an enforced
study period in the evening, and finally a prayer led by the superintendent
just before the boys were locked up for the night. "A perfect silence then
reigns throughout the establishment," concluded one account.

In the 1850s, still another new movement took hold, among clergy-
men, physicians, educators, and early feminists, driven by the progressive
ideal at the center of American life. They concluded that the houses of
refuge were too much like prisons, with their "bolted door, barred window, walled yard, shadowy cell and brute force," as Samuel G. Howe
of Massachusetts wrote. Some of these critics also noted that many young
inmates in the houses of refuge either absconded or were repeatedly
returned, up to 40 percent in the case of New York. So these child savers,
as they came to be called, set out to build a smaller, more wholesome
institution modeled on the family. The result was the reform school, or
the reformatory, and by 1890, nearly every state outside the South had
some type of reform school. Massachusetts pioneered the cottage plan,
soon widely copied, in which the children were divided into families of
forty or so, and each family had its own cottage and schedule. "Each
house is to be a family, under the sole direction and control of the
matron, who is the mother of the family," declared the Massachusetts
commissioners in their plans for a new reform school for girls. "It is the
design to give a home interest, a home feeling and attachment, to the
whole family." Many of the new cottage-based reform schools were located on farms, to remove the "city waif" and the "gamin of the alley"
from what was seen as the vicious influence of city slums. It was the city,
said Charles Loring Brace, the most influential leader of the movement,
that produced the "dangerous classes."

The basic plan of the reform school would last for more than a
century, into the present, but by the 1890s, reformatories were already
coming under attack. They, too, it often turned out, suffered from the
same brutal conditions as the houses of refuge and adult penitentiaries
they were supposed to replace, and they were not much better at rehabili-
tating their youthful charges. In Chicago, Jane Addams, the social worker,
felt that the answer lay in another way to separate children from criminals.
She advocated the creation of a separate juvenile court. It would be a
civil rather than a criminal court, one that would try to understand and
treat the offending child, much as a doctor would, instead of stigmatizing

him with a criminal record. The parental powers that reform schools had enjoyed should now be extended to the entire legal process, they suggested. "The fundamental idea of the Juvenile Court is so simple it seems anyone ought to understand it," said Timothy Hurley, the president of the Chicago Visitation and Aid Society. "It is, to be perfectly plain, a return to paternalism."

The idea was enormously appealing. After the Illinois legislature created the nation's first juvenile court in 1899, twelve other states followed suit in the next three years. By 1925, all but two states, Maine and Wyoming, had juvenile court laws.

The new laws represented an expansion of the *parens patriae* doctrine, of a benevolent court that would function as a wise parent outside regular law. In the family courts, the accused were to be defined less by their offenses than by their youth. It was the children's welfare, rather than their legal rights, that the new courts were to protect. This paternalism brought a whole new set of courtroom practices. Judges no longer wore robes, only their normal clothing. The courtroom was designed "as a parlor rather than a court, around a table instead of a bench," to give the atmosphere of "a family conference," according to the program issued for the opening of the first family court in Chicago. The key figure was the judge, who was to "get the whole truth about a child" in the same way that a "physician searches for every detail that bears on the condition of a patient," said one of the early Chicago juvenile court judges. To further add to the atmosphere of informality and protect the child, the court's records were sealed, and both the public and the press were excluded.

Punishment was deliberately kept mild, since children's personalities were thought to be still in the process of formation, making them more open to rehabilitation than adults. The juvenile courts introduced probation officers, whose task was to advise the judges, and they usually dismissed a child's first offense. The first crime is on the house, became the saying in the New York Family Court. Under New York law, judges had to be lenient in sentencing, limited to handing out only "the least restrictive available alternative" for a given offense, no matter what the facts. The maximum term of punishment was eighteen months.

In time, a whole new antiseptic nomenclature was invented for the juvenile courts. A boy brought before the court was not the defendant but the respondent. Even if the police had arrested him for robbery, he could not be charged with a crime. In the words of the New York Family Court statute, he was "not criminally responsible . . . by reason of infancy." The boy would not be arraigned, he could not be indicted, and there would be no trial and no verdict. If, following all this, he was found to have robbed someone, there would still be no sentence and no prison. Instead, in place of being arraigned, a child was first brought in through a process called intake and seen by a probation officer. Rather than being indicted, a boy would have a petition drawn against him, and then would face what was called a fact-finding hearing, not a trial. Eventually, there might be a disposition, not a verdict. Finally, a boy could be locked away by a placement with a state training school, rather than committed to prison.

By the 1960s, however, there was a growing chorus of criticism that the juvenile courts were also failing. The complaints, from children's advocacy groups and civil libertarians, focused on the lack of due process and legal safeguards in the family courts. They were antilegal. Young people appearing in these courts often did not have lawyers, and they had no right to cross-examination or appeal. All power rested with the judges, or with the often poorly trained probation officers, who kept the files and wrote up background reports on the respondents. New York was the first state to act, revising its law in 1962 to give all children in Family Court the right to an attorney—called a law guardian—and assuring them of most of the norms of due process.

Then, in 1968, the Supreme Court heard the case of Gerald Francis Gault, a fifteen-year-old boy who had been arrested by the sheriff of Gila County, Arizona, on the complaint of a woman neighbor. She accused him of making an obscene phone call. "Do you give any?" Gerald was said to have asked. "Are your cherries ripe today?" Gerald was picked up and interrogated for several days without any explanation or notification to his parents. A judge committed him to the state industrial school "for the period of his minority," what amounted to six years. But the woman who accused him did not appear at his hearing, and no sworn testimony was taken.

Justice Abe Fortas, speaking for the majority, pronounced juvenile courts a failure. "Under our Constitution," he said, "the condition of being a boy does not justify a kangaroo court." He found the doctrine of *parens patriae* constitutionally debatable. "The history of American freedom is, in no small measure, the history of procedure," he said. He then awarded to children in trouble with the law most of the rights already possessed by adults: the right to counsel, the right to confront and cross-examine sworn witnesses, and the privilege against self-incrimination.

The introduction of lawyers and due process into the juvenile courts created an awkward imbalance. In New York, a corps of smart, well-educated, and idealistic young attorneys working for the Legal Aid Society quickly appeared to represent young people before the Family Court. They were no longer primarily concerned with the child's best interest—

the original intent of the family courts—but with protecting their client's legal rights. Because they were lawyers, of course, that meant winning their case and getting their client off, whatever the facts. When they won, the kid would usually be sent back to the street, which wasn't much help, the way Judge Felix saw things. That was where the trouble had started. Privately, the Legal Aid lawyers acknowledged that most of their clients were probably guilty. But the *Manual for New Attorneys* of the New York Legal Aid Society's Family Court Branch decreed that the handling of a delinquency case should be the same as the defense of an adult criminal prosecution. Whatever the charge, the law guardian must disregard both his personal feelings and "the possible need for incarceration. His duty is to defend the child with zeal." Naturally, the Legal Aid lawyers also got to see what some of the reform schools were like; that only confirmed their belief that it was best to get their clients acquitted.

What was really crazy, Judge Felix thought, was that while the law guardians brought high new standards of professional help for the children, paid for by the taxpayer, the rest of the Family Court remained a kind of poor relative. In Manhattan, the Family Court in the early 1970s was so starved for funds that all the judges had to share one legal assistant to research their cases. The prosecutors, pleasantly misnamed corporation counsels, were badly paid, dispirited, and often fly-by-night lawyers who could not get jobs elsewhere. They had no clerk, no typist to help draw up briefs, no secretary to answer the phone, and seldom more than five minutes to prepare a case. Then there was the problem of witnesses. The prosecutors had no way to serve a summons except through the mail. Half to three-quarters of their cases were dismissed because witnesses failed to appear. Even the police treated the Family Court as a joke and often did not show up when needed to testify. By one estimate, young people appearing in the Manhattan Family Court were sent away as PINS or delinquents less than 10 percent of the time.

So by the time Willie first appeared in Family Court in 1972, there had been more than a century of progressive experimentation with juvenile justice in the United States, and the system was more in doubt than ever. The Family Court had been set up to handle newspaper boys who threw a rock through a shopkeeper's window or stole a hubcap. It was based on the premise that kids were basically good and could be reformed. But now Judge Felix watched as more and more children came before him for serious crimes, like armed robbery, drug sales, and murder, and they were coming back time after time. The system wasn't working.

Willie didn't know all this. But after his first few times in court, he got a sense of it, like the smell of candy in his mother's store. Wherever it was the judge was sending him, this place called Wiltwyck, it couldn't be too serious. He had run out of court, and nothing had happened to him. He could always find a way out.

EARLY ON THE MORNING of August 7, 1972, Laura took Willie to Wiltwyck's branch office in Harlem, where they were picked up by the school van. Miss Grayson, the juvenile police officer from the Twenty-eighth Precinct, went along for security, to make sure Willie got there. She was dressed in plainclothes, but Willie knew she had a gun in her purse. She had shown it to him. Now she had some brochures from Wiltwyck, and she tried to persuade him it was like a summer camp, not a prison. There were pictures of a swimming pool, and a big pond, and lots of trees everywhere. The campus had actually been moved since Butch was at Wiltwyck, so it was closer to the city, making it easier for the boys, their parents, and the staff to get back and forth. The new school, named the Eleanor Roosevelt campus, was in Yorktown Heights, in northern Westchester County, forty miles north of the city. It had formerly been the estate of Major Edward Bowes, who made his money conducting the popular show the "Amateur Hour" on radio. Bowes called his 112-acre property Dream Lake.

Almost everyone was impressed by Wiltwyck. It was at its apogee at the time, and there was something special about it, like the Peace Corps, the Civil Rights movement in the South, and the Kennedy White House. They all seemed to draw on the moral fervor of the 1960s to attract the best and the brightest to work for them. Wiltwyck's staff liked to boast that they took only the worst boys in New York City—the ones other institutions rejected—the most emotionally disturbed, the most ne-glected, and the most violent, virtually all of them black or Hispanic, and treated them without drugs or physical abuse. Visitors came from all over the country to see how Wiltwyck succeeded where others failed. Criminologists cited it in academic journals as a model to copy. Claude Brown, who had been there as a boy, dedicated his best-seller, *Manchild in the Promised Land*, to Wiltwyck. Some of its intensely dedicated employ-ees, like Ruth Gregory, the head social worker, came there to work after reading *Manchild*. "It is a wonderful heart-in-the-right-place experi-ment," Gregory told her family. She had grown up in an affluent, conser-vative family on the north shore of Long Island and had to explain why she was giving up a promising career as a management consultant to turn social worker.

Willie's first stop at Wiltwyck was an intake interview, along with his mother. He noticed that the woman conducting the interview, Carol Darden, looked like an African princess, with high, finely chiseled cheekbones, a radiant smile, and a regal bearing. She was beautiful enough to be a *Vogue* model; in fact, her sister was a successful New York model. But Darden, the daughter of a black physician who was raised in properly suburban Montclair, New Jersey, and graduated from Sarah Lawrence College, had chosen to become a social worker. She was smart and sophisticated but not naive about her work, and she was considered a terrific social worker. Now, as she looked at Willie, she saw a handsome, appealing child. But what struck her, more than his good looks, was how self-contained he was for a nine-year-old. Most of the children who ended up at places like Wiltwyck had trouble in school and didn't express themselves well. But Willie was very intelligent, articulate, and savvy. A slick little dude, Darden said to herself. He was the most poised boy she had ever encountered. When Laura told her Willie's nickname on the street was "Little Man," she was not surprised. He clearly had a strong sense of himself, along with a swagger that showed he knew he had built a reputation. At nine, he was already different, a star. Willie would need special attention, Darden noted. He was the kind of child who would either be lucky and catch on, or totally self-destruct.

In filling out all the forms with Willie and Laura, Darden took careful note that Butch was in prison and that Willie had never known his father. In her experience with other children, those kinds of gaps were like a cold vacuum that could cause chaos in a young personality. It is almost a physical loss, she believed, like missing an arm or a leg.

Laura said nothing about Butch having been at Wiltwyck. That would have been stunning information for the school and might have helped in treating Willie, but Laura was guarded as usual in what she revealed. There was something about Laura's manner that struck Darden as the interview progressed. Most mothers bringing their sons to Wiltwyck were struggling with anguish or guilt or anger, but Laura showed no particular emotion. She seemed to have successfully disassociated herself from the process, Darden thought. Laura mentioned that Willie looked just like Butch, and when Darden glanced at Willie and Laura seated in front of her, she saw that Willie didn't resemble his mother at all. Maybe, Darden thought, Laura's emotional disassociation grew out of this physical disconnection. It was as if Willie were all his father's doing, as if someone had given her a child other than her own, as if Willie were a stranger in her house. Whoever he was, whatever he was doing, it was because of his father, not her.

After Carol Darden finished her interview and reported her findings to the school's senior staff, Arruth Artis received a phone call in Cottage 6, where she was the child care supervisor. Artis was a strong, practical-minded woman of fifty with a firm jaw, warm eyes, and a ready, motherly

smile. She had raised four children of her own, plus an amazing total of
forty foster children, and whenever Wiltwyck got a boy it didn't know
what to do with, the phone call would go out: "Get Artis over here." It
was flattering in a way, Artis thought, though as a child care worker, the
lowest rung on Wiltwyck's ladder, she often felt she was looked down on
by the social workers with their graduate degrees, the teachers, and the
assorted psychiatrists and psychologists. She had never had the opportunity to get beyond high school in her small hometown in North Carolina.
Her mother was a maid and her father was a logger, until one day a tree
fell on him and crushed him to death. Artis had had to give up her dreams
of college and take care of her nine younger brothers and sisters. But her
family were always good churchgoing people, and her hardships had only
strengthened her spirit. She thought of herself as being from "the old
school," a vigorous disciplinarian, not afraid of any of the boys at Wiltwyck
and not afraid to use her hands on them when she had to. They respected
her for it, and many of them paid her the ultimate compliment. They
called her Mom.

This day, Lou White, the assistant director of Wiltwyck, was on the
phone. "Arruth," he said, "we got someone here, I hope you can handle
him. He's pretty tough."

When she walked into the room in the administration building to
fetch Willie, the first thing Artis saw was that he was peeking up the dresses
of the secretary and a receptionist. Laura was sitting there laughing. This
bothered Artis, and she started to say something, but Laura quickly told
her, "He's just like his father."

"Where's his father?" Artis asked. "In jail," Laura answered, as if
that told you everything you needed to know about Willie.

Artis now took Willie by the hand, to make sure he didn't run away,
and headed up the path to the six brick-and-concrete cottages where the
130 boys at Wiltwyck lived. As they walked, Willie acted very friendly,
with a big smile on his face. She thought he looked as if he came straight
from the angels, he was so beautiful. He looked as if he could charm a
bird off a tree. He began swinging her hand, in a nice way, except soon
he was swinging it more and more exaggeratedly, and she thought, dag-
gumit, he's going to break my arm. Suddenly, Willie swung her hand
right up to his mouth and bit her, hard. That shocked her, because she
thought she understood these kids, and she had not seen this coming.

As soon as they reached the cottage, she took him inside and gave
him her specialty, a real good shaking. No bruises, no marks. But when
she finished, Willie said, "Man, I'm never going to try that again."

It had not really sunk in on Willie that he would have to stay in

Wiltwyck, because Laura had told him she would wait while he inspected the cottage. So he accepted an offer from Mrs. Artis—that was what he called her at first—to go with a boy named Moises to look at his animal traps in the woods. Willie had never been in the countryside before, and it was exciting to see the traps that were set in hopes of catching raccoons and skunks. It was only an hour later, when he got back to the cottage and asked for his mother, that he discovered she had left and he was alone.

"You mean my mother has left and I have to stay in this mother-fucking place?" Willie began shouting. He had a serious temper tantrum right there on the spot, cursing and crying and knocking over the furniture. He felt tricked. He remembered how his mother had left him at Bellevue a few months before, and he was overcome by a fear of rejection. The entire time Willie was at Wiltwyck, he never forgot the sense of abandonment he felt on that first day. It colored his whole stay.

The other boys in his cottage, all bigger than Willie, wasted no time in testing him. They teased him over the light color of his skin, calling him "high yellow," or "light bright, almost white." Then, the first weekend after he arrived, when the number of child care workers on duty was reduced, a boy named "Richard" came up behind him, grabbed him around the neck, and started humping him. It was part of the initiation rites. When a new boy arrived, someone would "take his buns." Usually, new boys got raped in the shower or in their beds at night. The boys called it a blanket party. Four or five bigger boys would pull a blanket over the new boy's head and then screw him in the butt. This practice shocked many of the social workers, who tended to be liberal whites from comfortable middle-class backgrounds. But it also surprised many of the child care workers, or counselors, as they were called, who were mostly African-Americans. The first Sunday morning Larry Jones was at Wiltwyck, fresh out of college from North Carolina, a kid came down the hall of the cottage he was supervising.

"Mr. Jones, some kids are back there taking buns," the boy exclaimed.

The kitchen staff had just delivered some Danish pastry to the cottage as a treat, so Jones said, "You go down there and tell them to put the buns back. I'll be right down."

"No," the boy interjected with a scowl, "I'm not talking about that."

Willie wasn't so naive. He had already been introduced to sex by the girls on his block and by his grandfather. When Richard came up behind him again and tried to hump him, Willie ran outside. There, he took off his sneakers and put one sock inside the other. Then he filled up the sock with stones and tied a knot to keep them in place. Moises, the boy who had shown Willie his animal traps, watched what was happening and said to Willie, "What are you doing, man? Richard will kill you. He's much bigger than you." But Willie remembered the rules of the street and what his mother had taught him. "Don't be bullied," she had said. "Hit back. To get respect, you've got to be the toughest."

Willie put the sock in his back pocket and went inside. As soon as Richard saw Willie, he tried to jump on him. Willie pulled out his sock and hit Richard over the head as hard as he could. The sound of the stones hitting Richard's skull made a sharp noise, and blood spurted out of his head from a cut.

A second boy now came at Willie, screaming, "Yo, man, what you doing?" Willie swung again, hitting the second boy square in the nose, and more blood spouted.

Richard was holding his head, but Willie swung again and again, feeling stronger with each blow. Finally, Richard was on the ground shaking, doing the chicken, the boys called it.

"You remember this," Willie told him. "My father is a killer. I'm just like him, and I'll kill you too."

At last, a counselor showed up and put a bear hug on Willie. He took Willie down the corridor and locked him in the staff office. Richard had to be rushed to the infirmary. The incident began Willie's reputation. He was pleased to hear the other boys say that he was "the craziest nigger in Wiltwyck." That was high praise, the way Willie saw it. Violence, he kept learning, won him respect. After the incident, when Richard received packages from his mother, he always gave Willie some of his candy.

Of course, Willie had to work to keep up his reputation. At noontime one day, not long after his arrival, he overheard another boy say something he didn't like while they were eating lunch at a big round table in the cafeteria. There were ten boys at the table, and two counselors, including Larry Jones. Willie didn't say anything in response to the remark. He just got up from his chair, walked calmly all the way around the table, and bam, punched the other boy in the face. Jones noted that Willie's tolerance level was zero. He could explode on a dime. In a place where all the boys were impulsive, Willie was the most impetuous.

Another day, when he was supposed to be in school, Willie and another boy named Emilio skipped out of class. They first ran into the woods, so no one could find them, then later sneaked back into their cottage. Each cottage was equipped with a small kitchen, with a refrigerator and stove. Willie took out some marshmallows and the two of them roasted them on the top of the electric stove with a fork. After they had eaten a few, Willie toasted one until it caught fire. He carried it out to one of the boy's rooms and set the bed on fire. As the flames leaped around the room, Willie was pleased and ran out of the cottage. The staff suspected Willie was responsible but couldn't prove it. Wiltwyck wasn't equipped to handle him, Willie concluded. The worst they could do to punish you was confine you to your room for an hour or take away your television privileges. That hardly scared Willie.

After the first few weeks, Willie even got to like some things about being there, especially the chance to be with a few of the female staff. Every morning at 7, Arruth Artis woke him with a whisper in his ear. She told Willie to stick by her side while she got all the other boys in the cottage ready to go down the hill for breakfast and then to school. "I'm not even going to look, but you better be right there next to me," she said sternly. That was the best way she knew to ensure he didn't get into trouble.

Pretty soon, Willie began to call her Mom, and instead of thinking he was forced to go everywhere with her, he saw himself as her little pet. Willie started following her around, trying to sit next to her in the cafeteria, or snuggling up next to her in the cottage, hugging and kissing her. He knew she was very strict, but he liked it, because he realized it took someone very strong and very caring to control him. "Man, you're playing with death to hit that lady," Willie told himself. Artis even started taking Willie off campus when she took driving lessons, and he was with her when she bought her first car, a blue and black vinyl-roofed Buick.

Artis was getting attached to Willie, too, in spite of herself. She had taken care of a lot of tough children, but she had never seen a boy as angry, frustrated, and violent as he was. It was almost as if he were possessed. He began to talk to her when they were alone, and in talking, he revealed a sad, needy side. It was that neediness along with his incredible smile that got to her. When Willie talked, he often boasted about his father, how he was in prison for killing two men and how Willie had once gone to visit him in prison without his mother knowing about it. It was just a child's story, naturally, but it told Artis something. She felt Willie was disappointed his father wasn't there for him, and he clearly viewed his mother with contempt for not being able to handle him. Artis had seen that the first day, when Willie peeked up the women's dresses and Laura just sat there laughing. Before too long, when Artis reprimanded Willie for something, he would say to her, "I'm glad, Mom. I'm glad you made me behave myself."

One fall weekend, Artis even took Willie to her house, a modest red-frame structure near the Hudson River in Ossining, the home of Sing Sing state prison. The living room was neat and orderly, with Bibles on several coffee tables, and photographs of her four children and many foster children everywhere, arranged in magical profusion on the walls, on bookshelves, and on tables beside the couches. One of her own sons had become a successful jazz guitarist; another was a career army officer; a daughter was an executive with IBM. Ever since she had come north just before World War II, there had always been lots of children in the house. First it was her own younger brothers and sisters she had helped raise, making sure they got through college. Then there were all the relatives and friends from back home who kept appearing, and Artis took them in, feeling that the world was one big extended family and that you had an obligation to help. She had learned her values from her mother, Lord rest her soul, who had seen that her children never went hungry by doing the laundry of what seemed like all the white folks in North Carolina, even when she was ill.

Artis's great-grandmother, Moniza Smallwood, whom she had known as a little girl, had been a slave. From her, Artis had heard that she was part of a poverty-stricken people, but a people who were also rich, really rich, because they were filled with so much love for their families. Nothing had been given to her people, but everything was there in the earth, in the family. Family bonds were like building blocks; you built on the strength and honesty in your family.

And as Artis sat in her living room that day, watching Willie and looking at the accumulated pictures of her family, it struck her that this was what was missing in Willie's life. It was not so much that he had grown up economically poor, but that he had grown up with emotional poverty, without emotional attachments. Lacking them, he had nothing to build on; very scary, she thought. Boys like Willie didn't care how you punished them, because they had no fear. They had a saying about discipline at Wiltwyck, "It's just another ass-whipping to me." Nothing mattered to Willie because he had nothing to lose. Most people feel they have something to lose, at least a memory of something good to lose. But Willie had absolutely nothing that meant anything to him. No one had ever loved him back enough. So when he said he was going to be just like his father and kill someone, Artis believed him. He could kill and not feel it. The victim would be only an object, not a real living person. Artis wasn't sure Willie could ever stay long enough at Wiltwyck to make up for this emotional deficit.

But after Willie's first few months at Wiltwyck, Artis noticed that he was getting awfully fond of his teacher, Rose Niles, and she was sweet on him, too. Willie couldn't read or write when he arrived at Wiltwyck, and he thought school was a great big joke. Mrs. Niles, however, was different. She was a short, middle-aged woman with dark hair, dancing brown eyes, and a flamboyant, dramatic personality. She had come to teaching late, after raising a family, and her style reflected her upbringing in a tenement on Delancey Street on the Lower East Side of Manhattan, where her best friend was a Gypsy and she sang songs to earn spending money when she was only ten years old. Later, she had studied acting and worked in a theater troupe. Now, when she spoke, her eyes glistened, and she projected a tremendous vibrancy, like an actress. She caught Willie off-guard the first day in class by giving him some scented Magic Markers. The yellow ones smelled like lemons, the orange like oranges, the red like cherries, and the blue, his favorite, like grapes. They smelled so good, Willie tried to eat them.

The school principal, Joe Wynn, had learned that Niles had a way with really difficult boys, so he had assigned Willie to her. "Rose," he told her, "this is another lulu." "Bring him in," she replied. She never turned a child down.

She ran a big open classroom with boys of different ages and abilities, some of them with only a low level of intelligence, some of them like Willie, very bright though completely unmotivated. What they had in common, she had discovered, was that they were all full of rage and hostility, and they had all been told they were bad boys, so they had given up. After a while, they had decided, why bother? It was more fun to break into the principal's office than to try to learn. So she had devised her own behavior modification program. She gave out assignments, and for completing their work, the boys earned points toward a menu of rewards. The students got to pick some of these prizes. Earn enough points, and she would take you horseback riding, or ice skating, or bowling. Even if you didn't measure up, you might get a Hershey's bar. The big payoff was for the most points over three months, then you got to come to her house for meatballs and spaghetti and to meet her husband, Colonel Niles. Actually, he was retired from the service, but she had a photograph in the classroom of him in his World War II Army Air Force uniform, and the boys thought he was a great hero.

Rose Niles had another program the boys loved. Every week, she organized a trip someplace—to a farm to watch maple sugar being made, to a zoo, to an IBM factory, and to the Museum of Natural History and the Fulton Fish Market in New York. Each time, on the way back, she let them stop at a Baskin Robbins shop and bought them ice-cream cones. Willie thought about running away during these trips, but it got so he didn't want to disappoint Niles. He was very proud of being in her class; it made him feel special, like a big man on campus, because her class was the best. Willie and the boy with whom he was tightest in the class, Perry, were jealous of her attention. They both needed a mother, and Niles filled the role. One day, when she said to Willie, "You're so sweet," Perry got angry and shoved Willie. "He's not sweet," Perry said. "He's stupid."

Willie started treating her like his sweetheart. One day, she accidentally locked herself out of her car, leaving the key in the ignition. "Don't worry, Mrs. Niles," Willie said. "Just stay here." In two minutes, he was back with her key. She decided he was a mechanical genius. Another time, a boy stole her purse. Willie went into a fit, raged around all the classrooms smacking and grabbing the other boys until one finally fingered the culprit. Pretty soon, Willie was back with her wallet, too. He had fished it out of a toilet bowl.

After class, Niles often took him outside to sit with her on the ledge of a terrace. He had a perpetual smile on his face, to go with those big dimples, and he smiled his way into her heart. Willie would hug and kiss her, and Niles would say, "You're going to be either a doctor or a lawyer."

That was when Willie talked about his father. Willie idolized his father, she came to realize, always saying how great he was. "He's in jail for killing two men," Willie told her. "When I grow up, I want to be just like him." This scared Niles. She surmised that Willie believed violence was a way to get close to his father, to get in prison like him. Someday, he really would turn out just like Butch, she told the other teachers.

So the report card on Willie in his first months at Wiltwyck was mixed. On the positive side, he never got in a fight in Rose Niles's class, and he finally learned to read and write. He actually began to enjoy school. A psychological test done at the time concluded he was "precocious, warm and empathetic. He has a good capacity for giving and receiving love and support." It was the most sympathetic analysis ever written about Willie.

But his overall progress was only "marginal," the report concluded. He continued to bully other boys and had set fire to the cottage, and, the psychologist who wrote the report warned, "He resists emotional impact and his dependency needs are very strong." The key problem remained that Willie had felt rejected since birth by his mother, who had deceived him about his father. That made him full of rage. To make matters worse, the report said, Willie was imitating his father's career of crime and violence, the very qualities Laura Bosket despised. "In order to reach his above-average intellectual and creative potential," the report suggested, Willie now needed more support from the adults in his life.

THE MOST IMPORTANT ADULT in his life, his mother, seldom came to visit. It took a whole day of Laura's time, riding up and back in the school van, and it seemed as if every time she did go, an administrator at Wiltwyck said something about Willie that wasn't very nice. As a mother, she felt hurt to hear all those reports about his bad behavior. Besides, he was in Wiltwyck's hands now. He wasn't her responsibility anymore.

Willie missed his mother. When he watched other boys get visits from their families on weekends or make trips home to New York, Willie felt bad. Arruth Artis noticed that if another boy went home for the weekend, Willie often sneaked into his room and trashed his clothes and furniture. It was a way to vent his rage. Willie also started to figure out ways to escape from Wiltwyck and get back to Harlem. He didn't hate Wiltwyck; actually, he liked Artis and Niles. But he wanted his mother, and he just didn't like being controlled. He had a compulsion to challenge authority.

Christmas was particularly hard on Willie. A few days after the holiday, when he knew the school van was going down to New York to pick up the boys who had been on home leave, Willie hid himself under the backseat. He managed to escape detection all the way to Wiltwyck's office on 136th Street in Harlem. There he climbed out and ran home. When he knocked on the door, Laura said, "Who's there?"

"Telegram," Willie sang out, making as deep a voice as he could. Laura was not amused. "What the hell are you doing here?" she demanded. The next day, she called the school, and they sent a child care worker to pick him up. Willie repeated the performance a few days later, with similar results. Each time his mother sent him back, he felt more rejected, and the anger inside him grew.

Many of the other boys also tried escaping when they first arrived at Wiltwyck. It was only natural, and easy enough to do. There was no fence around the school, and the woods were only a few feet away. But most of the boys usually gave up after a while and settled down. Not Willie. His escapes grew more frequent and more brazen. This changed Wiltwyck's attitude toward him. Repeat runaways were the most difficult boys to deal with. For the staff, Wiltwyck was a hard place at which to work under the best circumstances. There was always a charged, hostile atmosphere, with the boys constantly cursing the employees or fighting with one another, which required the counselors and social workers alike to intervene physically, sometimes getting punched or kicked in the process. It was like being on the front line in a war zone, some of the staff thought. They were already overworked and underpaid, and when a boy escaped, someone had to be sent after him, increasing the load on the remaining employees in the cottages. It also meant more team meetings to discuss what to do about the boy, and more time spent individually with the child. So escapees were very time-consuming and annoying.

The worst part was that Willie's escapes threatened the whole philosophy on which Wiltwyck was built. As Dr. Joel Katz, Wiltwyck's resident psychiatrist, saw it, every boy was there by definition because his family and society had been unable to handle him and his problems. This led to feelings of rejection and loss of self-esteem, Dr. Katz explained to the rest of the staff. And this sense of rejection, in turn, showed up in some boys as depression and in others as grandiosity, a belief that they were so powerful that no one could take care of them. Boys who were grandiose were also likely to be paranoid and psychopathic, or antisocial, Dr. Katz had found. Willie was along those lines, he thought. All the boys used violence to protect themselves from their inner feelings of rejection and despair. Wiltwyck's brand of therapy depended on reversing the boys' sense of rejection by proving to them that the school was strong enough to handle them, whatever they were doing bad. With delinquent boys, Dr. Katz counseled, you had to expect them to test you before they would let you help them. Underneath their hard shells, the boys were actually terrified of their own destructive impulses, and if the staff showed that it, too, was afraid of the boys, they could quickly act their worst. If a boy got away with assaulting other kids or escaping, it had a rippling effect on the others, Dr. Katz preached. They started to lose all confidence in you. What do they need you for? They'd say, "You're no better than my mother, my father, the school, or anybody else."

The worst thing Wiltwyck could do with a troublesome boy, the absolutely worst thing, Dr. Katz stressed, was to kick him out. Transferring a boy merely confirmed that Wiltwyck was not strong enough to handle him, both to the boy himself and to all the other residents. "Shipping a boy out," Dr. Katz wrote in a memo for the staff, "means the staff has flunked."

Benign and impish-looking, Dr. Katz was proud of Wiltwyck's program. It was built on the theories of Alfred Adler, August Aichorn, and Bruno Bettelheim. He called it "total commitment." This commitment, he wrote, "must be complete and absolute, with no exceptions." When Wiltwyck took a kid, he pledged, the school would not use drugs to tranquilize him, nor would it kick him out. At the time he took over as director of Wiltwyck's psychiatric services in 1971, one-third of the boys were heavily sedated with powerful drugs like Thorazine. He thought that was wrong. The long-term side effects on children were unknown; fostering drug use among boys where drug abuse was already a major problem was absurd; and given the ethnic makeup of the school's population, he was afraid it looked as if Wiltwyck were using black children as guinea pigs. So Dr. Katz, a psychoanalyst by training, had ordered the drugs stopped. He was happy to tell visitors that in his first three years, he had not had to resort to drugs again. Nor had Wiltwyck shipped a single boy out to either a state-run reformatory or a mental hospital.

No one explained all this philosophy to Willie. But in the early months of 1974, after several more escapes that ended with Laura sending him back, he launched what amounted to a direct attack on the very foundation of Wiltwyck. It began to seem as if there was a new, more aggressive episode every day, with Willie skipping out of class or running out of his cottage into the woods. One afternoon when he went to talk to his social worker, Sandra Oehling, she was smoking a cigarette. Willie picked up a pair of scissors from her desk and, with a magician's touch, snipped the cigarette in two, leaving just the butt still dangling in her lips. She shouted at Willie as he tore out of the room.

Another day, Oehling had to tell him she would be leaving Wiltwyck soon because she was pregnant and was going to have a baby. She was concerned Willie would be jealous of the baby, or take her departure as still another rejection. They were sitting in her office on the hill, and after hearing the news, Willie got up and started pacing around the room. Suddenly, he picked up a metal chair and threw it at her. Willie was still a tiny boy, whereas Oehling was a tall, robust woman who had grown up on welfare in a tough Puerto Rican neighborhood in the South Bronx. She wasn't afraid for herself, but when he flung the chair, she was scared it was going to hurt her baby. The chair just missed, landing at her feet.

Finally, on February 25, 1974, Dr. Katz decided to break his policy and put Willie on drugs. He started with a small dosage of Ritalin, a psychotropic drug commonly used to control hyperactivity. That made no difference in his behavior. Two days later, Willie was transferred to what Dr. Katz called the Quiet Room, a special room he had set up in the infirmary to be used as the school's own tiny psychiatric unit. That way, he figured, Wiltwyck could handle its own problems and wouldn't have to ship any boys out. The Quiet Room had bare gray concrete walls, which had been covered with padding, and a locked wooden door. It was right next door to Dr. Katz's office. Some of the staff joked that the very name Quiet Room was an oxymoron. It didn't take Willie long to wreck it. He pried loose the wooden boards covering the radiator, took the valves off the pipes in the room, and smashed down the door.

When he got out, he kicked a pediatrician who was on duty in the groin and punched a nurse in the breast. Another day, he got into an argument with Dr. Katz over the medication he was being given. Dr. Katz had changed it to Thorazine, a more powerful drug, and was increasing the dosage every few days in an effort to calm Willie down. Soon he prescribed four hundred milligrams a day, enough to knock out an adult. Willie thought he was being "zombiized," as he put it. Even Sandra Oehling worried that Willie was beginning to look like a miniature junkie, the drug was so strong. While he was arguing with Dr. Katz, Willie ran back into the Quiet Room, pulled loose a wooden board with nails stuck in it, and swung it at the psychiatrist. Then he picked up a telephone off a desk and wound the cord around the neck of a nurse.

"Anyone comes near me, I'll kill her," he screamed.

Willie's adventures in the Quiet Room were increasing his reputation, or juice, among the other boys. They walked by outside, trying to talk to him. "Hey, Willie, what's up, man?" they called to him. "You all right? What you do this time? Man, you real bad. Man, you crazy." This was high praise, and it made Willie feel good.

So big was his reputation by now that some of Willie's friends plotted to help him escape. One boy confessed he broke into an old red Volkswagen used by Richard Stroh to deliver mail around the school. Stroh was a tall, skinny, eighteen-year-old with a beard and long blond hair down to his belt who had found a job at Wiltwyck after working in Senator George McGovern's campaign for president in 1972. Willie's friend had removed the tool kit from Stroh's car but was caught before he could get the tools to Willie.

Still, on the evening of March 3, a week after he was detained in the Quiet Room, Willie sneaked out. He went to the maintenance building, broke open a window, and climbed inside. He knew that the chief engineer left the keys to Wiltwyck's vehicles on a wooden panel, all nicely marked. He found the keys to what the school called its little yellow school bus, actually a van, and climbed back out the window. Then he and another boy, Darryl, got in the van, with Willie in the driver's seat.

Willie had never driven a car before. But he had watched his uncle, Joe Spates, drive a gypsy cab, and he was sure he could do it though he was barely tall enough to see over the dashboard. It was already dark and raining hard, but Willie started the van, navigated through the stone gateposts at the entrance to the school compound, and headed for the Croton-Harmon stop on the New York Central Railroad, ten minutes away. The route was familiar; he had driven it before with Rose Niles and some of the other staff. The hardest part was coming down a long, steep, winding hill and crossing a bridge over a lake. Some of the counselors liked to scare the boys, telling them there were ghosts in the water of a Wiltwyck teacher and five boys who failed to make the turn onto the bridge. Willie believed the legend, and so he gunned the accelerator as he hit the bridge, crossing it at sixty miles an hour. The corrugated metal floor of the bridge made an eerie moan.

At the railroad station, he parked the van, and the two boys boarded the first train for New York. Since they had no money for tickets, they hid in the men's room. A conductor found them, but let them go. At Grand Central Terminal, Willie changed to the subway, getting in by jumping over the turnstile. He arrived, triumphant, just before midnight.

Ruth Gregory was the Wiltwyck executive officer on duty that night, and she got a call at home saying that some kids had taken the chief engineer's keys. Later, there were reports that a Wiltwyck van had been seen driving around without its lights on. She was afraid the boys who took it might get hurt or, even worse, might kill someone, so she called the police, and they put out an all-points bulletin.

When the school discovered that Willie was missing and that he had driven off in the van, Gregory wasn't surprised. He was so smart, she thought, so charming, and had so much vitality, that he could have become president of the United States. He was a veritable factory of energy. But it was scary that he was also consumed by incredible rage. Sometimes when he was mad, he would come into her office to talk, and then bam, without any warning, he would scream, "Get off of me, you white bitch." After that, he went around the room knocking over the chairs, ripping out all the drawers to her desk, and scattering everything around the room. She had seen other boys like him, but Willie was at the extreme edge. He was so smart, and so crazy, thought Gregory, that he seemed to have an absolute straight line into what a grown-up was going to do next, the way psychotic people sometimes did. He was a master manipulator.

Gregory was beginning to think that Wiltwyck was too ambitious in accepting certain kids like Willie. Given the idealism of the time, Wiltwyck tended to see only the best in these boys. The staff sort of excused these kids and their parents because of all the poverty and racism that had crippled them. God forbid, Gregory sometimes caught herself and her colleagues saying, that we damage the children. But they had been damaged already, and with some boys like Willie, it might be too late. Willie, she was starting to think, was already gone by the age of nine or ten. Perhaps there was nothing Wiltwyck could do for him—a terrifying thought.

The day after Willie stole the van, Dr. Katz convened a staff meeting to discuss what to do about him. A number of the child care counselors and some of the social workers pushed for getting Willie transferred. He was dangerous, a thorn in their sides, and he made some of them feel inadequate. Dr. Katz was reluctant to dump Willie. It would violate his policy of "total commitment," and he had become personally interested in Willie since Willie now occupied the room next to his office. Dr. Katz was stunned, in talking to Willie, to hear him boast about his father's being in jail for killing two men. It immediately made Dr. Katz think that Willie identified with his father, as if he were the son of a dentist or a doctor.

But, Dr. Katz had to admit, Willie had become unmanageable. The school never had enough money to hire all the child care workers needed to handle a boy like Willie, if Willie could be reached at all. After two more team meetings, he finally agreed with the rest of the staff to send Willie back to Bellevue for further observation in hopes the Family Court would transfer him elsewhere. "It appeared to me," Dr. Katz wrote in a psychiatric note to the court, "that we were rapidly getting into a totally untenable situation with regard to Willie. He was repeating the same pattern with us as he had with his mother." That is, he had become contemptuous of Wiltwyck's ability to control him, just as he was disdainful of Laura's authority over him. Wiltwyck was feeding his delusions of omnipotence. Dr. Katz then recounted how Willie had threatened to choke the nurse. "Perhaps the most frightening aspect of Willie's behavior," he wrote, "is that he seems to be in control of it at all times."

On March 19, 1974, Willie got into the Wiltwyck van for the journey back to Bellevue in Manhattan. He was laughing. He had nothing personal against Wiltwyck; it was a nice place. But, in his mind, he had won the battle. He had proved himself stronger than the school. He was not thinking about where he might end up later, that it would probably be worse than Wiltwyck, that his behavior was self-destructive. When a nurse came over to say goodbye, Willie boasted happily, "I'm no average cat."

There was a sequel to Willie's sojourn at Wiltwyck. Exactly two years later, a gala performance of the Royal Ballet was staged at the Metropolitan Opera House in New York's Lincoln Center as a benefit for Wiltwyck. The event was an annual ritual begun by Eleanor Roosevelt, and the sponsors that night were a galaxy of names straight out of *Who's Who*. There were politicians like New York governor Hugh Carey and Senator Edward Kennedy; celebrities like Harry Belafonte, Leonard Bernstein, and Johnny Carson; successful businessmen like Marvin Traub, the chairman of Bloomingdales; and prominent journalists like Bill Moyers. Nelson Rockefeller, then vice president of the United States, wrote an introductory tribute for the evening's program. "When Wiltwyck is able to succeed, the child benefits, of course," Rockefeller said. "But so does the community, which is enriched by the return of a whole and more self-reliant individual. Wiltwyck clearly serves us all—and merits the support of us all."

On the cover of the expensively printed program was a photograph of a Wiltwyck teacher holding the happy, smiling face of a young boy against her chest. The teacher was Rose Niles. The boy was Willie Bosket, who had been dumped by Wiltwyck two years earlier. Willie looked so angelic, he was still the best advertisement Wiltwyck had.

CHAPTER 10

WILLIE

The Boy No One Could Help

Do ye hear the children weeping,
Oh my brothers. . . . The young children
Oh my brothers, they are weeping bitterly,
They are weeping in the playtime of the others.

Elizabeth Barrett Browning

I T H A D B E E N three years, but Dr. Mahin Hassibi remembered him well. The last time she had seen Willie at Bellevue, he was only eight years old and the saddest little boy she had ever encountered as a psychiatrist. Now, the Wiltwyck School had sent him back, complaining that he was violent and uncontrollable, and he was on her ward again, PQ6, Bellevue's child psychiatry unit. To Dr. Hassibi, he still looked the same: small for his age, with that incredibly handsome smile. She asked Willie why he had been sent to Wiltwyck.

"I mugged this old lady," he replied, his voice matter-of-fact, as if he were talking about what he had eaten for breakfast. "I stole her pocketbook, and then I gave her a good push."

"Why did you push an old lady?" Dr. Hassibi asked. "Didn't you think about what might happen to you, that you might get caught?"

"She was old and going to die anyway," Willie said. "Besides, I'm going to end up in jail, just like my father."

There was nothing surprising about his statement, as such. Dr. Hassibi had been at Bellevue for seven years, and she had heard many kids talk that way. It was a way of sounding tough, a way of sending the message that he didn't care what she or anybody else thought. But coming from Willie, the boy she remembered so vividly as sad and suicidal, the words startled her. You don't get those kinds of answers from suicidal patients, Dr. Hassibi thought. A suicidal patient won't tell you that he assaulted an old woman who was going to die anyway. There is a kind of empathy in a suicidal patient, a sense of feeling sorry for himself and the rest of the world that doesn't allow a suicidal person to hurt anybody else. Now, listening to Willie, she got the feeling that something had happened to him, at home or on the streets or at Wiltwyck, and that he had changed forever.

That first day at Bellevue, Willie was pleasant enough. But the next morning, when he was taken to the hospital's school, he threatened to rip the classroom apart with a knife he had made by breaking a chunk of metal from the bottom of his bed. So the teachers sent him back to the child psychiatry unit, where Dr. Hassibi invited him into her office to chat. It was a spartan room, with just a desk, some wooden chairs, and a few posters on the wall. Dr. Hassibi sat down at her desk with her back to the door. Willie came in, closed the door, then locked it. She came to attention when she heard the lock snap shut. She had never had a patient do that. She turned around just as Willie picked up a chair behind her and held it over her head.

"Discharge me or I will break the chair over your head," he said, his face a blank mask.

"Willie, what do you want to do that for?" Dr. Hassibi asked, not yet really believing what he had said. "You are an intelligent boy. You know you are here by court order, so it doesn't make any difference whether I discharge you."

"No talk," Willie said. "Discharge me, or I will kill you." Threats usually worked for Willie. It was what he had learned since he was a small boy on the street; it was what made him feel stronger and stronger at Wiltwyck, just as Dr. Katz had feared. "Do it," Willie repeated.

Dr. Hassibi, who was almost as tiny as Willie, finally realized he meant what he said. "Okay, let's go," she said, getting up and opening the door.

At the end of the long L-shaped corridor, Dr. Hassibi took a left turn. She was walking a few steps ahead of Willie, and just as she reached the nurses station, she jumped in the door and banged it closed behind her. "Call the guards," she told the nurses. When the security personnel arrived, Willie was still standing with the raised chair in the corridor.

"I'm not crazy," Willie said as he surrendered. "I just wanted to get out of here and go home."

In all Dr. Hassibi's years of experience of working with severely troubled children, none had ever threatened her before, and certainly none had scared her the way Willie did. After Willie had been led down to the safer adolescent ward on the floor below and locked in a strip cell, she began to think about what she had seen. Three years earlier, Willie had been a sad, frightened, suicidal eight-year-old, still soft and open. Now he had been transmogrified into an angry, hostile, homicidal eleven-year-old whom no one could reach. That was how fear worked in some very scared children, she thought. They were so frightened you might kill them that they turned into dangerous people themselves, always ready to attack, making everyone into an enemy. And Willie had all that baggage about his father being in prison and his mother telling him he would turn out like his father. So he had processed all this and come up with his identity at a very young age.

The next day, Willie appeared to have calmed down and was allowed out of his locked cell. A few minutes later, he asked a nurse if she had noticed something was missing from her pocketbook. She checked and found her lighter had been taken. Just then, another nurse shouted that a bed with a heavily sedated girl asleep on it was on fire.

That was the final straw for Bellevue. Willie was simply too dangerous. So the staff decided to transfer him out as quickly as possible, well short of the time normally required to make a full psychiatric evaluation. Dr. Hassibi wrote out her conclusions, with sadness: "Diagnosis—Antisocial Behavior."

Strictly speaking, according to the American Psychiatric Association's *Diagnostic and Statistical Manual of Mental Disorders*, this was not a formal diagnosis. The proper term would have been antisocial personality disorder, a psychopath, the same diagnosis given Butch. But Willie was only eleven years old, and children that young were not supposed to have fully developed personalities. They were still supposed to be open to change. Dr. Hassibi, however, wanted to make a point for the Family Court, so she resorted to a euphemism, suggesting Willie was an antisocial personality without actually saying so.

Dr. Hassibi intended to make another issue very clear to the court. "Willie is an extremely angry child ready to explode at the most trivial provocation," she wrote. "But at no point did he show any indication of being unaware of what he was doing. There was no evidence of psychotic breakdown during the episode, except for his poor judgment and some indication of paranoid fears."

In her view, Willie was not crazy. He was too well-organized, too much in control. Rather than being psychotic, Dr. Hassibi found, "Willie has learned to use violence as a very effective way of getting what he wants. You may question whether what he wants is really good for anybody. But he gets what he wants."

Since he was not psychotic, Dr. Hassibi advised, Willie should not be sent to a state mental hospital. Instead, she urged a "placement in a well-structured closed setting such as a State training school," one of the locked reformatories run by the Division for Youth, New York State's juvenile justice agency.

Dr. Hassibi saved her bleakest thoughts for herself. Willie was too young, by the standards of psychiatry, for her to pronounce final judgment. But she had the uneasy sense that there was nothing she or any other therapist could do for Willie. What Willie needed was a humanizing experience; psychiatry did not provide that. Psychiatry could only go where there was human fragility and try to work from inside out. Willie lacked that inner core of human sensibility. It wasn't just she alone who was defeated, she thought. It was her entire profession that had nothing to offer him. She feared that Willie was destined to wander from institution to institution, each time acting up so that the people in charge would dump him, sending him on to someplace else. He had become the boy no one could help.

AFTER WILLIE'S BEHAVIOR at Wiltwyck and Bellevue, Judge Lewis Pagnucco, a stern, old-fashioned law-and-order man, ordered that he be placed with the Division for Youth under Title III. That meant Willie was to be involuntarily committed to one of New York State's training schools for a term of eighteen months. Of course, Willie didn't take the judge's ruling too seriously, because neither the Family Court nor the Division for Youth could find an institution willing to take him for the next two months. Willie's reputation was beginning to precede him. In the meantime, the court let him return home with his mother on parole.

Finally, on May 29, 1974, the Division for Youth sent Willie to the Highland School for Children, near New Paltz, on the edge of the Catskill Mountains. It was an odd choice. The agency's own officials had recommended, after examining Willie, that he be sent to a maximum security facility. Highland was designed for the youngest and least threatening children under the agency's care, and it had little security.

Willie let the staff at Highland know immediately that he did not like being there. The first day in school, he refused to follow the teacher's instructions and threw a chair at another boy. A week later, after he again threw a chair at a fellow student in class, he was placed in a detention room. Willie then attacked a supervisor with a broom and escaped from the building. When several counselors tried to bring him back, he assaulted them, and in the process, his elbow was broken. In the infirmary, when a nurse put a cast on his arm, he swung at her and ripped off the cast in a rage.

Marion Beeler, who was an ombudsman in the Division for Youth assigned to oversee Highland, met Willie during one of her visits to the school. She was impressed that he was extremely bright, cute and charming, totally adorable. He had fabulous potential, she thought. If his background had been different, he could have become president of the United States, she told colleagues. But he was also the angriest kid she had ever met. When she came into an office to listen to his complaints about his treatment at Highland, he started throwing rocks at her, and she had to hide behind a wall.

Willie's outbursts at Highland persisted on virtually a daily basis. On June 29, the school's record relates, he "went wild. Threatened everyone with two large butcher knives and a large fork. Wounded two boys and broke two windows in cottages. Upset furniture until restrained by the Principal Children's Supervisor who was called to the cottage." Willie was just warming up for the main event. A few weeks later, he stole the gas cap from Highland's station wagon, threw it away, and tried to throw lit matches into the gas tank while the vehicle was filled with other boys. The next day, he chased several other boys with a flaming broom—after burning one boy, he jammed the blazing broom into the gas tank of a school van.

As a result, Willie was sent to a psychiatrist. The doctor reviewed reports on Willie's behavior at Wiltwyck and Bellevue and expressed incredulity that Dr. Katz and Dr. Hassibi believed his attacks in those institutions were merely manipulative. How could these other psychiatrists say Willie was only "antisocial" when he raised a chair over Dr. Hassibi's head and threatened to kill her? the Highland doctor asked. Not only that, but during all these attacks, Willie himself "was on 400 milligrams of Thorazine, the most powerful anti-psychotic agent known," the Highland doctor noted. It was a dosage big enough to knock out an adult several times his size.

"What stands out clearly" in the reports by Dr. Katz and Dr. Hassibi, he wrote, "is that no one seems to want to call crazy behavior crazy. Apparently this situation has only served to perpetuate the child's psychotic omnipotence and grandiosity and has only served to make him more anxious and behaviorally disorganized.

"It is clear," the Highland psychiatrist continued, referring to Willie's friendships at Wiltwyck with Arruth Artis and Rose Niles, "that the child readily develops symbiotic dependency ties to any non-threatening person. This does not, in any way, indicate object relations development beyond the age of one, since any normal one-year-old can relate to his mother in this way.

"His intellectual potential is at least in the upper half of the average range and possibly higher," the doctor observed. "But something has interfered with the constructive use of his intellectual capacity." That something, the psychiatrist wrote, was "very serious deficits in reality testing about his parents and other emotionally hinged factors of his existence." In fact, Willie's grasp of reality was so poor that the doctor believed he was psychotic.

The doctor then ventured a prophecy:

> With a history of a father in prison for a double murder, his mother predicting that he will turn out the same way, his poor reality testing, poor impulse control, infantile omnipotence and grandiosity, history of fire setting, enuresis and beating of other children, together with a history of suicide attempts and current daily threats on the lives of others, it is predicted that without intensive, long term residential psychiatric treatment, this child will eventually take the life of another person.

The internecine arguments among psychiatrists over the definition of what constitutes being crazy didn't much matter, the doctor reasoned. If Willie killed someone, it would make no difference whether his act was labeled psychotic, psychopathic, "or any other such designation." The fact remains, the psychiatrist concluded, "this child is profoundly emotionally disturbed and homicidal." His diagnosis: "Borderline psychotic—personality organization with infantile, symbiotic, paranoid and homicidal features and frequent lapses into psychotic behavior."

The doctor saw only one possible solution—to get Willie out of Highland and into a mental hospital. "Continued placement with the Division for Youth is contra-indicated and immediate psychiatric hospitalization is indicated," he wrote. "It would seem that any conclusions, other than these, drawn from the data, would violate common sense."

But no state mental hospital would take Willie. He was too violent. So the Division for Youth was stuck with him. It was only on September 20, 1974, two months after the psychiatric exam, and after Willie crashed Highland's bus during an escape attempt, that the agency transferred him to one of its two maximum security institutions, Brookwood Center. The day he was moved, Willie was asked to sign the transfer order. "I ain't signing shit," he said.

THEIR WEDDING MARKED the high tide of liberalism. Three months after the assassination of the Reverend Martin Luther King Jr. in April 1968 and three weeks after the shooting of Senator Robert F. Kennedy that June, a young lawyer named Marian Wright married a

Harvard Law School graduate, Peter Edelman. She had been a close friend of the Reverend King's; he had been Bobby Kennedy's legislative assistant. They had met in the spring of 1967 in Mississippi, where she had set up an office of the NAACP Legal Defense and Education Fund and he was the man who brought Senator Kennedy to see hunger among poor black families. The trip, with its sights of distended, starved bellies among black children, had transformed Kennedy, giving him new passion and a sense of mission as he emerged as the leading Democratic presidential candidate before being killed. Now, in Washington, the wedding was the social event of the season. The Reverend William Sloane Coffin, the Yale University chaplain who was a spiritual leader of both the Civil Rights and the anti–Vietnam War movements, performed the ceremony. Burke Marshall, the former assistant attorney general in charge of the civil rights division who had served as President John F. Kennedy's point man in Alabama and Mississippi, was there too, along with Vernon E. Jordan, the director of the Voter Education Project of the Southern Regional Council.

Wright, described by a *New York Times* account as "the first Negro woman to be admitted to the Mississippi bar," wore a knee-length dotted-Swiss dress and a tiara of white rosebuds. Edelman was attired in a white silk Nehru jacket over a white turtleneck shirt and black slacks. A trumpeter played Purcell's *Trumpet Voluntary* for the processional. Former Supreme Court Justice Arthur J. Goldberg, for whom Edelman had clerked, delivered a homily, standing by an arc of flowers in the garden. He described the era by quoting the opening passage of Dickens's *A Tale of Two Cities* about the French Revolution. Goldberg solemnly intoned, "It was the best of times, it was the worst of times."

That spring, when the Reverend King was assassinated, Wright had been working with him on the Poor People's Campaign, a crusade proposed to her by Senator Kennedy. The idea was to have the poor march on Washington and stay until an embarrassed Congress enacted sweeping anti-poverty legislation. It was the last of the Reverend King's attempts to find the magic formula that would convince the country as a whole to embrace poor blacks in the cities the way it had Rosa Parks when she refused to go to the back of the bus in Montgomery. With the Reverend King dead, the Poor People's Campaign flopped. But Marian Wright, now Marian Wright Edelman, came up with another idea in 1973 to try to rekindle the public's flagging interest in poor people. She would do it through children. Her vehicle was a new organization she founded, the Children's Defense Fund.

Peter Edelman stayed in politics for a while, helping run Arthur Goldberg's unsuccessful campaign for governor of New York in 1970.

But with Richard Nixon in the White House, the sixties seemed to be fading, and he took a job as vice president of the University of Massachusetts. Then, in 1975, he received an unexpected call from an old Kennedy friend who was working for Governor Hugh Carey of New York. Would he, by any chance, be interested in becoming director of New York's Division for Youth? Edelman had no experience in juvenile justice, but he was very interested in children's issues, through his wife, and while in Massachusetts he had been excited by the work of Jerome G. Miller. Miller, the commissioner of the Massachusetts Department of Youth Services, had startled the state by closing all of its reform schools and deinstitutionalizing their youthful residents. He was convinced that the reformatories were brutal and abusive, offered no real treatment, and existed mostly as a source of patronage jobs for state politicians. Miller's work, which came to be known as the Massachusetts experiment, was another late burst of 1960s idealism and carried great appeal for Peter Edelman. He decided to accept the job offer in Albany.

The Division for Youth had been created by Governor Nelson Rockefeller in 1960 as a small, progressive alternative to New York State's big, traditional training schools, often derisively called kiddie joints, which were administered by the Department of Social Services. The reformatories, with up to six hundred beds, still practiced corporal punishment and relied heavily on solitary confinement for discipline. Milton Luger, Rockefeller's pick to head the Division for Youth, was openly contemptuous of the training schools. "With the exception of a relatively few youths, it is probably better for all concerned if young delinquents were not detected, apprehended or institutionalized," he charged at a congressional hearing. "Too many get worse in our care." Like the reformers of a century earlier, Luger worried that youthful inmates were being hardened by their experiences in the reformatories, so he had set about creating an experimental mix of rural forestry camps and seven-bed halfway houses in the cities where the kids could be close to their families. All the residents in these new camps and homes were carefully selected volunteers. Not surprisingly, they had far lower rates of recidivism than the old reformatories.

In 1970, in response to revelations of abuse in some of the training schools, Rockefeller decided to go a step further. He ordered that the fourteen training schools, with a combined capacity of five thousand youngsters, be taken over by the Division for Youth. The experimental agency held only five hundred boys and girls at the time. It was like the tail swallowing the dog, some Division for Youth officials joked. Luger immediately began closing some of the training schools and shifting their residents to new, less intimidating facilities in their own communities.

When Peter Edelman assumed command of the agency, he speeded up this conversion. It was like shooting fish in a barrel, he thought, because the system was so bad you did not have to be a rocket scientist to figure out what to do. The training schools were absolutely horrible. They did not work in any respect. They were too large to offer kids any sophisticated treatment tailored to their own particular needs. They were filled with kids who really did not have to be institutionalized, like truants. And they weren't even very secure, so there were many runaways. Edelman also discovered that the training schools had a whole culture of cruelty. The staff took away kids' clothes so they would not escape, or made them clean the floor with a toothbrush as punishment. As a symbol of Edelman's new approach, he installed as his deputy for running the agency's facilities an ex-convict named Larry Dye. Dye had been arrested forty-five times, starting at age twelve, but had taken advantage of a prison education program and eventually earned his Ph.D. at the University of Massachusetts. Dye was a hang-out, free-spirit product of the sixties who put some of his disciples into key posts. By 1977, there were only four training schools left in New York State, with 375 inmates.

Willie arrived at Brookwood in the midst of this process. Brookwood was a modern, two-story, yellow-brick structure set in rolling cornfields dotted with cattle barns and crisscrossed by meandering streams that ran into the nearby Hudson River. It was Rip Van Winkle country. The school itself looked more like a motel or a suburban office building than a prison. It was set well back from a narrow county hardtop road, and the only indication of its purpose was a deliberately vague white sign that read Brookwood Center.

Beneath this placid surface, however, Brookwood was in turmoil. Since it had opened in 1964, a succession of directors had run it along strict training school lines. The school's original residents had been girls, and the staff enforced discipline by the use of isolation. If a girl said "Fuck you" to a counselor, the response was a swift "That's four days." The girl was locked in her room, and her food was brought in on a tray. If the girl then got angry and threw the tray, it was four more days. There was no toilet in the room; the girls were given a pan in which to urinate. Sometimes, the sparring escalated back and forth until the girl ended up spending the whole summer in solitary. There was a mandatory two-day stay in Brookwood's infirmary any time a resident came back from a home visit, so the staff could check for contraband.

The fall that Willie arrived, Brookwood got a new director, Tom Pottenburgh. He was a huge bear of a man, six feet nine inches tall and well over two hundred fifty pounds, the son of a farmer from the town of Rhinebeck down the road. Pottenburgh had a large head, a prominent square jaw, and a big, booming voice with which he could swear as well as any of the inmates. He was an intimidating physical presence, which was part of the reason he had been installed at Brookwood. But he also had pink skin and twinkling blue eyes that reflected something of the gentle nature that lurked under his formidable exterior. His mission was to clean up Brookwood. He was to get rid of the old training school mentality and practices. Room confinement, the Division for Youth had decreed, could now be used only when a youngster was an immediate danger to himself or to others, and could not exceed one hour. By this time, Brookwood had boys as well as girls, and Pottenburgh decided to act after two residents were put in room confinement for talking out of turn at a group meeting. He wrote a memo to the staff warning that use of this kind of punishment was against the law and would result in an official reprimand.

The results were swift. The staff simply stopped working. They claimed they couldn't maintain discipline without solitary confinement. A few nights later, there was a riot during which twenty kids ran away. By the time Pottenburgh got over to the school from his house across the road, kids were coming out of their windows and climbing a wall at the front of the building. One of them was a tiny boy who Pottenburgh thought looked a lot like the young Michael Jackson when he was singing with the Jackson Five. It was Willie Bosket. Willie was halfway through a hole he had made in the security grate outside his window. Pottenburgh grabbed his legs.

"Hey, Pottenburgh, lemme go, lemme go," Willie shouted up at the enormous man standing over him. "My girlfriend, she's out here, I gotta go find her."

What the fuck's another one, the director said to himself, as he looked around and realized he was the only member of the staff trying to stop the mass escape. So he let Willie go, a diminutive figure running down the road clad only in slippers, a bathrobe, and his underwear, though it was already late in the fall and the ground was frozen.

Eventually, Pottenburgh got into the school truck and started rounding up some of the kids. He found Willie down the road. "Come on with me, Willie," the director said. Willie jumped aboard, and they drove around in the dark looking for his girlfriend.

That was the way it was much of the time Willie was at Brookwood in late 1974 and early 1975; total pandemonium. Pottenburgh believed deeply in the reforms, to make Brookwood less corrections oriented and to provide more real treatment for the kids. But the new leaders at Division for Youth headquarters were moving too precipitously, he began to think. It was like banging from one wall to another, with nothing in between. It also made it harder to deal with Willie.

Willie was still doing the things that made him troublesome at Wilt-wyck and Highland. When a girl called him stupid in class, he slapped her. He hit a nurse with a stapler and squirted the school psychologist with a fire extinguisher. Without the use of solitary confinement to punish him, many of the staff had no idea how to deal with Willie. They complained that he was running wild. "The verbal and physical abuse was unbelievable for a child his age," wrote Ernestine Coleman, an administrator in the wing to which he was assigned. All in all, she said in her first report, "his behavior has been rotten."

It was his Jekyll and Hyde quality, his extreme changeability, that struck many of the staff. Helen Gentile, a social worker in charge of directing all of Brookwood's school, work, and recreational activities, thought Willie was always polite, courteous, and charming when he came into her office, asking if there was anything he could do for her. He even made engraved rings for her and her husband out of two old silver spoons. She was a neat, orderly person herself, and his manners made a good impression on her. Then one day, just after he said, "Good morning, Mrs. Gentile, how are you?" Willie saw another boy coming down the corridor. He picked up a big paper cutter from a desk, one of those heavy wooden blocks with a metal cleaver attached to the side, and tried to cut the other boy as if he were wielding a machete. It took six adult men to subdue him. After he calmed down, Willie said, "Where's Mrs. Gentile? I was talking to her."

"Willie," she responded, "what was that all about?"

"Oh, don't worry about it," Willie said, as if nothing had happened.

She got the sense that Willie was not what you would call an angry person. It was more as if he was filled with a terrible inner rage that he could control only up to a point before he just exploded. After the outburst, he could function again. Willie himself, in a ten-page autobiography he wrote at the time, called his temper tantrums "throwing hairys."

The Legal Aid Society took a special interest in Willie and sent several lawyers to Brookwood to take statements from him. Officially, Willie was still a PINS, a person in need of supervision, not a juvenile delinquent. He had not been convicted of anything, but here he was in a maximum security institution with older boys who had committed armed robbery, rape, and murder. The Legal Aid Society was mounting a major lawsuit against the Division for Youth for mixing PINS with delinquents, and Willie was to be a prime exhibit. "Plaintiff Bosket does not like Brook-wood," a Legal Aid lawyer named Michael Dale wrote in a brief. "He believes he is being introduced to older, more institutionally experienced youths. . . . He thus views his future as institutional and believes that he will enter the adult prison system."

Pottenburgh readily acknowledged that mixing PINS cases with delinquents should be stopped. Hell, that isn't good for the kids, he said. But he thought the Legal Aid lawyers themselves were naive do-gooders. One woman lawyer told him, after talking to Willie, that she wanted Willie to be able to call her in New York whenever he felt there was a serious issue. Residents were strictly limited in the number of phone calls they could make, but Pottenburgh agreed to make an exception for Willie.

Over the next three weeks, Willie was always demanding to call his lawyer. The trouble was, she was often busy with other cases. So he cursed her secretary, calling her a "motherfucking bitch," and told her to tell the lawyer, "You're fucking fired 'cause you're not doing anything to get me out of here." The next day, the attorney herself phoned Pottenburgh. She would no longer accept collect calls from Willie, she announced. Pottenburgh had to laugh. That was Willie's impulsiveness getting in his way again. It made him awfully hard to help, even for do-gooders.

Eventually, in January 1975, after Willie had been at Brookwood four months, he was made part of an experiment with the four other most difficult boys. They were kept in the infirmary and put on what was called a behavior modification program. Each day, they were given a number of points according to their actions, and with the points could choose from rewards like candy, sodas, and games of pool. They were also placed in the care of an ex-convict from Florida named Chuck Nattell. The other boys seemed to improve over the next few weeks; Willie didn't. But he was fascinated by his new supervisor. First off, Nattell surprised Willie by locking himself into a room with him whenever Willie acted out. It sent Willie a message that, unlike other adults, he wasn't afraid of Willie, even when Willie threatened to kill him. That had a calming influence. Willie, he decided, actually craved structure; he wanted someone to lay down the parameters.

The main thing, Nattell believed, was that Nattell reminded Willie of his father. Willie started asking Nattell about prison life every time he had a chance, what solitary confinement was like, what would happen in prison if you threw a chair at a guard. Nattell got the idea that Willie's father was a folk hero to him. Every little boy is like that. Except Willie's father was a convicted murderer. Nattell sensed that Willie had a compulsion to become a murderer, too—a heavy burden for a twelve-year-old.

By the middle of February, there were no signs of progress with Willie. "Most staff feel that Willie has not changed from the boy he was when he came," reported Bertha Fields, the head child care worker. "Willie is a little boy wanting to be a man." A review panel concluded that Willie was not ready for release, that he should stay at Brookwood at least until the beginning of April, and if his behavior improved by then, he would be allowed to make an Easter home visit.

That was also the message Pottenburgh was getting from the Division for Youth's central office in Albany. In a memo in January, Pottenburgh was told, "Willie, in our judgment, is not near ready for release to the community. He is very destructive and a threat to himself and the community."

Given the seriousness of Willie's behavior, the memo added, he had been classified as a "sensitive" case. This meant that Pottenburgh, as Brookwood's director, could not simply release Willie on his own, as he could with most kids. Instead, he was expected to send Willie home only after developing an agreed-on plan with Willie's aftercare, or social worker, in New York. The plan had to include provisions for school and further counseling. This was a new regulation, designed to guard against what were termed "precipitous" discharges. Pottenburgh knew all about them. Before he took over Brookwood, when some of the previous directors had truly difficult kids, they would give them what they jokingly called a "dishonorable discharge." That meant they took the kids to the front door and gave them money to go back home. One girl had been driven down to New York, given five dollars, and told to get lost. She was warned that if she ever reported what happened, she would spend the rest of her life in a mental asylum. But she had gotten into drugs, become a prostitute, and then was arrested, and now there was a suit against the Division for Youth.

Despite all these caveats, the man assigned to be Willie's aftercare worker in Manhattan, Edwin Cruise, was growing suspicious that Brookwood intended to dump him. Cruise had been tipped off on January 7 by a phone call from a counselor at Brookwood alerting him that the school "wants to release Willie to the community immediately because of recent acting out behavior."

Then on March 4, Cruise received a memo from Phil Williams, the head of Willie's wing at Brookwood and a close friend of Pottenburgh's. The school planned to let Willie have a week's home leave in late March, and Williams suggested that Cruise make arrangements so that Willie could stay indefinitely. "It is my opinion that Willie is not a psychotic youngster and that his behavior at Brookwood is manipulative to the situation," Williams said. "His acting out may well be due to the institutionalized environment itself."

Cruise was furious. As an aftercare worker, he was an employee of the Division for Youth, too. And as a good bureaucrat, he didn't like to make waves. By nature, he was cautious, timid, slow, and thoroughgoing. He was constantly overworked, with a caseload of eighty kids to keep track of. That meant he could visit each of them or their families barely once a month. He also knew that the agency's senior officials in Albany didn't think much of aftercare workers; anyone who was ambitious in the Division for Youth went to work in the institutions that held the kids—that's where the prestige was. Cruise knew his limits.

But just shipping Willie back to New York was too much. Cruise fired off a tart reply. "Willie may or may not be psychotic," he wrote. "I am not qualified to diagnose his condition. However, I do know that his behavior at Brookwood is not manipulative to the situation. Please check the record. Willie has had problems with impulse control and reality testing for many years.

"The point is this," Cruise said. "Willie is not ready to come home to his community. He still has a big problem with controlling his impulsivity. He reads into situations threats that are not there. He can be totally destructive. *He is not ready to come home.*"

Brookwood ignored Cruise's appeal. Willie was sent home for a visit on March 25, 1975. On April 2, Williams was scheduled to drive down to New York to bring Willie back to Brookwood. Instead, Williams called Cruise and told him the visit had been changed to an "extended leave." Cruise phoned the Division for Youth's headquarters in Albany to protest. He was informed instead that the agency was now considering making Willie's extended leave an outright release. Willie's behavior, Cruise was told, had magically improved. Besides, Brookwood was being converted back to an all-girls school, in another of the reforms convulsing the agency. Willie was the last boy remaining and could no longer be kept. Cruise summed up his reaction in a handwritten memo: "What's going on with Willie stinks!"

Ed Cruise figured it was just a matter of time until Willie got in trouble, now that he was back home, and he didn't have long to wait. Two weeks after Willie's extended leave began, he got angry at a dry cleaner for allegedly damaging a pair of his pants. Willie cursed the employees in the shop, then smashed a plate-glass window. The strange thing was, his mother noticed, there was nothing wrong with his pants. Afterward, Laura called Cruise and said she wanted Willie back at Brookwood. "I thought he was trying to improve his behavior," she told the aftercare worker, "but I see better now."

There were fresh incidents every couple of days. One evening, Willie cut a man in the back with a broken bottle. Laura had to rush out into the street to intervene when a friend of the injured man pulled a .38-

caliber revolver and started shooting. Several times, Willie stole bicycles and television sets from neighbors, selling them to buy toy guns and real police handcuffs. On June 7, Willie kicked a nine-year-old boy named Michael Mosley and hit him with a knife. This time, the police arrested Willie and charged him with assault. He had to go to Manhattan Family Court, but the court was jammed and a judge gave Willie the customary leniency for a first offense—all charges were dismissed. No one told the judge that Willie was supposed to be in the custody of the Division for Youth.

Cruise had gotten to know the Bosket family well by now, and he thought Willie's relationship with his mother was a source of much of the trouble. Laura struck him as a gruff, surly, cold person. Willie's younger sister, Shirley, now ten years old, was enrolled in a special class for intellectually gifted children at her local public school. She had an effervescent, outgoing personality that charmed Cruise. On one of his visits to the Boskets' apartment, Shirley greeted him with a big smile, holding a flute in her hand. She played a few notes for him, then played on for several minutes without making a mistake.

"Mother! Look," Shirley exclaimed. "I played it all the way through and didn't need any music."

Laura growled. "What's that? It don't sound like nothing!"

Shirley was unfazed by the rebuff. With the flute and sheet music in her hand, she bounced over to where her mother was sitting in the living room and tried to place the open music in Laura's lap.

"See," Shirley said proudly. "Here it is."

Laura snarled again. "Go away! I don't want to see any of that stuff."

This second rejection was too much for Shirley. She fled to the street.

The incident was like a lightbulb going off in Cruise's head. If Laura was that cold with Shirley, it suggested how she treated Willie. Cruise thought she alternated between rejecting him and intense feelings of guilt and frustration over his bad behavior. Laura was clearly still mad at Butch for the murders in Milwaukee and for deserting her when she was pregnant with Willie. When Cruise raised the point with Laura, she replied, with indignation rising in her voice, "I never would have made it without my mother." It was as close as he had seen Laura come to expressing an emotion. That anger spilled over into her feelings for Willie, Cruise thought.

Willie needed his mother's affection, but he also told Cruise that he hated her for having him committed to all those institutions. It didn't help that in July 1974, just when Willie was sent to Highland, Laura told the family she had married a construction worker named Anthony Hicks, who was now living with her. Willie was openly contemptuous of Hicks.

"He ain't got no job," Willie told Cruise. "He just hangs around the house. I hate his guts." A year later, the relationship ended, and Laura told Cruise not to call her Mrs. Hicks anymore.

Laura's mother, Nancy, was the rock of the family, Cruise reported. Nancy had brought up Willie's older sister, Cheryl, who was now sixteen and had a year-old son of her own. It didn't help, though, when one of Nancy's sons, Joe Spates, who was an uncle to Willie, was stabbed to death in Philadelphia by his girlfriend. There was blood all over the bedroom when the family arrived the next day. The killing made a big impression on Willie, who attended the funeral.

By early July, Willie was getting in so much trouble that Laura demanded that Cruise send him back to Brookwood. The clincher came when Willie tried to set fire to the apartment one night while everyone else was asleep. Cruise suggested that what Willie really needed was psychiatric care. "No," Laura responded. "He's not crazy. He's just plain bad, like the rest of the kids out there."

AT 10 IN THE MORNING on July 14, 1975, Jay Oppenheim, the assistant superintendent of the Highland School, got a surprise phone call. Ed Cruise was on the line. He wanted to let Highland know that two Division for Youth guards were on their way to the school with Willie. Oppenheim was livid. He remonstrated that Willie's experience at Highland the year before had been "a total failure." The school simply could not take Willie back. But it was too late. Willie arrived at noontime, with no official paperwork. That was the way to get things done with a troublesome kid. You just dropped him somewhere.

Now it was Highland's turn to get rid of Willie as fast as it could. After urgent appeals from the school's leaders, Division for Youth headquarters agreed to send Willie to the Children's Psychiatric Center at Rockland State Hospital. His father had been there twice, and Butch's records were still in the hospital's archives, but no one was aware of this. Rockland, however, did make a conscientious effort to examine Willie. Over the next month, he was seen by a series of psychiatrists, psychologists, teachers, social workers, and a neurologist. They subjected him to every test known, and kept at it, even though he often got up in the middle of a session, threatened the examiner, and ran out of the building. Early on, one of Rockland's social workers, Carol Hayden, put together the most comprehensive and thoughtful profile of Willie and his family ever done. She noted that since Willie had first been at Wiltwyck, "He has been bounced around in various facilities, probably reinforcing his feelings of rejection and worthlessness."

The Bender Gestalt test revealed that Willie had "poor planning and low frustration tolerance." His Rorschach test showed that his "basic attack skills in a new situation is to go in quickly with little forethought or planning. Willie is looking for support both from female and male caretakers. Coincident with his need for nurturance is a negative attitude toward males or authority figures." Another tester, who asked Willie to do some drawings and make a clay figure, found he had "a very disturbed emotional state with underlying depression, anger and feelings of inadequacy."

No one found any signs of psychosis. Instead, Rockland's staff reverted to the finding that had often been made about Butch and about Willie at Bellevue. Willie was suffering from "Unsocialized aggressive reaction of childhood." This was the same as saying childhood antisocial behavior, a junior psychopath in the making. After reaching the diagnosis, the staff met for a long time to try to decide what could be done for Willie. First off, "it was agreed by all that this hospital does not represent an ideal place for him," since he was not psychotic, only violent. Willie's real problem, the group concluded, "has to do with his underlying sense of inferiority and insecurity and the rage which he personally feels towards his mother and which his mother expresses to the world partly through his behavior."

Because the real trouble was Laura and her rage at having been mistreated, Rockland recommended a bold new three-step treatment plan:

1. Intensive family therapy in the city for Willie's mother and other members of the family, preferably with a black female therapist.
2. Some contact with the real father, by mail if no other way.
3. Full-time exposure, at least eight hours a day, to a young black male therapist with whom Willie could identify and whom he could take as a role model.

Unfortunately, the staff added, without elaboration, it would be impossible to achieve these recommendations—they knew the state lacked funds for so much therapy and neither Laura nor Willie was likely to agree to it. Therefore, Rockland said Willie should be returned as swiftly as possible to the Division for Youth.

The next stop was the Tryon School for Boys, on six hundred rolling acres in the foothills of the Adirondacks. Willie arrived there on September 10, 1975. He continued his pattern of assaults on the staff and other boys, but Tryon was actually determined to try to keep him. Willie's eighteen-month placement with the Division for Youth was due to expire in November, and to make sure the school would be able to hold him, Tryon promptly filed for an extension of an additional year with the Manhattan Family Court. In its court papers, the school reviewed Willie's history and concluded, "When he is able to leave Tryon and return to the community, he will require extensive supervision and continuing treatment." In short, Tryon believed that Willie was nowhere near ready to be released.

On November 20, 1975, a Division for Youth official assigned to the Family Court arrived to present Tryon's application for an extension. But the judge dismissed the request without hearing arguments; a court clerk had forgotten to put the application on the judge's calendar. It was a technical error and the fault of the court, the judge conceded, but he had no choice.

That led to another ruling. Since Willie's placement had now expired and had not been extended, the judge ordered that Willie be released. It would be against the law to keep him a day longer than his commitment. Willie was sent home on a Trailways bus that afternoon.

Willie's handling by the Family Court, the Division for Youth, and the other institutions to which he had been sent was turning into a comedy of errors. Even the one school that wanted to keep him was ordered to let him go. As a result, Willie was feeling increasingly rejected, and simultaneously more and more powerful. No one could deal with him. In February 1976, Ed Cruise closed the Division for Youth file on Willie, since, as he wrote, "the Court's denial of the extension request is taken to mean that the Court feels we have no further role to play."

Willie was now free for the first time in three and a half years. He wasn't in an institution, and he wasn't going to school. He had beaten the system. Willie had only just turned thirteen, and things looked pretty good. He figured he had some catching up to do with the other boys in the neighborhood to launch the career he had chosen for himself—being a criminal. Laura had moved to an apartment on West 145th Street, and Willie began hanging out with a group in the neighborhood that included four of his cousins, Herman, Jeffrey, Leroy, and Penny Spates. They were each a few years older than he, all over sixteen, which made them adults under New York law. But Willie was the smartest, and so he became the leader. He would walk to the subway station each day with whichever of his cousins wasn't in jail at the time. They started out stealing fire extinguishers from subway cars, selling them for a dollar or two to customers at a Merit gas station near the IRT subway station on 145th Street. When they got tired of stealing fire extinguishers, the band moved on to pickpocketing on the subway, and then to robbing passengers who looked too weak to resist.

Willie was arrested for the first time in 1976 on March 21, just a month after the Division for Youth closed its file on him. He was charged with going through the pockets of a sleeping passenger at the 207th Street station of the A train, at the northern tip of Manhattan. His cousin Leroy Spates, who was seventeen, was arrested with him. At intake in Family Court, Willie was paroled to his mother, pending a further hearing.

Willie now began to get arrested about once a month. On April 14, he and Leroy were picked up by the police for snatching two dollars from the hands of a passenger named Edward McGarrity as he stood next to the turnstile of the 207th Street station. Laura appeared at the intake hearing and told the judge, "Willie doesn't go to school and commits crimes with his cousins." But he was paroled to his mother again anyway. On June 8, Willie and Penny Spates were arrested for trying to steal the pocketbook of Rosalyn Ramirez as she walked down the stairs to the Number 3 train at the 145th Street station. When the victim screamed, Willie threw bottles at her. On July 29, Willie and Penny Spates threatened to kill a woman who worked in the token booth at the 145th Street station; she was a witness to the boys' attack on Rosalyn Ramirez. And on September 18, Willie was arrested for stealing a Timex watch and seven dollars from Janvier Peralte, a passenger waiting on the platform of the 145th Street station. During the intake hearing, Willie ran out of court and went home.

Until now, despite these five arrests, the legal system had not really bothered Willie. He had spent a few nights in Spofford, the juvenile detention center in the Bronx, while awaiting intake hearings, but once he got to Family Court, the judges always paroled him to his mother. Willie was actually committing dozens, he would later say hundreds, of other petty crimes for which he never got caught.

Laura was in despair. She had a good idea of what Willie was up to and tried to stop it, but felt powerless. Early in the spring, Laura had called the police after Willie robbed another boy in their tenement building and hit him on the head with a hammer. The police arrested Willie and sent him in an ambulance to Bellevue for psychiatric evaluation. He was put on PQ5, the adolescent ward on the fifth floor. A psychiatrist asked Willie, "Why are criminals locked up?"

"Are you trying to be funny?" Willie responded. "You stupid white people lock them up."

Each morning, Willie was sent up the elevator to Bellevue's school on the eighth floor. After several days, Willie figured out the routine. When the kids were brought down in the elevator for lunch on their ward, he hid behind some adults and waited until he reached the ground floor. Then he just walked out the door, went to the nearest subway station, and jumped the turnstile. Bellevue dutifully recorded that he had "eloped." But it was not the hospital's duty to look for escapees. So after a few days, they closed his file by saying he had been discharged.

Willie was free all during 1976 because of the way the Family Court worked, or, as some of its critics were beginning to charge, didn't work. He had been assigned a new law guardian in 1976, Kay McNally, after his previous lawyer had left the Legal Aid Society. McNally was a short, slender Midwesterner with shoulder-length brown hair and freckles under her gray eyes. She had gone to law school late, when she was already in her thirties, and so she was older than most of her colleagues who worked long hours for low pay representing kids in Family Court. Her manner was reserved and serious, but she was just as passionately dedicated as the other members of the Legal Aid Society. Her role, she resolutely believed, was to be a good lawyer and minimize her clients' exposure to the system. If there was an alternative to incarceration, she tried for it. If that meant getting a case dismissed, that's what she argued for. It was not her job to worry about whether a kid was innocent or guilty. That's what they paid judges for. Besides, she was convinced by experience that the training schools were a mess and offered no real treatment to the boys cycled through them. So there was a moral reason for coming up with the best possible defense. Being in court every day, with a load of a hundred cases at a time, McNally had also come to feel that the Family Court itself was inherently unfair to the kids. Cases were decided too quickly and sloppily, and the judges were predisposed to find kids guilty. What McNally saw was an endless stream of sad, tragic people. It was exhausting, depressing work.

When McNally first met Willie in March 1976, he had just been arrested for pickpocketing, or jostling, as the police called it, and there was nothing to distinguish him from the other kids she represented. Most of them came into court once or twice, and then she never saw them again. Willie had not yet been charged with a violent crime. The jostling arrest was bullshit, she thought. Willie insisted he was innocent, and she doubted the testimony of the cop who had arrested him. Willie's appearance was a definite plus, too. He was handsome, with that big, winning smile, and he was always neatly dressed in court. McNally had seen some reports on Willie's behavior at Wiltwyck and Brookwood, and some of the psychiatric analyses of him. But to her way of thinking, they were contradictory. They didn't establish a clear pattern. Besides, she reminded herself, her job was to be his lawyer, not to get him locked up.

She did a good job that year. Of Willie's first five arrests, she got the judge to dismiss all charges in three of the cases. On the charge of snatching two dollars from the hand of a subway passenger, McNally won a dismissal by arguing that the case had been calendared an excessive and unfair number of times: eleven, to be exact. Sometimes it was the fault of the corporation counsel, or prosecutor, who had not been ready to proceed. But several times it was Willie himself who caused the delay by refusing to come to court. McNally got the judge to dismiss the charge of threatening the witness in the token booth when she pointed out that the trial in which the woman was a witness had already taken place. Besides, the woman had not been called to testify. So, under the statute, she was not a witness, and therefore Willie could not have threatened a witness. Several of the prosecutors opposing her said McNally was resorting to technicalities. McNally scoffed at that. "Every point of law is a technicality," she shot back. "Some people would say that the Fourth Amendment is a technicality," was a line she liked to use.

Willie was found guilty on the two other charges—jostling and trying to steal a pocketbook. But the charges were combined, or consolidated, in legal terms, because the Family Court could give only one placement at a time. The disposition was handed out on October 22, 1976, by Judge Harold Felix, the same justice who had originally sent Willie to Wiltwyck. Judge Felix ordered Willie placed in a secure facility with the Division for Youth for eighteen months.

The agency first sent Willie to a new experimental program it was running at the Bronx State Hospital, a reform inspired by Peter Edelman. It was designed precisely for kids like Willie, who seemed to be both violent and mentally ill and therefore had fallen through the cracks between the juvenile justice system and the mental health system. They were too dangerous for the state mental hospitals and needed too much psychiatric treatment for the training schools. The new program would combine the two approaches, providing both maximum security and good psychiatric care. It was being run by Ned Loughran, an affable, thoughtful young administrator from the Division for Youth with a face that was a map of Ireland.

The morning Willie was brought in, he had a bad hangover from drinking and from smoking too many reefers the night before. So when a psychologist started asking him questions, Willie lost his temper more quickly than usual. "White motherfuckers, I'm going to kill you," he shouted, and picked up a chair to menace his examiner. "No fucking way I'm coming into this program."

The psychologist was terrified. Loughran called for a guard he had hired, Rich Green, a big, strong, smart ex-convict who knew how to handle boys like Willie.

"That's a real bad-ass kid," Green said, after he finally calmed Willie down. "He knows how to play the system like a violin."

Sure enough, after Willie's outburst, the mental health staff at the hospital refused to take him. Willie had sabotaged his treatment once again, though it might have been the best possible program for him.

After that, Harriette Godley, the head social worker at Spofford, who had taken a liking to Willie, pulled some strings and persuaded a private agency to take him. On November 9, he was admitted to the Lieutenant Joseph P. Kennedy Jr. Home in the Bronx. It was a pleasant, unguarded house funded by the Kennedy family and meant for less dangerous kids. Godley was a stout, gray-haired, motherly woman who had grown up in a tough neighborhood in the South Bronx. She was normally a strict disciplinarian and didn't hesitate to tell kids who misbehaved, "It's a good thing you're not my child, 'cause if you were, I'd beat you so hard you'd be six feet under." But Godley was impressed by Willie's intellectual potential. She also felt he had gotten a bad break both from his mother, who had effectively washed her hands of him, and from the juvenile justice system, which kept shuffling him from one place to another. So she circumvented the rules by getting him into the Kennedy Home when he was scheduled to be sent back to Brookwood.

Willie laughed. He didn't have to be Houdini to escape from the Kennedy Home. All he had to do was walk out the front door and take a bus home. Ten days after he arrived at the Kennedy Home, he was gone. The Division for Youth issued a warrant for his arrest but had no way to enforce it. Coincidentally, he was arrested with two of his cousins on November 28 for stealing fire extinguishers from a subway car, but the police did not hold him, since they had not been notified of the Division for Youth warrant. It was like a Keystone Kops movie.

No one took any action against him, in fact, until January 10, 1977, when Laura called the police after Willie hit one of his cousins on the head with a hammer. This time, the police showed up quickly at the Boskets' apartment at 313 West 145th Street. Willie was brandishing a two-foot-long metal pipe. When the cops grabbed him, he fought, so he was now charged with assaulting a police officer, a big-league offense. But a Family Court judge ordered the assault charge dropped. Willie, after all, was already supposed to be in the custody of the Division for Youth serving the maximum sentence he could be given as a minor, eighteen months. Willie had beaten another arrest. Still, he was finally back in custody.

· · ·

ON THE COLD WINTER AFTERNOON of February 18, 1977, Willie arrived back at Brookwood, which by now, in another switch, was an all-boys facility. "He came with a smile on his face," Tom Pottenburgh wrote, "happy to see old friends and was heard saying to a female staff [member], 'I've come back home.'"

In truth, Pottenburgh did not want Willie back. He remembered only too well what Willie was like, and he was finally starting to make some progress calming the school down, getting the staff accustomed to running things without resorting to the use of room confinement. He didn't want Willie stirring things up again. So Pottenburgh agreed to take Willie only after Division for Youth headquarters ordered him there on an emergency basis and guaranteed that the agency would find another home for Willie within thirty days. This understanding was important to all that happened later, since from the beginning of Willie's second stay at Brookwood, the school's leaders believed they did not have to keep him for long.

From Willie's earlier stay, Pottenburgh knew he hated school. Willie couldn't sit still in class, and he didn't do well in academic subjects in which other boys might get higher grades, injuring his hypersensitive feelings. But Willie had enjoyed Brookwood's vocational program, where he could do things with his hands. So Pottenburgh decided to improvise for the temporary period he thought he would have Willie. Instead of enrolling him in Brookwood's school, he sent Willie downstairs to the basement to work in the maintenance shop for eight hours a day. This was exactly the kind of innovative, progressive treatment that Peter Edelman, the director of the Division for Youth, was trying to bring to the agency—to work out individualized programs for difficult kids that got them interested in what they were doing. Maybe this way they could take some pride in their lives, perhaps even start to turn things around. Other institutions had tried to break Willie, as if he were a wild horse. Pottenburgh wanted to give him something positive. Pottenburgh also seized on a report from a private psychiatrist in Manhattan who had seen Willie on the initiative of the Legal Aid Society just before he was shipped to Brookwood. The doctor found that Willie equated school with "kid stuff" but was interested in becoming a carpenter or electrician. So the psychiatrist had recommended that Willie be put in a vocational program.

Pottenburgh's plan seemed an inspired choice. The head of the maintenance shop was Jake Onufrychuk, an easygoing mechanic with the high Slavic cheekbones and crescent-shaped eyes of his parents' native Ukraine. Jake used his own money to buy Willie an orange hard hat and a pair of dark green coveralls, and he got his niece to embroider Willie's name on his new outfit. Willie grinned from ear to ear when Jake presented him with the clothes, as if someone had just handed him a million dollars.

After that, Willie came in every morning, nice and polite. He would put on his coveralls and hard hat, then add a nail apron. He stuck a hammer in his belt. This was a special privilege, since the boys were not supposed to have any potential weapons. Willie always lined up his tools neatly on the wall after he had used them: screwdrivers, saws, files, and wrenches.

Brookwood had been having trouble with the boys smashing the wooden chairs and bookcases in their rooms and breaking big panes of glass in the corridors. Jake assigned Willie to repair the furniture and replace the broken glass. Overnight, the damage stopped. Willie told the other boys, "If you break things, you're going to have to make me repair it." They were afraid of him, so he didn't have to say any more.

Soon, Jake and Willie had a mutual admiration society. Jake found that Willie had a natural talent with his hands. He not only learned how to cut glass and glue furniture back together, he could also change an electric switch with the juice on, fix television sets, and do all the maintenance on the school's cars and trucks. Jake noticed that Willie started walking around with a lot of pride, "like King Shit," Jake joshed him. Willie was careful not to act up in the shop because he knew he could lose his special program. And Jake was treating him like a man, with respect, Willie felt.

In the mornings, after they had put in some work, Jake started taking Willie with him off the school grounds in a truck to the local diner for breakfast. The other customers knew Jake and realized Willie had to be one of the boys from Brookwood, but his politeness surprised them. Every word out of Willie was "Yes, sir," or "No, ma'am." His usual vocabulary of four-letter words was forgotten. Jake even brought Willie back to his own home for dinner, and Willie helped wash the dishes afterward.

Peter Edelman came for a visit to Brookwood, and after being briefed about the program for Willie, gave it his blessing. Willie was already famous at Division for Youth headquarters. Edelman had heard lots of stories about how bad Willie was, yet how much potential he had. Finally, here was somebody really helping Willie. Later, Willie typed up a report on what he had learned working in the shop. "I owe all my thanks to the guys in maintenance for teaching me my trades and having patience with me and trying to help me make it in life without being a criminal," he wrote. "They taught me by being very nice to me without criticizing me when I made a mistake. They told me to work and I will be able to get whatever I want without any trouble from the police. That is why I'm going legit. Thank God."

Minerva Woullard, a child care worker in Willie's wing at Brookwood, thought he was doing much better in his second stay at the school. A kindly, middle-aged woman who had grown up in Harlem, Woullard was another of the mother figures toward whom Willie gravitated. Woullard would arrive at Brookwood at 7 a.m., get the boys up, have them take showers, and then escort them to the dining room for breakfast. Willie called her Ma Woullard, and if he started getting in trouble, she would put her arms around him and hold him for a while, and he would calm down. He was still small for his age, and she wondered if that made him extra defensive. But she thought Willie was brilliant, and she liked him so much she started bringing him home on weekends to her neat, red-brick, ranch-style house. Her husband, Chuck Woullard, was a big, muscular cross-country trucker and a part-time policeman. They had no children of their own, but they helped raise three of her brother's young kids, Tony, Laurie, and Leah. When Willie came over, he would help Chuck cut the grass, then the Woullards would leave him to babysit their nephew and nieces while they went into Albany to shop. Willie made the kids lunch, cleaned up the kitchen, and took them out to the pool. They all got to feeling so close, Woullard told her husband, "Willie is just like the son we never had." They even began to talk about bringing him to live with them as a foster son.

But there were skeptics at Brookwood who didn't think Willie had changed. Marvin Reisman, the school's resident psychologist, reported that Willie had threatened him with a hammer and tried to shake him down for money. "I fail to see where he is making any progress," Reisman wrote. He thought Willie's shows of good behavior were just an act.

Bob Pollack, a slight, soft-spoken, boyish-looking child care worker, also had his doubts. Pollack was new to Brookwood and had been assigned to Wing One, where Willie was kept. One evening when Willie was playing pool with another staff member, Martin Gallanter, Willie grinned and swung the pool stick at Gallanter's head like a baseball bat. At the last second, Gallanter took a step back, and the thick end of the cue stick just grazed his nose. It turned out that Willie was angry because two weeks earlier, Gallanter had locked him in his room for an hour for fighting. Gallanter was so shaken by the episode, he walked right into Pottenburgh's office and resigned. In a report afterward, Pollack wrote, "Willie holds a perverted sense of revenge toward other people who he thinks have wronged him.

"Willie has built a strong relationship with a few staff, mostly with females, such as Mrs. Woullard, the mother type," Pollack added. "But I have my doubts about the value of these relationships. Willie has been institutionalized for so many years this has retarded his emotional development. If we are ever to service this youth, he must learn there are limits on one's behavior. And our program is not giving Willie the blocks to build that maturity." Pollack wrote in another report, "Willie is showing some improvement but has a long way to go. He needs constant supervision."

At the time, in the spring and summer of 1977, Pollack's father was dying of cancer, and he and Willie had some deep discussions. Pollack was impressed by how sympathetic Willie was toward his father. Willie, in turn, mentioned that his own father was in prison for murder. Then one day, in the middle of a conversation, Willie said, "You know, Bob, when I get out of here, I'm going to kill somebody. All they can give me is eighteen months."

That June, less than six months after Willie arrived at Brookwood, Tom Pottenburgh began pushing to get Willie back to New York. The Division for Youth had not lived up to its pledge to find another place for Willie, so Pottenburgh took things into his own hands. As director, he had the authority to transfer Willie to another facility, if he could get the other institution to take him. Better yet, under Division for Youth rules, he could release a boy outright to his family if the youth had completed two home visits without trouble. Willie had already made one home visit in May. Now all that was required was another home visit and a plan for what Willie would do after his release. It was true that the Family Court had placed Willie with the Division for Youth for a term of eighteen months. But that was merely the maximum time. The agency had full discretion if it wanted to release him before then. It didn't even have to notify the Family Court. Instead of being a secure juvenile criminal justice system, the Division for Youth sometimes was a giant sieve, full of holes to be exploited.

Pottenburgh also had a constructive reason to send Willie back to New York. A major part of the reforms Peter Edelman had brought to the Division for Youth was keeping kids in their community as much as possible. In the community, not the training schools, he believed, boys could most effectively be given treatment and then learn to live better lives. So while Edelman closed more of the training schools, he rapidly increased facilities like halfway houses in the cities. The word "community" was repeated over and over, like a mantra from the late sixties.

When Ed Cruise, who was still Willie's aftercare worker, came to visit him at Brookwood in early June, Pottenburgh and his deputy, Phil Williams, planted an idea with Cruise. After Willie's scheduled second home visit in July, or a third visit in August, he would be sent back to Manhattan, where he would live in one of the Division for Youth's halfway houses, called Youth Development Centers. Here, the agency could create a vocational program for Willie like the one he had in the maintenance shop at Brookwood. And they could find a "one to one relationship with a father figure," like Willie had with Jake Onufrychuk. The agency should pay Willie for his work, Williams urged, since in the past "he has resorted to robbery to get money." Williams even proposed that Willie sign a formal contract with the Youth Development Center. Under it, Willie would live in the halfway house for the first sixty to ninety days, then increasingly live at home as he showed he was ready for the responsibility.

This time, Cruise offered no opposition. "Hopefully," he wrote his superior in the New York office, "funding can be found for such a purpose."

In Pottenburgh's mind, he was not dumping Willie. He honestly believed Willie had made progress. Sure, there had been a few bad incidents. One evening, Willie grabbed a two-by-four and smashed through a Plexiglas door into Brookwood's offices. Another day, after several boys teasingly called him a homosexual, he climbed over a fence and took off in the school's old Ford pickup truck. Fortunately, he could not get the vehicle out of first gear, and Williams ran him down. Pottenburgh thought this was pretty minor stuff, given Willie's history.

The real problem, Pottenburgh felt, was Sylvia Honig, a social worker who came out of the old training school culture. Smart, acerbic, and outspoken, Honig believed that Willie was being treated too permissively. The way she saw it, Willie, at fourteen and just over five feet tall, had intimidated the giant six-foot-nine Pottenburgh. Willie was running the place, she charged. He wasn't being made to go to school, he had special privileges, and he wasn't punished when he acted up, like constantly calling her a whore. All this was making Willie worse, not better, Honig argued. The only lesson he was learning was that crime pays, and it was feeding his feelings of omnipotence. Willie once told her, "The only person I listen to is the man upstairs." He liked to boast that he was the king of Brookwood. So Honig began writing letters out of channels to Edelman to complain, and threatened to go to the governor's office. Pottenburgh considered her a troublemaker and put a letter of reprimand in her personnel file.

In late August, after Willie had made a third home visit and negotiations had been completed to transfer him to the Youth Development Center in Manhattan, Pottenburgh asked Brookwood's psychiatrist, Dr. Lewis Jarett, for a final evaluation of Willie. Dr. Jarett had observed Willie, on and off, for three years, and in all his previous reports, including one only three weeks earlier, he had described Willie as an angry, aggressive, antisocial boy. But on August 31 he wrote, "This boy was seen again today and indeed the change in him is quite remarkable. I feel there has been growth in this boy that indicates a sense of stability and consistency and is not just a passing momentary phase." Willie's special program working in maintenance, the psychiatrist concluded, "obviously has been the best possible therapeutic situation for him. He feels important, and most important, he feels accepted and respected." It was unusual for a psychiatrist to change his opinion about a patient so dramatically in such a short period of time. Some staff members at Brookwood thought he had tailored his views to help ensure Willie's departure.

Whatever the case, Pottenburgh genuinely believed Willie had reformed and openly proclaimed his conviction, sending assurances to Peter Edelman at Division for Youth headquarters. During Willie's last week at Brookwood, when a team of documentary filmmakers were there preparing a show for PBS, he told them, "You really have to meet this kid Willie. He's a great model of our rehabilitative efforts."

The documentary team, Susan and Alan Raymond, filmed Willie in his room. He was proudly wearing his hard hat and work outfit. "When I first got put into institutions," Willie said on camera, "I was with kids who had done worser crimes. So I learned how to rob, mug, steal from the institution. Most institutions don't do nothing for you. They just make you worse." But Brookwood was different, he insisted, a grin on his face. "Working in maintenance, I got respect. I learned, Earn it, don't take it. I grew up here."

The Raymonds at first thought Willie was beguiling. But shortly after they interviewed him, Alan Raymond was filming a group of boys walking down the corridor. Willie suddenly ran at him and jammed the camera into his face, laughing as he did it. The force of the blow left Alan with a black eye. The Raymonds now began to think Willie was frightening. He had just been mouthing the right words as a way to get out of Brookwood faster. When they heard that Willie was being sent back to New York, they decided he had conned Pottenburgh.

Willie was scheduled to be sent there on September 15. Two nights before, he tore up his room, then turned the fire extinguisher on several people. Phil Williams, the head of the wing, had to be called at his house. He came back, put Willie in isolation in the infirmary, and sat with him until Willie calmed down at 1:30 in the morning.

On Willie's last morning, Williams and Jake Onufrychuk drove him in the school's van to Manhattan. There was a collective sigh of relief from many of the staff. John Deeters, who had worked on Willie's wing, had a dismal thought. He told Sylvia Honig, "Willie will end up killing someone."

CHAPTER 11

WILLIE

The Baby-Face Killer

Where there are no human attachments, there can be no conscience.

Selma Fraiberg, *Commentary*, December 1967

THE MANHATTAN YOUTH Development Center Number Two
had made no special preparations for Willie's arrival. In fact, the
center didn't even know he was coming. Someone had fouled up.

Phil Williams delivered Willie to the center at 10 a.m. on September
15, 1977, precisely according to the schedule drawn up during the
summer-long negotiations he had conducted through all the echelons of
the Division for Youth. Ed Cruise, Willie's social worker in New York,
was there to meet them. But the director of the Youth Development
Center was out, and the junior counselor left in charge said no one had
told him anything about Willie. Williams, who a lot of the boys thought
looked like a hippie, with a full beard and long brown hair down to his
waist, asked about the arrangements for Willie to work in a maintenance
program at the center.

"There is no such program," the official replied. "Willie will have
to go to school every day, just like all our other boys do."

Willie blew up. "Fuck that," he said. "I ain't going to no school.
That's not what I agreed to."

This was not an auspicious start. Williams knew Willie would never
willingly go to school; the mixup could undermine all the progress he
thought had been made with Willie at Brookwood over the past nine
months. Yet he still registered Willie with the halfway house. Williams
had to get back upstate to Brookwood, and he figured the problem could
be resolved later. Officially, Willie had been transferred from one Division
for Youth facility to another, not released and not dumped. On paper,

everything had been done correctly. That was the important point. Now Willie was no longer Brookwood's responsibility.

In spite of the confusion, Willie was smiling inside. What none of the Division for Youth officials had realized was that the center, a battered three-story brownstone, was only two blocks from Willie's home on 145th Street, smack in the middle of Harlem. On the drive into Manhattan, they had passed by Willie's apartment, and he had seen his sister Cheryl hanging out the window. After a single night at the Youth Development Center, Willie walked out and went home. Simple as that.

At first, no one came looking for him. The center was run by officials from the original, progressive wing of the Division for Youth, who still thought of the boys as volunteers. They felt that no adolescent should be forced to stay against his will. One afternoon when Willie realized he had left some clothes at the halfway house, he walked back over and rang the entrance bell. When no one answered, he broke in through a window and helped himself to the television set, a few radios, and some of the other boys' clothes.

It took the center a week to put out an AWOL warrant for Willie through the Division for Youth. Willie learned about it when an agency employee called the Boskets' apartment and asked for Laura. Willie had answered the phone, said his mother was out, and inquired why the division needed Laura. "We'd like to know when to send some men around to arrest Willie," the woman answered.

Willie immediately called Phil Williams at Brookwood—collect, of course. He told Williams about the warrant, then complained, "I'm getting screwed. They want me to go back to school and they've got no work program for me where I can earn money to support myself." Willie said he was depressed, that he missed Brookwood, and that being on the outside was just a waste of time. He wasn't learning anything. He also asked Williams if he could do him a favor and get the warrant quashed.

Williams thought Willie had a point. The Youth Development Center had not lived up to the agreement. Besides, Willie had already successfully completed three home visits during the past summer; under Division for Youth rules, that meant he could be released outright to his home. So there was no legal need for him to stay at the halfway house. Williams, Cruise, and the leaders of the Youth Development Center had another discussion during which they decided to drop the AWOL warrant.

By early October, then, Willie was effectively free, though his court-ordered placement with the Division for Youth would not expire until the following April. No one had deliberately planned for Willie to be loose, but there was no official in the agency in charge of monitoring the release of dangerous cases like Willie. This was the kind of thing that happened in a big, overworked bureaucracy. Willie was sent from Brook-wood, a maximum security institution, to the Manhattan Youth Development Center, which had virtually no security, and then was allowed simply to go home. The different parts of the system had hardly meshed; Willie maneuvered through the cracks.

LAURA WAS TRYING to get her life in order. She was now working as a security guard for a private agency at City College, only a few blocks from the family's apartment on 145th Street. When Willie had left Brookwood and come home from the halfway house, she figured the Division for Youth had let him go. No one contacted her to tell her differently.

Laura had a new boyfriend, "Charles," a tall, thickset, very dark-skinned man who at forty-eight was eleven years older than Laura. He acted as the superintendent of their building and ran the pool hall on the first floor, Al Clark's Billiards. Charles also watched over the building next door, a front for drug pushers. Given his line of work, Charles always carried a gun, and he wasn't shy about using it. One night soon after Willie came home, Laura, Shirley, and Willie were looking out the window of their second-floor apartment when they saw a man named Gangster running out of the pool hall. He was trash-talking about how he wasn't going to pay for the games he played, and what he was going to do to Charles. Charles pulled out his pistol and shot Gangster in the kneecap.

Willie was awed by Charles. To Willie, he was the baddest dude on the street and the first man he met who might have been as tough as his father. By this time, Charles had moved in with Laura, bringing his collection of guns—fifty or sixty revolvers, automatics, and shotguns: a regular arsenal. The local drug dealers gave them to Charles to hold for safekeeping, and he stored them in the bedroom closet.

Willie was having trouble with two boys—Leroy, an older boy who lived in the neighborhood (Willie was fifteen), and Ricky, a drug dealer and trained boxer. Leroy and Ricky enjoyed taunting Willie, calling him a punk and challenging him to fight.

"Yo, my man, don't disrespect me," Willie told them. "Do I disrespect you?" When the two older boys persisted, Charles offered Willie a gun to even the odds.

"The next time you see them," Charles counseled Willie, "you show them this gun and you let them know what's going to happen if they start picking on you. They won't disrespect you."

It was the code of the streets again, the code that descended from the old Southern notion of honor. A man had to be ready to fight to

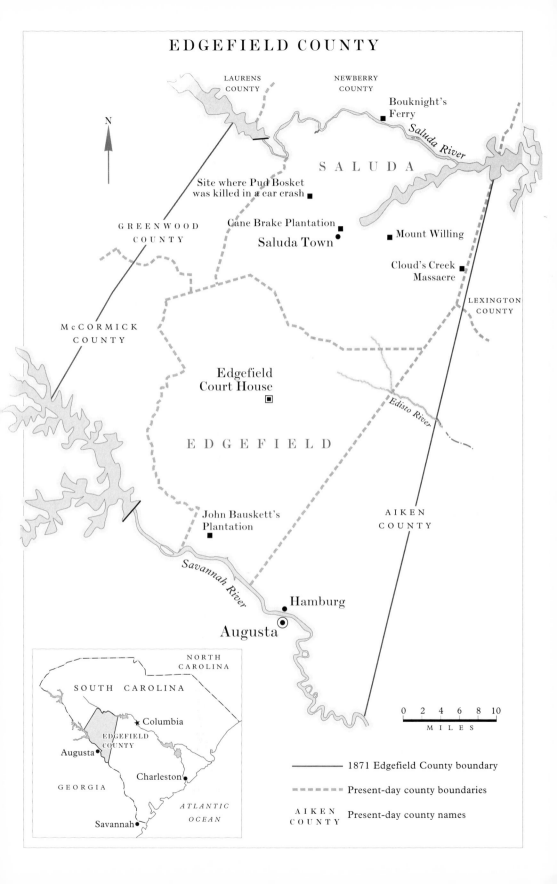

EDGEFIELD COUNTY

LAURENS
COUNTY

NEWBERRY
COUNTY

Bouknight's
Ferry

Saluda River

S A L U D A

N

Site where Pud Bosket
was killed in a car crash

Cane Brake Plantation
Saluda Town

Mount Willing

Cloud's Creek
Massacre

GREENWOOD
COUNTY

LEXINGTON
COUNTY

McCORMICK
COUNTY

Edgefield
Court House

Edisto River

E D G E F I E L D

AIKEN
COUNTY

John Bauskett's
Plantation

Savannah River

Hamburg

Augusta

NORTH
CAROLINA

SOUTH CAROLINA

Columbia

EDGEFIELD
COUNTY

Augusta

Charleston

GEORGIA

*ATLANTIC
OCEAN*

Savannah

0 2 4 6 8 10
MILES

——————— 1871 Edgefield County boundary

– – – – – – Present-day county boundaries

AIKEN
COUNTY   Present-day county names

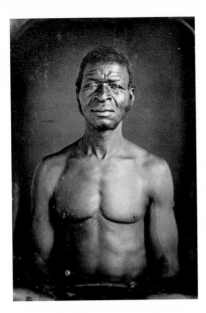

One of the earliest known photographs of a slave, taken in 1850. "Jack" was kept on a plantation in South Carolina, not far from Edgefield County, where the Bosket family began their American lives.
(*Peabody Museum, Harvard University*)

Illustration of a slave market in Charleston, like those at which the Boskets were bought and sold, from the London *Illustrated News*. (*South Caroliniana Library*)

SOUTHERN CHIVALRY — ARGUMENT versus CLUB'S.

Preston Brooks, a Congressman from Edgefield. In 1856 he caned Senator
Charles Sumner at his desk in the Senate because he felt that Sumner had
impuned his family's honor. The most upstanding citizens used violence to
resolve disputes. (*Cartoon of the caning: New York Public Library; Portrait of
Brooks: South Caroliniana Library*)

The deadly results of a duel. Southern white men fought for their honor—what today on city streets is called "respect"—a personal form of justice whose violence continues to haunt America. (*South Caroliniana Library*)

"Negroes, Negroes."—a typical headline above an ad for slave sales in the Edgefield *Advertiser*. In 1852, John Bauskett sold the young slave Aaron Bosket to Francis Pickens through a similar ad. (*South Caroliniana Library*)

Francis Pickens, the new owner of Aaron Bosket and governor of South Carolina who led the state into secession, starting the Civil War. With emancipation, the Boskets initially stayed in South Carolina; succeeding generations carried the lessons of white belligerence and readiness to use violence.
(*South Caroliniana Library*)

The Confederate hundred-dollar bill, with a portrait of Lucy Pickens, the wife of Francis Pickens, in the center. Her lavish spending led Pickens to sell Aaron Bosket, separating the boy from his parents. (*South Caroliniana Library*)

"Pitchfork" Ben Tillman, Populist
and racist governor of South Carolina
who in the 1890s disenfranchised
black voters like Aaron Bosket and
imposed segregation. He liked to
boast, "I am from Edgefield."
(*South Caroliniana Library*)

The crowd outside the courthouse of the new county of Saluda watching the
hanging of Pud Bosket's relative Will Herrin, November 27, 1908. Pud was
there. The end of the Civil War and emancipation did not end the problems
of race, justice, and violence. (*Saluda County Historical Society*)

Street scene in white-owned Saluda, circa 1910, about the time Pud Bosket turned to robbing stores. (*Saluda County Historical Society*)

Black Saluda was poorer and eventually led the Boskets to seek a better world elsewhere. This is all that remains of the sharecropper cabin lived in for many years by Pud's brother, Dandy Bosket. (*Photograph by the author*)

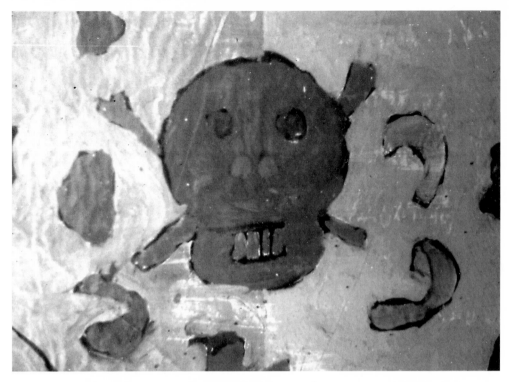

A skull, the earliest artwork by Butch Bosket, Pud's grandson, painted in 1951 when he was nine or ten years old. Butch had been sent to the Wiltwyck School for Boys, after being abandoned by his father and mother as an infant. (*Courtesy of Edith Kramer*)

Butch's painting of a sailor, probably meant to be his father, James, whom Butch mistakenly believed to have been in the navy. (*Courtesy of Edith Kramer*)

Two sailors coming ashore from a ship, painted by Butch at Wiltwyck at about age eleven. Painting gave Butch a way to maintain his precarious emotional balance. His therapist thought that this painting, because it depicted two figures, indicated a new capacity for friendship. (*Courtesy of Edith Kramer*)

Butch tried to destroy his painting of swordfighters because his paranoia, after a young lifetime of living on the streets and getting into fights, made it come alive to him. (*Courtesy of Edith Kramer*)

Butch's portrait of a "prisoner," painted at Wiltwyck when he was about eleven. The subject was his father, in jail at the time for robbery.
(*Courtesy of Edith Kramer*)

A painting of a magician, done at Wiltwyck, conveyed Butch's flamboyant, dramatic personality, his tendency to do many things at once, his therapist believed.
(*Courtesy of Edith Kramer*)

Butch's painting, probably of Floyd Patterson, who had graduated from Wiltwyck and gone on to become world heavyweight boxing champion.
(*Courtesy of Edith Kramer*)

Self-portrait by Butch about age thirteen, shortly before his release from Wiltwyck, depicting himself as a juvenile delinquent. It was the identity he had chosen for himself.
(*Courtesy of Edith Kramer*)

Butch, about 1980, in the exercise yard at Leavenworth prison. He had been sent there for robbing banks after escaping from another prison, to which he had been sent after being found guilty of a double homicide.
(*Courtesy of Michael Schoenfield*)

Butch receiving his Phi Beta Kappa key at Leavenworth from University of Kansas professors. This made him the first inmate in American history to be elected to Phi Beta Kappa while in prison. His teachers thought he was brilliant and would make a good scholar. (*Courtesy of Michael Schoenfield*)

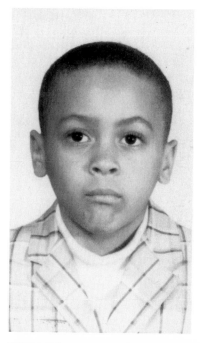

Willie Bosket, Butch's son, in 1969, age seven. Here he looks sad and depressed, a hidden side that a psychiatrist at Bellevue saw before the homicidal boy emerged.
(*Courtesy of Laura Bosket*)

A smiling Willie, age nine, in the arms of Rose Niles, his teacher at Wiltwyck. He was sent to the same institution as his father for stealing, truancy, and attacking other children with weapons. Wiltwyck later used this picture as an ad. (*Courtesy of Rose Niles*)

Willie was filmed for a television documentary at Brookwood, a maximum security state training school. A few days later he was allowed to return home to Harlem, where he then murdered two men. (*Alan and Susan Raymond*)

Willie's original mugshot at age fifteen after his arrest for murder.

Mugshot of Willie at age twenty-one after his arrest for attempted robbery. By this time, Willie was well on his way to becoming the most dangerous criminal in New York State prison history.

Willie, age twenty-three, in the visitors room at Sullivan prison, where he repeatedly attacked his guards and set his cell on fire.
(*David Jennings for* The New York Times)

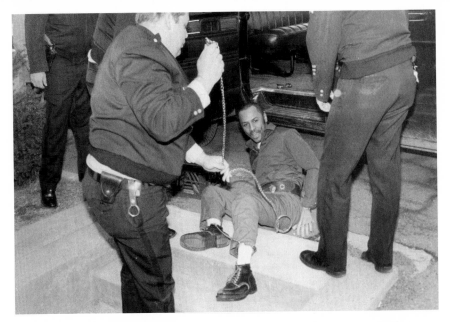

Willie in shackles being dragged to court to stand trial for stabbing a prison guard, 1989. After a lifetime of incarceration, he considered himself "a monster created by the system" and believed he was at war with prison authorities. (*Associated Press*)

Handcuffed, Willie acts as his own attorney in the 1989 stabbing trial. One judge had congratulated Willie on his exceptionally able performance, but he received a life sentence. (*Courtesy of Dan Chidester,* Kingston *Daily Freeman*)

prove himself in the eyes of others. Southern whites had called it honor; Willie's great-grandfather Pud had talked about reputation; and his father, Butch, had spoken of respect. Now on the streets of Harlem, the term was undergoing another metamorphosis—it was being referred to as disrespect. Whatever word was used, it was still a lethal credo, especially for poor African-American boys like Willie with scant chance for a good education or a decent job and little to look forward to but a life in prison. And Willie, so bright and driven, had carried the code of violence to the extreme. For him, violence was like a sport, a competition, and victory went to the most violent. So what Charles said struck a powerful chord in Willie, an echo of the voices of his ancestors.

On February 1, 1978, Willie was hanging out at Intermediate School Number 10, a large, yellow-brick building that had been constructed on top of the subway yards at 148th Street and Lenox Avenue, not far from his house. While Willie was trying to talk with a pretty brown-skinned girl who messed around with Leroy, she insulted Willie, disrespecting him. He slapped her in the face.

That was a serious challenge to Leroy. He gave Willie an ultimatum that evening: "You can fight it out alone with Ricky, or we will both kill you." Leroy led him up to the roof of their five-story tenement, where Ricky was waiting. Willie knew he was overmatched.

When Ricky started throwing punches, there was no time to think. The language of the street was action, and Willie pulled out the gun Charles had given him. Ricky jumped backward in fear, toward the edge of the roof. Willie gave him a kick, knocking him down the narrow air shaft between the building they were on and its neighbor. Leroy turned and ran.

The next morning, Charles found Ricky's body lying in the bottom of the air shaft and told Willie he had to get rid of it. People often dumped their garbage out there, and someone might find the corpse and call the police. Willie said he would get some gas and burn it.

The police did not learn about the incident, but Willie was beginning to worry that Leroy would seek revenge and went looking for Ed Cruise, his Division for Youth social worker. Cruise was a soft touch, in Willie's opinion, easily manipulated, even afraid of him. After Willie had walked out of the Youth Development Center, Cruise had taken Willie's side, claiming the center had treated Willie unfairly. In December, Cruise had arranged to enroll Willie in another agency activity at the Henry Street Settlement House on the Lower East Side of Manhattan. It was designed as an afterschool program to pay kids $2.35 an hour for taking part in group counseling and doing community work projects. In Cruise's view, it was a way of keeping Willie off the streets for part of the day and having him earn some legal income. If Willie cooperated, he would become eligible for a new full-time federally funded maintenance and building job. Willie, though, thought the Henry Street program was bullshit. He failed to show up much of the time, and when he did, he often was drunk or high on marijuana and got into fights. Still, Cruise hadn't given up on Willie.

So when Willie went to Henry Street and told Cruise about his battle with Ricky, he figured Cruise might be sympathetic. Willie didn't tell him the truth, exactly. He made up a story about stabbing a drug pusher who had sold a friend of his some tea instead of "herb" (marijuana); he said he had been warned to get out of town or his life would be in danger. Could Cruise help? It was an odd request to make of a Division for Youth employee. Fortunately, Cruise remembered that Minerva Woullard, the child care worker at Brookwood who was fond of Willie, had expressed an interest in having him as a foster child. So he took Willie to Grand Central Terminal and bought him a round-trip ticket to the Woullards' home upstate, an emergency trip, just for a weekend.

When Minerva Woullard got the call about Willie from Cruise, she was delighted. "By all means, send him up here," she said. Willie had phoned her occasionally after his release from Brookwood, and she was worried about his fate in Harlem. She and her husband, Chuck, had moved away from New York City because she didn't want her nieces and nephews, whom she was helping raise, to get in trouble on the street.

After Willie spent the weekend, she and Chuck were more firmly resolved than ever to make Willie their foster child. They took him to a party at a friend's house, and he was so polite and well-behaved, people remarked on what a fine boy he was. Chuck loved to hunt in the woods near their house, for deer, turkeys, and rabbits, and he showed Willie his collection of nine rifles and shotguns. The Woullards asked Willie if he would like to come and live with them, and he said absolutely. There was only one condition, the Woullards added—Willie would have to agree to go to school, something he had never done happily. That was cool, too, he told them.

Minerva was so determined to have Willie as a foster child, she even tried to keep him when the weekend visit was over, until Division for Youth headquarters formally approved. There was no way she wanted Willie going back to Harlem now. But she was told no, Willie had to return to the city, so the agency could finish the paperwork. Meanwhile, she went for the required physical and a chest X-ray and met with a social worker assigned to the case.

Ed Cruise cooperated by visiting Laura and obtaining her permission for Willie to move in with the Woullards. Laura readily assented. She

was becoming increasingly anxious about Willie as she saw him falling
back into his old habits. He had started hanging out with his cousins
again, staying out late, and she wondered what else he was doing. "If he
doesn't get off the streets of New York," she told Cruise, "he's going to
end up dead or in the hospital."

Now—early February—it was just a matter of waiting until the legal
formalities were completed, normally a matter of a few weeks. No one
thought the delay was very important.

WILLIE HAD GONE BACK to his favorite line of work—riding the
subway, looking for what he called bums, or winos, passengers who had
fallen asleep and were easy marks to rob. He and his cousins had developed
a system. To make sure the victim was asleep and would not resist, one
of them would stroll by and kick the person's feet. If the victim woke up,
they would say, "Excuse me," and move on.

On March 6, 1978, Willie went out with his cousin, Herman Spates,
who was not in jail at the time. Herman had been abandoned by his
mother as well as his father, and had come up on the streets. In the year
and a half since Herman had turned sixteen and become an adult under
New York law, he had already been arrested six times—mostly for minor
charges, robbery and burglary. He had taken to sleeping in movie houses
around Times Square where no one would put him out at night.

That evening, Willie and Herman were riding the A train in upper
Manhattan. Willie had a switchblade, what the police called a gravity
knife, since it sprang open when you flicked it. In Harlem, it was known
as a Double O Seven, after James Bond. The knives came in three sizes:
the "baby," the "mama," and the "papa." Willie had a "mama." He
kept it ready in his back pants pocket, with a horsehide string hanging
out. It made him feel like a real manchild.

As the train pulled into the station at 207th Street, the last stop on
the line, Willie and Herman spotted a woman sleeping. Willie nudged
her feet, and when she didn't respond, he went through her pockets. She
had no money at all.

They were walking out the subway door onto the platform when
two plainclothes Transit Authority police officers, patrolmen Michael
Callahan and John Koratzanis, came up from behind and arrested them.

The cops took the two boys to the district Transit Authority police
office, which was underground in the large station of the A train at 145th
Street, a few blocks from Willie's home. Since Herman was legally an
adult, the police put him in the bullpen, their temporary jail. Willie, still
a juvenile, had to be kept separate; the law protecting the rights of juveniles

was very strict. They handcuffed him to a bench in their locker room, processed him, and called his mother. Laura was at home, and she said she would come pick him up. The cops only gave him a desk appearance ticket, which released him to the custody of a parent. If Laura hadn't been available, he would have been remanded overnight to Spofford Juvenile Center until he could be brought to the Family Court.

When Laura saw Willie, he remembered later, her eyes narrowed and her voice grew cold. "Get your ass over here, right now," she commanded between clenched teeth.

Willie kept his eyes on the floor, his lips out and his face pouting.

"Didn't I say get your ass over here," Laura barked. "And straighten out that face. You always getting in trouble. One of these days, I ain't going to come, and your ass is going to end up dead or right in jail."

On the short walk home, if Willie didn't move fast enough, Laura gave him a shove. After they got back to the apartment, Willie thought she might give him a good whipping with a belt, as she had when he was younger. But by now, he calculated, she had learned that it didn't make much difference. She just ordered him, "Go to bed before I knock the shit out of you."

Willie was back out on the subway looking for marks to rob the next day. He learned from his mother that the Family Court had scheduled a hearing on the attempted robbery charge in two weeks, on March 21. That was nothing to worry about, because in the meantime, Willie was making good scores almost every day. One evening, he and Herman found $380 in the wallet of a passenger who was sound asleep. Willie said he was going to use some of his share to buy a gun from Charles. He had given Charles back the pistol he had used in the fight with Ricky because he wanted a piece of his own. Charles agreed to sell him a .22 with a brown handle and a steel-blue finish. Willie paid him sixty-five dollars for it. Then he bought a holster so he could strap the pistol to his hip. That was the way policemen carried their guns, and Willie still had his child's fantasy of being a cop, just like on the television shows he loved to watch. Now he felt powerful; it was a rush to his head. When he strapped on the pistol, he walked with a swagger.

A few days after he bought the gun, on Sunday, March 19, Willie was riding the subway uptown from his grandmother's apartment to his mother's place. It was 5:30 in the afternoon, and he was by himself on the Number 3 IRT train. He spotted a sleeping passenger, a middle-aged Hispanic-looking man wearing a big gold digital watch. In those days, digital watches were new, and the fancy ones had red faces that glowed. The man was wearing sunglasses—pink sunglasses, Willie noticed. With the digital watch and the sunglasses, he reminded Willie of a counselor at Spofford whom Willie hated, because he often beat Willie. Willie remembered how the man shouted at him to stay in line as the kids were marched from room to room.

"How many times I got to tell you to stay in line?" the counselor would growl, then swing at Willie. Sometimes when he did so, his watch-band popped open and he paused to snap it shut. Then he hit Willie again. *Smack, smack, smack.* Willie could still hear the sound of the blows.

There were two other passengers in the car, at the back of the train, but they got off at the 145th Street station. The last stop was only three blocks farther on, the 148th Street and Lenox Avenue terminal. Willie was now alone with the slumbering passenger. He went over and kicked his feet. There was no response. Willie got his gun out and began to take the watch off. But suddenly, the man started to open his eyes. Willie didn't hesitate. He had long wanted to feel what it was like to pull the trigger on somebody. At that instant, it was partly his fantasy about being a cop in the big shootout. It was even more his whole life that had taught him violence was the way to get things done. Willie shot the man through the sunglasses in his right eye. The victim threw his hands up, and blood spurted out of his face like a geyser. He screamed.

"If he's not dead, he's going to cause me a problem," Willie thought. Willie shot him a second time, in the temple. Just then, the train came out of the underground tunnel into the late-winter twilight as it approached the last stop. Ahead was a big subway train yard with the Harlem River on the right, and across the water, perched on a bluff, the hulking shape of Yankee Stadium. The man fell back against the wall of the car, then slumped to the floor.

Willie took the watch, pulled a ring off the dead man's finger, and quickly went through his pants. He found fifteen dollars. In a second, he was out the door and up the steps of the station to the street. No one saw him. On the short walk home, Willie sold the ring for twenty dollars.

That night, Willie thought to himself that killing someone was no big thing, nothing to lose sleep over. He showed Cheryl the watch, which still had a little blood on it.

"Booby," his sister asked, "where'd you get that watch?"

"I killed a motherfucker," Willie answered. He was laughing.

Cheryl laughed, too. "Get out of here," she said. Willie was always telling tall tales, so she didn't believe him.

Sensing her skepticism, Willie said, "No, I really shot a man."

It was then she saw that he was acting kind of puffed up, like he was real bad, real tough, like he had done something to show he was no pushover and he deserved a lot of respect.

The next day, the newspapers identified the victim as Noel Perez, a forty-four-year-old hospital worker who lived by himself in the Bronx. The papers said it appeared to be a random shooting, done for no reason. That was true, in a way. But Willie had been waiting to kill somebody for a long time. He felt it was his destiny. And the man who had been murdered was not entirely a random choice. To Willie, he resembled a guard in Spofford, one of the juvenile prisons where he had spent his youth. Noel Perez, it turned out, lived on Spofford Avenue, just down the street from the detention center.

The next day, Willie appeared in Manhattan Family Court for the scheduled hearing on his attempt to rob the woman passenger on March 6. To Willie, it was just another day in court; he wasn't thinking about the murder he had just committed. The killing was like the hot dog his mother had bought him before he went into court that morning; it was already done with and gone, in the past.

As usual, the hearing was postponed; Judge Cesar Quinones put it over for three weeks. Hearing that, the corporation counsel made an uncharacteristically strong plea to keep Willie at Spofford.

"Your honor," the prosecutor began, "this boy is likely to kill if set free." As proof, he cited Willie's long record of arrests and his history of assaultive behavior at Brookwood and other juvenile institutions.

Judge Quinones thought the prosecutor was greatly overstating the evidence. "I don't see any arrests for 1977," he said. It just so happened that over the past year, Willie indeed had not been arrested. He had been at Brookwood most of that time, and after he got out, he had simply not been caught.

The probation officer assigned to Family Court also came to Willie's aid. He informed the judge that the Division for Youth was close to completing the paperwork to place Willie as a foster child with a family out of the city.

Viewing the evidence, Judge Quinones concluded, "I can see no reason to remand this boy to Spofford." He released Willie to his mother's custody. The comedy of errors was still running in Willie's favor.

By that spring, Willie's life had settled into a pattern. He slept late, often until 2 or 3 o'clock in the afternoon, when Herman—whom a judge had also let go—came to his house to wake him. To Willie, this was part of living in the ghetto. Unless you had a job, street life didn't come alive until the evening. After he got up, Willie fixed himself a cup of coffee and a grilled cheese sandwich or a fried hot dog, something quick. Then he and Herman headed for the subway. When they made a score, they would buy some beer and some grass and find a couple of girls to mess around with. Willie had two favorites who both lived in the big public housing project where the old Polo Grounds used to stand. They were each fifteen years old; one already had a one-year-old baby daughter. Sometimes Willie brought one of the girls back to his family's apartment, since his mother was out working the late shift on her security job. Most nights, Willie didn't go to sleep until near dawn.

On Thursday, March 23, Herman came over as usual to wake Willie up. "Let's go get some money," Willie proposed, strapping on his gun and holster. They walked down a short hill, then over to the terminal of the Number 3 train at 148th Street and Lenox Avenue. This time, they paid the fare, not wanting to arouse suspicion, and walked down the steps to the long concrete platform. It was a dark, cavernous space, lit by dim industrial bulbs that hung over the subway yards off to their left. The air smelled of oil from the maintenance work that was done on the trains there.

They spotted a motorman in a brown and yellow checked woolen hunter's jacket walking out into the yard. He had a large CB radio in his hand that Willie and Herman thought would be worth at least a hundred dollars if they sold it. He was a white man, heavyset, with curly brown hair; a thick, droopy mustache; a broad, prominent nose that looked as if it had been broken a couple of times; and a long purple scar under his right eye. His name, ironically, was Anthony Lamorte. Lamorte's family came from Naples, and he had been brought up in a working-class section of Brooklyn. He had never finished high school, but he had been drafted and shipped off to Vietnam as an artilleryman with the Big Red One Division. On the eve of the Communists' Tet offensive in 1968, he had gotten into a fight with his mess sergeant and ended up with a shattered cheekbone. A medical evacuation helicopter took him to the large army hospital at Long Binh, outside Saigon. "The war is over for you," a doctor told him.

In the subway yard, Lamorte's job was to cut the trains, making half-trains out of whole trains when the rush hour was over, or bringing out extra cars to make full trains when they were needed. That afternoon, he was at the end of his shift and was about to make up his last train when he saw two kids following him into the yards. One of them looked very young, only about five feet seven inches tall, perhaps one hundred twenty-five pounds, with a baby face, dressed in a black hooded coat. Lamorte didn't pay much attention to them at first. But they kept walking toward him, farther into the subway yard, so Lamorte shouted down at them from the car he was in, "You're not supposed to be here. Get the hell out."

"Why don't you come down here and make us get out?" the smaller boy shouted back.

"Okay, I'll put you out," Lamorte responded, climbing down the steps of the car.

Willie, who was still about thirty feet away, now pulled out his gun. "Give me your money and the radio," he demanded.

Seeing the gun, Lamorte got a bad feeling. It was still a time when few kids in Harlem carried guns, and the sight shocked him. There was also something arrogant and cold about the little boy with the pistol. So Lamorte quickly turned around and started climbing back up on the train. As he mounted the steps, he could hear the boy running toward him on the ballast rocks set along the tracks. Lamorte had a premonition he was going to die, something he never had in Vietnam.

Just as he reached the top, there was a popping sound, and he felt a numbness in the back of his right shoulder. But it wasn't a really bad pain; he couldn't believe he had been shot. And after the pop, to his relief, he heard the two boys running away. Afterward, Lamorte walked to the dispatcher's office and said he thought he had been shot. That's when he first saw there was blood on his clothing. It was the second shooting in a week at the terminal, so some of the transit workers started talking about having a serial killer on the subway.

Over the next three nights, Friday, Saturday, and Sunday, Willie and Herman pulled three more violent robberies on the subway. One evening, Willie kicked a nattily dressed middle-aged man down the steps of a station on the A train, badly cutting his head. They took twelve dollars in cash and several expensive rings from the victim, leaving him unconscious in a pool of blood. Another evening, Willie shot a fifty-seven-year-old passenger named Matthew Connolly in the hip when he refused to hand over his money. Several Transit Authority patrolmen later found Willie and Herman waiting on the platform for a train and arrested them. But when they searched Willie, they unaccountably missed the gun he had hidden in his pants. The police drove the two boys to the emergency room at North Central Bronx Hospital, where Connolly had been taken by ambulance. He said he couldn't identify them. Willie thought Connolly recognized him but was too scared to tell the cops. This close encounter with the police did nothing to change Willie's opinion that he was smarter than the law. He was feeling downright invincible.

The next evening, Monday, March 27, Willie suggested that they start at the 135th Street station of the Number 3 train. It took the two boys ten minutes to walk down there from Willie's apartment on 145th Street. They jumped the turnstile and entered the last car of the subway going uptown. Only one passenger was in the car. He was a Hispanic-looking man in his mid-thirties, of medium build, wearing a black coat over a white, blue, and red plaid flannel shirt and dark pants.

Willie knew he had the man trapped, because at the next station, 145th Street, the platform was short and the last few cars were always left back in the tunnel, with their doors locked. Passengers unfamiliar with the station often got caught that way.

Willie posted Herman at the front of the car, then approached the seated passenger. He took out his gun and put it three inches from the man's head. "Give up your money," Willie demanded.

"I ain't got any," the man said.

Willie felt a kind of compulsion take hold of him. He pulled the trigger.

The man slid down off his seat onto the floor, his body ending faceup in a pool of spreading blood. Herman bolted forward into the next car, running as fast as he could to get away. Willie knelt down, systematically going through the dead man's pockets, turning them inside out. He found a brown wallet with a New York City welfare card in it, and two dollar bills. The man's name, Willie noticed, was Moises Perez, same surname as the other man he had killed on the subway.

Willie met Herman at a bus station near the subway exit. They discarded the wallet behind a bowling alley as they walked back to Willie's house. Willie was laughing.

The next day, when Herman came over, they sat in the kitchen reading about the murder in the paper. Willie started giggling. He felt like a big-time killer—something he had done had made the front page of the newspaper. He felt no remorse for the killings. The way he had been brought up, and then his life on the street, and all those years in institutions were like a fort that protected him from being sorry for what he did. It was more as if he had scored a big victory in the most competitive game of all, violence. Living in a world where violence was essential for survival, Willie treated each encounter like a life-or-death duel, and he had proved to be the best by being the most violent.

Laura and Cheryl were in the kitchen, too. Willie had told his sister what happened after each of the shootings, and she hadn't believed him. But now, seeing him read the story in the paper this way, she said to herself, "He told me the truth."

That same day, Division for Youth headquarters in Albany gave final approval for Willie to go live with the Woullards as a foster child.

DETECTIVE MARTIN DAVIN of the Sixth Homicide Zone got the call at 8:45 p.m. on Monday, March 27, right after a Transit Authority conductor found Moises Perez's body. The Sixth Homicide Zone saw a lot of action—it covered the whole of central Harlem, three police precincts. As each murder came in, the detectives took turns catching the cases. This one was Davin's.

At forty-eight, Marty Davin was straight out of a central casting call for a New York City cop. His father had been a trolley driver, an immigrant from Galway, Ireland. Davin grew up in Washington Heights, on the northern edge of Harlem, in ethnically mixed working-class communities with names like Vinegar Hill and St. Rosalina's Parish. After high school, because the Korean War was on, he joined the navy and served on a submarine. But he had always wanted to be a policeman, and after getting out of the service, he passed the New York City police exam. His first assignment was as a foot patrolman in Harlem. Later, he qualified in motorcycles, and then in fingerprints, and when the city set up specialized homicide squads in 1971, Davin won a job investigating murders. He was sent to Harlem again, but Davin didn't mind, unlike some other white policemen. He had been there practically his entire life and knew his way around. Davin had a gruff manner, behind which lurked an impish spirit. His body was compact and sturdy, his face strong, broad, and ruddy. Over his high forehead, he wore his graying hair combed straight back.

By the time Davin reached the subway terminal at 148th Street and Lenox Avenue, where Moises Perez's body had been found, a television reporter was already there, broadcasting live. The newsman was very excited and kept saying New York had a serial killer on the loose. Davin didn't need that. It would mean more pressure coming down on him from high up in the police department. So he made arrangements to work through the night.

Because the killing had taken place in the subway, the Transit Authority police also had jurisdiction, which gave the investigation more resources but further complicated things. That first night, Davin deployed everyone he could to canvass the neighborhood—good old-fashioned police work: ask everyone if they had seen anything. The next day, a man found Perez's wallet and turned it in. To Davin, that meant the killers were probably people from the neighborhood.

The Transit Authority detective assigned to work with him, Nick Vazquez, suggested checking their new computer. It had files on criminals who were known to operate in the subway and their modus operandi. Right away, the computer spat out the names of two boys who had been picked up for the shooting of Matthew Connolly just a few days before but were released when Connolly couldn't identify them—Willie Bosket and Herman Spates. A further check showed that the pair had repeated arrests. And Willie, Davin noted, lived only a few blocks from the terminal where people kept getting shot.

This was good information, and the transit cops wanted to arrest Willie immediately. But Davin saw a problem. Willie was only fifteen, still a juvenile; you had to be very careful with a juvenile. If you arrested him, there were tough restrictions on how long you could hold him. He had seen Family Court judges throw out a case because a kid had been held too long. You also had to have one of his parents present before you talked with him. All this made it harder to work over a juvenile suspect and get anything out of him. Davin thought it would be much smarter, and safer, to find Herman first and go to work on him. Herman was seventeen, an adult. So he told the transit police, "I don't want you to go near Willie." When he discovered that several gung-ho plainclothes transit police had staked out Willie's house anyway, Davin reiterated his order. "Don't go near him. If you see him come out of the building, just follow him."

On Saturday morning, March 31, Davin was still trying to track down Herman. Herman had no address, since he slept in movie theaters or wherever he could find a place to flop for the night. At 11:30 a.m., two of the undercover transit police staking out Willie's building saw Willie come out. Willie's grandmother, Nancy Roane, had stopped by the house during a break from her work as a domestic, and she asked Willie to go out to buy her a newspaper. He put on his pants, his sneakers, and a jacket, and headed for a newsstand two blocks away on St. Nicholas Avenue.

Willie walked the first block, started to cross the street, and then, halfway across, felt someone grab his right arm, then someone else seize his left arm. The two men pushed him into a phone booth on the corner and shook him down to see if he had a gun. When he recovered from his surprise and looked at their faces, he recognized two police officers who had arrested him before on the subway. Willie was just too tempting a target, given all the publicity that was building about the subway killer, and the transit officers had acted prematurely.

Davin was apoplectic when the transit police brought Willie in. He had Willie in custody, but now he wasn't going to be able to hold him for long. Willie kept saying, "You got me on shit. You got me on nothing."

Davin had to speed up the search for Herman. Herman was on probation, the detective had noticed, but he knew from experience that people in the probation department were usually uncooperative when a cop called looking for one of their clients. Still, Davin put in a phone call. To his surprise, the person who answered was helpful and said Herman just happened to have been there a few minutes ago and had gone out with his probation officer for a job interview. Davin got the address and rushed downtown.

Herman was still there. Davin identified himself and said he would like to talk with Herman, but he couldn't say about what right now.

Please get in the car and come with us, he asked. Herman was agreeable and came along voluntarily. That was a tipoff to Davin that Herman wasn't too smart. He never asked any questions or pressed about his rights. Herman had wild, unkempt hair, sad eyes, and a receding chin. His expression added to Davin's sense that Herman was not a rocket scientist. They drove back uptown, to the office of the Sixth Homicide Zone, which was housed in the Twenty-fifth Precinct, on 119th Street in Harlem. When they arrived, Davin realized they had another problem. If Willie was looking out the window, he would see Herman being brought in. So they went in through a rear entrance in the basement, up to the homicide office on the third floor.

Davin started questioning Herman in the role of the bad cop, foaming at the mouth, a role he enjoyed. Detective Nicanor Vazquez, from the transit police, was the good cop.

"We know where you were on Monday, when that guy got shot on the Number 3 train," Davin pressed, his finger in Herman's face.

"No," said Herman. "I was sleeping in a movie theater on Forty-second Street, on the top floor landing."

"Bullshit," Davin interjected. "You're full of crap. We know you were with Willie that afternoon. Willie told us already. He gave you up."

Herman's eyes grew wide. Davin thought they were going to pop right out of his head.

"Yeah," Davin continued. "Your cousin has given you up, you goddamn idiot. Remember, he's only a kid. All he can do is a juvenile sentence. You're going away for twenty-five years to life."

"Well," Herman said, looking sorrowful, his eyes on the floor, "I ain't going to jail for something he did. I didn't shoot the guy."

"We know you didn't," Vazquez said, joining the conversation. "Let's get some coffee and soda." Food was brought in.

They were making quick progress, to Davin's relief. Often in murder cases, he knew, the person who didn't do the shooting doesn't understand the law. He thinks that if he didn't pull the trigger and only participated in the robbery, he can't be charged with murder. Herman was one of those, thought Davin; he didn't realize he was implicating himself.

Now they read Herman his rights. "First of all," Davin said, "we are here to try to help you. We're going to try to save you. Willie is trying to put all the weight on you, and goddamn it, that's wrong. You didn't do it, so why should you go to jail."

Here, Davin paused. "You know, I got kids as old as you. I feel bad about this. So let's just get this thing straight. We know the facts, we're just trying to find out who is lying."

Herman gave them the whole story on the death of Moises Perez.

When he finished, Davin said, "You're still lying. You left out the other one, on the nineteenth."

"No, I wasn't there," Herman said, his voice sadder all the time. "Willie told me he did it."

Herman also told them about the gun. It was Willie's pistol, he said. Willie had bought it and kept it just outside his bedroom window, on the sill of an abandoned building that was squeezed up next to his.

There it was, thought Davin, a big piece of the cake. Herman had just locked himself away for murder, and he had given them a lot of ammunition to use against Willie.

Davin now worried about finding the gun. He didn't know how much longer he would be able to hold Willie. Besides, anyone in Willie's family, knowing he had been arrested, could throw the gun away. So Davin put in a call to the Manhattan district attorney's office. Someone from the DA's office would have to go get the search warrant, and Davin also needed a prosecutor to come up and take Herman's formal confession.

Harvey Rosen took the call. He was a senior trial counsel in the district attorney's office assigned to homicide that day, which meant that he was on duty from 8 in the morning until 8 a.m. the following day, like a young intern in a hospital. He had to approve of any homicide arrests that came in. Rosen was a tall, lean, thirty-one-year-old with a bony, angular face, who bore more than a passing resemblance to Abraham Lincoln. He was born in the projects in the South Bronx to a father who was a machinist and a mother who was a telephone operator. That gave him street smarts and a quick, self-assured manner. He had gone to college in the sixties and took part in the whole radical scene, anti–Vietnam War demonstrations and civil rights protests. He was going to be a defense lawyer, to rid the system of injustice, until a summer internship in the district attorney's office during law school turned his thinking around.

Davin told Rosen about Willie's gun and where Herman said it could be found. Get a search warrant as fast as possible, Davin said, and we will come down to pick you up. Rosen pulled out a search warrant form and filled it in:

In the name of the People of the State of New York:
To any police officer of the City of New York:

Proof by affidavit having been made this day before me by Det. Martin Davin, Shield #709, 6th Homicide Zone, that there is probable cause for believing that certain property, to wit, a .22 caliber pistol with a brown handle may be found at 313 West 145th Street,

Apt. 2E, or on an adjoining window sill of a vacant apartment, said window sill adjoining defendant's bedroom.

You are therefore commanded to make an immediate search.

Rosen rushed over to the Criminal Court Building across the street from his office and got a judge to sign the search warrant. Davin was waiting for him in an unmarked police car with another detective dressed in a ten-gallon hat. That was Vazquez, who was driving. By now it was almost 5 o'clock, rush hour, and they were down near the bottom of Manhattan. They had to get all the way back up to 145th Street. At that time of day, it could easily take an hour.

Vazquez was driving fast, like crazy, Rosen thought. Davin kept saying, "We've got to get up there fast, before someone gets rid of the gun," and Vazquez drove even faster. On Park Avenue, Vazquez went up onto the sidewalk to get around the traffic. Rosen thought they were all going to be killed.

The detectives dropped Rosen off at the Sixth Homicide Zone, to get Herman's confession, then went to Willie's apartment. Laura met them at the door, on her way out. She had finally received word that Willie had been arrested and was headed for the police station. Davin showed her the search warrant.

Laura was in a dilemma. It was too much like the time the Milwaukee police had questioned her about Butch's role in the murders there. She was trapped whatever she did. There had been an argument in the family about what to do with the gun. The way Cheryl remembered it later, Laura's boyfriend of the time urged her to get rid of it, so there would be no evidence against Willie. But Laura said no. She was worried that if she threw the gun away, the police might find out and implicate her in the murders. Besides, Cheryl believed, Laura also wanted to put a stop to the killing. She was a mother, after all, and a few years in jail was better for Willie than getting shot down in the street, which was where she was afraid he was headed if all this continued. Laura wasn't selling him out, Cheryl thought, just trying to do what she believed was the right thing. So the family looked for the gun, and when they found it, they wrapped it in a cloth. It was at that moment that the detectives arrived.

"Look," Davin said to her, trying to strike a balance between sounding tough and sounding sympathetic, "we can make a big thing out of this. I could tear your house apart. I could get sweat all over my suit. Or you could just show me where the gun is and let me go in there."

Laura took a long breath. "Okay," she said.

Davin could sense the tension in her. He guessed she was worried

Willie would kill her if he found out. "I promise I will never tell Willie," the detective added. "Don't worry. In court, I won't even look at you, and if I do, I'll look very hostile."

At the station house, Rosen had easily obtained Herman's full confession with a stenographer to record it. Questioning Willie was much tougher. Willie, it was obvious to Rosen, was much brighter and more belligerent than Herman. After Laura arrived and came into the room, it was legal to talk with Willie, and Rosen began with a few simple questions. They were all sitting around a table.

"I ain't saying nothing," Willie said.

"Now the district attorney is just going to advise you of your rights again," Davin interjected.

Willie was adamant. "I ain't talking to nobody that cannot open them two doors and let me out."

Then Willie smiled at Rosen. "I wouldn't use a gun on you; if I was going to do anything to you, I'd use a knife."

In all the years Rosen and Davin had interrogated suspects, they had never heard anyone this hardbitten, or seen anyone threaten the district attorney like that. Often a person being questioned would show remorse, or at least fear of going to jail. Willie showed nothing. Rosen looked over at Laura, but she was sitting there impassively, not saying a word.

Rosen knew he was facing a tough case. But he had learned that if you look at kids long enough and don't say anything, just look at them, their macho pretensions will take over, and they will eventually start mouthing off. So Rosen stared at Willie, and Willie stared back. After five minutes of silent confrontation, Willie blurted out, "The only thing you have on me is the gun, and I found it two and a half weeks ago and it's been with me ever since." He said he had found the gun when he saw some cops chasing a man who threw it under a car, and he picked it up. "That's all you got on me, you honky white motherfucker."

This was a big blunder by Willie; it tied him to the gun. The murders had taken place in the past two weeks, and here was Willie admitting he had had the gun during that time. Willie's bravado, which had served him so well for so long, now became his downfall.

IN THE PAST, Willie's case would have been prosecuted in Family Court by a corporation counsel. Willie had often done well against the inexperienced, overworked corporation counsels. They did not have a warrant squad to ensure witnesses showed up in court. They had no time to run lineups. They seldom interrogated suspects. Usually, the first time they met a defendant was when the case was heard in court. In short, they lacked all the tools of the trade that a regular prosecutor had in adult criminal courts. This tended to tilt the balance in favor of the more skilled law guardians from the Legal Aid Society, like Kay McNally, and their young clients, like Willie.

But by the mid-1970s, with mounting public concern over a dramatic increase in violent juvenile crime, the Family Court system was being revised. From 1960 to 1975 alone, arrests of young people for murder, rape, robbery, and assault tripled. It felt like an epidemic, and for the first time teenage crime suddenly became a big issue for Americans. In New York State, reporters and politicians who had long been critical of the Family Court and the Division for Youth for being too harsh on young people now began finding that the juvenile justice system was too soft on violent kids. The initial result of this change in sentiment in New York was the passage of the Juvenile Justice Reform Act of 1976. It created a new category of juvenile crime, the "designated felony," which allowed kids as young as fourteen who committed violent acts like murder and rape to be given longer sentences. Instead of the traditional limit of eighteen months, they could now be sent to a training school for three to five years. Judges were also instructed to consider "the need for the protection of the community," not just the best interests of the child, the old criterion. And, significantly, district attorneys replaced corporation counsels in trying designated felonies. The odds in court were being changed.

In Manhattan, the first professional prosecutor to be sent from the district attorney's office into the Family Court was Robert Silbering, a jaunty, animated, thirty-one-year-old with light brown hair and the manners of a politician. He moved easily around the courthouses arrayed in the caverns of lower Manhattan, seemingly knowing everyone, and always ready with an affectionate quip. "You're the greatest, you're the best," he said to friends on the phone or in the hallways, and the judges in Family Court, who were initially suspicious of his coming, began to appreciate his expertise. Silbering's parents were immigrants from Russia. His father worked in the garment center, and they had all lived with his grandfather in an apartment in the Bronx to save money. After college, Silbering worked his way through law school at night by teaching. Like Davin and Rosen, he was another street-smart New Yorker. Officially, his title was assistant district attorney and head of the Juvenile Offense Bureau, which he had set up only at the end of 1977, a few months before Willie's arrest for murder. This would be his biggest case.

Even though the police had found the gun in Willie's apartment, and even though a ballistics test showed it was the weapon that murdered Moises Perez, Silbering worried that all he had was a circumstantial case.

He had no witnesses to the two murders and no confession from Willie. Willie had pleaded not guilty, and his lawyer was expressing confidence that she had a strong defense. So Silbering worked methodically to build the evidence against Willie. Some transit police took pictures to Anthony Lamorte, who was in the hospital recovering from his wound, to do a photo lineup. Willie was scowling in the black-and-white photograph they showed Lamorte, and his cherubic smile didn't show, making it hard for Lamorte to recognize him. But when Lamorte hesitated, one of the police pointed knowingly at the picture of Willie, and Lamorte said, "Yeah, that's the guy."

It was easier at a regular lineup in the police office downtown, with Willie there in person. Lamorte picked him out right away from the five other boys who had been assembled. "That's him," he said. "The baby-faced one." Somebody leaked Lamorte's description to the newspapers. The press still did not know Willie's name because of the confidentiality rules of the Family Court, so the papers began calling Willie the baby-face killer.

Silbering also pressed Harvey Rosen to squeeze Herman, to get him to agree to come in and testify against his cousin. Rosen offered Herman a deal. If he testified against Willie, he could plead guilty to manslaughter one—with a recommended sentence of eight and a half to twenty-five years. If he didn't, he faced a felony murder charge with a sentence of twenty-five years to life. Herman decided not to take the weight and voiced only one concern. When he got shipped upstate to prison, he asked, would he still get credit for the automotive course he had taken while on Rikers Island? Davin felt bad for a young man who asked such a pathetic question in the face of a long prison term. He assured Herman he would get credit. Davin, Rosen, and Silbering all considered themselves lucky that Herman was not any smarter than that. With his testimony, they believed, Willie was going to go down.

The trial was held in the new Manhattan Family Court Building that had opened in 1976, an eleven-story black granite fortress with a few oddly spaced windows that looked like gun portals. It was located at 60 Lafayette Street, across the street from the Criminal Court and the federal courthouse, where graduates of the Family Court might someday end up. Already, by the time Willie's trial began in April 1978, the new Family Court building was covered with a layer of grime and graffiti, the orange and blue plastic seats in its public waiting areas were broken, and the toilets in the men's rooms were out of order. The crowd of black and Hispanic faces that thronged the Family Court reminded Willie of going to the welfare office.

Technically, Willie was charged with three separate designated felonies—two counts of murder and one of attempted murder—so there were three different trials. But all three cases were heard in Part IV, the new designated felonies part, by Judge Edith Miller, one of the first black justices in the Family Court. Judge Miller was a good-hearted, gracious woman whose grandparents had come from the West Indies. She was also a devout Roman Catholic who, after finishing law school, had gone to work for the Legal Aid Society. There she did landlord-tenant, child custody, and divorce cases for the poor people of New York. Judge Miller already knew a little about Willie. He had appeared before her when she was sitting at intake for several of his minor crimes on the subway, and he had impressed her as an unusually bright, handsome boy with great personal charm. One day at lunchtime, when Laura was buying Willie a hot dog outside the courthouse, Judge Miller ran into them and said to Willie, "Young man, when are you going to stop causing your mother all this trouble?" Willie just looked at her. That was when he noticed she had great legs.

Judge Miller was not prepared for the Willie Bosket now before her. Almost as soon as the hearings began, on April 6, Willie acted nasty in court. When Davin testified, he called the detective a "fucking liar" and had to be restrained. Another day, after Silbering cross-examined his mother, Willie walked over and spit on Silbering's head. He even threatened to kill Judge Miller herself. She shook that off. What upset her more was that Willie seemed to lack any moral sense. At the probable cause hearing, he made Amalia Perez, the widow of Moises Perez, come in to testify that she had gone to the morgue and identified the body as that of her husband. Normally, a defendant in a murder trial will waive the appearance of the family member who identified the corpse, to spare the person further anguish. Willie insisted on it. Mrs. Perez was in a daze, and Judge Miller's heart went out to her. Willie was hurting himself. Since the case was in Family Court, this was not a jury trial. In Family Court, everything was up to the judge.

One thing gnawing at Willie was that since he had been arrested on March 31, he had been confined in Spofford. He had never had to stay at Spofford for a prolonged period before because he had always found a way to get out and go home. Willie hated the regimentation at Spofford. They made you go to school every day, and whenever you went anywhere, you had to march military fashion, from locked door to locked door. As his three trials dragged on, from April into June, Willie grew increasingly restive. It got worse when the police brought his younger sister, Shirley, to Spofford. She and a friend had stolen some money from a drug dealer, and then to cover up their act, set his apartment on fire. Having Shirley inside Spofford with him really hurt Willie. She had been the last hope of the family, and now she was trapped in the system, too. With all these tensions building, Willie began to get uncontrollable. One day, when another boy he didn't like sat down next to him in the cafeteria, Willie stabbed him in the neck with a fork. He also hit a counselor in the face with a metal mop wringer, breaking his nose, and he choked a psychiatrist who was trying to interview him. Judge Miller was disturbed when she received the reports about Willie's conduct at Spofford. They further damaged his cause.

Despite Willie's accumulating troubles, his lawyer, Kay McNally, still thought he had a chance; she felt that Herman would be a weak witness, and the testimony of a codefendant alone should not be enough to find Willie guilty. Yet as the three trials ground on, with so many hearings, it seemed as if every time Willie came into court from Spofford, he was getting more and more angry and detached, as if the whole thing was not really happening to him.

Eventually, Willie began to tell McNally that he didn't want a trial. "What do you mean?" she asked. "You either have to plead guilty or have a trial."

Willie didn't want to do either. To McNally, it was getting frustrating and bizarre. Laura was sitting there with him all the time in court, but she never said anything. It seemed as if the shootings had touched something deep inside her, like a wound in her soul, and there was nothing more she could do or say.

Now, each time Willie was brought into court, he asked McNally, "How much longer is this going to be? What are we doing this for? When is this going to be over?" Partly, it was that Willie didn't want his cousin Herman to have to come in and testify against him. It would make Herman into a rat, a snitch, leaving a lifelong stain on his reputation. Whatever else people said about Willie, he didn't want to do that to Herman.

But there was something else going on. On June 6, when the bus delivered him from Spofford, Willie told Seymour Gottfried, the Family Court probation officer whom he had known since he was nine years old, "I don't care anymore. Let them do what they want with me." Willie had lost his patience.

During a recess in the proceedings that day, Willie abruptly turned to McNally and said, "I just don't want to go to trial. They are going to find me guilty anyway."

McNally thought he was being irrational. But she went along with him. She said, "Then you have to enter a plea."

"Okay," Willie said. "I'll plead guilty." He was fed up with the whole thing. In the end, his impulsiveness did him in.

Silbering insisted that Willie plead guilty to all three crimes, the two murders and the shooting of Lamorte. June 6 was Silbering's birthday, and Willie's surprise admission was a big birthday present. All that was left was the sentencing. The maximum punishment for a designated felon was five years, certainly longer than the eighteen months that had been the limit until 1976. But given the seriousness of the crimes, and the extensive publicity in the newspapers and on television, Silbering tried to figure out a way to make it tougher. He thought maybe he could make the sentences consecutive, make three five-year sentences into fifteen years in prison. He couldn't; there was no precedent.

Sentencing was set for June 27. Judge Miller knew that Family Court was coming in for criticism, for having failed to do something about Willie, but she thought that was unfair. Family Court was only a forum to decide cases. It did not have the resources to give successful treatment to kids, or the power to compel the Division for Youth to keep kids. It wasn't Family Court that had failed, thought Judge Miller. What had failed were the values of America. This wasn't a racial problem, but a cultural and an economic problem. She found reading Dickens consoling. His descriptions of the conditions of the city in nineteenth-century England were all too familiar. Just substitute cocaine for the gin in England.

Judge Miller sentenced Willie to the maximum—that he "be placed with the Division for Youth for an initial period of five years." Whatever happened, he would have to be freed when he reached his twenty-first birthday, in December 1983, five and a half years away. That was the law.

TWO DAYS AFTER WILLIE was sentenced, Governor Hugh Carey was flying in his state plane from New York to Rochester to make a campaign appearance. Carey, a liberal Democrat, was in the midst of a tough reelection battle, and his Republican opponent, Perry Duryea, was attacking the governor for being soft on crime, especially the rising tide of juvenile crime. Duryea had an answer to the problem, a proposed new law that would permit kids to be tried as adults for violent crimes. Duryea's plan was widely backed by Republicans throughout the state, as well as by some Democrats.

Carey knew there was mounting public support for the get-tough approach, but he had strongly resisted it as being too drastic and unfair. This morning, however, riding in his plane, the governor was reading the New York papers. It was bad enough the press had learned the confidential terms of the five-year sentence given Willie for killing two people. But the *Daily News* had a more detailed story under the headline "He's 15 and He Likes to Kill—Because It's Fun." The *News* reported that Herman had told detectives that Willie shot his victims because "he got a kick out of blowing them away." As Carey read on, it got worse. The *News* also said that Sylvia Honig, the maverick social worker at Brookwood, had written to Peter Edelman a few weeks before Willie was released, warning that he was dangerous.

Carey exploded. He called together the reporters aboard his plane and held an impromptu midair press conference. He was now shifting his position and would support trying juveniles as adults for violent crimes, he told the startled reporters. "There was a breakdown of the system, and it is really on the doorstep of the Division for Youth," the governor said. "The blame is squarely on the shoulders of the department."

It was an embarrassing slap at Peter Edelman, who felt the criticism was unfair. Many well-intentioned people had worked hard with Willie over the years, he believed. But what exactly do you do with a child like Willie who is so explosive? There was no right place to put him, and no real treatment for him, Edelman concluded. Neither the system nor anyone in particular was to blame, he insisted. Thank God, Edelman thought, there are few children like Willie.

Still, Carey made a bold promise to the public. The new law would make sure that Willie Bosket "never walks the street again."

A week later, Carey called the legislature back to Albany for a special session. He got the new law, the Juvenile Offender Act of 1978, passed in record time. Under its terms, kids as young as thirteen could now be tried in adult criminal court for murder and would face the same penalties as adults. This was not a small matter. The new law represented a sharp reversal of 150 years of American history, dating to the founding of the New York House of Refuge in 1825. It was the first break with the progressive tradition of treating children separately from adults, both in special family courts and in juvenile reformatories outside the regular prison system. The new law also marked a departure from the cherished American ideal of rehabilitation—the notion that kids could be changed and saved. Rehabilitation wasn't working, backers of the new law believed. Bad kids should be locked up and punished, not treated.

With the passage of the law, New York became the first state in the country to take this conservative step. Later, as violent juvenile crime continued to rise, other states would follow. It was a watershed in American juvenile justice policy. In New York, the press, the police, and prosecutors all took to calling it the Willie Bosket law. Willie had made history.

PART IV

CHAPTER 12

BUTCH

The Prisoner and the Scholar

Prisons are the gauge of the level of a civilization.

Attributed to Fyodor Dostoyevsky

AFTER THE DRIVE UP from Milwaukee across miles of rolling farmland, Wisconsin State Prison loomed like a gothic fortress. It had an ominous, gloomy look, like many of the big, old-time joints, with high gray stone walls and watchtowers manned by armed guards. Out front, there was a somber iron-work gate, and inside the wall, the huge cellblocks were arranged like spokes on a wheel around a central hub. When a new convict was admitted, he had to pass through four sets of doors, each made with heavy waffle bars. The sound of the metal doors slamming shut echoed down the corridors for a long time, imparting a sense of permanence. The sight of the prison and its sounds sucked out Butch's breath the day he arrived, March 2, 1963. He was facing a life sentence and was far from New York and his wife and newborn son, Willie, whom he had not seen.

The prison was located in Waupun, fifty miles northwest of Milwaukee, and the convicts referred to the prison by the name of the town. It had originally been built in 1853 and was modeled after the pioneering New York State prison at Auburn. Auburn was designed in the 1820s by reformers who believed that crime resulted from the vices of society—negligent parents, taverns, gambling halls, and houses of prostitution. Given the origin of crime, they were convinced that malefactors could be rehabilitated by perfect isolation in a new form of jail they called a penitentiary. To realize their plan, Auburn's architects made the inmates sleep alone in their cells at night and forbade them to talk with fellow convicts whether at work, at meals, or in the cellblocks. This scheme, which came to be known as the silence system, left a deep impression on visitors who came to study Auburn from other parts of the United States and from Europe. After an inspection in 1831, Alexis de Tocqueville wrote: "Everything passes in the most profound silence, and nothing is heard in the whole prison but the steps of those who march, or sounds proceeding from the workshops." After the prisoners were brought back to their cells at night, "the silence within these vast walls . . . is that of death. . . . There were a thousand living beings, and yet it was a desert solitude."

When Butch arrived at Waupun, the prison still employed some of the old silence system. There was supposed to be no talking in the cell halls, no conversation at work in the prison's shops, and no banter in the dining room, called the Big Top, a large room at the center of the spokes, with a high, copper-topped dome. At meals, the inmates sat facing in one direction, with guards armed with lead-tipped canes standing in the aisles behind them. In the middle of the Big Top was a glass-enclosed gun tower.

Waupun was tightly run. There were no newspapers. The radio carried music and sports, no news. And convicts could write only one letter a week, which was censored.

The cellblocks were derived from the ingenious design of the first warden at Auburn, William Brittin. In the center of each hall was an island of cells that was stacked four tiers high and surrounded on all sides by a vacant area about ten feet wide for walk space. The cells themselves were so narrow that when you stood, you could touch both walls. They held a bunk on chains from the wall, a toilet, and a small sink. Both the honeycomb of cells and the area around it were in turn enclosed by the outer shell of the building, broken here and there by windows. So the cellblock became a prison within a prison. If a convict broke out of his cellblock, he still had to find a way to get over the outer wall of the prison to escape. You could travel all across America, from Sing Sing to Leavenworth, and all the older prisons looked alike, as if they had been built by the same man using the same set of stone building blocks.

Butch was issued rough green woolen pants and a green workshirt, like the other eight hundred prisoners at Waupun, and he was assigned to work as a bindery helper in the prison print shop. His job did not go well. The guard in charge of the shop found him to be "a nuisance, who is not a good team worker. He is not ambitious, and tends to shirk work, which he feels is not good enough for him. He indulges in minor rule infractions on the sly, then when he is caught he tries to give a good impression and appears very repentant. He is a con man."

Butch quickly developed a reputation among the other convicts. He already knew from his early life on the streets and his time in reformatories and prisons in New York that there was a code for survival, the predators' code. In Waupun, they put it simply: "Kill or be killed." You either exploited someone else, or they exploited you. There was no room for humanity or intimacy; you had to learn to shut those feelings off. If you were young and attractive, you had to deal with convicts who wanted to extort sex from you. If you had a wife on the outside, you had to cope with convicts who would extort you to bring in drugs or money or else they would harm your family. You could die over a pack of cigarettes. Taxpayers thought building prisons was a good idea, a way to get criminals to reform their behavior. In truth, it usually worked the other way around. Prison made criminals into more confirmed criminals. You learned to adapt. The experience shaped your values.

It was in Butch's favor that he had been sentenced for murder. That made him a professional criminal, in the eyes of the other convicts, along with the bank robbers, the technically proficient burglars, and the big-time forgers. It elevated him to the highest rank in the joint. At the bottom of the pecking order were the sex offenders, who wore blue tags sewn on their shirtsleeves. They were called "devs," for deviants. It also helped that Butch was physically dominating, with the body of a football running back, now six feet two and approaching two hundred pounds, well-sculpted by weightlifting during his earlier years in prison. He had big arms, a broad chest, and a narrow waist. There were prominent scars on his chin. And there were his eyes; they always seemed to be on the alert, scanning a room, bulging if he sensed trouble. He radiated rage and danger. When Butch was around, it was like walking by a live high-transmission wire with no insulation. He just hummed and smoked with a blue glow, some of the other convicts thought. Perhaps it was an act, to scare others off preemptively. Acting crazy was an old prison trick. But Butch also backed it up.

One day, early in his incarceration at Waupun, Butch was working in the kitchen. He spotted a big Indian kid, even bigger than himself, and thought, "That guy's going to give me trouble." Twenty minutes later, the guards found the Indian in the meat locker, unconscious. Walter Birk, another young inmate, who was in for forgery, saw that Butch was breathing heavily and both his hands were puffed up. "Well, that's over with," Butch said softly, so the guards wouldn't hear. "He won't be coming up behind me."

Another time, Birk, who was nineteen but looked only about twelve and was cute in a boyish way, was sitting in his cell with the door open. An inmate, called the tiertender, came by to bring hot water for shaving and washing. When he entered Birk's cell, he threw a couple of packs of cigarettes and some candy bars and potato chips on the bunk. "When you make canteen, you can pay me back," the tiertender whispered.

"I don't know if I like this," Birk said softly to Butch, who was in the next cell. "He's thinking about raping you," Butch responded. Butch got a bar of soap and put it in a sock. "Keep this under your pillow, and when the guy comes back into your cell, whack him as hard as you can. That's probably the last fight you'll ever have to have in the joint."

The next day, the tiertender came back and started for Birk. Birk smashed him in the head with the sock, knocking him out. Butch dragged the man out of the cell and yelled for the guards. "Hey, this guy's had a heart attack." When the guards rolled the man over, sure enough, he had a mop handle stuck in his belt. Birk thought, "Butch was absolutely right." It was as if Butch had a sixth sense about what was going to happen in prison.

Over time, Butch's reputation spread so he could control a room just by walking into it, his mere presence intimidating. If he came into a room and there was no chair available, Butch had only to look at someone and he would yield his chair. This led prison officials to put Butch down as "the strong armed type who will throw his weight around and take advantage of weaker inmates."

But despite the prison authorities' conviction that Butch was "a bad ass prisoner," as some of them put it, another side of him slowly began to emerge at Waupun. Wisconsin had long been known as a progressive state—it had abolished the death penalty all the way back in 1853—and the convicts believed that a man could work his way out through education. Classes in the 1960s were readily available as part of the state's generous rehabilitation program, and if you kept out of trouble and studied hard, you had a good chance at parole. The inmates called it "programming your way out." There was even a story at Waupun about a man who committed a double homicide and won a parole after only four years because he did so well in school. Besides, going to class was a lot easier than working in the print shop or the laundry, the places Butch was being assigned. Birk persuaded Butch to try a class.

Butch started with high school–level courses in English and American history. Soon, he was also taking classes in algebra, mechanical drawing, typing, and bookkeeping. For a man who had never gone to school regularly, unless you counted up to the fifth grade in reformatory, he did very well. The first report on him, in September 1963, six months after he was imprisoned at Waupun, described Butch as "making exceedingly good progress. This man is very intense about learning everything." Butch had finally found a way to compete, and compete successfully, in the straight world. After a lifetime of disappointments, rebuffs, and failures, it was exhilarating.

In February 1964, a teacher noted in Butch's file, "This young man is quite intelligent." Butch was doing so well, in fact, that the teacher also reported, "He is now anxious to qualify for a high school equivalency certificate. The real important thing to him at this point seems to be his schooling."

As long as Butch was at Waupun, however, he could go to school only half-time; he had to work the other half of the day. So the trick for him was to develop a good enough reputation with prison officials to win a transfer. In November 1964, a year and a half after being sentenced, Butch was transferred to Wisconsin State Reformatory at Green Bay. It was still a maximum security joint, but he could go to school full-time. There he got his high school equivalency diploma. Butch now had higher aspirations—to take college courses. For that, he needed another promotion, to the Wisconsin Correctional Institution at Fox Lake, a medium security prison.

Some prison officials had come to believe in him. "Much to my dismay," wrote a social worker, Kurt Plachetta, "Mr. Bosket is one of the best-read individuals I have ever met and he certainly incorporates his newfound knowledge as much as possible. I think it is well-known the strides he has made along educational channels and he certainly wishes to improve himself. He readily gives the impression of sincerity, intelligence and the capacity for reform." In a later report, Plachetta said, "Butch has assisted this social worker on numerous occasions with young, wild, hostile and violent blacks in getting them to adjust."

Other prison authorities were more skeptical. "The inmate emerges very clearly as a sociopathic personality from a clear-cut dissocial background," reported a prison psychiatrist, Konstantin Geocaris. "He is a smooth talker who has a capacity to be quite seductive and manipulative and tends to want to say the kinds of things that people expect of him or want of him. I doubt he has ever really had any close, meaningful interpersonal relationships that have been enduring. It is my feeling that most of his contacts with others are fairly superficial and are used for him to meet his ends.

"Needless to say, sociopaths are not the greatest therapeutic prospects in the psychiatric sense," Dr. Geocaris added.

Still, the psychiatrist reasoned, "If he could gain enough narcissistic gratification and learn ways of coping more successfully so that he could function as a well-adjusted psychopath, he may be able to ultimately find his place in society without attacking people or defeating himself." In other words, Butch would always be a psychopath, but he might become a psychopath who could function in the outside world. There were certainly a lot of them around.

Dr. Geocaris concluded that perhaps Butch should be considered for a transfer to Fox Lake. "There is little more to be gained in keeping this man in this institution. He has made the greatest use of our available rehabilitative procedures." Eventually, Dr. Geocaris ventured, "If he is able to continue his gains at Fox Lake at the pace he has here, he might even be favorably considered for parole." That was a pretty good evaluation for a man who had committed a double murder and was serving a life sentence.

IN 1970, SEVEN YEARS after being incarcerated in Wisconsin, Butch finally got his transfer to Fox Lake. It was luxurious compared to what he was used to—a modern-style prison with individual rooms rather than cells. From the outside, it looked more like a college dormitory than a penitentiary, and there were even stories of people who drove by Fox Lake and asked how they could get their sons into school there. Inmates, in fact, could enroll in extension classes given by the University of Wisconsin at Oshkosh.

The convict in the room next to Butch was a tall, very skinny, middle-class Jewish kid, Michael Schoenfield. Schoenfield had been arrested for possession of three joints of marijuana in a restaurant in Milwaukee in 1968. It was shortly after the tumultuous Democratic National Convention in Chicago that year, and it was Schoenfield's bad luck that possession of pot was still a felony in Wisconsin. A few months later, the state reduced the charge to a misdemeanor. Schoenfield was a college student who had dropped out to be an anti–Vietnam War activist and then a campaign worker for Senator Robert Kennedy. After Kennedy was assassinated, he switched to Eugene McCarthy. The Chicago convention, with all of Mayor Daley's police, the violence, and the nomination of Hubert Humphrey, had left Schoenfield feeling burned out. He had taken part in a demonstration soon after the convention, during which he set fire to his draft card, and it was that afternoon he got arrested. So he always believed that the real reason the cops had picked him up was because he had burned his Selective Service card.

By the time Schoenfield got to Fox Lake, he was disgusted with the world and his mind was messed up. Richard Nixon had been elected president and had expanded the war in Vietnam. It seemed as if none of the things Schoenfield believed in had come about. He still had a fantasy that he might start the revolution in prison, organizing the prisoners.

They were the downtrodden, the vanguard of the proletariat, according to the books he had read. And as a sixties radical, he believed he was just the person to lead them in redistributing the wealth of the country. That was when Schoenfield got his worst surprise. The convicts loved Nixon. They thought America was right in Vietnam. All in all, they were the most conservative group of people he had ever met, the bedrock of American imperialism, he concluded. Here he was, an intellectual, with no one to talk to in prison. Besides, he was physically very vulnerable, being so young and weighing only about one hundred twenty pounds.

Then Butch arrived. Butch was already a legend in the Wisconsin prison system, and he was pretty scary-looking. But the way Schoenfield later figured it, Butch saved his life. Butch turned out to be the only person in Fox Lake he could talk to. Schoenfield had his books with him, and he started sharing them with Butch: copies of Karl Marx, Max Weber, *Steppenwolf* and *Demian* by Hermann Hesse, and Robert Heinlein's *Stranger in a Strange Land*. Schoenfield had most of the books that made up the counterculture top ten of the sixties, as well as a subscription to *Ramparts* magazine, the voice of the left, and Butch loved all of it. They started having bull sessions, just like in college, except they were in prison. They talked about class structure, sociological theory, weaknesses in the revolution. They were connecting intellectually. It got so they were calling each other brother, and meant it.

Schoenfield was taking a college extension class on modern fiction, and they were reading Henry James's novel *The Turn of the Screw*, esoteric stuff for convicted criminals. Butch signed up for the class, too. It was a new kind of challenge for him, as street fights had once been. He got an A on his term paper. That was when Schoenfield realized Butch was literally falling in love with academia, an intellectual manqué, he thought. Butch began saying that when he got paroled, he was going to move in with Schoenfield and attend the University of Wisconsin, maybe even get a Ph.D.

Butch's favorite book was *Steppenwolf*, Hesse's phantasmagoric account of a man driven by his longing for a higher reality, which he ultimately finds in a magic theater. It was Hesse's belief in magic and fantasy and his dissatisfaction with reality, as ordinary people perceived it, that appealed to Butch. If Steppenwolf could soar above the claustrophobic reality of everyday life through fantasy, so could Butch.

In March 1972, Schoenfield was released from prison, receiving a full pardon from Governor Patrick Lucey. He left his books behind with Butch, and Butch later began a long correspondence with Schoenfield and his wife, Barbara. In his letters, Butch reveled in his newfound erudition and talked repeatedly about his fascination with Hesse.

"*Steppenwolf* has become a virtual bible for me and I never tire of reading it," he wrote in one letter. "Actually, I feel something very personal, something spiritual, when I am going thru [*sic*] it. Perhaps *Steppenwolf* is an eye into my soul. It has helped me to uncover deeper and deeper layers of myself."

"Very simply," Butch confessed in a letter to Barbara Schoenfield, "as a child someone, somehow, taught me that all I had between myself and the ravages of the streets . . . was imagination and fantasy, and throughout the worst in my life I've very desperately clung to same."

"Hesse is a magical writer for magical people," Butch said in another letter. "He has helped me break through walls that I had spent a lifetime erecting."

Butch called this "walling up," or running. "Ever since I was a child, when confronted with situations in which I knew that I would more than likely have to take some hurt (my dad's drunken brutalities, my ma's indifference, a nasty street fight, battles with prison bureaucracies, etc.) . . . a kind of mood-film drops about my mind. I pull inside, make myself numb, to endure, to make myself stronger." But *Steppenwolf*, Butch wrote, has now "completed my spiritual liberation."

Michael Schoenfield himself came to believe there was a simpler, more direct explanation for Hesse's appeal to Butch. For Butch, who had been in reformatories and prisons for so many years, fantasy offered a way out. Through fantasy, Butch could imagine himself to be totally free even when he was behind bars.

Soon after Schoenfield was released from Fox Lake, Butch began getting in trouble. It was as if his unlikely relationship with a Jewish college radical had been a stabilizing influence on him. Only three weeks after Schoenfield left, the warden received reports that Butch was organizing a ring of inmates, controlling gambling within the prison, extorting protection money from other convicts, and forcing selected prisoners into homosexual acts with him at knifepoint. Butch insisted he was innocent. The prison authorities, in fact, had no direct evidence against him, but they had chosen to believe the testimony of several other inmates. Six months later, in September 1972, Butch was shipped back to Waupun, Wisconsin's most secure prison, and put in solitary confinement.

The transfer was a huge setback for Butch. It effectively blocked his dream of getting a college degree while in prison. Schoenfield thought the charges were a frame-up. He never had a sexual relationship with Butch, and he never knew Butch to force another inmate into a sexual relationship, because Butch didn't need to do that—there were guys who wanted him sexually. Many people in prison get to be bisexual. You can make love to your hand only for so long. And Butch had been in prison practically his whole life. So Butch had partners, but they freely initiated the encounters. Butch took the male role. A couple of times, Butch had asked Schoenfield to be a lookout while he was in the shower with a guy. The charges just didn't sound right to Schoenfield. He also remembered a time when a big, burly white inmate, a weightlifter, had tried to coerce a smaller prisoner into a homosexual role. Butch didn't like that and had called the bigger inmate out of his room. Then, bingo, Butch decked him. Butch had no relationship with the smaller man; that wasn't why he did it. It was just his good side.

In solitary, Butch went downhill fast. He became depressed, and a psychiatrist who examined him felt he was paranoid and delusional. All Butch's old fears were coming back. He was only a few months away from eligibility for parole, but it seemed to him that he would never get out of prison. He thought the system was out to get him, a black man acting too smart. A month after he was returned to Waupun, Butch had to be taken to Wisconsin General Hospital in Madison for a serious infection in his gums. While he was in the doctor's office, Butch found an iron pipe, brandished it at the guard who had been escorting him, and took off.

The police picked him up twelve hours later. Butch was charged with escape and attempted assault, and he could have been given ten more years in jail. But at his trial, in Dodge County Court, Judge Henry C. Gergen Jr. found him not guilty by reason of insanity. It was a lucky break. Instead of more prison time, the judge ordered Butch to Central State Hospital for the Criminally Insane. There he was diagnosed as suffering from "Schizophrenia, paranoid type," a very serious condition, and was placed on a heavy dosage of Thorazine, an antipsychotic drug. There didn't seem to be much hope for him. Butch's social worker wrote in his record, "It does not appear he will be returning to the prison."

Butch was so far gone, everyone believed, that the hospital began letting him work outside on the grounds, unsupervised. The staff seemed to have forgotten he had been sentenced for a double murder. But Butch wasn't as crazy as people thought. He had become close with a woman who worked for a private prisoners' services organization, another sixties radical, who had gotten to know him while visiting inmates in Waupun. She had fallen in love with Butch and, from time to time, brought him clothes and money. Then on October 5, 1974, while working on the hospital grounds, Butch just walked away. This time his escape was successful.

· · ·

THE DAY AFTER CHRISTMAS, a tall black man dressed in a dark-blue ski parka with a fur-trimmed hood stepped up to the teller's window of a branch of the Chemical Bank in New York. He handed the teller a note. In large capital letters, it read: "PASS $20, $50, $100 BILLS—IN WRAPPED PACKS. NOW." When she looked up, the man said to her, "See what it says. Do it!" He also had taken out a big .45-caliber automatic and was pointing it at her. She quickly reached into her cash drawer and handed him the contents, $2,144, which he stuffed into a large manila envelope. "Don't worry about it," the man said with a smile, just before he dashed for the door. "The bank's insured."

Butch was back in New York. He had returned as a bank robber, the profession with the highest ranking in the demimonde of prison in which he had come of age. After he escaped, he had tried working—as a dishwasher in a restaurant and as a machinist for an electric company, but the pay was bad and he became restless. He craved excitement.

Two weeks after the first robbery, he hit another bank, the Sterling National Bank and Trust Company on Sixth Avenue, near Rockefeller Center. He walked out with forty-five hundred dollars.

Butch was starting to feel better about himself. The straight world had rejected him, despite all his efforts to reform himself through education. Now he would live by his own code. What he wanted more than anything was a family; it was like a piece of him that had been missing all his life. He considered going to see his son, Willie, whom he had still never met, but that would have been too risky. The police might be watching Willie's apartment. He made a few phone calls and learned that Willie had been sent to a reformatory. That saddened him. He sensed that Willie was caught in the same pattern of neglect and delinquency that had consumed his own childhood, but Butch thought there was nothing he could do for his son now. He couldn't very well walk into the reform school.

So Butch searched elsewhere for the elusive family he so badly wanted. He wandered out to St. Louis, and later to Chicago, where he bought a Chevy Impala and stayed in the YMCA on South Wabash Avenue. There he met a pair of sixteen-year-olds, Jimmy and Mary, who had run away from their homes in a small Midwest town and had no money and no place to stay. Butch took them in, then bought some grass and shared it with them. They got stoned together, and Butch told them fabulous tales of robbing banks and getting rich and killing cops and traveling all over the world. Jimmy and Mary were so young and innocent, and yet so loving to him. The couple's names and plight had a biblical ring to Butch. That was when he began to think the three of them would make a great family. After a few days of good grass and good talk, they piled into Butch's new car and headed for New York.

They checked in at a hotel, the Embassy, on Broadway and Seventieth Street, near Lincoln Center. One night, after Jimmy and Mary fell asleep, happily high, Butch took out a portable tape recorder he had purchased and let his thoughts flow onto a cassette:

These are the first recorded words in the family of three. I am he that was sent to make us free. Let the arms that I had meant to go home to assume the changes and discoveries that I've made over the past few years, this trek to my destiny. Our family has begun, time has no meaning. Well, I can remember when it was that our family joined flesh with me. There is Mary, the supreme mother, a thousand times woman, incredible, but by their standards she's just a child. And by their standards too, a child is Jimmy. Oh, Jimmy. Knew you how much for a brother that I loved and cared for you.

And yes, I understand what the voices have been trying to say. I have entered the magic theater, and now I must seek out those who are worthy to come into the magic theater. It is truly a terrifying experience, for in it you find yourself, just you, out there, live and in color, while they are trying to bury you in tombs and in prisons and insane asylums, crucifying you.

Well, today they can't bury me in prisons or asylums any more. We can have it all, if we come together in a family. That's our destiny. We are the new order and our time has come. The day of the herd is past, the day of the weak and the pious.

Now I say that we, the outsiders, so-called sociopaths, psychopaths, we have a divine right to power, because we are superior. I'm not talking about no fucking utopia. I'm talking about starting our family, and growing together. And then I say we can do anything we want to because we are together as a family. The key is money, baby, money. We can accumulate large sums of money by busting a few banks every now and then.

I guess you could call it being chosen. You dig it? I've been chosen to live this life. I could walk into the largest Federal Reserve bank in this fucking city, pull my gun out, rob it, and shit on the floor before I leave, and I still wouldn't get busted. I'm that protected. Can't nothing happen to me until I've done what I'm supposed to do, to be the most lowdown ruthless and vicious mother-fucker on the face of this earth.

And here is the paradox. I'm one of the hottest mother-fuckers in this country. I got FBI crawling out of every crack and corner and asshole in the country trying to get their hands on me. I've been convicted of two murders, broke out of prison, been sticking up banks ever since. And now here are these two sixteen-year-old kids. I love these kids so much. If every sixteen-year-old in the world was like these two, it wouldn't be necessary for a dude like me to try to tear up this mother-fucking society.

Frankly, I'm no idealist. I ain't got no mother-fucking morality. I don't like killing, and I don't dislike killing. I just do what I got to.

Someday, I'll be outnumbered. At any hour the pig could put his foot in the door and it's O.K. Corral time. Time to die and take company, because I ain't never gonna see the inside of a penitentiary again as long as I live. Anyway, I have nothing to lose, and like Jimmy said, the cool ones gotta die.

The only reason I haven't checked out death yet—death is just another trip to a higher level of power—is because I ain't taken care of everything I'm supposed to take care of down here. And I know what I got to do, and I got to do it.

A few days later, Mary and Jimmy drove Butch to the Manufacturers Hanover Trust Company branch on the corner of Second Avenue and Sixty-third Street. He was out in a minute with sixteen hundred dollars in cash. Butch was also waving his .45 Ruger automatic. They took Butch back to the hotel and left him there. Mary and Jimmy were frightened. It was more excitement than they had bargained for. They weren't cut out to be Bonnie and Clyde after all, they decided. So they just started driving fast, to get away.

Two New York City policemen in their patrol car spotted Jimmy driving. He looked awfully young to have a license, and he was going too fast. When the cops pulled Jimmy and Mary over, the couple was so scared, they just blurted out the whole story, all about Butch and the bank robberies and his gun. Up until then, although the FBI had been looking for the New York bank robber for six weeks, they had no clues about his identity or whereabouts. But that afternoon, January 31, 1975, a team of New York City detectives surprised Butch in his hotel room and arrested him. It happened so fast that, despite his vow, he didn't resist. Butch had wanted a family badly, and now he realized his new family had let him down, too. In the Federal House of Detention, Butch tried to kill himself by slashing his wrists.

Thomas Engel, an assistant United States attorney for the Southern District of New York, drew the assignment to prosecute Butch for bank robbery, a federal crime. When the United States marshals brought Butch into his office, Engel noticed that his hands had been cuffed behind him and his legs were in iron shackles, both unusual precautions. Butch was big, mean-looking, and intimidating. Engel had had many criminals come in front of him to be arraigned, but he had never been in the presence of anyone who inspired such complete terror.

When Engel learned from the FBI that Butch had escaped from prison in Wisconsin on a double murder sentence, he had a problem to resolve before he started to prosecute Butch. If Butch still had a long term to serve in Wisconsin before being eligible for parole there, "it would be a waste of time, expense and manpower, both of this office and of the Court" to try him for bank robbery in New York, he wrote to the Wisconsin attorney general, Bronson LaFollette.

An official in Wisconsin's Division of Corrections saw an opportunity in this. "Mr. Bosket is a native of N.Y.," the official confided in an internal memo. "I would be pleased to have N.Y. prosecute and sentence him there. Let them keep their own. This is why I think we ought to make his parole chances sound fairly optimistic. I would not like to deprive N.Y. of his presence."

Sure enough, when Engel received a return letter, Wisconsin said Butch was already eligible for parole and he would likely win his freedom "in the near future." Given Butch's record, that was not true, of course. He was supposed to be in a Wisconsin mental hospital for the criminally insane, and he also faced another sentence of five years in jail for the escape. But this was the story of Butch's life—no one wanted him.

Engel had to go ahead with the robbery case. Luckily, Butch saved everyone a lot of trouble by pleading guilty. He was sentenced on May 13, 1975, to fifteen years in a federal penitentiary.

THE SPECIAL ROOM was housed in the basement, under the Education Section of the United States Penitentiary at Leavenworth, Kansas. Leavenworth was the oldest federal prison—it had been built by convicts at the turn of the century—and was perhaps the most dangerous jail in the country. In the mid-1970s, Leavenworth averaged three stabbings a month and three murders per year. There was a palpable sense of fear in the prison. In this atmosphere, the basement room was an unlikely oasis of calm and reflection, the place where the intellectual elite of the prison labored, convicted murderers included. There were thirty men altogether in the basement room out of the twelve hundred in Leavenworth. Each had to have an IQ of more than 120 and a high school education. Then he had to pass a test in logic and undergo a year's training course. If he passed all these hurdles, he got to work in the special room. Each man had a big, capacious wooden desk, not just a prison-issue metal desk. The centerpiece of the chamber was a large IBM mainframe computer. For the convicts who worked in the room had been trained as the first inmate computer programmers in the country, and they wrote programs for use by the departments of Labor, Agriculture, and Justice. They did not have terminals, so they wrote out the programs in longhand, then converted them to punch cards and got a printout to work with back at their desks. In a big prison like Leavenworth, where hierarchy was all-important, being picked to work in the computer room was an honor, a mark of respect. A real "kick ass program," the prisoners called it.

When Butch was sent to Leavenworth, he applied to get into the computer room as quickly as possible. He had the mandatory IQ and had earned his high school diploma in prison in Wisconsin. The computer room was part of UNICOR, the federal prison industry agency, and was run by a stocky, well-educated African-American named Jim Martin. He had been in the Special Forces in Vietnam, the convicts said, and spoke Chinese and had worked with the CIA. That created an aura of power and mystery about him, much like the aura around Butch himself, and Butch and Martin hit it off well from the start. So after his year's training, Butch went to work as a computer programmer.

Leavenworth also had college courses taught by faculty from the University of Kansas, real live professors from a big-time school. This excited Butch; it offered him a chance to revive his dream of earning a college degree. At the time, the Federal Bureau of Prisons followed what was called "the medical model of rehabilitation." A criminal committed a crime, it was presumed, because he was sick, and he could be cured if the sickness was properly treated, just as with someone who was physically ill. In the 1960s and early 1970s, the belief was that a criminal's sickness was caused by poverty, a bad environment, a lack of job skills, and most important, a poor education. So the bureau tested inmates and prescribed medicine in the form of schooling. All Butch needed was two hundred dollars a semester to pay for his classes. That was no problem; he earned that much in two months working as a programmer. Butch's sentence for bank robbery was fifteen years. But with good behavior and a college degree, he figured he had a chance of getting paroled in as little as five years, in 1980. It was a chance worth focusing all his restless energy on.

By his second year in Leavenworth, Butch was following a remarkably rigorous schedule. He rose at 6:30 every morning, worked as a computer programmer from 7:30 a.m. to 4:30 in the afternoon, napped until 6, took classes from 6 to 9, and studied until 1 or 2 a.m. He also ran three miles a day during the week, and twelve miles on Saturday and Sunday.

After a while, to increase his self-discipline, he took up yoga and became a vegetarian. For his first semester, Butch enrolled in classes in American history, college algebra, business law, and world literature. To the astonishment of the prison authorities, he earned an A in each. He repeated the feat the next semester, and the next, and the next. And he had no disciplinary reports by the guards. None. "In all facets of confinement," wrote the case manager on his cellblock, "Mr. Bosket is considered an excellent inmate."

By now, Butch was getting giddy with delight at his new self. He wrote about his new world to his old prison friend, Michael Schoenfield.

> Leavenworth
> January 18

Dear Michael:

My primary interest, my raison d'etre, if you will, is to establish myself as a serious author, and perhaps, as an academic. Most definitely, I am not interested in a quick fix. . . . Make no mistake about it, I am a very serious scholar.

Another factor at work in my optimism is this: Michael, when I ran from the hospital and re-introduced myself to the "streets," I knew instantly that I had merely run from one tomb to another tomb. I cannot ever go back to that. Hence I am through running. The only path open to me is to obtain my freedom through the machinery of the system. Prison is no longer acceptable to me as a rational thinking human being.

I am fully aware that I have a long history of antisocial and violent behavior. Still, by sheer dent [*sic*] of will and sincere desire, I have accomplished what borders nigh upon the impossible. I do not believe that this society has grown too hardened and coarse as to not be responsive to this.

At work intrinsically within me is the notion that: cogito ergo sum. I think, therefore I exist. I am, and will remain positive, and optimistic. The sociopathic behavior of my past, and whatever character disorders which accompanied said behavior were environmentally induced, and I have effectively conquered them by rising above my environment. . . . It was an environment I utterly detested. At the time, I was trapped and could only find freedom by manipulating that environment.

"Butch" is dead. I do not miss him at all.

> Ever struggling,
> Butch

The Schoenfields were ecstatic with news of Butch's progress—they knew he was brilliant. But they worried about the temptations of prison and the danger of Butch not being able to maintain his self-control. So Butch wrote to reassure them.

Leavenworth

February 23

Dear Mike:

Please remove any thoughts that may be tipping thru [*sic*] about the possibility of me "backsliding." It is not even remotely possible. I have cleaned myself of street dirt and thoughts to the point that I know such would never present a problem again. I am thru [*sic*] running. There is no place for me to go but forward.

I am always in control of myself now. As you noted in your letter, in the past I always tended to be my own worst enemy. I've truly cured myself of that. I've literally learned to internalize discipline to levels that approach asceticism.

Sincerely,

Butch

Gradually as their correspondence increased, Butch began to reveal more layers of himself, and also to dream bigger dreams.

Leavenworth

February 28

Dear Michael:

As you note so cogently, I project an "air" of a thug often. In many respects, this has been my albatross. Simply put, I need help in ridding myself of the image. Circumstances have made me a very closed and isolated man.

Your brother,

Butch

Leavenworth

April 6

Dear Michael:

Hey, about downhill skiing: it sounds terrific! Really. Mike, I want to spend as much time as humanly possible out-of-doors when I leave this madness. I need to be close to nature—with the earth. In fact, as soon as I can make it happen, I want to get me a spot, at least 20 miles or so from the nearest building or highway back in the woods, where I can do some organic gardening, and where I can walk through the woods whenever the mood moves me.

Oh, Mike, I don't have any problems with the thoughts you expressed about Lenin's slant on Marxism. If you will remember, Trotsky was always my guy anyway. Now, like you, I eschew hard attachments to dogma of any variety.

Love to all,
Butch

As time passed, Butch began to think of Mike and Barbara Schoenfield and their young daughter as his family.

Leavenworth
July 2

Dear Mike and Barb:

After our phone conversation last evening, it has dawned on me that I have not been as effective as I ought to have been in communicating things. . . . Mike, Barb, we are a family, and as such we will always work together.

Let me quote Hesse about this. In a letter he wrote in 1955, Hesse says, "Everywhere on earth there are people of our kind. That for a small part of them, I can be a focal point, the nodal point in the net. This is the burden and joy of my life." I want both of you to understand me within the context of this statement by Hesse— "People of our kind."

Family is where the center of the world is. That has always been a major piece of me that has been missing. But now I have family.

I guess I'm feeling pretty poetic today. I'm happy. . . . If I am possessed by a madness, I can only assure you that it is a fine and delicate madness.

By the way, what day is Barb's birthday? You know that I do have a kind of mental block about birthdays—a personal idiosyncrasy. I just have a thing about counting off years out of life.

Love,
Butch

AFTER HIS FIRST YEAR of classes, Butch decided he would major in psychology, with a minor in computer science. He was also taking courses in sociology because some of the best teachers were a dedicated band of sociologists from the University of Kansas campus in Lawrence, an hour's drive away. Roger Barnes, a graduate student and teaching assistant in sociology, taught Butch in a course called "Causation of Crime and Delinquency." Barnes got a rush every time he approached Leavenworth, looking up at the big front wall and then walking in through all the security gates. It was the kind of feeling you might get as a football player, getting off the bench to go into a big game. Barnes was a short, amiable, enthusiastic man in his mid-twenties, with long, curly reddish-brown hair and the twang of the Kansas plains in his voice. He had grown up in Dodge City. Like some other professors who taught at the prison, Barnes had become involved at Leavenworth as a leftover part of the late sixties anti–Vietnam War movement. He thought of himself as being very progressive and idealistic. To him, teaching at the prison was taking truth to the people—better yet, to people who were locked up and really needed it. The gospel he was spreading was radical sociology, with lots of Marxism.

Barnes taught at Leavenworth one evening a week for two full years, and he always looked forward to his classes, especially after he met Butch. To Barnes, Butch was brilliant, the best student he had ever encountered. In class, Butch had an incredible persona, Barnes thought, projecting an aura of power and strength. He was tall and perfectly built, of course, but his most striking feature was his eyes. They were burning bright, laserlike, and when he got interested in something, his eyes lit up and went right through you. Sometimes, when he couldn't find the right word for a sentence, or got mad, his eyes would bulge and it was as if you could literally see the smoke coming out of his head. At those moments, even Butch's hair, which he combed straight back, seemed to stand on end. That made Barnes think Butch was on the edge all the time, an explosive temperament driven by hidden demons. One day when they were discussing how capitalists exploited people, Butch said, "Just line the motherfuckers up and kill them." But when he did written work, it was always well-controlled, very well written, and well-researched.

It was as if Butch could separate his academic work from his personal life in prison. In this, he was like a lot of convicts, thought Tom White, a psychologist who worked in Leavenworth and talked regularly with Butch over several years. Butch had a great ability to compartmentalize. He was able totally to believe whatever he was saying at the moment, which made him very convincing to others. But at bottom, he was simply being pragmatic. That was what you had to do in prison to survive. You had to be selfish and something of a psychopath. When you are swimming with sharks, you have to be a shark, too. So in class, Butch could be a scholar. He even carried a briefcase. But back in his cell house, he had to be a convict. More than most, White believed, Butch had come to understand the difference and was trying to rise above his environment.

The question was whether he could ever fully escape from the prison culture that had so formed his character after a lifetime of incarceration.

Amazingly, Butch seemed to be succeeding. Despite working full-time as a computer programmer, Butch graduated from college in four years with an almost straight-A average. Out of the forty courses he took, he got only two B's. On January 11, 1980, the University of Kansas awarded him a bachelor of arts degree "With Highest Distinction," their equivalent of *summa cum laude*. He had finished in the top 3 percent of his class.

Roger Barnes wanted to do something even more special for Butch, after all he had achieved. So he went to see Francis Heller, a professor who headed the university's chapter of Phi Beta Kappa, the national honor society. "What do you think?" Barnes asked. "Is he Phi Beta Kappa or not?"

Heller talked it over with his colleagues, and sure enough, Butch was elected to Phi Beta Kappa. Two months after graduation, Barnes, Heller, and several other professors, including the chairman of the sociology department, Scott McNall, drove to Leavenworth to induct Butch into the society. Heller put on his black academic gown, and a formal presentation was made in one of the prison's classrooms. In accepting the award, Butch wore a sweatshirt over his green prison fatigues. He had now become the first prison inmate ever elected to Phi Beta Kappa since the scholarly fraternity was started in 1776 at the College of William and Mary. He was joining John Quincy Adams, Daniel Webster, Ralph Waldo Emerson, Theodore Roosevelt, and Woodrow Wilson. To Butch, it was the ultimate mark of respect.

The wire services and newspapers gave the story national coverage. Some people were not pleased that a criminal had been elected to Phi Beta Kappa. The society's national headquarters in Washington received angry letters, and the organization's officers had serious reservations of their own. They felt that students shouldn't be eligible by merely taking extension classes without even setting foot on a college campus. So they made sure that Butch became not only the first prisoner elected to Phi Beta Kappa, but also the only one.

Still, Butch had his Phi Beta Kappa key, and now it helped open the door of the prison. Butch's professors deluged the Federal Parole Commission with letters of support. "Few people have impressed me as much as Mr. Bosket in terms of his intellectual intensity, his commitment and his drive," said Professor McNall, the chairman of the sociology department. Robert Antonio, another of his professors, wrote of Butch: "He is one of those very rare students who has the combined traits—high intelligence, diligence and enthusiasm—which provide a potentiality for high level scholarship. . . . He recently came within two letter grades of compiling a perfect undergraduate point average. This is a most difficult and rare accomplishment! He definitely exhibits the potential to complete a Ph.D. in sociology. I urge you to parole Mr. Bosket so he can begin his scholarly pursuits in the appropriate setting." Even the director of the Federal Bureau of Prisons, Norman A. Carlson, wrote to congratulate Butch. "Yours is an extraordinary accomplishment in which you can take pride."

Butch was paroled on January 19, 1982, after serving six and a half years of his fifteen-year sentence. He still had to serve time in Wisconsin, where he was wanted for escape and had not completed his murder sentence, but Butch was confident the good people of Wisconsin would not keep him long.

"I pose absolutely NO threat whatsoever to free society, nor have I for years," he wrote to Mike Schoenfield. "Any warped sense of values or psychological or emotional instabilities have long since been eradicated by maturity, education and a very clear sense of the need for social values and norms.

"I want freedom. I've earned it."

CHAPTER 13

BUTCH AND WILLIE

The Warriors

*No man knoweth the Son, but the Father; neither knoweth any man the
Father, save the Son.*

St. Matthew 11:27

I T W A S R I G H T smack at the top of the Sunday paper. Willie read
it when a counselor handed him a copy of the *Daily News*. They
distributed the paper every day at the Goshen Center for Boys, New York
State's most secure reformatory. Goshen had been Willie's new home
since he was sentenced for murder three weeks earlier. The New York
papers were still looking for angles on the "baby-face killer," and this
morning, the *Daily News* trumpeted its latest revelation. It had discovered
that Willie's father, also named Willie Bosket, had himself killed a man
and was currently doing time in Wallkill state prison.

Most readers were shocked. Willie was thrilled. This was the first
independent proof he had ever had of the stories his mother and grandmother had told him about his father. They had said his father killed
some people and was in prison. Based on these meager facts, so often
repeated as a way to scare him, Willie had made his father into his
boyhood idol. Now here was evidence his father was alive and in a prison
not far away. Willie returned to his small room and lay on his bunk. He
read the story over and over, and tears came to his eyes. Crying was not
something he did very often, but this was a special moment.

Willie asked the counselor on his wing for advice on what to do. He
knew that inmates in prison are normally not allowed to correspond with
other convicts. His counselor said exceptions could be made for close
relatives. Willie got out a tablet of yellow lined paper and wrote a letter
of pure joy to his long-lost father.

Trouble was, the *Daily News* had made a mistake. The man the paper identified as Willie's father was indeed named Willie Bosket, and, in fact, he had killed a man and was serving an eight-year sentence in Wallkill. But the man in Wallkill was only a relative of Willie's father. When he got Willie's letter, he was terrified. He was due to come before the parole board later in the year, and the public suggestion that he was the father of the notorious "baby-face killer" might cause the board to regard him unfavorably. The more he thought about it, the more he panicked. He tried to talk to his social service worker about the mixup in identities, but he was under so much stress, he lost his voice and could not think coherently. Finally, he showed the social service worker the clipping from the paper. That loosened things up a bit, and he now poured out his tale. It turned out he knew young Willie's father; they were the same age and had served time in a reformatory together twenty years earlier. There were other episodes in the family's past he also didn't particularly want the newspapers or the parole board going into. His own father, Mamon Bosket, for instance, had been a cousin of Pud Bosket's in South Carolina. Mamon had been convicted of murdering a man during a gambling argument over a dime in Saluda in 1926. After serving time on the county chain gang, Mamon had moved to New York. There, in 1963, at the age of sixty-two, he had been convicted for shooting and killing his girlfriend after he found her in bed with another man. The Willie Bosket in Wallkill had himself been sentenced for shooting his girlfriend's brother after an argument outside a party. The culture of violence of Saluda still exerted a strong gravitational pull.

A week after young Willie wrote the man he thought was his father, he received a letter in return explaining the confusion. The other Willie Bosket said he knew where Willie's father was, in Leavenworth, and he promised to write to Willie's father. Now it was Butch's turn to be surprised.

When Butch had first been imprisoned in Wisconsin for murder in 1962, he had called Laura a few times. But with the passage of time, he began to cut himself off from all contact with his family. He sent Laura a letter and told her not to write him anymore. After that, he took Laura and his newborn son, Willie, off his prison visitors list. Not that anyone from his family ever came to see him in prison. It was just a gesture on his part, a sign of the resignation he felt. Eventually, he urged Laura to get a divorce from him, which she did. Butch also told the prison authorities he didn't want any more mail from his father or mother. His father was "a no good bum," and his mother was "a prostitute," he explained to the prison officials. "I'm trying to get my life together at last, back off the bottom of the barrel," Butch said, "and I don't want to be disappointed again." When his father did write, Butch refused to accept the letters. As his years in prison stretched on and he achieved academic success, Butch also created a new identity for himself, reconstructing his past. His father, he sometimes said, was a lawyer in New York, and his mother was a social worker. It was a good, stable bourgeois family. He had married a nice, rich Jewish girl from Long Island. Unhappily, when her parents found out, they had forced an annulment. His son, Willie, was a product of that short-lived union, he claimed. Butch himself had gone to the University of Wisconsin on a football scholarship. Unfortunately, again, he had fallen in with a gang of thieves while in college and someone had gotten killed. Of course, while he was free robbing banks in New York in 1975, Butch had learned that his son was in a reformatory. But he had quickly repressed that information.

So the letter from his relative in Wallkill reporting that his son had been convicted of murder made Butch very uncomfortable. It confronted him with an excruciating dilemma, he told Richard Hughes, another convicted murderer who worked in the computer program at Leavenworth and took college classes with him. Hughes was a Choctaw Indian, raised on a reservation in Arizona, and was as tall and well-muscled and smart as Butch, so they made a natural team, both "warriors in a warrior society," they liked to say. After Butch got the letter, he confided to Hughes, "Of all people, I can understand my son's situation. I went through the same rage at being neglected. I've been battling the same monsters all my life." But Butch was also on the verge of winning his freedom through his scholarly attainments and his clean record at Leavenworth. If he got involved in correspondence with his son, now an infamous killer, it could hurt his chances for parole. All the incoming and outgoing mail at Leavenworth was checked by the guards, and Butch sensed danger.

Still, Butch felt he had to respond. He wrote his son a cautious letter, telling Willie about the classes he was taking with professors from the University of Kansas, and he urged him to get his high school equivalency degree. He also suggested Willie get into yoga and a regular physical fitness program as a way to discipline himself. Scholarship, reason, and control, Butch wrote, were absolutely essential to preventing a violent outburst that could result in more time in prison. These were the secrets Butch had finally discovered to improve his own life.

Willie was excited when the letter arrived and he saw the familiar name on the envelope. He was also impressed with his father's erudition. But the substance of the message was not what he had expected. Above all things, he hated school. At Goshen, he had gotten into the usual trouble, slapping one of his teachers, throwing a globe at another, and hitting a third over the head with a bookshelf. He was also refusing to attend class.

"Oh, man," Willie said when he finished reading his father's letter. "I don't want to hear that shit. I don't want anyone lecturing me."

Over the years, Willie had built an idealized portrait of his father in his mind. He thought of Butch as a big-time criminal, a bad-ass dude, a real stone killer. From his experience in institutions, he had learned that big-time criminals have influence on the inside. He pictured his father as James Cagney playing a mobster in the big joint. If Cagney gave the word for a hit, it got done. Fast. To Willie, all his pops had to do was give the word, and someone could break him out of Goshen. So when he wrote back to his father in Leavenworth, Willie said, "Send people you know to break me out of here. And find me a place to stay." Willie had a wonderful plan, he told his father. "Just think what a great pair of bank robbers we'd make if we were together as a team. Better than Jesse James and his brother."

About this time, the part-time Roman Catholic chaplain at Goshen, the Reverend Terrence J. Foley, arranged with the Catholic chaplain at Leavenworth to have Butch call Willie. Having one inmate call another was highly irregular, but both the warden at Leavenworth and the director of Goshen, Joseph Bertholf, consented to it, feeling it might have a calming effect on Willie. After all, Willie, who was fifteen, had never met or talked to his father, who was thirty-seven, and now his father was a model inmate.

When Willie picked up the phone in the director's office, with Bertholf sitting alongside, it was like a chess match, with father and son fencing with each other. Willie knew it was his father, but he could not bring himself to call the man on the other end Dad. He had never called anyone that. It sounded strange in his mouth. For once, Willie was embarrassed. But he didn't want to be disrespectful either; he had to say something. So he finally said, "Hello."

"Hey, how you doing, my man?" Butch began. "It's good to hear your voice."

"I'm doing fine," Willie responded. "It's really good to hear your voice."

Neither one had given in and used the familiar terms of father or son.

But pretty soon, Willie came right out and popped the issue that was on his mind, the request he made in his letter. "You got to get me out of here," Willie said.

"Ah, that's not the right thing to do at this point," Butch replied, trying to stay calm. He knew the guards at Leavenworth were monitoring the call. "Get your mind off of that stuff. Let me send you some books."

It should have been an emotional moment. But afterward, Willie didn't attach any importance to it. To him, it was just like a conversation between two strangers. Later, Butch did send him some books, on improving his grammar and vocabulary, but they weren't what Willie was looking for from his father.

For Butch, the new relationship with his son was becoming increasingly painful, as if someone held up a mirror to his own life. He also began to wonder, thinking back on his past and how as a boy he had wanted to imitate his father's criminal career, whether Willie was consciously or unconsciously copying him. He had a further terrible thought. Had Willie inherited something from him that made his son kill two people, just as he had done?

Still, Butch thought Willie was luckier than he in one important way. Willie had literally gotten away with murder. He had killed two men and attempted to kill a third but was serving only a five-year sentence. If Willie would just stay straight, he would be out by the time he turned twenty-one. Butch kept writing Willie to stay quiet.

On Christmas 1978, six months after Willie had been sentenced for murder, snow fell all day at Goshen. By evening, more than a foot had piled up around Goshen's fence, the heaviest snowfall there in more than two decades. In previous years, many of the boys would have been allowed to go home for the holiday. They always looked forward to those visits. But this year, all home visits, including those at Christmas, had been canceled because of the tough new juvenile offender act that had been passed so swiftly the past summer. That was the epochal law that allowed New York State for the first time to try children as young as thirteen in adult criminal courts for violent crimes. It was Willie's law; even the other boys at Goshen called it that. But the boys didn't like the results of the new law—Christmas season always made them a little restless anyway, thinking of home, and this year, with home visits taken away, the inmates at Goshen were particularly fretful. So on Christmas night, after the boys were locked in their rooms, some of the kids in an upstairs wing began to pound on their doors. They pushed and kicked hard enough that the doors flew open. Then they broke through the large locked door at the front of their wing and rushed downstairs.

"Let's go get Bosket to join us," one of them shouted. They broke into Willie's wing and overpowered the staff member on duty, taking his keys. Several of the boys from the upstairs wing had the foresight to put on warm clothes and pack small bags to take with them. Willie didn't want to miss his chance, though, and ran out the door that the others had opened right into all the fresh snow, clad only in his pajamas and bathrobe and slippers. Ten boys in all made the escape.

A state policeman found Willie two hours later by a gravel pit, less than three miles from the reformatory. He was shaking and freezing, his lips and hands blue from the cold.

In his haste, Willie had overlooked a critical fact. He had celebrated his sixteenth birthday on December 9, which in New York made him an adult. Escaping from a penal institution was a felony for an adult, even if it was only from a Division for Youth facility. Those boys who were under sixteen were simply sent back to Goshen. For Willie, now an adult, the price was greater. He was put on trial, convicted, and sentenced to four years in a state prison. Unlike all the crimes he committed as a juvenile, which had been wiped clean, the felony conviction would stay with him forever. It was a stain that would haunt him.

WHEN BUTCH LEARNED that Willie had tried to escape and been caught, he felt very low. His son had ignored all his advice. It is humanly impossible to be a father from jail, Butch thought, especially if your son is also in prison.

"In a sense, I have lost a child," Butch wrote to his friend Mike Schoenfield. Butch got so concerned about Willie that he began to think it might have been better if the two of them had not found each other.

> Leavenworth
> Aug. 16, 1981
>
> Dear Mike:
>
> I am distressed by my son's situation. I have empathy and compassion for his situation because I understand the whys and whatfors at root in it because of my obvious life proximity to it. It was my seed that gave life to him. Still, spiritually . . . we are different beings.
>
> Michael, there is not a single thing more that I, or you or we together can do to alter my son's life. . . . This gives me pain because I am his biological father, and wish it were otherwise.
>
> Love, your Bro,
> Butch

After Willie started doing his time in adult prison, relations between father and son worsened. Willie was getting shipped around to some of the toughest joints in New York—Dannemora, Green Haven, Auburn,

Comstock, and Attica—where he came under the influence of a group of older convicts who were militant Black Muslims. They taught Willie a revolutionary ideology that gave meaning to the rage he had long felt, a new prism through which to understand his plight and that of other African-Americans in the inner cities. Now Willie began to see his lifetime of incarceration as part of a centuries-old white racist plot to enslave black people. His new mentors also encouraged Willie to improve his education by reading, and they gave him books like *The Autobiography of Malcolm X* and *Soledad Brother* by George Jackson. Willie was especially attracted to Jackson, a high-ranking member of the Black Panthers and one of the three Soledad Brothers—black convicts in Soledad prison in California who were charged with throwing a white guard over a balcony in retaliation for the failure of prison authorities to punish a group of white racist inmates who had killed a black convict during a fight. In August 1970, George's brother, Jonathan Jackson, was killed in a shoot-out, along with a white judge, at the San Rafael courthouse. Jonathan had been trying to take hostages as part of an elaborate plan to free George from prison. A year later, George Jackson himself was killed during an attempt to escape from San Quentin. Three guards and two white prisoners also died, and George Jackson's lawyer, Stephen Bingham, who was suspected of smuggling a gun to Jackson, went into hiding. To Willie, it was a noble, romantic tale, and he began to fill his letters to his father with his newfound philosophy.

April 19, 1982

Dad:

Since I have been confined I have been able to "see" and experience the ways and activity of the Devil. I have reflected back on my past and the past of Black people period and after researching and researching thoroughly I can't help but be devoted to one thing: Revolutionary Struggle.

Dad, I am not trying to disrespect you, as a matter of fact what I'm going to say is so I never have to disrespect you intentionally or unintentionally, because I love you Dad and never want to feel as though I'm going against you or that which you feel should be.

Dad, there is nothing or no one who can make me see out of eyes other than the eyesight of a Revolutionary. My destiny is set towards the destruction of the oppressor to better the conditions of the oppressed Black people here in America and abroad. The same way I would give my life for you, as my Father, and for my Mother, I'd just as quick give my life in struggle for the advancement of my people. Dad, I'd never want to have conflicting views with you, so let's refrain from discussing this subject again, OK.

> Love always,
> Your son,
> Willie James Bosket

P.S. The warrior in you, is in me.

Butch had little use for this rhetoric. He had always been a loner and a pragmatist, and organized religion and ideology held no interest for him, even if they were intended to benefit people of his color.

May 21, 1982

Dear Son:

Once again I have found myself going through a process of searching for words to write to you. I read your last letter with great interest. In your letter, you seem taken with the ideas and writings of George Jackson most, and the need for confrontation with societal forces at large at some level of "revolutionary suicide." Frankly, that's a bit too much excitement for me, and it has been my observation that the energies from such a thought basis tend to dissipate unfruitfully before the onrush of hard pragmatic realities. But then, I'm just "old folks," so what the hell would I know about uplifting the "people" or becoming a martyr for some cause—and going out in a blaze of glory.

You know, I have had it in my head that you and I might spend some time off in some quiet rustic locale getting to know each other; and I have played with the notion that it might be nice if you went to whatever school I was going to for graduate degrees—just, as I said, getting to know each other.

Well, even if we cannot come to some exact meeting of minds about what immediate course and direction you want to take with your life, I would have you give some thought to the notion that you are actually putting the elements of what future you have, and possibly your life, in danger with the propensity you have to aggressively vocalize the "revolutionary" position you have implanted in your head so openly. Further, I am going to suggest to you that there are many members of the law enforcement community in the State of New York who would jump at the opportunity to blow your ass away. I think that you ought to come to grips with the notion that there are many people in the New York community who sincerely believe that you are like some rabid animal that needs to be exterminated for the safety of the community. Now that is a hell of a thing for me to say, but it is true—and it is the root nugget to the situation that you must confront when you are turned loose.

Logically, it would seem to me that it would be more sensible for you to just keep your mouth shut about whatever "political" notions you have in your head until you have acquired the intellectual sophistication to put some protection on your life. I would also have you give some thought to the notion that you would have not only been out of jail by now (some time ago, in fact), but that you would not have a felony record if you had heeded similar advice that I gave when you were in Goshen.

Reading your letter really forces me to seriously consider the notion that you might really be off into a self-destructive trip. I have met people in my rounds who really got off into such. In fact, I frankly read George Jackson as being so afflicted.

Son, I am not saying that you are necessarily so driven, but I must confess the shit that you were babbling to me in your letter has a suicidal reek to it. I would be more impressed, and pleased as your father, if you begin to demonstrate the capacity to listen. As you grow older, you will find life's path is strewn with the bodies and stripped mind hulks of warriors who could not acquire the capacity for self-control.

Son, I love you; and, in my love for you, I must return to the notion of the one, and most valuable gift that I have to give to you. Wisdom.

Love,
Your Dad

About this time, Laura also became increasingly anxious about Willie, that he would do something foolish that would keep him in prison past his twenty-first birthday. So she took the painful step of writing to her former husband for help. Butch answered stiffly.

June 10

Dear Laura:

In Re your suggestion that I "could write."

At this point in time I really and sincerely believe that any involvement or suggestions by me can only complicate things more. BOTH of us should have gotten involved in things while Willie was in Goshen, and had legal status as a juvenile.

Right now, I have only one notion of any certainty. Make whatever preparations you can towards relocating out of NYC. Many, many members of the NYPD will use any opportunity or excuse to kill the child after he has been released. If I can get myself loose before Willie gets out, I most certainly will help you with whatever money I can to get you moved and re-established—if you want to accept help.

Sincerely,
Butch Bosket

After he received several more belligerent letters from Willie, Butch was coming to believe there was a serious pathology at work in his son. It was a syndrome he recognized, like his own childhood coming back to plague him. Butch thought he had overcome these problems in himself by years of study and self-discipline. But he felt a need to warn his friends the Schoenfields against having anything to do with his own son.

August 8, 1982

Dear Mike and Barb:

About my son. I do not know how dirty his head is. I want both of you to understand, my son is EXTREMELY intelligent and he may well be SNEAKY dangerous. He has repeatedly lied to me about many serious things. My concern is of the kind where I would not allow him to sleep in the same house with family right now—or for that matter, I would not go to sleep in the house with him. The kid had some really bad sicks moving around in his head no more than a couple of years ago, and I cannot move with the assumption that all is well now. He has had not one whit of therapeutic care while he has been away, and prison has made him DAMNED sophisticated.

Love,
Butch

Father and son, Butch and Willie, were more alike than they realized. They shared so much, and yet like other fathers and sons, they were at different points in the tortured trajectories of their lives. Butch was older now and burdened with the knowledge of age. He thought he had found a way out of prison through academia. Willie was still young and full of the invincibility of youth and saw everything as a contest to be the most violent man on the street, just as his father once had. Willie was even competing with his father, he admitted to himself, and his father came up short. He had expected his father to be a big-time criminal, but Butch was only a punk, in Willie's eyes, with his sermons about school and staying out of trouble. Willie's natural rage at his father for neglecting him for so many years was multiplied by his disappointment. The way

Willie saw it, he was now tougher than his father. His father could not beat him or threaten him, and therefore Willie could not respect him. It was a cruel calculus. In the fall of 1982, Willie brought their brief period of contact to a wrathful end.

October 10, 1982

Listen Man:

No 1—I'm not a child. These cracker devils stole my youth when I was 9 years old and sent me to jail. So don't be dictating your sarcastic bullshit to me as if I'm a child.

No 2—You sound to me like you been down too long, getting too old, and starting to go soft, in other words, you sound like a "House Nigger." (Institutionalized and your spirit gone.)

I have come to see you for what you really are, a petty, phony ass, house nigger. I've gone 19 years so far without you, asshole. I know I can go the rest of the way without you. Forget I ever existed man, cause that's the way I feel about you.

Willie James Bosket

BUTCH AND WILLIE never corresponded with each other again. But despite Willie's anger and the new black nationalist ideas he had acquired, he seemed to undergo another transformation during his last year of incarceration. In March 1983, after he had completed his four-year term for escape from Goshen, he was released from prison and sent back to the Division for Youth until he reached his twenty-first birthday that December. It was an extraordinary move. The state was taking a twenty-year-old convicted murderer, hardened by years in the adult prison system, and placing him with thirteen-, fourteen-, and fifteen-year-olds. There was no telling what influence he might have on the younger boys. The alternative was to let him go free months before his original release date. The *Daily News* heard of the possibility and ran a huge front-page headline, "Baby Face Killer To Be Freed." Governor Carey was appalled. After all, he had vowed that Willie "would never walk the streets again." So state officials hastily worked out an emergency plan—Willie had to go back to a reformatory because he had not served enough time under his juvenile murder conviction.

Willie, at first, was outraged. He thought he was being treated like a political prisoner, a victim of Governor Carey's promises. No politician wanted to be accused of being soft on Willie Bosket.

To make things even harder on Willie, the Division for Youth arranged for a special five-man team of guards to keep a twenty-four-hour surveillance on him. At least one guard was to be by his side at all times as long as he was in his new home at the McCormack Secure Center, in upstate New York near Cornell University.

But Willie decided that this was an opportunity, a chance to show the system it was wrong about him and to ensure that he would be released when he turned twenty-one, nine months later. He enjoyed confounding people, and this was a new kind of challenge. So at McCormack, he enrolled in several classes, including a college-level course on child care management, and volunteered to work with some of the younger boys in group counseling. Soon he noticed that McCormack's library was hopelessly inadequate. It held only about twenty secondhand paperbacks, all more than ten years old. Willie began writing to nearby colleges, including Cornell University and Ithaca College, as well as several local high schools, to solicit books. After a while, Willie was spending eight hours a day running McCormack's newly burgeoning library and encouraging the younger boys to read more. He also got in touch with Cornell to ask if any African students would be willing to come and give lectures during Black History Month. Several showed up, and Willie made sure their talks were well-attended.

Nicole Librandi, the education supervisor at McCormack, was pleasantly surprised to find that Willie was a serious, persistent student and very productive in class. In his entire time at McCormack, he never caused a disruption in class, nor did he fight or try to escape. Eventually, even the special team of guards hired to keep Willie under constant watch relaxed and let him wander freely around the facility.

When he was scheduled to be released, Susan Yeres, the assistant director of McCormack, wrote Willie a letter of appreciation. "You have demonstrated a potential for maturity and responsible behavior," the Division for Youth official said. It was the consensus of the staff, the letter added, that Willie "has the potential to be a productive member of society."

CHAPTER 14

WILLIE

Counsel for the Defense

Though the mills of God grind slowly, yet they grind exceedingly small.

Henry Wadsworth Longfellow

THE RING WAS A plain gold band with a circle of twelve small diamonds. It had been Laura's wedding ring in 1961. Butch had given it to her, and now Laura offered it to Willie. He was touched by his mother's gesture. The ring was the only souvenir she had of her bittersweet time with Butch all those years earlier, except for Willie himself, her handsome, devilish manchild of a son who seemed possessed by Butch's fateful spirit. Out of curiosity, Willie took the ring to an appraiser, who said it was real. In fact, the jeweler said, it was worth a lot of money; that made it doubly valuable to Willie. He figured his father must have stolen it.

Willie had been released from prison a month before, on his twenty-first birthday, December 9, 1983. That was as long as the criminal justice system that had practically raised him could hold him for murder. His release made Willie suddenly feel better about the world and about himself. He had gotten to thinking that the governor or the Division for Youth or the courts or the police, someone, would find some other way to keep him incarcerated. Freedom had come to seem impossible. As a boy, Willie was locked up so much of the time that he didn't have dreams or aspirations like other kids. Now that he was actually out, he felt lucky, and he determined to try to make it, to live a life free of his murderous patrimony. Just as he had done in his last months in McCormack, he would show people how wrong they were about Willie Bosket. The thing he could do best, Willie had come to believe, was to work with other kids from the ghetto and help them stay out of trouble. So he had gone down to the Family Court to look up the assistant district attorney who had prosecuted him, Bob Silbering, to volunteer his services. Nothing came of it. A young assistant in the office who talked with Willie thought he was really plotting a revenge attack on Silbering, and so Silbering was assigned a bodyguard. But Willie did enroll at Manhattan Community College and started taking classes on early childhood development and child psychology.

About a week after his release, Willie was walking down the street with his sister Shirley when a tall, very pretty girl named Sharon Hayward stopped them. Willie noticed she had elegant features and a slender build, with a healthy butt, the way Willie liked women to be shaped.

"How you doing?" Sharon asked Shirley.

"Fine," Shirley replied.

"How's your brother?" Sharon then asked, knowing that Shirley's brother, like so many other young men in the neighborhood, was in jail. It was the kind of routine, polite inquiry that people on the streets of Harlem made every day, like people in Westchester or Scarsdale asking about a relative off in college.

Shirley laughed. "This is my brother," she said proudly.

Sharon looked at Willie. She had met him before, when he was about fifteen, before the murders. Willie had been attracted to her then, but Sharon had rebuffed all his advances. Now she felt differently. Willie had that big inviting smile that could light up a room, and he was a legend on the street. This was a moment to celebrate, and, years later, the way Willie remembered it, Sharon right then began putting the moves on him. She jumped into his arms and kissed him, then gave Willie her phone number.

He called her later in the day and asked her to dinner, which was fine with Sharon. Willie had to borrow some money from his mother and sisters. He put on new clothes that his grandmother Marie had bought for him, including an expensive gray and black leather jacket. He also showered, combed back his Afro, and splashed on some Old Spice aftershave lotion. Willie was actually going on a date. He was a little nervous, a new feeling for Willie, and he wanted to look his best. He thought his small Errol Flynn mustache suited him well.

When he picked up Sharon that evening, Willie proposed going to a seafood restaurant. She demurred. Willie was crestfallen.

"Do you know where I really want to go?" she asked.

"Wherever you'd like to go is fine," Willie answered.

"I'd like to go up to your sister's apartment," Sharon said, keeping her eyes fixed on Willie.

"Okay," he said, "we can hang out there."

"No," Sharon interjected. "You don't understand. I want to go there with you and stay all night."

Willie couldn't believe how slow he had been in picking up her intention. Nor could he believe his good luck.

After that, they spent every day together. Sharon already had a baby girl, but that was fine with Willie. He badly wanted a family, and he decided he would be the little girl's father. He quickly learned how to change a diaper. Didn't mind the work at all. He also got along well from the start with Sharon's mother, Marie Hayward, who was smart and well-educated. She was impressed by Willie. He was much nicer than the other boys Sharon had dated—very personable and thoughtful, with a brilliant mind, she thought. She loved to play Scrabble, and very few people could beat her at it, but Willie did.

Three weeks into Willie's affair with Sharon, Sharon popped the question. She asked him to marry her. Willie said he had to call Sharon's mother first, to ask her permission. He also wanted to tell her about his criminal record.

"I'm afraid it was me who killed those men on the subway," Willie told Marie Hayward. "That's okay," she replied. She had heard plenty of that kind of story. "That was then. It's what you do now that is important. I trust you."

That was when Willie's mother gave him the ring. On the wedding day, Sharon and Willie, accompanied by Laura and Sharon's mother and baby girl, went down to city hall. Now they were Mr. and Mrs. Willie Bosket. Willie felt real proud when walking down the street with his new wife, a beautiful black woman; people stopped and stared. For the first time in his life, Willie was living, not just surviving. He actually began thinking about the future, something that might seem commonplace to other people, but Willie felt as if he had been transported to another planet. The specter of doom that had long hung over Willie and his mother, like so many generations of the Boskets, seemed to be lifting. Perhaps Willie could now break the terrible cycle of crime and punishment in which he had been caught, just as Butch seemed to be doing. Maybe, Willie allowed himself to think, he wasn't predestined to spend his life in prison after all.

WILLIE'S TWO SISTERS, Cheryl and Shirley, were still living in the building on 145th Street where Willie had stayed when he committed the murders five years earlier. The five-story tenement had been in bad shape then, but in the intervening years, the landlord had died and things had really fallen apart. The pool hall on the ground floor was boarded up.

Only four of the eight apartments on the other floors were still occupied. The ceilings were crumbling. Garbage was strewn everywhere. Rats roamed the building. There was no heat. Consolidated Edison had shut off the electricity, so the only light the tenants had was what they could get by illegally tapping into the neighboring power line. The hallways and narrow stairwells were dark most of the time. The only authority in the building was enforced by Charles, the big, mean-tempered man who had run the pool hall on the ground floor and rented out space to the neighborhood drug pushers. Charles, no longer Laura's boyfriend, had developed a crush on Cheryl, and eventually he and Laura got into a fight. After that, Laura moved out and Charles moved in with Cheryl. He was twenty-six years her senior.

Even though Charles had sold Willie the gun he used in the killings and had been a role model for him, when Willie got out of prison, he took a disliking to Charles. He wasn't happy about the way Charles was treating his mother and sister. One day, in Willie's presence, Charles called for Cheryl.

"Come here, bitch," he said. Then he grabbed Cheryl by the neck, threw her on the kitchen floor, and started beating her. When he saw Willie staring at him, Charles asked, "You got a beef?"

"Naw," Willie answered. "I don't got no beef."

Willie, though, began to try to think of ways to get rid of Charles. He couldn't confront Charles straight on; Charles was just too big and always carried a gun. So Willie decided to turn Charles in to the police. By the code of the street, it was a lowdown thing to do, but Willie was trying to live a decent life now, and Charles was a definite menace. Besides renting out the empty apartments to drug dealers, he also held an arsenal of their guns in the bedroom he shared with Cheryl.

The police were surprised when Willie walked in and identified himself, and everything went dead quiet. Even the typewriters stopped click-clacking. The cops all knew who he was. It was like in an old Western movie when the gunslinger walks into the saloon, thought Willie. But the police were happy with the information Willie brought about Charles and his guns, and they worked out a prearranged signal with Willie. If Charles was carrying a gun when he next came out of the house, Willie was to put on a knit cap.

Willie went back to the building and told Charles he needed to go out to make a phone call at a local bar. The Boskets were too poor to afford a phone. Charles volunteered to accompany Willie on his mission.

"Do you want me to bring a piece with me?" he asked.

"Yeah," Willie replied, putting on the cap.

When they walked outside, the police moved in and arrested both

Charles and Willie, so Charles wouldn't know Willie had been the snitch. They locked Charles up, but let Willie go with a fake desk appearance ticket, meaning he would not have to appear for arraignment. A search of Charles's apartment turned up two pistols, three sawed-off shotguns, and a rifle, all with their serial numbers rubbed out. The police missed a dozen more guns hidden under the bed. But what they found was enough to get Charles a three-year sentence in Sing Sing.

Willie felt good about getting Charles arrested. He had removed a serious threat from his family's life, and he had done it legitimately, without falling back on his violent ways.

Unfortunately, Willie started having nightmares about Charles. The dreams were always the same: Willie was walking down a crowded street, then he saw Charles following him. Willie would run into a basement to escape, but Charles would chase him. There was irony in this incubus, Willie knew. He had never had nightmares about killing people. But now he was worrying all the time that Charles, in jail, was out to get him for doing something legal.

Willie began to think that the building on 145th Street, from which he had set out to murder people on the subway, was a haunted house. It was casting an evil spell over him.

One evening, when Willie visited Cheryl in her second-floor apartment, they noticed a surge of water dripping down through the ceiling from the apartment above. It had happened before, but this time it was worse, and Cheryl had about lost her patience with her upstairs neighbor, Joel Brown. He was a frail, seventy-two-year-old eccentric, scrawny and beset by glaucoma and diabetes. His illnesses left Brown legally blind, but he managed to live off the $372 a month he drew from social security after years of working as a porter. He shared his apartment with his longtime friend, Isaiah Anderson, an unemployed fifty-year-old ex-convict. They made an odd couple, lost souls in a neighborhood of many lost souls, and Cheryl didn't like them. That night as the leak in the ceiling turned into a flood, Cheryl went up to berate Brown, and then he came down to curse her out.

When Willie heard that, it was too much. Brown was disrespecting his sister. "Man, get your ass out of here," Willie shouted, and shoved the door in Brown's face. It was the kind of quarrel that went on all the time in the building, especially now that Charles had been removed and there was no landlord, no superintendent, no authority whatsoever. Willie didn't give the argument any more thought. He was just pleased that he had not totally lost his temper, as he had so many times in the past, and done something violent. It was a small sign of progress.

A few days later, Cheryl invited Willie and his new wife over for dinner. Willie was happy. This was the kind of family occasion he had come to relish in his brief weeks of freedom. Willie arrived first; Sharon was to join them later. The stairs were dark, with the electricity cut off, and as Willie reached the second-floor landing, he glimpsed the outline of a very dark-skinned man.

Charles, Willie instinctively thought. His heart dropped into his socks. It was his nightmare coming true. He had been ambushed.

Willie reached behind his back for his knife. It was a normal part of a young man's outfit on the streets where Willie was raised. He was trying to go straight, but he still didn't feel well-dressed without his weapon. It was a long ten-inch blade, with a pistol grip made of brass and pearl. Willie wore it upside down in a holster in the nook of his back, just over his hip. That made for the quickest release. It was like the knife his father had once carried.

After he whipped it out, the dark figure moved. Willie now realized the man was too small to be Charles. It was Joel Brown. Willie was furious that the old man had scared him. He wanted to have some fun in return.

"You fucking faggot," Willie yelled, stamping his feet for emphasis. "I'm going to kill you."

Brown jumped in fear and scampered up the stairs to his third-floor apartment, moving fast for a man of his age and infirmities. He was also screaming now, calling out for his roommate Anderson to help.

Anderson had been sitting watching television when he heard Brown shriek. He kept an ax behind the door for emergencies, and now Anderson grabbed it, threw the door open, and started down the stairs for Willie.

"The motherfucker's got an ax," Willie said, stunned.

By this time, Cheryl had heard the commotion and had come out on the second-floor landing, along with her young daughter, Lavelle. She saw Anderson standing at the top of the steps with the ax. "What happened?" she asked Willie as he bolted past her into her apartment.

"I was coming upstairs and that faggot surprised me, so I was having a little fun with him," Willie explained. "He must have thought I was trying to rob him or something, 'cause he yelled for his friend who came out with an ax and tried to cut me."

Cheryl screamed a final obscenity up the stairs at her neighbors and went back inside her apartment with Lavelle. Then she and Willie laughed. It was a minor scrape in a life of constant wariness and battles. No harm had been done. Over dinner, they forgot all about it.

Three days later, a policeman from the Manhattan North Senior Citizens Unit stopped by Cheryl's apartment and asked where he could find her brother. Said he had a small question to ask him, nothing very important. Cheryl said she didn't know where Willie was, but if the cop would leave his name and number, she would have her brother get in touch with him. The policeman, Detective William Mercurio, left his card.

That afternoon, Willie came by to see Cheryl, and she gave him the card. Willie thought it must have something to do with some of his cousins, who were often in and out of jail. He had never heard of the Senior Citizens Unit. It didn't occur to Willie that the police might be looking for him. He hadn't robbed anybody.

He went to the neighborhood bar, where the nearest public telephone was located, and called the police.

Detective Mercurio said, "We've got a complaint from Joel Brown that you robbed him, or tried to rob him."

"That's crazy," Willie said. "Me rob that old man? All I did was try to scare him after he scared me."

"That's fine," the detective said reassuringly. "In that case, all we need is a statement and that will be it."

"Okay," Willie responded. "I'll be down there as soon as I can get a bus." He was trying to be as cooperative as possible. He still had no hint of alarm.

"Never mind," Mercurio said. "Where are you? We'll come pick you up."

Willie said he would meet them in front of his sister's building on 145th Street. He would be wearing a large orange arctic parka with a hood, so they could recognize him, Willie added. Then he went back to Cheryl's apartment, fixed himself a bologna and cheese sandwich, and waited for the police.

They drove up in an unmarked car. Willie opened the door himself and got in the backseat. Everything still seemed very friendly. But when they arrived at the precinct house, the policemen took Willie to the bathroom in the back.

"Why are you bringing me here?" Willie asked. "I don't need to go to the bathroom."

"We are going to strip search you," Mercurio answered.

"You can't do that," Willie said. "I'm not under arrest."

"You are now."

Willie now realized how serious the situation was. He couldn't believe he had voluntarily turned himself in. But he also couldn't understand why he had been arrested. After all the things he had done in his life, to be arrested for the attempted robbery of a seventy-two-year-old man whom he hadn't tried to rob seemed absurd. And all this at a time when he was doing his best to go straight? He was going to college; he had gotten married; he was looking for a job where he could help other troubled kids. It smelled like a frame-up to Willie. Governor Carey had promised he would never walk the streets of New York again. And now the New York police were making good on the governor's pledge.

Willie had a terrible premonition. He used his one phone call to call his wife, Sharon. "Get my mother and grandmother, get your mother, get anybody you can," he said. "You've got to raise bail for me, or I'm going to be in prison the rest of my life. They're never going to let me out." He had that sense again that he was predestined to spend his life in prison. It was March 19, 1984. He had been out of jail barely three months.

At Willie's arraignment, bail was set at fifty thousand dollars. It was a huge amount, considering the charges, attempted robbery and attempted assault. But the judge, Leslie Snyder, said, "This case leaves me quite speechless. This defendant commits two murders and serves five years, and now he's involved in an attempted robbery." The system, which had worked in Willie's favor while he was a juvenile, was now going to pay him back. His family could not come close to raising the money, so Willie had to stay in jail pending trial.

PATRICK DUGAN WAS SUPERVISING the distribution of criminal cases in the Manhattan district attorney's office when Detective Mercurio came in with Joel Brown's complaint. The small room in the Criminal Court building was like a MASH unit. There were cops and young assistant district attorneys and witnesses in cases all talking and hanging around the intake basket. Dugan's job was to evaluate each case, decide on the charges to be brought, make bail recommendations, and then assign it to a prosecutor. In other words, he was to bring order out of chaos. It was a job for which Dugan felt well-suited. Both his father and grandfather had been New York City police detectives, and Dugan himself, though a lawyer by training, had a formidable physical presence, with the build of a football lineman. He was tall and thickset, with a strong, square jaw and rugged, handsome features.

When he picked up Joel Brown's case from the basket, he was amazed to see the name Willie Bosket. Everyone in the district attorney's office, practically everyone in New York, knew Willie Bosket. Dugan called for the detective who had made the arrest.

"Is this *the* Willie Bosket?" Dugan asked Mercurio.

The detective was stumped. "What are you talking about?" he said.

"Is this the guy who is the reason why the juvenile offender law was created?" Dugan asked again, more pointedly.

Mercurio looked bewildered. He had no idea whom he had arrested.

Dugan instantly realized the stakes in the case. There would be a lot of publicity, and it might get to be a political trial. Dugan decided he would take the case himself. He was the senior trial counsel in the district attorney's office at the time, and he often ended up with the toughest cases anyway.

In the weeks leading up to the trial, Dugan kept searching for a motive. Why would Willie want to rob a man right in the building where his sisters lived, just after he had gotten out of jail? It didn't make a lot of sense. He was too easy to identify. And how could a frail, practically blind man outrun Willie up the stairs? But Dugan never doubted that it was a good case. Willie deserved to be prosecuted, Dugan felt, given his long criminal history.

There was another troubling question. The attack, or attempted attack, had taken place about 5 o'clock on a Friday afternoon after Joel Brown came back from buying some collard greens in a grocery store. But even though he had the only phone in the building, Brown did not report the incident to the police until Saturday morning. Brown and Anderson admitted they had waited overnight for an apology from Willie and Cheryl. Or at least they waited hoping the Boskets would come forward with a way to end the infighting in the building over the water leaks. When the Boskets made no apology and did not offer a cease-fire, Brown decided to go to the police, his way of getting even. Still, even knowing about this bad blood in the building, Dugan was convinced Willie was guilty of committing a crime. It was Willie's past catching up with him.

Willie's past, in fact, was becoming a big problem for him. It undercut his defense in the trial from the beginning. The only witnesses to the alleged crime were Brown and Anderson on one side, and Willie and Cheryl on the other. On the stand, both Brown and Anderson testified that Willie had threatened the old man with a knife and tried to rob him, saying, "I want your money." Willie could have offered the real explanation of what happened—that he was scared of Charles, that in the dark he had mistaken Brown for Charles, and that after he discovered his error, he was just trying to have some fun with Brown. After all, Brown and his sister had been quarreling. But Willie's attorney, Alton Maddox Jr., did not let him testify. It was too great a risk. If Willie took the stand, it could open him up to cross-examination by the prosecutor Dugan, who might be able to get into Willie's criminal record. That could be fatally damaging. Moreover, Willie didn't want to tell the story about Charles anyway. Only he and the police knew Willie had turned Charles in. A public admission of being a snitch would tarnish his hard-won reputation and was likely to invite retribution from Charles or his friends.

Cheryl believed deeply that Willie had been framed. For once, she told her family, Willie was innocent. She had seen and heard most of what happened. But she was too scared even to go to court as a spectator. For one thing, there was her own juvenile criminal record, which had landed her at Zarega, the girls' detention center. More important, there was still a collection of Charles's guns hidden under her bed that the police had failed to find. It had been only a few weeks since Charles was arrested, and she remained his girlfriend. She was still going to visit him in jail. What would happen if she testified for Willie and then the police, in retaliation, came and searched her apartment again? Besides, she had her young daughter to think about. Cheryl did not know that it was Willie who had led the police to Charles. But even if she had, it probably would not have made any difference. She was paralyzed by paranoia, the paranoia of growing up on the street.

The trial was coming down to one simple issue—whether the jury believed Joel Brown and Isaiah Anderson. The defense would present no evidence and call no witnesses.

Willie's chances did not look good. From the start, things seemed to go wrong for Willie. During a pretrial hearing on July 11, 1984, his lawyer, Maddox, got in a fierce argument with the judge, Justice Robert Haft of the Manhattan Supreme Court. Maddox already had a growing reputation for defending young black men and turning criminal trials into political crusades, a reputation Maddox relished. He had grown up in a dusty, redneck Georgia town where, as a teenager, he was chased and badly beaten by a white mob. Now as a lawyer, Maddox intended to redress the wrongs inflicted on African-Americans. He took cases like Willie's on a pro bono basis; he worked hard; and he had the cold stare of a zealot. A year before, he had embarrassed the New York police by discovering that six transit officers had used unnecessary force to kill a black artist, Michael Stewart, whose crime had been to scrawl graffiti on a subway wall. Maddox believed Willie's trial was another case of racism. Willie, he thought, would never have been arrested on these flimsy charges except for his reputation.

"It's very clear to me that there's a wide spirit of racism that exists in these courts," Maddox said to Justice Haft. But Haft waved off his accusation and told the court officers to take Willie away until the next scheduled trial date. Willie did not move immediately. He wanted a further word with his attorney. So one of the three court officers put his hand on Willie's shoulder and gave him a nudge.

"Let's go," the court officer said.

"Don't push," Willie responded. "I can walk."

But the three officers had been warned about how dangerous Willie could be, and they now began pushing him harder. Willie raised his fist and shouted, "Keep your fucking hands off of me. I'll kick your fucking ass."

At that, the three officers jumped on Willie and shoved him backward onto the big oak defense table. It cracked under the weight of so many wrestling bodies, and the legs splintered off. One of the officers grabbed a broken leg and started to club Willie.

Maddox had been shouting for Justice Haft to intervene. When the judge failed to act, he hurled his briefcase at Haft and then jumped on the back of one of the officers, to pull him off Willie. By now, all the men were scuffling on the floor. It was bedlam. After order was restored, Willie was charged with assault, resisting arrest, and criminal contempt of court.

When the trial resumed, there was a new judge. It was summertime, and with many judges on vacation and few of the others wanting to deal with the combination of Willie Bosket and Alton Maddox, the case was assigned to a visiting justice from Rochester, Donald J. Mark. He came to New York as part of a program to speed up trials in the city's backlogged court system. Mark was a former marine who had landed with the first wave on Okinawa and had been recalled during the Korean War. He was cool, even-handed, and firm. He would give Willie and Maddox some latitude, but he wasn't going to let the court get out of control the way it had earlier.

Maddox knew his case rested on the credibility of Willie's accusers, so he concentrated on making Brown and Anderson look bad. Brown helped him out. Dugan had asked the elderly man to wear a jacket and tie to court, a routine request to make a witness look good for the jury. Brown complied by wearing his one and only suit, all white, with ruffles. Brown was proud as a peacock strutting up to the witness stand, but Dugan could hardly believe what he was seeing. The prosecutor thought his key witness looked like an old pimp. Dugan also had to tell the jury— otherwise Maddox would have brought it out on cross-examination— that Anderson had done time in jail twice, for burglary and unlawful possession of a .38-caliber revolver.

In his closing argument, Maddox summed up his defense. "Mr. Foreman, ladies and gentlemen of the jury—there is a problem with this case. There is no evidence. No evidence whatsoever. Nobody was injured. No money was taken. No weapon was recovered. All you have is two individuals who were not angels, shacking up with each other, living it up every day, doing their thing, and now they want to get even. Go back to their story," Maddox urged the twelve members of the jury, nine of them African-American, the other three Hispanic. "Why didn't Joel Brown or Isaiah Anderson report this robbery to the police immediately?"

Maddox asked. "When you look at the facts, it is very simple. Isaiah Anderson said the only thing they wanted was an apology. That's all they wanted. If Willie Bosket had apologized Friday evening, everything would have been cool.

"So now we know that wasn't no robbery. If you listen to what they say, it was an argument.

"Ladies and gentlemen of the jury," Maddox concluded, "this is what this case is all about. It's about two men who come into this court-room who disrespect everybody in order to snatch life and liberty away from Willie Bosket. . . . You don't have to buy a lemon from a used car salesman. These men are lemons."

The jury reported after two days that it was deadlocked. Justice Mark urged them to try once more. The jurors were torn between their sympathy for the decrepit seventy-two-year-old man and their doubts about his credibility. It would have helped if Willie had testified. They found it strange that he hadn't. In the end, the jurors did what juries often do when faced with the hard reality of sending a man to prison—they split the verdict. They found Willie not guilty of attempted robbery, but guilty of attempted assault.

Nothing had been stolen, and no one had been hurt, as Maddox pointed out. Still, the jury's verdict meant a felony conviction. That made two felonies for Willie. It went into his permanent adult criminal record along with his brief escape from Goshen just after he had turned sixteen. Under New York law, a second felony automatically meant a longer prison term. Instead of two and a half to four years, Willie was looking at three and a half to seven years for the crime of attempted assault. Things were getting more serious for Willie.

And they could get much worse fast. If you had a third felony convic-tion in New York, no matter how small the crime, you could be found a "persistent felony offender." That could get you twenty-five years to life. The law had been enacted in 1965, under Governor Nelson Rockefeller, as people became more and more angry about the sudden, huge increase in crime in the 1960s. It was an early version of the three-strikes-and-you're-out proposals that gained enormous popularity across the country in the 1990s. Most people in New York had forgotten that the persistent-felon law even existed. But it was there, on the books, a trap waiting to be sprung for serious repeat criminals.

WITH THIS CONVICTION, the old hot anger came back over Willie. His long-awaited freedom, his marriage, his start at an honest living, all were now forfeit to the accusations of a zany seventy-two-year-old man who claimed he outran Willie up a flight of fifteen stairs in the dark. One hundred days of liberty were all Willie had been permitted.

It seemed to Willie as if there were an unwritten compact to make him spend his life in one prison after another. As far back as he could remember, someone was locking him up: his teachers, psychiatrists, social workers, judges, the police, even his mother. Hell, his mother couldn't raise bail for him in the Joel Brown case. That felt like another betrayal. In his darkest moments, Willie wondered if he himself was part of this compact. Maybe there was something he inherited from his father that was at work in him. Or maybe it was just the result of spending all those years behind walls. Whatever it was, deep inside him, Willie often felt a compulsion to be incarcerated. It was a terrible truth that he had come to feel comfortable in prison.

Something of that dread temptation took over in Willie now, after his conviction for the episode with Joel Brown. He became ever more reckless, ever more willing to challenge "the system," even if it resulted in more time in jail. He felt he had nothing left to lose. Willie called it his war.

His first battle was at his sentencing hearing. Since society did not play fair with him, Willie decided, he would not play by society's rules. He would wage an unconventional, guerrilla attack. He turned his chair around so he had his back to Justice Mark, then insisted that the judge, whom he addressed as "Mr. Nigger," discharge his attorney, Alton Maddox.

"The only reason I am asking that Mr. Maddox be dismissed as counsel is due to the simple fact that I do not acknowledge these proceedings," Willie told Justice Mark. "This is an American court, but I am not a descendant of America. I am of African descent."

Willie was being as contemptuous as possible, but Justice Mark decided to let him have his day in court. Willie was about to be sentenced anyway.

With his lawyer dismissed, Willie now took up the questioning himself. Pat Dugan had called a police officer, Richard Raymond, a fingerprint specialist, to prove that the Willie Bosket who had escaped from Goshen was the same Willie Bosket who had been convicted of attempting to attack Joel Brown. That had to be confirmed before the judge could sentence Willie as a second-time felon. Willie, of course, denied he was the same person who had run from Goshen. He said he was really Bobby Reed. It was a novel, if unsuccessful, ploy.

Willie had more tricks. "Your Honor," he said, "I would like to ask for an investigation of Mr. Raymond. I have circumstantial evidence that

Mr. Raymond and what's his name, Mr. Dugan, are having a homosexual affair."

Dugan jumped to his feet. This was preposterous. "Objection, irrelevant," he shouted.

Willie smelled blood and persisted. He was enjoying mocking the judicial system.

"Are you having a homosexual affair with Mr. Dugan?" he asked the flustered police officer.

"Did your wife have any affairs with Mr. Dugan? Did you ever commit an orgy with Mr. Dugan?"

It was getting more and more bizarre. Justice Mark had never had anyone as wild as Willie come before him in court, but he figured Willie would eventually run out of things to say.

When it was time to sum up, Dugan recounted Willie's entire criminal record, going back to the time he was first sent to Wiltwyck at age nine. He also quoted from a videotaped deposition Willie had given in a suit brought by the widow of his second victim, Amalia Perez. She was suing the New York Transit Authority for negligence in not taking more precautions after Willie's repeated acts of violence in the subway. Willie had consented to be deposed out of sympathy for Mrs. Perez, he maintained. But he couldn't help using the chance to embroider his reputation. Between the ages of nine and fifteen, Willie testified under oath, he had committed more than two hundred robberies on the subway and taken part in at least two thousand crimes. That included twenty-five stabbings, Willie estimated. "On one occasion," Willie said, "I cut a man's eyeball out of his head." That wasn't true. Willie just said it for effect. Now Dugan, the prosecutor, quoted it back at him as evidence. It was better than a confession, Dugan thought. It was Willie boasting in living color to a life of crime.

"The defendant," Dugan concluded, "is the most violent youth that the criminal justice system has ever encountered."

Willie thought that was high praise, in a way. Here was public recognition that he had triumphed in the arena he had chosen for himself—the world of violence. Willie couldn't help making a rejoinder. "Your honor, how can this homosexual D.A. come into this courtroom and speak of violence when white men have committed so much violence upon black people for four hundred years?

"Violence is what your grandfather did to my grandmother," Willie charged. He didn't know that several of his female ancestors had actually been forcibly taken by white men. That sad family history had been lost, like so many things about the Boskets.

"Violence is when you lock up nine-year-old black babies for the rest of their lives in hard-core penal institutions," Willie added, in a reference to his own life. "Hell, I guess I'm just like you all, ain't I?"

When Willie had finished, Justice Mark sentenced him. "Mr. Bosket," the judge said, "you are a ticking time bomb." He awarded Willie the maximum, three and a half to seven years in prison. He tacked on an extra thirty days for Willie's histrionics in court.

Willie's actions were beginning to add up, unlike when he was a juvenile. As a fifteen-year-old, he had essentially gotten away with murder. Now that he was in the adult criminal justice system, he was marked for life by a reputation with the police, prosecutors, and judges. That reputation had helped indict and convict him for something he believed he didn't do. Willie knew there was irony in what had happened, but he didn't appreciate it. He was the most depressed he could ever remember feeling.

There was one good thing, though, to come out of the trial—Willie discovered he liked being a lawyer. He thought he had done pretty well at it, for a kid who had not gone past third grade. He sensed he had one big advantage. The prosecutor was bound by the rules of evidence and his legal ethics, but Willie, acting as his own lawyer, could say anything he wanted in court. Most people are afraid of the judicial system. They bow and scrape in front of the judge in his solemn black robes. Not Willie. The worst thing that could happen was that the judge would sentence him to some extra time for contempt. But that was nothing to worry about, since he figured he was going to spend the rest of his life in prison anyway. The courtroom now became just another battlefield for Willie to show how formidable he was.

When it came time to stand trial for his fight with the three court officers during the Joel Brown case, Willie demanded that he be allowed to go pro se—to be his own attorney. Justice Edwin Torres, who was handling the new trial, didn't like the idea. There is an old courtroom adage that he who represents himself has a fool for a client. If the judge let Willie act as his own lawyer, and he was found guilty, it could be grounds for appeal. It was a particularly big risk in this case, for Willie was charged with two counts of assault on the court officers, as well as two counts of criminal contempt and two counts of obstruction of government administration. The assault charges were felonies. If Willie was convicted on either of them, it would be his third felony, which under New York's persistent-felon law could mean a life sentence. And it certainly looked as if Willie was going to be found guilty. The fight had taken place in plain sight in a courtroom packed with fifty people. Several court clerks and assistant district attorneys had witnessed it, and it had taken place under the nose of the judge, Justice Robert Haft.

Houdini himself couldn't wriggle out of that tight a predicament. But Willie insisted on being his own lawyer; it was his right. Justice Torres, with misgivings, finally agreed.

The prosecutor was Steven Sokolow, a tall, trim, red-haired man who had the serious, precise, self-confident manner of a good attorney. His parents had both come to New York as Jewish refugees from Europe, and his mother, who was born in Berlin, had been a friend of Anne Frank's in Holland, where both their families were hiding from the Nazis. Even though the evidence against Willie looked overwhelming, Sokolow recognized there were going to be problems with his case. On the assault charges, the injuries to the three court officers were minor—small cuts, a few bruises, and a sprained back—and none of the men required hospitalization. The most severely injured officer, Ismael Diaz, who had the bad back, was out of work for only two weeks. Juries in New York had long since grown cynical about cops and court officers, Sokolow knew. Most people in New York were likely to think such small aches and pains were just part of the job. So the jurors might not take the trial very seriously.

As soon as jury selection began, Sokolow realized that Willie, acting as his own attorney, was going to make the case seem even less weighty. To get right down to it, Willie was turning the trial into a circus. One of the first prospective jurors Willie questioned was a white woman.

"Do you know that Africans used to rule the world as kings and queens?" he asked her. When she looked puzzled, Willie put another query to her: "Do you know that white people used to have sex with animals?"

Sokolow was on his feet shouting, "Objection," and Judge Torres, a law-and-order-minded former prosecutor himself, kept sustaining Sokolow. But Sokolow quickly sensed he had to be careful about not objecting every few seconds, every time Willie said something improper or outrageous. There was a danger that if he did, the jury might feel Sokolow was being unfair to Willie, creating a backlash of sympathy for Willie. But when Sokolow didn't object, Willie was able to get ideas before the jury that he normally wouldn't be able to. By refusing to play by the rules of courtroom etiquette, Willie had trapped the prosecution.

That was how Willie kept managing to suggest that he was the real victim in the case. "I don't believe there is any such thing as a black man or a poor person getting a fair trial in America," Willie told the jury. Sokolow knew it was an inflammatory comment, but he decided to let it pass.

"This whole case is a mockery of justice, a mock," Willie went on.

"The District Attorney's office has just tried to exploit this situation to pull a thorn out of their sides, a black man, a black revolutionary."

Again, Sokolow wanted to object, but held back. He wanted to tell the jury that Willie was a strange kind of black revolutionary. He had previously been convicted of murdering two Hispanic men and attempting to assault an elderly African-American. But that kind of evidence, though true, was highly prejudicial. Sokolow knew the judge would not allow it.

Sokolow's witnesses weren't helping him much, either. Officer Diaz, who suffered the worst injury, said Willie had never hit him. His back had been hurt when Alton Maddox jumped on him from behind, Diaz testified.

Then the real disaster came from an unexpected quarter, Justice Haft. Haft had watched the fight from his bench, the best seat in the house, and Sokolow assumed the jury would be impressed by Haft. After all, he was a judge. So the prosecutor was stunned when he put his first question to Haft and the judge said he couldn't even remember whether Willie's case had been on his calendar the day the battle took place. Haft gave the same answer when Sokolow asked him what had started the fight. "I don't recall," the judge said timidly. Altogether, Haft said "I don't recall" eleven times to the prosecutor's questions.

Then it was Willie's turn to cross-examine the judge. "Did you see me strike anyone in the courtroom?" Willie asked, staring at Haft as a lion would at its prey. A silence sat in the courtroom for a long moment. Finally, the judge responded, "I don't recall seeing you strike anyone, no." All Haft could remember seeing was people struggling with each other and then crashing to the floor on the broken defense table.

Sokolow was furious and disappointed. The judge, of all people, was a weak witness.

Willie, on the other hand, was having a ball. He had reserved his opening statement until after Sokolow presented all the government's witnesses. It was an unusual maneuver, but he had calculated it for effect. "Ladies and gentlemen of the jury," he began, "in my hand I have a copy of the indictment. It is just a piece of paper."

Then he ripped it up.

"It means nothing," Willie said. He now had the jury's full attention. "It's not evidence, it does not establish guilt. As a matter of fact, an indictment can be obtained against a ham sandwich, if the D.A.'s office really wants to get an indictment."

It went on this way for eight days. When the jury finally retired to weigh the evidence, Sokolow still had some hope that the panel would see through what he thought were Willie's obvious obfuscations. But when they came back, the jury foreman said they had found Willie not guilty on all counts.

Sokolow was galled. Judge Torres was visibly angry, too. The court officers there that afternoon were so incensed, they went right over to the jury box to tell the jurors that Willie had earlier been convicted of murdering two Hispanic men. He was no black revolutionary. That left the jury unhappy and embarrassed, too; they realized they might have let a guilty man go free.

Willie was all smiles. There was a van waiting outside the courthouse to take him to Downstate prison, where he would serve his sentence for what he considered the phantom assault on Joel Brown. But this time Willie knew he had beaten the system's ass. More important, he had avoided getting a third felony conviction, which could have meant life in prison.

As he was handcuffed and put in the prison van that afternoon, Willie forgot for a moment where he was headed. He was savoring his triumph. It reminded him of his happiest times as a boy when his mother worked in the candy store. Whenever he walked into the shop, his nostrils filled up with the scent of candy: sweet tarts, lollipops, and a candy version of Kool-Aid. It had been a long time since he had smelled that smell.

PART V

CHAPTER 15

BUTCH

Free at Last

What happens to a dream deferred?
Does it dry up
Like a raisin in the sun? . . .
Or does it explode?

Langston Hughes, "Harlem"

BAKER HOUSE HAD BEEN a Roman Catholic convent, St. Leo's, on the near west side of Milwaukee. There was still a large cross on the outside of the red-brick building to mark its origins. But the parish's worshippers, working-class families of German heritage, had fled as black immigrants moved into the neighborhood in the 1950s and 1960s. In time, the nuns retreated, too, so the diocese, anxious for funds, had rented out the convent. It had now been transformed into a minimum security prison.

Butch was sent to Baker House as he worked his way toward parole in the Wisconsin prison system. When Butch had finally been released from his federal bank robbery sentence at Leavenworth in January 1982, he expected he would have only a short stay remaining in Wisconsin. It was true he had a double murder sentence to finish and when last in Wisconsin had escaped from the state hospital for the criminally insane. But he had turned into a model inmate at Leavenworth and had acquired a national reputation by his election to Phi Beta Kappa. He was confident there was no reason to hold him for long.

Butch's reception in Wisconsin was a nasty surprise. The state prison authorities knew nothing about his record at Leavenworth, or about Phi Beta Kappa. In fact, they were downright incredulous at Butch's claims; they just slapped him back in Waupun, the state's maximum security prison where he had started serving his murder sentence twenty years before. "Well, Mr. Bosket," an official told him on arrival, "it's good to have you back."

All Butch's fears, frustrations, and paranoia after a lifetime of living on the street or in institutions came back in Technicolor. "I am in hostile country, Bro," Butch wrote to his prison friend, Michael Schoenfield, who had become a parole officer after his release. "My mind is scattered just thinking about surviving. These fuckers want a pound of my flesh."

"Frankly, Mike, there is a conspiracy going on," he wrote later. "They are really serious about keeping my ass in as much as they can for as long as they can. Wisconsin, with its provincial prejudices, is unhealthy for the spiritual psychology of niggers who have a problem with tap dancing and shining shoes."

Schoenfield counseled patience. The Wisconsin Division of Corrections had made a mistake, he said. Schoenfield promised to use his contacts to start a campaign to win a parole for Butch, and he urged Butch not to give in to his anxieties. Schoenfield knew it was important for Butch to remain in control of himself. It was not just the years of being in prison, where others were always trying to control him, that made him crave mastery over himself. It was also, Schoenfield thought, that Butch was honestly afraid of himself. He had learned since he was a boy that he was capable of terrible violence when his impulses took over.

So Butch made one last great effort to harness all his fears and his energy.

Waupun
Sept. 6, 1982

Dear Mike:

Bro, for now, just know that I love you and I am under control of self—I work at maintaining control. Anger as a means of venting frustration is a luxury that I cannot play with.

Love,
Butch

Pretty soon, the public relations campaign was in high gear. The Wisconsin parole board was inundated with letters supporting Butch. The National Association for the Advancement of Colored People and black state legislators wrote arguing that Butch was "a model individual" who was being held in prison "without any rational basis." There were letters from professors at the University of Wisconsin–Milwaukee where Butch had been admitted to graduate school. And there were appeals from individuals who had taken up Butch's cause after reading about his induction into Phi Beta Kappa. They included a retired Pan American pilot and the highest-ranking female executive of a National Steel Corporation subsidiary, Susan St. Clair. She had fallen in love with Butch and showered him with gifts: an expensive sweater, a suede jacket, and a custom-tailored cord blazer. When Butch got out of prison, she was ready to give him a job at her company. But more than that, she intended to marry him, she wrote to the chairman of the parole board.

July 14, 1983

Mr. Fred Hinickle, Chairman
Parole Board
1 West Wilson Street
Madison, Wisconsin

Dear Mr. Hinickle:

I would like to take this opportunity to give you a brief synopsis of myself. I have a rather successful career in the steel industry. At present, I am the highest ranking woman in management in my corporation. My financial situation is more than comfortable. I am a single parent with three children. Pragmatically, I assure you, I am not a woman given to flights of fantasy, nor do I have any misguided causes to campaign about.

I have, over a period of time, come to know and care deeply for Butch Bosket. He is a gentle, caring man, a man who has the capacity for unlimited potential in society, with a positive, giving posture. Butch is the perfect example of what a person can accomplish in the vein of individual rehabilitation. His educational achievements as well as his emotional stability are solid proof of this fact.

Butch and myself wish to begin a life together in a loving, married relationship. I am proud to have Butch Bosket as my future spouse and equally so to have him be the stepfather to my children.

Mr. Hinickle, I wish for you to consider these things when the parole board meets to discuss Butch's request for parole. Butch Bosket is so much more than a number, 4488-A, and a file in someone's office. He is an exceptional man and the people that know him are enriched through their contact with him.

Sincerely,
Susan St. Clair

Butch had that effect on people. He was so intelligent, so articulate, and so charismatic that he exerted a strong gravitational pull. Seeing how he had reconstructed himself through education despite his early years of poverty, neglect, and crime, people got swept away.

All these letters, plus Butch's continued good conduct in prison, began to influence the Wisconsin authorities. Hinickle, the chairman of the parole board, insisted on taking a cautious approach. Butch had to serve a little more time to prove to Wisconsin that he was reformed and deserved to be freed. After all, he had been convicted of a double homicide. But Hinickle was impressed. Butch, he decided, was an extraordinary inmate. His accomplishments in prison "are, without question, among the most impressive the Board has seen," he wrote back to one of Butch's advocates. Similarly, he said, "the expressions in support of parole are almost without equal." It got to the point Hinickle thought Butch had enough going for him to support four paroles.

The Wisconsin authorities started moving Butch along the prescribed route to freedom. He had to be transferred from the maximum security prison at Waupun to a medium security facility, then to a minimum security prison, and finally to a minimum security prerelease program. Butch arrived at Baker House in Milwaukee on May 22, 1984. It had taken two and a half years since he was paroled from his federal sentence. But if Butch could stay clean, he could win his Wisconsin parole in only six more months, the following November.

Butch felt freedom coming close. "I am in control of myself here, Mike," he wrote triumphantly to Schoenfield after he arrived in Milwaukee. "In fact, there is a raw and powerful sorcery and magic in the degree of control I have over self. A kind of transcendation has occurred within me. Just watch my magic."

BAKER HOUSE WAS RUN in a pleasant, progressive way by a private nonprofit agency, Wisconsin Correctional Service. The inmates were called residents, not convicts, and they were there for the last few months of their sentences so they could go to work or to school in a prerelease program designed to show they were ready for the responsibilities of freedom. The guards, such as they were, were known as security counselors. They were mostly women and were more like social workers than corrections officers. Each had a small caseload of residents. Their main job was to make sure Baker House knew where the residents were at all times. A count was taken every hour. Several times a week, the counselors also did spot checks on the men, either by phone or by showing up where they were supposed to be.

To Butch, Baker House was a great opportunity, and he embarked on an ambitious agenda. While the other residents either had a job or went to school, Butch undertook both. He enrolled at the University of Wisconsin–Milwaukee, taking a full load of courses, to earn his master's degree in urban affairs. He worked as a teaching assistant at the university, helping a professor teach an undergraduate class entitled "Computer Fundamentals in the Behavioral Sciences." And he got a full-time job, with good pay and benefits, as a computer programmer at the Astronautics Corporation of America. The company designed and manufactured aircraft and navigational instruments for the Defense Department.

Every morning, Butch set off early from Baker House, dressed in a clean white shirt and a freshly pressed three-piece suit. His black shoes were always carefully shined. He wanted to make sure nothing went wrong that would interfere with his chances for parole.

Michael Barndt, the chairman of the urban affairs department, was excited by Butch's arrival. He had received incredible letters of recommendation for Butch from his professors at the University of Kansas, and he had read over Butch's impressive three-page resumé. That anyone had done all that while in prison was pretty amazing, Barndt thought. But Butch offered something more. He was an African-American at a school that badly wanted to recruit more black graduate students. He had unusual skill with computers in an academic field that was becoming increasingly quantitative. And he had a lifetime of firsthand knowledge about crime and prisons, which gave him special insight for research into one of America's biggest problems.

In person, Butch proved to be even better than his advance billing. He was smart and well-read, and he picked things up quickly. Barndt reckoned that Butch was in the top 10 percent of the students he had ever met. Butch was also a wonderful teaching assistant. The course was a difficult one for undergraduates, since it involved a lot of technical work with computers. But Butch was very committed, friendly, and accessible, putting in long hours helping the students with their problems.

Keeping this schedule was not easy for Butch. Baker House required its residents to take the city bus system. That was part of the discipline. For Butch, it often meant wasting several hours a day as he shuttled back and forth from his residence to the university and then on to work at Astronautics.

The spot checks also bugged him. He felt embarrassed in front of his professors and his coworkers, and the surveillance aroused his old paranoia. "I am still surrounded by this madness," he told Schoenfield. The closer he got to his final scheduled meeting with the parole board, the more apprehensive he became that the system was going to find some way to yank him back to prison. Butch still had a bad case of what convicts called jail fright.

Richard Ruck, who ran Baker House, worried that Butch's suspiciousness was getting the better of him. He often charged that someone had broken into his room or that his bank account, managed by a state accountant, was incorrect. On these occasions, Ruck tried to calm him down.

But Butch only got more upset. Once, when a counselor inspected his room and found a dirty towel, Butch was livid. "That towel wasn't dirty when I left," he said. "Somebody put it there to mess me up. That's what happened and I want it investigated." Then Butch looked at Ruck. "Well, is there going to be a report written and put in my file when I go up for parole, that I'm a slob?"

"No," Ruck reassured him. "Calm down, it's not a big thing."

But Butch's eyes were bulging again, and his jaw muscles were clenching. Ruck thought Butch was sitting on a powder keg. His eyes gave him a terrifying fierceness. Watching Butch's behavior, Ruck suggested he needed some work on anger control. His fuse was just too short. There was a new program available, Batterers Anonymous. Butch rebuffed the idea. All he needed, Butch said, was to go to work and to school to get his master's degree.

Despite Butch's fears, when November came, the parole board voted to release him. "Your enormous efforts to accomplish positive things for yourself have led to great success within the criminal justice system," the board wrote to him. The board sounded only one small note of caution: "We sincerely hope that the Butch Bosket who is now defined as a person of accomplishment is the real Butch Bosket."

At his moment of triumph, Butch looked back on a lifetime of incarceration. He was now forty-three. He had been locked up in one institution or another since he was nine.

"I have been fighting for my freedom for a number of years," Butch wrote in celebration to a friend he had met while at Leavenworth, Jeremiah Cameron. Cameron was a leader of the NAACP in Kansas City and a fatherly professor of English at a community college there. Butch knew Cameron would understand how he felt. Like Butch, Cameron had been poor and black, and as a young man many years before, he had struggled to overcome racial prejudice to become the first African-American elected to Phi Beta Kappa at Indiana University. Butch invoked the words of the Reverend Martin Luther King Jr. during the March on Washington. "Free at last. Free at last. Thank God Almighty, I am free at last."

AS SOON AS BUTCH was paroled, on November 21, 1984, he moved in with his new girlfriend, Donna Bernhagen. He had dumped Susan St.

Clair a few months before, when he felt she got too possessive. Butch hated it when someone tried to control him; he had had enough of that in prison. St. Clair was "no great loss," despite her wealth, Butch told Mike Schoenfield. At least he had gotten a wardrobe out of her. That was the cynical, hardened convict side of Butch. After all those years behind bars, he looked at people to see how he could use them—the predator's code. In prison, caring for anyone but yourself is dangerous; they might kill you. "I will never again allow myself to get involved in a relationship that is not founded on a clear quid pro quo benefit," Butch confided to Schoenfield.

Butch had picked up substantial academic learning as he remade himself. But his personal philosophy remained the way of the street and prison. "Man is at essence an atavistic beast," he wrote to Schoenfield, "a savage primitive child incapable of surviving in the absence of a directly exerted social force."

He had a particular contempt for women, part of which had to do with prison. In prison, the convicts who are sexually assaulted are the sissies, the effeminate, and they are called "punks" or "fuckboys." This applied in the outside world as well. People without dicks were weaklings, Butch thought, and you can screw them because they have no respect.

Part of Butch's scorn for women went even deeper, back to his childhood. His mother, he believed, had abandoned him to go off and be a prostitute, leaving Butch alone on the street. In his adult life, he was still bitter. "She was a whore," Butch told Jeremiah Cameron. "I had to steal food and sleep in alleys just to survive." Butch said he had no respect for women. "They are just something to be used."

Butch had met Donna at Baker House. She was a thirty-nine-year-old instructor at a beauty college. She had stopped by Baker House one evening with another resident who was a student of hers. Butch was standing near the front desk and liked what he saw. Donna was a voluptuous, slightly overweight, dyed blond who wore heavy makeup and had big hair. When she was young, she had been very pretty and had dreams of being a movie star. She had been forced to settle for being a beautician, but she still put great effort into her appearance, and men noticed.

Butch got her name and phone number, and started calling her every night. Donna was in the midst of a bad divorce, so she was feeling down and was flattered by Butch's attention. He was the most intelligent man she had ever met. Pretty soon, she was head over heels in love with Butch, like a teenager.

When Butch was paroled, he was supposed to move into an apartment he had rented in White Fish Bay, an exclusive upper-middle-class suburb just north of Milwaukee on Lake Michigan. Butch jokingly called it

"White Folks Bay." Mike Schoenfield, who had worked as a parole officer, had urged Butch to get his own place. Schoenfield knew that would be critical to the parole officer assigned to Butch, Ben Bennett. Cohabitation was still technically against the law in Wisconsin; it was the wrong way to start a new life so soon after being paroled. Unhappily for Butch, Bennett was a rigid, old-fashioned parole agent, a guy with a badge who was not impressed by Butch's academic achievements. Bennett's philosophy was simple—you've committed the crime, you've got to do the time.

Legally, there was no limit on how long Butch would be on parole, since he had been convicted of murder. It could go on forever, unless his parole officer became sympathetic and released him from it.

Despite knowing that it would raise his parole officer's mistrust, Butch moved in with Donna. He couldn't resist taking the risk. His life had been a series of fast, dangerous adventures. He had won his freedom after superhuman effort, but, like many convicts, he was addicted to excitement. Normal life on the outside with its daily grind was too humdrum. "I am not spiritually capable of existing in conventionality," he once confessed to Schoenfield.

Donna lived in a lime-colored duplex town house in the heart of Milwaukee's south side. It was a heavily Polish community, very white, working-class, and family-oriented. All the houses in the neighborhood had nicely kept lawns with shrubs that were perfectly trimmed, either round or square, never natural. Donna's house had an expensive hand-hewn stone bottom and aluminum siding on the upper floor. There was a locust tree in the front yard and a barbecue in the back. It looked more like a suburb than part of the city.

Donna had twin six-year-old children, Matthew and "Kristin." She had won temporary custody of them when she filed for divorce a few months earlier, though her husband was in court contesting her control over them. Donna was a devoted mother and kept their rooms compulsively clean. She had even labeled their dresser drawers. Kristin had lovely features, and her mother had hopes of making her into a child model, so she had commissioned a portfolio of photographs. When Donna proudly showed them to Schoenfield, he was taken aback. In some of the pictures, Kristin was standing in the bathtub only partly clothed. To Schoenfield, they were borderline pornographic, but he didn't think anything more about it at the time.

This should have been the best time in Butch's life. He had finally been released from prison. He had a good job at Astronautics, he was doing well in graduate school, and he was highly regarded as a teaching assistant. Butch and his professors were talking about his going on for a

Ph.D. after he earned his master's degree. He now also had an attractive and adoring girlfriend. But at the end of November, just after he was paroled and left Baker House, Butch seemed to get more tense and nervous. He was drinking more coffee and smoking more cigarettes. Barndt, his professor, thought Butch was trying to do too much and was feeling the pressure. He urged Butch to slow down.

Butch said he still felt caged. He was free, but he didn't know how to deal with freedom. He had been in prison too long. Butch was still thinking and acting like a convict; the predator's code was binding him with metal chains. His predicament reminded one of his professors of a phrase by Max Weber, Butch's favorite social theorist. A person can only succeed, Weber wrote, if he recognizes "the demon who holds the fibers of his very life." Butch could not shake the demon.

A few nights after Butch moved in with Donna, he was helping give Kristin a bath. Butch thought the girl had a cute body, so he got out a camera and began taking pictures of her, including close-ups of what Kristin called her "privates." Butch said he could sell the photos for big money.

After Donna put Kristin to bed that night, Butch stayed in her room. He was wearing only his underpants. He came over and sat on the bed with the little girl, pulled up her nightgown, and took off her panties. Butch was breaking all the rules now, but in his mind, he was just living by the prisoners' code of taking what he could get. He ran his finger around Kristin's vagina, then pushed his penis in. Kristin cried out. "It hurts," she said.

Kristin could see her mother standing in the darkened doorway of her room, and she asked her to make Butch stop. But Donna was in thrall to Butch. He was so smart and so powerful, like no one she had ever known. Butch would stand over her and say, "Obey me, obey me," and Donna felt helpless to resist.

When Donna heard her daughter's plea, she said, "No. I won't stop him."

After a while, Butch withdrew his penis and told Kristin to roll over on her side. Then he thrust it in her rectum. That hurt, too. But the six-year-old was too dazed and confused to cry this time. She lay there silently.

Butch was also making moves on the live-in babysitter, Kathy Theissen, a twenty-one-year-old. "I need more than one woman to keep me happy," Butch told her. "I want to make love with you." Theissen was outraged, but scared, too. She had heard Butch boast that he had killed four men and that he had recently been paroled from Leavenworth for bank robbery. He looked enormous and menacing to her. She had seen his eyes bulge when he got angry, and she had heard moans coming from Donna's bedroom at night. Afterward, Donna said Butch had been punishing her, but she deserved it.

Still, Theissen refused Butch's demand for sex. "Who is going to be next?" she asked defiantly. "The children?"

On weekends, the twins' grandmother, Eleanor Bernhagen, came to pick up Kristin and Matthew to visit with her and their father, Michael Bernhagen. On December 1, when she brought Kristin to her house, she noticed that the child was unusually quiet and withdrawn, just sitting on a chair and sucking her finger. Kristin also refused to take a bath. She said her "peepee" and "pooper" hurt too much. The grandmother noticed that the girl's vagina and rectum were red and irritated. When she asked what was wrong, Kristin would not answer. It had been only ten days since Butch was paroled and moved in with Donna.

Things came to a head on New Year's Day when Butch kicked the babysitter out of the house and fired her. Theissen went directly to Kristin's father and grandmother with her suspicions. The next weekend, when Eleanor Bernhagen picked Kristin up, she questioned her granddaughter more closely. In tears, the girl acknowledged why she hurt. That was the information the family had been waiting for. The father and grandparents and the babysitter marched straight to the county department of social services to file a complaint. After that, they took Kristin to the Sexual Assault Treatment Center at Family Hospital for a medical exam. A nurse found that her vagina was enlarged and bruised, consistent with sexual abuse.

When Butch's parole agent heard about the charges, he didn't wait for any further investigation or an indictment. He simply revoked Butch's parole. The police picked up Butch in the computer room at Astronautics. He was polite, said there had been a mistake, and apologized to his fellow employees as he was led away in handcuffs.

It was January 24, 1985. Butch had been free for just two months.

BUTCH INSISTED HE WAS innocent and hired a lawyer. Donna, who was not charged, backed him totally. They were being framed by people out to get them, Donna claimed. Her estranged husband couldn't stand the idea of her living with a black man. Her mother-in-law was a conservative Roman Catholic who went to Mass daily and did not like Butch making fun of religion with the children. The babysitter was mad because she had been fired. And the nurse who performed the examination on Kristin just happened to be the new girlfriend of Donna's husband. So Donna and Butch said they smelled a conspiracy.

Seymour Pikovsky, Butch's new lawyer, thought Butch and Donna's story had credibility. In bitter custody fights, people often make wild claims. It was a strange case for Pikovsky, he had to admit—one of the two men Butch had murdered in 1962 had been an in-law of his wife's. But he began to prepare a defense and felt Butch had a chance.

The Schoenfields were also confident Butch was not guilty. They recalled that two years earlier a man had tried to molest their two-year-old daughter in the yard behind their house. Luckily, an older boy was watching and chased the molester away before she was harmed. When they told Butch about it, he wrote from prison, "Bro and Sis, I am not going to lose my cool, but I must have that man's name. If the police arrest him and send him to prison, fine. . . . But something more must be done, over and above any legalistic judgment. This man must be made to suffer."

Michael Schoenfield thought he knew why Butch was so insistent on seeking revenge. In prison, a sex offender is at the bottom of the barrel. He is a deviant, Mr. Slant Eyes. It would go against the most sacred rule of the convicts' code for Butch to mess with a little girl.

After Butch had been put back in jail, Schoenfield could tell his friend was despondent.

"I'm never going to get out," Butch said in a phone call from jail. "I'm a black man charged with raping a little white girl. I can't win."

But Schoenfield sensed that the situation was even bleaker than that. In the past, each time Butch got arrested, going back to jail was like coming home. That was one of the things straight people didn't know about prison. For a criminal like Butch, going to jail simply meant that his street life would end and his prison life would begin again. Most of the people he knew were in prison. You come through the line and somebody's got a joint for you or a pack of cigarettes or an extra sandwich, and then you know you're home and you're safe because you have your whole group around you again. For a lot of people, their entire neighborhood is in prison. The kid next door is waiting for you on the chow line with extra food.

As tough as it is to go back to prison, your friends try to make it easier for you. "Hey, man, what happened?" they ask sympathetically. "Tell us about it." For someone like Butch, who had a reputation as a big-time professional criminal, a bank robber and a killer, things were even better. He had a lot of respect in prison.

But now, if he was convicted of sexually assaulting a six-year-old, the situation would be utterly different. The Butch Bosket myth would be gone. He would just be an ordinary sex offender. None of the other convicts would talk to him. No one would bring him an extra sandwich, or walk around the recreation field with him. He would be cut off, ostracized, a nonperson.

Butch made a vow he would rather die than go back to prison again, especially not as a sex offender. His closest friend at Leavenworth, Rodney Britton, a tall, skinny twenty-seven-year-old convicted bank robber, had set an example for Butch. Rodney and Butch used to go to class together, and Rodney often drew a picture on the blackboard. It was always the same drawing—a dead dog on its back, with an arrow through its stomach. Rodney said it meant "I'll end up a dead dog before I'll get caught."

Rodney was paroled from Leavenworth a few months before Butch. He drove down to northwest Arkansas and held up a Pizza Hut in Fayetteville. Later that evening, he was pulled over for a routine traffic stop by the police chief in the small town of West Fork. As the officer approached his car, Britton killed him with a .44-caliber magnum pistol and then hiked into the Ozark Mountains to escape. It was the same territory where Jesse James had operated, along with Belle Starr, the Bandit Queen, who had hidden the James brothers in her brothel. One hundred state troopers and sheriffs' deputies from Arkansas, Missouri, and Oklahoma spent a week tracking Britton. A police officer riding a mule finally found him in a remote log cabin farmhouse. When the policeman climbed a ladder up to the second floor attic where Britton was hiding, the two men saw each other and fired simultaneously. The officer was seriously wounded; Britton was killed. Butch took the news badly.

Now, in the sexual assault case, Butch was growing more morose and desperate as the days passed. He was housed in the old county jail in the Safety Building in downtown Milwaukee. It was the same place he had been held pending his murder trial two decades earlier. Sitting there all day, Butch could feel the past in the cell with him like a malevolent spirit. Things were spinning out of control, the control he had sought so hard to impose on himself. Then he remembered Hesse, and *Steppenwolf* and the magic theater. Hesse had overcome reality with magic. So could Butch. He reached into his conjure bag for his best magic trick.

Since Butch had been put back in jail in January, Donna had been coming to visit as often as permitted. Given the charges against him, they were not allowed to touch, so Donna sat in a small cubicle and talked to Butch by phone. He had also been calling her at home every night. Despite their troubles, Donna missed Butch badly. She missed touching and hugging him, and she was getting depressed. The court had given her husband custody of their children after a judge heard the charges about what went on in her house. She couldn't bear the thought of losing Butch as well as the kids.

One night in February, Butch told her he had a plan, an old prison ruse. If you swallow enough salt, it will irritate your stomach, like an ulcer, causing pain and bleeding. A convict who knew how could manage to cough up blood, making his condition look very serious. The county jail lacked its own medical facilities, so prisoners who were ill had to be taken to an outside hospital. That was the opportunity Butch wanted. He had already escaped twice from hospitals in Wisconsin.

Butch asked Donna to find out how much salt he needed, given his weight. She called the state poison office in Green Bay, posing as a student doing research on the toxicity of salt. With information from them, she calculated it would take eighteen teaspoons. Butch began saving the little salt packets served with his meals. They had plenty of time. Butch's trial on the sexual assault charge was not scheduled to begin until April.

On Friday, March 1, Butch told Donna he would have enough salt by Wednesday, March 6. Besides, that was a lucky day—Butch's forty-fourth birthday.

Donna started making preparations. She reserved two tickets on Amtrak from Chicago to Los Angeles. She bought a big, brown curly wig and a nurse's cap, pin, and uniform as a disguise for herself. She also purchased two guns. Donna had grown up around men who liked guns, so she knew a lot about them. She picked out a snub-nose black .38-caliber Colt Agent revolver, and another short, two-inch, nickel-finish .38-caliber Smith & Wesson revolver. She wanted short barrels because they would be easier to hide in her nurse's outfit.

Saturday morning, while she was doing a customer's hair at the beauty school, one of her students, Gilbert Mickelson, asked her how Butch was. Donna had brought Butch around the school before he was rearrested and introduced him as her fiancé. Mickelson was just making polite conversation; he knew nothing about the charges or Butch being in jail. Now Donna blurted out the whole thing, about the assault and Butch's arrest.

Mickelson and Donna's customer couldn't believe what they were hearing. Mickelson wasn't sure what to say. He had taken a liking to Donna. Was there anything he could do to help, he asked? Yes, Donna replied. She said she was having a rummage sale the next day, Sunday, to raise money, and she could use an extra hand. He agreed to come by her house.

Mickelson was a slightly built eighteen-year-old with a punk haircut. His parents had been divorced when he was a small child, and he had been brought up by his father. Mickelson had done poorly in school, but his neighbors liked him. He was always willing to babysit or help the elderly, and he seemed like a nice boy, not the usual troublemaking teenager. Maybe it was his open, ingenuous manner, or perhaps it was his neediness and vulnerability, but Donna felt drawn to him. He was another lost soul like herself.

At the garage sale, Donna sold off everything: her furniture, the silverware, her kids' clothes, even her makeup and hair rollers. Mickelson sensed that when a lady like Donna, who put such stock in her appearance, sold her beauty supplies, things were serious.

On Wednesday, Mickelson asked if he could go with Donna to visit Butch. They were hoping they would find that Butch had swallowed the salt, vomited some blood, and been taken to the hospital. Donna explained they would have to pretend to be shocked.

They arrived at the Safety Building at 6:30 p.m. and signed in as visitors. Just before 7, a guard told them Butch had been rushed to the hospital. Donna started crying and asked which hospital. The guard said he could not give her that information, since Butch was a prisoner. On the way out, Donna spotted another officer whom she recognized and began crying more profusely.

"Excuse me, ma'am, you look real upset," he said. "What's wrong?"

"My fiancé has been taken to the hospital and they won't tell me which one," Donna said.

"Well, maybe I can call out there for you," he said. He was breaking jail regulations. But Donna looked in bad shape.

He reported that Butch had been taken to Milwaukee County General Hospital in Wauwatosa, a suburb on the northwest side of the city. There was a big complex of hospitals there, on 240 acres, like a small city.

When Donna and Mickelson reached the hospital, they found Butch in the X-ray department. The sheriff's deputy guarding Butch broke the rules again and let her into the room. She kissed Butch on the chest. "Baby, I love you," she said.

When they finished the X-rays, a nurse told Donna she had to leave. They were going to transfer Butch to Froedtert Memorial Lutheran Hospital, to a gastroenterology center where the pain and burning and bleeding in Butch's stomach, whatever was causing them, could be treated. Froedtert was up a gentle hill behind County General Hospital, with a long passageway connecting the two institutions. Donna insisted on staying with Butch. As they wheeled him on a stretcher to Froedtert, she walked alongside, holding his hand. Donna was acting more and more distraught. Only after he was settled in Room 3158 did she agree to leave.

On the way out, Donna told Mickelson to memorize Froedtert's layout. This was where they would make the break-out.

They drove back to Donna's house, and she fixed Mickelson a wine cooler. At midnight, Butch called from the hospital.

"Everything is fine," he said. "You can visit tomorrow."

That was a prearranged signal. The escape would come the next day.

Donna was elated. While they were sitting and talking, she asked Mickelson if he would like to come along. Not as an accomplice, she said, but to start a new life for himself. "Of course, it might get real hairy," Donna said. "There might be cops and shooting." Mickelson was terrified of guns, but he thought an escape was a neat idea and he wanted to get far away from his father. He agreed to join them.

They began to pack. Donna had all of her clothes and Butch's things as well, including a portable typewriter and the school transcripts of which he was so proud. By the time they finished, it was 4 in the morning. Donna had stuffed her canary-yellow Nissan with fifteen suitcases, cardboard boxes, and paper bags, plus a cooler. There were also clothes on hangers in the backseat. Anyone looking at the car would think they were going for an ordinary trip.

Butch thought the night was dragging on forever. His stomach was hurting, and he was impatient as usual. He spent most of the hours smoking or chatting with the nurses. The sheriff's deputy guarding him thought Butch was depressed, but otherwise a model prisoner. There was nothing suspicious in his behavior.

At 6 on Thursday morning, Butch called a sleepy Donna. "Everyone is treating me nicely here," he said, "including the one deputy." That was another signal. He had only one guard.

At noon, Butch called her again. "You can come for your visit at two," he said.

Before leaving the house, Donna put on the wig and checked her makeup one last time. She had to tone it down a little to look more like a nurse. Mickelson climbed in the cramped backseat of the car, so when they got to the hospital, Butch could jump in the front.

Froedtert was a gleaming white structure with big circular towers on each end of its front side. The towers housed stairwells and looked like farm silos. That was appropriate, because the money to build the hospital had come from Kurtis Froedtert, who ran the world's largest malting company at the time when Milwaukee was the beer capital of America.

Donna parked her car beside the tower at the left front corner of the building. Butch's room was almost directly above her on the second floor. To escape, all you had to do was walk down one flight of stairs inside the tower and out the side door to the car. As Donna got out of the car, Mickelson said, "Good luck." She left the motor running so he could listen to the radio.

The main front door to the hospital was a few feet around the corner. Donna walked into the lobby and paused to make sure of her bearings. Inside, the lobby was like the courtyard in an Eric Portman hotel, with a high ceiling that went all the way to the top of the hospital and a profusion of green plants, flowers, and birch trees. Donna went into a women's restroom and took off the blue trench coat she was wearing over her nurse's uniform. She stuck the two guns into her waistband. Then she took an elevator at the back of the lobby to Butch's floor.

At 2:15, sheriff's deputy Mariellen Kostopulos looked up from her chair at the seat of Butch's hospital bed to see a tall, buxom nurse with a bad bouffant wig and a stethoscope around her neck. She was cradling in her arms a plastic clipboard that looked like a patient's chart.

"Hi, Mr. Bosket, I have to ask you a few questions," the woman said as she approached the bed. "I'm going to be your nurse."

The next thing Kostopulos knew, the woman was pointing a revolver at her left temple. "Don't move," she said.

Butch was handcuffed to the rail on the bed. He was wearing a blue-and-white hospital gown and had an IV tube in his arm. Kostopulos was the daughter of a truck driver and considered herself a tough judge of humanity, but she was impressed that Butch seemed refined and articulate for an inmate. Just before the woman walked in, Butch had been telling her about the charges against him. "Can you believe this?" he said. "I'm a Phi Beta Kappa and have a good job. Why are they making this stuff up about me and the girl?"

Now Butch told Donna to throw him her other gun, and he put it right between Kostopulos's eyes. "I'm sorry I have to do this," he said.

At that moment, Kostopulos was actually glad Butch was the one holding the gun on her, because Donna was beginning to shake, and he was very calm. He told Donna to get out a handcuff key she had purchased and uncuff him. He also ordered her to take the deputy's revolver, so they had a total of three guns. Then he yanked out the IV, sending a spurt of blood to the floor. After that, he took Kostopulos into the bathroom, put her own handcuffs on her, and chained her left leg to the rail by the toilet with a leg iron. As a further precaution, Butch gagged her with a paisley bandana.

Everything had gone perfectly up to now. Donna had brought a shirt, a pair of pants, shoes, and a coat for Butch, and he was starting to change into them when the phone rang. It was another sheriff's officer who was scheduled to take over from Kostopulos later in the afternoon.

"Where is the deputy?" the man asked when Donna answered.

"The deputy?" she said haltingly. "Ah, umm, well, ah, she's not here right now. This is Mrs., I mean, Nurse Bernhagen. I'll tell her you called."

Now Butch's impatience showed. He had only gotten as far as pulling on his new pants. "Hurry up," he shouted at Donna, and they ran out of the room.

The escape route from here was simple. It was only a few steps to the left across the hallway to reach the stairs that led down to the side door and the car. But in her alarm, Donna became disoriented and turned the wrong way as she came out of the room. She went to the right, toward the stairs on the opposite side of the hospital.

When they got to the bottom and came outside, Donna was mystified. The car was not there. She looked helplessly at Butch. He decided to take over.

It was a cold gray day. There were still small mounds of old snow on the ground. Butch had on only his thin hospital gown over the pants and his hospital slippers. His feet were freezing. But he couldn't run in the flimsy slippers, so he took them off by the door.

At that moment, Jim King, the hospital's director of public relations, was looking out an office window. He saw a man in a hospital gown start to run toward the back of Froedtert. A nurse was chasing him. "It must be one of our friends from the Mental Health Complex escaping against medical advice," King joked to a secretary.

Butch had chosen the wrong way, too. He and Donna were only a few steps from the front of the hospital. The car was around the corner to the left. But he had turned right, heading downhill toward the rear of the building. He didn't know how far it was that way. Behind Froedtert was County General Hospital. It was almost three city blocks from the front of Froedtert to get around County General, and another three back. The layout was vast and confusing. People got lost there every day.

Deputy Kostopulos waited a minute and a half. She wanted to make sure Butch and Donna had left the hospital so there would be no shooting inside with all the patients, doctors, nurses, and visitors. Then she managed to pull the nurse's cord in the bathroom.

James Paradinovich, another sheriff's deputy, heard the call "Prisoner escaped" over the radio in his squad car while he was patrolling the medical complex grounds. The dispatcher said an unknown white female, posing as a nurse, had overcome a deputy guarding the prisoner. The dispatcher had no description and no names.

Paradinovich, though, knew right away it was Butch and Donna. It was a strange coincidence, he thought. He had been posted as a bailiff in court the day Butch was arrested and again the day he had his preliminary hearing. Those were the only two times he had ever been a bailiff. He had also seen Butch that very morning when he was asked to take a radio battery to the deputy in the hospital room. So he called in a description and headed his car down a roadway along the left side of Froedtert.

He was opposite the passageway connecting the two hospitals when he spotted Butch and Donna jogging back up the hill toward him. They had worked their way around to the front of County General and were finally headed toward Donna's Nissan.

Butch saw the sheriff's cruiser coming, its lights flashing. He and Donna ducked behind a tan Buick in a parking lot. Paradinovich was out of the car now, his revolver drawn. As he advanced past a row of cars to within twenty feet, Butch jumped up and fired. He had guns in both hands.

Just in time, Paradinovich rolled behind a green Ford van for cover. From there, he could see only part of Butch through the window of the Buick he was hiding behind. Paradinovich's training took over now, as if he were on automatic. He crouched to one knee and fired back twice at Butch's midsection, the center of mass, the proper target to stop an armed suspect. His rounds had to go through the Buick's windows before they could hit Butch. The Milwaukee County Sheriff's Department used hollow-point bullets that flattened out when they hit something. So after they went through the window on the driver's side and then the window on the passenger's side, they had little impact left. One shot did strike Butch in the arm, a small wound that did not slow him.

Butch kept bobbing up and down like a turkey, firing over the Buick's roof at Paradinovich. Some of the bullets smashed the glass in the van the deputy was using for cover. He tried to call for backup on his radio, but at first he couldn't get air time. Everyone else was announcing that they were responding or they were reporting bogus sightings of the suspects. Paradinovich was feeling very alone. To make things worse, he couldn't risk shooting again. There was a building behind Butch, and he could see nurses filling up the windows to watch.

At that moment, Donna came out from behind the Buick and walked toward Paradinovich. "Don't shoot, I'm a hostage," she said.

But he recognized her, wig and all. If it had been any other officer, he might have fallen for the ploy. Paradinovich was also suspicious of the way she held her hands together at her waist, with something silver gleaming between them—a gun, he guessed.

"Drop it," he ordered, "or I'll blow your fucking head off."

Donna fell to her hands and knees and crawled back behind the Buick.

Butch had now used up all the rounds in the snub-nose Colt and the revolver taken from his guard. He told Donna to give him the third gun.

Butch could see other officers starting to arrive—hospital security guards and more sheriff's deputies in squad cars. He knew now he couldn't escape. He would not surrender and go back to prison. He had made that promise to himself and his friend at Leavenworth, Rodney Britton.

As he surveyed the situation, it was as if his whole life had been scripted for this minute, all the violence and recklessness, ever since he drew his self-portrait at Wiltwyck holding a knife pointed at himself. Butch only had to do what came naturally—act on impulse.

Paradinovich's view was blocked. But Nancy Hoffman, a nursing student, could see everything from the window of her dietetics class, as if she were watching a television show. After Donna crawled back, Hoffman saw the two people talking, or arguing, or maybe embracing, she wasn't sure which. Donna started to stand up. Butch grabbed her around the neck with his left arm, pulling her closer to him. At the same moment, his right hand came up, and he shot her in the temple.

Then Butch placed the muzzle in his right ear and pulled the trigger.

Mickelson was still waiting in the getaway car, right outside the hospital door, listening to the radio. He sat there calmly for two hours after Butch and Donna were dead, with no one paying attention to him, until he went up to Butch's room to ask what happened and a security guard arrested him.

The next day, Jeremiah Cameron read about Butch's death in a Kansas City newspaper. In an important way, Cameron believed, Butch was a metaphor for the plight of blacks in America. He was highly intelligent—a Phi Beta Kappa—but he still could not succeed. It reminded Cameron of a line in a play by Ossie Davis, *Purlie Victorious*: "All these wings and they still won't let me fly."

As he pondered that, Cameron came to think that maybe Butch's death was for the best. In the end, Butch had found freedom the only way he could. He had finally gotten out of prison, but he couldn't get prison out of himself.

CHAPTER 16

WILLIE

A Monster Created by the System

Don't be shocked when I say I was in prison.

Malcolm X, "Message to the Grass Roots"

LAURA BROUGHT WILLIE the news the Sunday after Butch killed himself. Willie was at Downstate prison in Fishkill, fifty miles up the Hudson River from Manhattan, and he was dressed in brand-new state greens, the fatigues issued to all New York State inmates. The uniform was so new, it had the same fresh smell and crispness as a suit on a rack in a department store. It had been only ten days since Willie was sent to Downstate, after he was acquitted on the charges of assaulting the court officers. His victory didn't matter, of course, because he still had to serve out his sentence for what a jury had declared to be an attempted attack on Joel Brown.

In the visitors room, Laura took a seat on a plastic chair. "I got something to tell you," she said.

The way she spoke, very slow and serious, Willie could tell there was going to be bad news. He didn't like to be told things this way, as if he were going to break down and cry. Willie was a good convict, and good convicts never betray an emotion.

He snapped at her the way he imagined James Cagney did in a movie he had seen about the big joint: "Come on, let it out. Let it out."

"Your father's dead," Laura said.

"Yeah, okay," was all Willie allowed himself to say.

"He was shot," Laura added laconically. She was not a person to show emotion, either.

After his mother left, Willie got to thinking about what had happened to his father. The way he had it figured, Butch had gone soft and was trying to be a white man. But dying in a shoot-out with the police while trying to break out of prison, that was something else. Even though his father had counseled Willie not to try to go out in a blaze of glory, Butch had ended up doing just that. It restored his father to a place of dignity in Willie's mind.

Willie was not superstitious, but bad things seemed to happen in March. It was in March that he had murdered two men and been arrested. It was in March that he had been picked up for the incident with Joel Brown that had landed him back in jail. Now, in March 1985, his father had died while trying to escape. There were too many coincidences.

Willie was facing only a three-and-a-half- to seven-year sentence for the attempted assault on Brown. With good behavior, he could be out as early as 1988. All he had to do was stay out of trouble. But after he learned about his father's death, Willie became more and more convinced he would never leave prison alive. His old sense of predestination descended on him more strongly than ever. He could feel the burden of his family's legendary past weighing on him like an evil talisman. With it came a terrible rage and a desperate desire to prove once and for all how violent he could be. He embarked on an all-out war against his guards and the system they represented. Willie called it going kamikaze. He said to himself, "I'm going to be the worst fucking nightmare the Department of Correctional Services ever had to deal with." In his way, Willie became as heedless and self-destructive as the zealous white patriarchs of old Edgefield who fought for honor. Willie went into combat for respect. He was smart enough to know it was a battle he could not win, but it was a fight he could not prevent.

A few days after Laura told him about his father, Willie swallowed a metal toenail clipper. He was vomiting blood and had an acute pain in his abdomen. Willie figured the guards would have to take him to the prison hospital ward for X-rays, and he might have a better chance there to escape. Willie did not know that his father had swallowed salt in a similar scheme.

Sure enough, Willie did get taken for X-rays. Over the next few days, they showed the nail clipper slowly making its way through his stomach. But after the piece of metal eventually passed through his bowel, Willie was returned to prison. He was classified "Maximum A Security," placing him in the most dangerous category. The superintendent also decided to assign Willie to what was known as administrative protective custody. He was locked in a special cell and allowed out only an hour a day for exercise. It was the same as being in solitary confinement, except that he was assigned to a different block than the convicts in solitary, who were kept in the Special Housing Unit, the SHU, better known as the box.

Willie was insulted by his placement. He wanted to be in the box, like any really violent prisoner. Here I am, Willie thought, a person respected throughout the entire prison system. But how can I keep my respect in protective custody? Usually, protective custody was reserved for homosexuals or inmates who were in trouble with other prisoners, like those who could not pay off a debt. The guards, Willie felt, were disrespecting him.

Being in the box had several other advantages, to Willie's way of thinking. He didn't have his father's size and menacing physical presence. Now full-grown, he stood only five feet nine inches tall and weighed a slender one hundred fifty pounds. So he was much safer being in a single cell in the box than in general population. It meant he didn't have to worry about fights, and he didn't always have to be watching his back. For someone raised on the street, with a heavy dose of paranoia, that was a major benefit. Willie could also sit and read whenever he wanted to, or listen to the radio—he had become a fan of "All Things Considered" on National Public Radio. He didn't have to go to work or exercise according to the prison's schedule. And being in solitary gave Willie a sense of control. He felt as if he himself determined where he was assigned, and though it might be only a tiny, locked space, he was master of that space. His jailers could think they had Willie under their control, but in Willie's mind, he was king of his own dominion.

So the day the nail clipper passed through Willie's system and he was returned to protective custody, he staged an incident. "Let me out of this cell so that I can do something to go to the box," he yelled at a guard, Wayne Theiss.

"Don't do anything stupid," Theiss replied. "The sergeant will be here and you can talk to him."

Two minutes later, Theiss looked up and saw a flaming bedsheet hanging from the door to Willie's cell. Theiss grabbed a chemical fire extinguisher and with two other guards rushed to put out the fire.

As soon as the blaze was out, Willie yelled, "Open this door, motherfuckers, so I can cut you up." He spit in the face of one of the corrections officers, and then shouted, "This will get me in the box."

Just to make sure, Willie reached in his pocket and pulled out a homemade seven-inch metal shank. "Come on in and I'll cut your eyes out," Willie challenged them. Eventually, a lieutenant arrived and negotiated with Willie, getting him to surrender his weapon. In exchange, Willie got his wish. He was given a disciplinary hearing and ordered to spend thirty days in the box.

Willie now believed he was engaged in a holy crusade. Over the next eighteen months, he launched an orgy of attacks on his guards and the prison system. Each assault, however badly it ended for Willie, only made him feel more powerful. He set fire to his cell seven times. He repeatedly spat in the face of corrections officers, once right in the eyes of a prison superintendent. Another time, after he filled his wastepaper basket with water, he dumped it on a deputy superintendent who had stopped by to visit him. "That's so you know I'm playing for keeps, you white, honky, slime-bag motherfuckers," Willie said.

A favorite trick was to throw urine on his guards. Several times, he tried to escape by ripping open a hole in the ceiling of his cell. The guards would find him with only his legs dangling down from the ceiling. Given the chance, he bit guards on their fingers or legs. Repeatedly, Willie somehow managed to fashion crude but deadly weapons while in solitary confinement: sharpened toothbrushes, razor blades stuck in the handle of a toothbrush, and knives as long as sixteen inches he made from pieces of metal torn from the spartan fixtures in his cell. When his guards entered his cell to disarm him, Willie threatened them.

"I'm going to go off on the count of three, if you don't stop," he once told three corrections officers who came in to restrain him. Then he stared at one of the men, Leroy Stewart Jr., with a look as if Stewart were the prisoner and Willie were on the outside. It was the cold, hard stare of a man who was used to being in command. A few seconds later, Willie started counting: "One, two, three." When he got to three, he charged Stewart and tried to bite him on the shoulder. His mouth was wide open. After the three guards quelled him, Willie still glared out of his cell at Stewart. "I'm going to get you and your family for this," Willie yelled. "You're mine. You ain't shit."

New York's lack of a death penalty gave Willie another way to taunt the corrections officers, known by convicts as COs. "You can't do anything more to me for killing a CO than for assaulting a CO," he liked to say. "So I might as well kill you." The guards knew he was right.

With female prison employees, Willie often turned on the charm, as he had done earlier in Wiltwyck and Brookwood. He still had that gorgeous boyish smile, those big dimples in his cheeks, and a sweet way of talking. He was so smart that he often knew what people were thinking before the thought even occurred to them. That helped him get into people's minds. A female guard in one prison fell for Willie so hard that, he claimed, she even helped him plan an escape. It was foiled when another convict gave an anonymous tip to the guards. They pulled Willie out of line unexpectedly one day to frisk him; it turned out he had a diagram of the prison.

The prison authorities fought back with the means at their disposal. They put Willie in handcuffs, but he often twisted or cracked them open. They tried putting a black iron box over the handcuffs, and then attached the cuffs by a metal chain to a heavy belt around his waist. Willie twisted himself free anyway. They put him in leg irons. He broke the leg irons. When he became truly uncontrollable, the guards hog-tied him. They put him facedown on his cell bunk, then chained his hands and his feet together behind him. That way, he couldn't even roll over.

Sometimes, the authorities put Willie on a hardship diet for weeks at a time, consisting of water, cabbage, and neutraloaf, a bread-shaped, pasty, tasteless concoction that was useful only for the vitamins and minerals it contained. Every day that Willie was on this diet, he retaliated by sending a piece of neutraloaf or soggy cabbage in the mail to one of the guards or a senior prison officer.

Whenever Willie acted up, a guard had to write out a misbehavior report, which led to disciplinary hearings. All the hearing officer could do to Willie was give him more time in the box. Pretty soon, it got to be a joke. Willie was getting more years in solitary than he had in his prison sentence.

What the guards didn't understand was that Willie liked solitary. One time, a deputy superintendent jokingly suggested that he was going to put Willie back in general population. "You can't do that," Willie replied nervously. "It's against prison regulations." Deep down, Willie knew it would also have meant the loss of his celebrity status. He would have become just another convict.

After a particularly serious episode, the Department of Correctional Services often transferred Willie from one prison to another to try to defuse the tensions that had built up between him and his jailers. It could get very personal in the box. And so Willie made his rounds of the New York prison system, just as he had a few years before in the state's juvenile justice institutions. In a short time, Willie saw the inside of Downstate, Attica, Midstate, Auburn, Collins, Sullivan, Shawangunk, and Woodbourne.

The superintendent of Collins, Charles A. James, an African-American, took an avuncular interest in Willie. He could see Willie's potential, and he thought more might be gained by treating Willie with respect than by the usual tough disciplinary approach. So he granted Willie some privileges. He let Willie have a television set and a cordless phone in his cell, though he was supposed to be in solitary. James also permitted Willie to wear a gold chain around his neck and rings on his fingers.

Most important to Willie, he was allowed to have visits in the box with his new girlfriend, a stunning-looking woman almost six feet tall, with long, shapely legs and broad, high cheekbones. Willie and his wife, Sharon, had split up after he was convicted for assaulting Joel Brown.

Willie had it made at Collins. Willie knew it; the guards knew it; and for a time Superintendent James thought things were working fine. Then Willie started getting frustrated. There was no more challenge, no fun in getting along so well with his jailers. One day, out of the blue, Willie accused a corrections officer of spitting at him. The guard denied it. So Willie threw urine on him, then electrified his cell door so that any guard who touched it would get a shock. The cease-fire was over and Willie's war had resumed. Willie himself acknowledged that he was responsible for ruining a good situation. His refusal to behave was both a choice and a compulsion.

Amazingly, despite all Willie's misconduct, the repercussions had never been that serious. Punishment was confined to internal Department of Correctional Services procedures, as it was in most of New York State's prisons, which held thirty-nine thousand inmates at the time. The local district attorneys turned a blind eye to what transpired inside the state prisons in their counties. There were too many infractions to prosecute all of them. And the system was growing fast—it more than doubled in the 1980s, as prison systems had across America. Counties all over the state were competing to be the site for new prisons. A prison meant big dollars for construction workers and good-paying jobs with good benefits for new guards. In some counties, hit by America's loss of traditional blue-collar manufacturing jobs, prisons were the only new source of employment.

It was natural that in this gold-rush fever to get prisons, a few of the lucky counties had no previous experience in running a big-time jail. Oneida County, in central upstate New York, was one of these. It had been awarded Midstate prison, which opened not long before Willie was sent there. Oneida was good, solid Republican territory with conservative farmers spread out around the old city of Utica. In the late nineteenth century, both of New York's senators had come from Utica, and though the city had been in decline for decades, it wore its heritage proudly. Oneida's voters took law and order seriously. If a criminal came to trial, Oneida juries were more likely to convict him and Oneida judges were more likely to hand him a tough sentence than those elsewhere in the state. The county's single-mindedness about crime showed up in politics. The longtime district attorney, Barry Donalty, was a Republican, but he was also endorsed by the Democrats. Not surprisingly, Donalty was troubled by Midstate's opening. He wanted to be certain that the new prisoners, mostly from New York City, did not bring with them what he saw as their culture of crime, drugs, and promiscuity. So he adopted a strict and unique policy: the county would treat a crime in its state prison the same as it would a crime on the streets.

Willie arrived at Midstate at noontime on October 21, 1985. Special preparations had been made for him. A few weeks earlier, a federal judge had ordered that any time Willie's cell door was opened, he was to be videotaped by corrections officers. The directive was designed to protect Willie after he charged that a group of guards at Attica had killed an inmate in the cell next to his in the box. A video camera was set up in Midstate's solitary area, and word of Willie's reputation spread quickly among the guards. They were mostly white, farm-bred men who liked to hunt for deer in the fall, drive their snowmobiles over the rolling countryside in the long snowy winter, and go fishing in the summer.

Willie was sure the guards at Midstate were waiting to get him. He could feel it in the air, his usual paranoia working overtime. So the first evening when a guard brought around his meal of spaghetti, Willie claimed sand had been put in it. He threw the food out the small feeder trap door at the bottom of his cell door, making a mess in the corridor. The next morning, he chucked his oatmeal out after finding what he said was garbage in it. At lunchtime, the same thing happened.

Willie was certain the guards were disrespecting him, so he decided to harass them. He called this busting chops. There was nothing personal about it, from Willie's point of view. Being in prison was just like an endless chess match. He had to make a move every time the guards made a move on him. Now, sitting in Midstate, Willie knew that if he created a disturbance, the guards would have to fill out official reports, and that would take them time. They might even have to miss a coffee break or mealtime. In his war, any annoyance to the guards, no matter how petty, gave him pleasure.

At 1:10 p.m., a guard named Joseph Gullo was making his rounds of the fourteen cells in the solitary confinement block when he smelled smoke coming from Willie's cell. Gullo saw that it was thick and black and noxious, yelled for help, and then squirted a fire extinguisher through the feeder hole. By the time Gullo and several other guards put the fire out and opened the cell door, Willie was lying unconscious against the back wall, overcome by an acute asthma attack. A sharpened toothbrush was next to his limp body. The guards took Willie to a local hospital, where he was given oxygen and put on intravenous fluid. Willie had made the fire from wadded-up toilet paper, a paperback copy of prison regulations, and his sheets, blankets, and pillow. The guards also found a charred edition of *Siddhartha*, the novel by Hermann Hesse. It had been a bequest from Butch.

Later that afternoon, after Willie had recovered, the guards put him back in a different cell in solitary. As punishment, they confiscated all Willie's clothes save his undershorts, and took everything out of his cell except a mattress. This was called a strip cell and was standard prison procedure.

Willie was used to it. As far as he was concerned, the battle was far from over; he began methodically tearing up the mattress.

Officer Peter Berezny saw what Willie was up to through the small viewing port cut in his cell door. Berezny and three other guards then got a four-foot-high Plexiglas shield from their command post, a tool specially designed to protect guards dealing with violent inmates. It was curved outward, in a convex shape, so that a guard holding its handle could effectively surround a prisoner and keep him at a safe distance.

Armed with the shield, the guards opened Willie's door and pushed him up against the far wall. A sergeant ordered one officer to remove the remains of the mattress and told Willie to take off his underpants. Willie refused. When Berezny tried reaching around the shield to pull Willie's shorts off, Willie punched him in the ear, splitting it. He also kicked the guard hard in the leg, sending him spinning and injuring his back. Eventually, the officers wrestled Willie's underpants off and left him to lie naked on the steel frame of his bunk.

Midstate had had enough of Willie. At 9:30 that night, he was sent off to another prison. He had been there less than a day and a half. Willie considered this a very satisfying triumph, showing the guards that they could not handle him.

During the fire in his cell and his attack on Berezny, Willie had paid no attention to another guard standing outside in the corridor who had been videotaping everything that happened, precisely in accordance with the federal court order that Willie himself had sought as protection against his claims of mistreatment by corrections officers. Now it was all on tape.

That same evening, as Willie was being transferred, the district attorney's office in Utica gave the order to bring criminal charges against him for arson and assault on a guard. Oneida County was going to make an example. It was not going to be casual about crimes in its prison, the way other counties in New York long had. Willie had been at the wrong place at the wrong time.

WILLIE WAS NOW in a serious predicament. He had been indicted on three counts of arson, two counts of assault on a corrections officer, illegal possession of a weapon in prison, and damaging prison property. The arson and assault charges were felonies. If he was found guilty on any of them, it would be his third felony conviction, which could make him a persistent felon liable to a sentence of twenty-five years to life.

Willie still had a choice. At a pretrial conference, the assistant district attorney handling his case, Steven Fortnam, offered Willie a plea bargain. If Willie agreed to plead guilty to the single crime of attempted arson in the second degree, the district attorney's office would recommend that he be treated as only a second felony offender and be given a sentence of six to twelve years. In practical terms, Willie could still be out of prison in as little as two or three more years. It was a terrific deal, considering the alternative of life in prison.

Willie looked at Fortnam, a mild-mannered, sandy-haired man who wore steel-rimmed glasses. When he talked, his words came out slowly and cautiously, with long pauses in between. He didn't look like a formidable opponent in a courtroom. He was too much of a straight arrow, Willie thought, to have the flair for the dramatic that was essential to swaying a jury. Willie figured that, based on his experience in winning his trial for the assault on the court officers, he was a far better lawyer than Fortnam.

Willie also was not impressed by Fortnam's offer of six to twelve years instead of the risk of losing at trial and then being hit by twenty-five years to life. Ever since he was a boy, Willie had always lived for the present. Psychiatrists said Willie had no patience, that he craved instant gratification, a classic symptom of a psychopath. Willie saw it differently. There were always so many challenges and threats around—on the streets or in prison—that he had to deal with them immediately. How could he think of something three, six, or twenty-five years in the future?

Besides, whatever the district attorney's offer was, to Willie it simply meant more time in prison. It fed into his belief that he was predestined to spend his life in jail. He was coming to see himself as a martyr, an African-American fated to be locked up forever by an oppressive white society. This gave him a sense of mission. So Willie turned down the plea bargain. "I'm not pleading guilty to anything," he said. He would take his chances at trial.

Judge John T. Buckley, the Oneida County Court judge who was presiding over the case, thought Willie wasn't using his head. His decision made no sense. "If you don't take the offer, you could be sentenced to life," Buckley explained, giving Willie a chance to reconsider. But Willie rejected the offer again. Frank Blando, a public defender whom the judge had assigned to assist Willie, began to feel that Willie wanted to be sentenced to life. That way, instead of merely getting his Andy Warhol quotient of fifteen minutes of fame, he could be a celebrity for life.

The trial was held in the Oneida County Court House, another of those nineteenth-century monuments to the majesty of justice, with a fortresslike sandstone exterior and long marble corridors and high vaulted ceilings on the inside.

Willie, as usual, acted as his own lawyer. To Judge Buckley's surprise, Willie turned out to be exceptionally able at the law. His questioning of prospective jurors was well-focused, better than what a lot of professional lawyers Buckley knew could do, and his defense strategy was shrewd. He put the Department of Correctional Services on trial, depicting himself as the victim of a group of guards who were out to get him because of his bad reputation.

"Ladies and gentlemen of the jury," Willie began his opening statement, "what the D.A. and the corrections officers are not going to tell you . . . is that these officers had a motive to kill me." Willie recounted for the jurors the incident at Attica when the inmate in the cell next to him killed himself, or, as Willie asserted, was killed by guards. Willie had filed a lawsuit as a result of the man's death, and a federal grand jury had investigated eight of the corrections officers who worked in the box at Attica.

"I went through so much hell as a result of me uncovering that murder that Judge Michael A. Telesca, of Federal Court, issued an order . . . that whenever my cell door was opened a special man from the Department of Corrections was to videotape any movement I made.

"The Federal judge also ordered that I be transferred from the Attica Correctional Facility for my protection. . . . And when I got to the Midstate Correctional Facility they were waiting for me. They were waiting to take up where Attica left off. They did a damn good job at it, too."

Willie was embroidering a little. Judge Telesca had ordered the videotaping but had not ordered him transferred out of Attica. But he had the full attention of the jurors. Even though he didn't have his father's intimidating physical presence, he still had Butch's dramatic, electric persona.

"An officer most likely will testify before you telling that I burned my cell up," Willie continued. "He's a liar. He's a liar because I was in the box. And in the box you are not allowed to have matches. In the box you are not allowed to have nothing. They even stripped my clothes from me and left me naked, with my hands handcuffed behind my back."

Having played to the jurors' sympathy, Willie also disarmed them with candor: "You are going to hear testimony that I am a bad guy. Corrections officers are going to testify that I am the worst inmate they ever seen in the Department of Correctional Services. Fine. I am not an angel. If I were an angel I wouldn't be in prison now. But I am not what they are trying to make me out to be, either."

Later, at the end of the trial, Willie played his trump card. He had learned from his previous cases that by going pro se he could get away with transgressing legal proprieties. He knew the judge would give him some latitude. So he came right out and told the jurors that if they found him guilty, he would be sentenced to life. The jury wasn't supposed to know that.

"Ladies and gentlemen," he concluded, "I'm worried because I got a wife and a little baby. And I don't want to spend the rest of my life in prison." He was stretching the truth, of course. Sharon and he were separated, and the baby wasn't really his.

But after the jury had retired to deliberate, Buckley congratulated Willie. "You did a great job defending yourself, I mean that," the judge said. It was high praise coming from Buckley, an earnest, hardworking man who was referred to as "Maximum John" by local defense attorneys because of the tough sentences he handed out. Buckley knew it was a hard case for Willie to win. Everything he had done at Midstate was on camera—the camera he himself had requested—and the videotape was an exhibit in the trial. It was worse for Willie than a confession.

The jurors were torn. They stayed out for twelve hours and asked repeatedly to have the videotape replayed. When the jury came back in, several of the members were in tears. They found Willie not guilty of damaging prison property with the fire, and not guilty of possessing a weapon, the sharpened toothbrush, and not guilty on two of the three arson charges. But they couldn't get around what was on film. So they found Willie guilty on the remaining count of arson and the two assault charges, all felonies. They were Willie's third strike.

Under New York law, Buckley now had the discretion to hold a sentencing hearing to determine whether Willie was a "persistent felony offender." If he was, the penalty was twenty-five years to life, the same as for a criminal convicted of the most heinous offense in New York, murder, a class A-1 felony. On the scale of seriousness, the three crimes for which Willie had been convicted as an adult were all rather minor. The attempted assault on Joel Brown and the arson and assault charges at Midstate were only class D felonies; and his escape from the training school at Goshen when he had just turned sixteen was a mere class E felony.

Willie felt he was being screwed by the criminal justice system. How could those three minor convictions add up to a sentence reserved for murder?

The answer lay in the intent of the legislators who had drafted the persistent-felon statute. They had crafted it precisely to snare repeat offenders like Willie, giving the sentencing judge the authority to consider

not only the criminal's convictions but also his entire "history and character." Everything Willie had ever done in his short, unhappy, violence-
plagued life was now fair game. The prosecutor could introduce all of it,
right down to his record as a boy. Willie's past was catching up with him.

Willie knew he probably couldn't win. There was too much in his
record. But he liked being a lawyer, and he loved the theater of the
courtroom. It gave him a legitimate stage on which to perform. Normally,
a sentencing hearing for a persistent felon might take only a day or two,
the district attorney needing only to recite the defendant's past misdeeds.
Willie decided to play a few tricks and draw the hearing out as long as
he could. He would savor every minute of it. Besides, Willie figured,
prolonging the hearing was another way to harass the system.

Willie started things off with a surprise. The day before the hearing
was scheduled to begin, on February 18, 1987, he made a collect call
from his cell to Sylvia Honig, the former social worker at Brookwood
who, despite his early attacks on her, had become his good friend, frequently visiting him in prison. Willie confided to her that the Black
Liberation Army was going to stage a raid and rescue him as he was
being taken to the hearing. Honig called a state police officer with the
information. The authorities took the threat seriously. Willie, after all,
had developed a big reputation. State officials already considered him
the most violent inmate in New York. Sheriff's deputies were assigned
to guard Buckley's house, and a decision was made to move the hearing
from the courthouse to the basement of the county jail for greater security.
The next morning, as the hearing began, a New York State Police helicopter hovered overhead, FBI agents took up positions, and more state
troopers with dogs and shotguns, plus a SWAT team, cordoned off the
jail. Nothing happened. Willie had made it all up.

When the hearing did get under way, Willie produced another shock.
He told Buckley, "The defendant denies that he is Willie Bosket and
therefore denies that he is the same person who was previously convicted."

It was an original if fanciful defense. Since he was not Willie Bosket,
he had not been convicted in the past and could not be found a persistent
felon. Willie promised to call a slew of witnesses to prove he was not
Willie Bosket.

Buckley could have cut Willie off right here. But the judge knew the
persistent-felon statute was a drastic remedy, and he didn't want to rush
to judgment. There was something else at work, too. Buckley had come
to like Willie. He could see that Willie was very smart and had a pleasant
personality. If the circumstances had been different, he felt that Willie
could have been a successful attorney. Buckley even identified a little
with Willie. His own father, a judge, had died when Buckley was only

six months old. He still kept a campaign poster of his stern-visaged father running for election for judge on the wall of his chambers. Buckley knew what it was like to grow up without a father, and to grow up dreaming of emulating your father.

Steven Fortnam, who was still the prosecutor in the case, laboriously went over Willie's career of violence starting from age nine. He called detectives and district attorneys who had convicted Willie in the past and guards from each of the prisons where he had been. Fortnam introduced the videotaped confession Willie had made in which he boasted of committing two thousand crimes by the age of fifteen, and he also cited a letter Willie had written threatening the life of President Ronald Reagan.

All power to the Black Liberation Army.
For too long you white cracker devils have perpetuated violence and death against blacks, African people here in the United Snakes of America.
Ronnie, you're a piece of dirty white devil shit, and I'm going to kill you myself very, very soon.
For the black African men, women and children is Almighty God. Break the chains.

Willie James Bosket Jr.

Lorraine Mallet, a special agent with the Secret Service, testified she had investigated Willie after his letter was intercepted. Willie readily admitted that he had sent the letter. He wrote it, he told her, "For attention."

When the prosecution rested, Willie put on his witnesses to prove he wasn't Willie Bosket. First up was Shakim Allah, a convicted double murderer who had been in prison with Willie in 1982.

"Is my name Willie Bosket?" Willie asked Allah.

"I know you by the name Butch," Allah replied.

"As a matter of fact, you know me by the name of Butch Smith, don't you?" Willie asked again, this time with a smirk. He had just concocted the name. He didn't even know where it came from.

"As a matter of fact," Allah said, "when we was at Auburn state prison, everybody called you Butch Smith, including the corrections officers."

Next was Terrance Jones, a seventeen-year-old from Utica who had been convicted of murdering an elderly woman. He said Willie was really a person named Butch Smith who had once been his piano instructor.

It was getting silly. Fortnam cross-examined Jones and asked him if he was gay. "Looking at you, I find myself, yes, very," Jones answered. "I'm into D.A.'s."

Finally, Willie called his cousin, Herman Spates, who had been sentenced to eight-and-a-half to twenty-five years after admitting he had participated in one of the subway murders with Willie. Herman was doing his time in Attica.

"I ask you, Mr. Spates, is Mr. Bosket your cousin?" Willie began his questioning.

"Yes," Herman said.

"As a matter of fact, you know Mr. Bosket very well?"

"Yes."

"Am I Mr. Bosket?"

"No."

When Fortnam's turn came to cross-examine him, Herman refused to answer any questions. "Do you know what you can do?" Herman said to the prosecutor. "You can kiss my ass. Fuck your questions." Now both Herman and Willie were laughing, making a mockery of the criminal justice system.

"Judge," Willie said, "I come from a very splendid background. I would never be a cousin of a criminal."

After an hour of this, Buckley eventually held Herman in contempt and sentenced him to an extra thirty days in jail. The judge also struck Herman's testimony.

Eighteen days into the hearing, Buckley decided it had gone on long enough. Willie had called thirty-two witnesses on his behalf, some of them, it seemed to the judge, just for the sake of having reunions. He had subpoenaed Kay McNally, who had served him faithfully as his Legal Aid lawyer as a boy, and Alton Maddox, who had defended him in the Joel Brown case.

"You've tried as good a case, a criminal case, as I've ever seen any lawyer conduct," Buckley complimented Willie. "Considering the circumstances, no one could have done a better job."

Despite his personal feelings, there was no question how the judge would rule. Buckley announced that he found Willie to be a persistent felony offender. For the incident at Midstate, Willie was to spend twenty-five years to life in prison. The judge's ruling also meant that if Willie was convicted of any further felonies, they would result in additional sentences of twenty-five years to life.

Buckley then asked Willie if he had anything to say. It was Willie's moment. He focused all his rage like a laser beam—the anger that he had felt against his mother as a boy and the hatred he had come to feel against America as an adult.

"A long time black people has been persecuted in this country," Willie began. "I look at myself as a perfect example of a black man being persecuted in a white America. Through the years I've done a lot of studying . . . and I've come to see the system for what it is. Am I bitter toward it? Hell, yes. Because right here in America we're dealing with a system that has some very poisonous claws. And once those claws set in your neck, it's very hard to get them out. Believe me, I know."

Willie was thinking of the first time he was sent to Bellevue and the first time he was shipped off to Wiltwyck, when he was only nine years old. That had been the start of his lifetime of incarceration. His eyes were bulging now, and the muscles in his jaw and neck were working hard, just like his father's expression when he got intense.

"A very well-known black revolutionary once said to the people of this country, 'Don't be surprised when I tell you that I've been in prison. Because that's what America is—one big prison. We're all in prison.' That was stated by Malcolm X.

"Why am I so angry toward the system?" Willie continued. "Well, the reason is because I'm only a monster that the system created—a monster that's come back to haunt the system's ass. And I'll dog this system until it's in its grave, because it's a wrong system.

"It lets the rich get away, and puts the poor behind bars. And I do hate America. And if I could, I'd urinate on the American flag on the White House lawn.

"In my heart, I'm a black revolutionary. And your twenty-five years to life will be my license—nothing but a license—to go to the extreme in everything that I believe. So come with me."

THE VISITING ROOM in Shawangunk prison looked like an office cafeteria. There were vending machines along the walls, bright fluorescent lights, and blue plastic chairs. On Saturdays, Sundays, and holidays, it began filling up at 9 a.m. The visitors came in first, past a metal detector and through a sliding glass gate at the front of the room. Once they entered, the visitors had to check in with a guard seated behind a desk on a low platform. On Saturday, April 16, 1988, the officer on duty was Susan Moseley, a round-faced woman in her late twenties who had grown up on her family's horse farm. She assigned visitors to seats on the outer rim of one of four large oval-shaped tables that dominated the room. The tables were lined up nearly side to side, with a low rail dividing them at the midpoint of each. Inmates were restricted to a narrow aisle that ran down the center of the room and bisected the tables. The prisoners sat on the inside edge of the big curved tables opposite their guests.

All the inmates were frisked before they entered the visiting room at the back end. Although Shawangunk was a maximum security prison, there were no other overt signs of safety precautions. Neither Officer Moseley nor the only other guard assigned to the room, who oversaw a program for prisoners to have photographs taken with their visitors, was armed. Most of the convicts—all those not in solitary confinement— were allowed to wear civilian shirts over their dull green prison-issue pants. So with everyone seated, the room had a look of normalcy about it. The prisoners and their visitors could easily reach over the tables to touch or hold each other. A lot of serious hugging went on. The convicts' girlfriends and wives had a taste for tight, eye-catching outfits. A number of the women were very overweight, but they all wore plenty of makeup and had big hair.

This Saturday, Willie had a visitor, Matthew Worth, a slight, boyish-looking, twenty-nine-year-old reporter for the Utica *Observer Dispatch*. They had met a year earlier, when Worth was covering Willie's trial for arson and assault at Midstate. Worth was intrigued by Willie, and Willie had seized the opportunity to ask Worth if he would like to collaborate on writing his autobiography. Worth was interested, but insisted that Willie pledge not to get involved in any more violent acts that would jeopardize their work. Willie readily assented. In fact, for the past twelve months, for the first time in years, Willie had managed to avoid creating any serious incidents. The prison authorities were delighted and thought the book project might be helping. So Worth had been coming to interview Willie almost every other weekend. He would buy Willie food, sodas, or coffee from the vending machines while they talked.

On April 16, when Worth checked in, the guards in the Special Housing Unit, the box, got Willie ready. They made him take off his shoes in his cell and frisked him there, rather than at the entrance to the visiting room, where ordinary prisoners were searched. Then they escorted him down to the visiting room. All Willie's movements outside his cell were still videotaped, except in the visiting room. It didn't seem necessary to keep him on camera there since he had always been well-behaved with visitors.

As Willie entered, he saw Worth seated at the front table at the far end of the room with his back to the prisoners' aisle, so Willie walked up behind him and said boo. It made Worth jump. Willie laughed and smiled his big grin and offered Worth a hearty handshake of welcome.

As usual, Willie spent much of the time talking about his belief in the need for revolution and bloodshed to remake America. "They tried nonviolence in South Africa, but the babies continued to die," he said. Worth had heard this rhetoric from Willie a number of times already, so he didn't attach any particular importance to it today.

Still, Worth began to sense Willie was distracted. His mind was wandering, and he wasn't answering Worth's questions. About 10:30, Willie got up and said he was going to the bathroom. The prisoners' toilet was just outside the back end of the visiting room. A guard was stationed there to frisk inmates before they entered the visiting room, but he paid no attention to Willie since he had already been searched in the box. Five minutes later, Willie was back.

Worth resumed his questions, but Willie now looked at him squarely and confided, "I got a shank on me."

Willie didn't say what he planned to do with it, and Worth didn't really know how to respond. He was seated only a couple of feet away from Willie, and if it was true that Willie had a knife, there was no easy way for Worth to get up and walk over and alert Officer Moseley at the desk. So Worth did the only thing he could think of—he tried to reason with Willie. Having a weapon was a dumb idea, Worth said. He wanted no part of a violent stunt. It would jeopardize their book project. It could even mean the end of the book.

Willie was not deterred. "The next time you see me, our interviews may be under different conditions," he hinted to Worth. "I may be in shackles or in a different prison."

Willie's thoughts were growing more ominous. "I'm a very loving person," he said, "but because of being here my heart is very callous. Love doesn't mean nothing to me.

"I should be here because I believe my destiny is here," Willie added.

He was talking faster now, as if he were coming to the climax of their conversation, the finale of their entire work together. "My life is one of sacrifice and that's why I'm here—to show the world what the system does to somebody," Willie said. "I will leave a legacy. I've spent all my life in jail since I was a kid. I have nothing to lose. I might as well put it to use to make people comprehend why I kill."

At 12:30, Worth said he had to go to the bathroom. He was still trying to figure out how to warn somebody. Willie got up and said he was going to the bathroom also. The visitors' restroom was directly behind Officer Moseley's post. Worth had his chance, but he decided it was too risky. No telling what Willie would do if cornered. By now, there were more than one hundred people jammed in the room, including many women and children. So Worth came back and took his seat.

Willie had been planning this moment since he was convicted for what he believed was the phony attempted assault charge on Joel Brown four years earlier. When he was sentenced to life for being a persistent felon, it only reinforced his sense of purpose. He meant what he said to Judge Buckley. He felt he now had a license to go to extremes.

Willie had made the shank from a thin metal rod he had broken from the underside of an old typewriter the prison officials let him borrow to type up his endless legal appeals. He bent one end of the rod on the door of his cell to make a handle. Then he wrapped the looped end with masking tape and a strip of cloth he tore from a sheet to give him greater purchase. He sharpened the other end on a piece of concrete in his cell, stroking it until he got a fine point. When he finished, Willie had what looked like a homemade ice pick with a blade five and a half inches long.

Willie mulled over whom to attack for a couple of weeks. He originally thought about using it on one of the guards in the box. But he decided that wasn't strategic. He liked to think of himself as a good strategist. Back in the box he was isolated, and there was too much of a chance for the guards to retaliate by beating him to death.

So Willie decided the visiting room presented the best opportunity. The way he figured it, there were so many people around, he could be like an assassin on a crowded street. He would stab a guard swiftly and silently and no one would even see it happen. Then he would ditch his weapon. It could be the perfect crime.

On that Saturday morning, Willie had hidden the shank between two layers of socks he put on. The guards searched his shoes, but failed to pat the bottoms of his feet.

When he went to the bathroom the second time, Willie took off a shoe and one outer sock and retrieved his weapon. He put it in his pocket and walked out with his hands in his pockets.

As he came back to the visiting room, one of the two guards was almost directly in front of him. It was the officer running the photo operation, known as the click-click. His name was Earl Porter. He was a slightly built, dark-haired man with a bushy mustache and sad, frightened-looking eyes. Porter had been a corrections officer for only five months and was still working as a substitute, taking whatever duties were assigned to him. On Saturday, he had been told to run the picture-taking program. Willie had never met him, didn't know his name, in fact, had never seen him before this morning. Porter had just returned from his lunch break and was seated at a small desk with his back to Willie. He was wearing the standard winter uniform for guards: a dark-blue ribbed sweater over a blue shirt and black tie with dark-blue trousers.

To reach Porter, Willie only had to go through a low swinging metal gate and walk a few steps. He was now on the outside of the visiting tables, in an area where inmates were not allowed without permission. Officer Moseley, standing beside her raised desk at the opposite end of the room, saw Willie start through the gate into the restricted area. He didn't have her consent to be there, so she began walking toward him to advise him to go back.

Willie was moving fast now. He put his left hand on Porter's shoulder, spinning him around clockwise. Then with his right hand, he drove the shank into Porter's chest, all the way up to the handle.

Porter thought someone had punched him from behind in the back. It was the way the knife felt when it reached through to his backside. He never saw who did it. When he looked down, he just saw a fist doubled up on his chest.

Porter stood up. As he did so, he felt a sharp pain in his chest and he started gasping for air. It was getting harder and harder to breathe. He could also feel something coming out of his mouth. When he put his hand up to the front of his face, it came away covered with blood. He began walking toward the front of the visiting room where Officer Moseley was stationed. His vision was getting blurry. When he reached Moseley, all he could say was, "Stab wound to the chest."

He could hear people screaming now, and he reached for the sally port gate to try to get out of the room. As he grabbed it, he slid to his knees. Then the world went dark.

When she realized Porter had been stabbed, Moseley pulled the pin on her alarm mechanism. It alerted the prison's central office to an emergency in the visiting room. People were running in every direction inside the room, knocking over the chairs as they went. There was total panic. Willie hadn't anticipated this.

So Willie jumped up on one of the curved blond wood tables. "Surround me," he started shouting. "Surround me. This has nothing to do with visitors or inmates. I only want police."

Delores Trippardella, who was visiting her husband on their wedding anniversary, looked up and saw Willie brandishing his weapon. She could also see fear on the face of Officer Moseley. Mrs. Trippardella had no idea what was happening. All she knew was that she was terrified Willie might attack her husband, since he was an inmate. The Trippardellas grabbed each other and stumbled back against a vending machine along the wall, as far away from Willie as they could get.

In minutes, the room was flooded with twenty guards. Some had pulled out their batons; others had picked up chairs to defend themselves. They started yelling at Willie to put down his weapon.

Willie knew the game was over. He felt he had scored a big victory. A guard was lying on the floor, maybe bleeding to death. Willie saw no need to take any further risks. He said he would surrender his shank, but only to a female corrections officer, Sergeant Claire Armstrong. That was the touch of chivalry in him. Armstrong stepped forward, and he gave her the knife.

T H E T R I A L W A S H E L D in the Ulster County Court House in Kingston. It stood on the site where on July 30, 1775, the state of New York had been founded in the presence of Major General George Clinton. Clinton went on to be governor of New York seven times and twice vice president of the United States.

The main charge was attempted murder. Porter had survived, barely. Willie's shank had punctured and collapsed his right lung and missed his heart by a scant two inches. He bled so badly that he lost two liters of blood, almost half the average human's supply of blood. An ambulance had rushed Porter to the local hospital just in time for doctors to save him.

This time, the authorities took no chances with Willie. He was escorted to court each morning by a phalanx of a dozen corrections officers and armed sheriff's deputies accompanied by police dogs. Another guard kept a video camera on Willie at all times. Willie's legs were bound by heavy iron shackles, and his arms were handcuffed in front of him. The handcuffs were attached to a double chain padlocked around his waist, which, in turn, was connected by another chain to the shackles on his legs. This arrangement made it awkward for Willie to maneuver around in the courtroom. He was acting as his own lawyer again, and every time he wanted to look at a legal note or document, he had to pull it up laboriously out of a folder with his hands cuffed together. Willie wore a pair of black-rimmed plastic glasses to read, and when they kept slipping down his nose, he had to struggle to push them back up into place. Whenever he was called to approach the judge's bench, Willie shuffled his feet together slowly, dragging the heavy leg irons. They rattled on the courtroom floor, making it sound like a dungeon.

Willie protested that being handcuffed and manacled this way was prejudicial to the jury. The judge hearing the case, Francis J. Vogt, a square-jawed man with a full face and white hair, rejected his pleas to be unchained.

Willie's defense was in keeping with his strategy in his earlier legal cases—he would use shock tactics to put the criminal justice system on trial. He intended to make the trial into a referendum on his life.

"Judge, ladies and gentlemen of the jury," he began. "This trial means nothing. Your verdict whether it's guilty or not guilty means nothing. It means nothing because I am presently incarcerated in prison.

Whatever your verdict is, I will continue to be in prison for the rest of my life."

The twelve jurors, six men and six women sitting in green padded chairs, were listening carefully now, their eyes riveted on Willie. His voice was soft, and with his slight build and youthful features, he did not look dangerous. Seeing him manacled this way, some of the jurors were beginning to feel sympathy for him.

"The system is going to come in here and have you concerned with did Willie Bosket stab Earl Porter," he said. "Willie Bosket stabbed Earl Porter. So there should be no concern about that. I am telling you that Willie Bosket stabbed Earl Porter."

It was as self-incriminating as he could make it. That had always been Willie's way, to be dramatic, reckless, and challenging. To Willie, acting as his own attorney was just an extension of a street fight.

"I am telling you that the only regret Willie Bosket has is not killing Earl Porter," he went on, even more audaciously. "But there is a main concern here that the system doesn't want you to know. Why did Willie Bosket stab Earl Porter? That is the question."

Judge Vogt tried to stop Willie. "The prison system is not on trial, Mr. Bosket. You are on trial."

But Willie would not be restrained. What could the judge do? Hold him in contempt?

"Ladies and gentlemen. This trial will not bring any justice to Earl Porter. It is not going to bring justice to Willie Bosket either for all his trials and tribulations at the hands of this system. But it can bring justice to thousands of little children."

The prosecutor, Donald Williams, the chief county assistant district attorney, was on his feet objecting. Williams had read through all of Willie's legal records, and he made no secret of his conclusion. Willie, he thought, was the most dangerous and violent criminal in the history of New York State. New York did not have the death penalty at the time. So to Williams, Willie was a walking, talking advertisement for the restoration of the death penalty.

The stabbing of Earl Porter and now the trial were theatrics by Willie to call attention to himself, Williams believed. Willie knew he would never get out of prison and therefore he wanted to be known as the worst prisoner ever. It was the one thing Willie had left. Williams had coined a phrase for it: he said Willie was trying to legendize himself.

But Williams couldn't help adding to the myth. As his final piece of evidence to prove Willie's guilt in the stabbing, Williams read the jury part of a letter Willie had written to the deputy superintendent of his prison, Joseph Demskie:

On April 16th, 1988, at approximately 12:42 p.m. in the visiting room of the Shawangunk state prison, prison guard Earl Porter felt a vicious hate-filled thrust as an eleven inch stiletto blade was plunged into his chest to the hilt, just a fraction of an inch from penetrating his heart. The heart had definitely been the target. And as the stiletto blade invaded the chest cavity of prison guard Earl Porter, in search of his most vital organ, Bosket's most vital organ was singing a song of hateful joy.

To this day, the only regret Bosket has is not having killed prison guard Earl Porter and spitting on his corpse—not because he was Earl Porter, but because he was the system.

When Williams finished reading, there was a stunned silence in the courtroom. Williams let it hang there for a moment, like the sound of doom. "Thank you, Your Honor," he finally said. "I think the People are going to rest."

Now it was Willie's turn, as defense counsel. He startled the judge and jury by reading the rest of the damning letter into evidence, all eight neatly handwritten pages.

Everyone in New York State, Willie told the courtroom, "wants to figure out what makes me tick—the media, the politicians and the corrections system." He agreed that it was important for people to understand him because with more and more young black boys being locked up, "many more Willie Boskets are being created within the juvenile and prison systems at this moment.

"Why am I so bitter? Why am I so angry towards the system? Well, I am going to tell everybody why I'm so angry. The reason is because . . . Willie Bosket has been incarcerated since he was nine years old and was raised by his surrogate mother, the criminal justice system. . . . This being the case, Bosket is only a monster created by the system he now haunts."

Willie's letter was wandering far from the permissible rules of evidence. He was not offering a legally recognized defense, but both the judge and the prosecutor had given up trying to check him. There were tears in Willie's eyes now, and his voice was breaking.

He was willing to admit he stabbed Earl Porter, Willie said. But to stop other monsters from being created, to save other poor African-American boys in the ghetto from his fate, Willie offered a proposal. Let the prison authorities put together a panel of experts—psychologists, psychiatrists, social workers, guards—"to do a personal in-depth study on me." They could hypnotize him or do any scientific tests they wanted. Perhaps that way society could benefit by being able to "better comprehend and identify the 'Willie Boskets' and defusing them before it is too late."

Willie could read no more. He dropped the letter on the defense table and walked slowly toward the courtroom door, dragging his clanging shackles as he went. The defense rested.

WILLIE'S APPEAL TO THE jurors almost worked. Several of them spent sleepless nights. They felt bad for a boy who had been locked up since he was nine. They thought his tears were real. They also couldn't believe Willie had actually intended to kill Earl Porter. If he had, he would have succeeded. Three of the twelve jurors wanted to find Willie guilty only on the lesser charge of assault, not attempted murder. Then they read his letter over and over, and they realized they had no choice. He had confessed.

At his sentencing, Judge Vogt asked Willie if he had anything to say. "Judge," he responded, his rage palpable, "this is the part of the little charade where the defendant is supposed to come into Court and beg for mercy. I don't think this Court nor Mr. Prosecutor would delude themselves that Willie Bosket is going to come in here and beg this system for mercy. Just the contrary. I would like to tell you why I would never give you any mercy. Any sentence that this court can impose upon me means nothing. I laugh at this court."

Vogt was looking down at Willie from the bench. "Your opinion is noted, Mr. Bosket. I agree with you that there's nothing I can do. But I'm going to impose a sentence here. I'm going to impose the maximum sentence I can impose."

Since Willie was a persistent felon, that meant another twenty-five years to life. The sentence would be served consecutively, added on to his current twenty-five years to life.

"The problem that bothers me," the judge said, "is that as sure as I am sitting here and you are standing there, Bosket, I know that the opportunity will present itself where you will attack someone again and in all probability you will be successful. So in sentencing you I am really sentencing an innocent person to death.

"You said something in the beginning of this trial which I'm afraid is very true," Vogt added, a tinge of sadness and resignation in his voice. "You have a license to kill."

Willie laughed. "The system gave it to me, Judge," he said. "You are renewing it today."

So the cycle would go on. It was too late for Willie to redeem himself. He could only live out the fatal tradition of violence that had made its way from rural South Carolina to the poor streets of the city. Willie was the last car on a long runaway freight train that had jumped the tracks. He had all that dread momentum.

EPILOGUE

IN THE CLOSING YEARS of the twentieth century, the number of young boys committing murder has reached epidemic proportions. Between 1985 and 1993, homicides by fifteen- to nineteen-year-old males in the United States jumped more than 150 percent, almost all of them involving guns. Willie Bosket is no longer an anomaly. Stories like his have become all too familiar as the staple of the nightly television news.

In the face of this plague of violence, it is easy to despair. The politicians, reading the public opinion polls, have a ready answer: more prisons, tough three-strikes-and-you're-out jail sentences, and laws to try juveniles as adults in criminal courts. Some state legislators have boasted they have "abolished childhood" by providing for children as young as six to be sent to adult court. By 1995, there were 1.5 million people incarcerated in state and federal prisons and in local jails around the nation. Another 100,000 youths were confined in juvenile institutions. These numbers have tripled in the past two decades.

If more prisons was the sole solution to the problem, we should be among the safest nations on earth. But these measures have not reduced the crime rate or made people feel more secure. Prison, it is indisputably true, does incapacitate, keeping offenders off the street and preventing them from carrying out more crimes while locked up. Criminals with records of chronic or violent offenses need to be locked away to protect society. The trouble is, there is little evidence that prison has much of a deterrent effect, especially for young people who come from poor, crime-blighted neighborhoods with little hope for the future. In New York State, 85 percent of the youngsters released by the Division for Youth are rearrested. For them, as for Willie and Butch, prison has come all too often to represent simply a rite of passage. Prison is where they expect to go, if they are not killed first. There is also the terrible power of example. The best way to predict who will be arrested and sent to a reformatory, some corrections officials believe, is to check which boys have a father or older brother who has been in prison. Willie and Butch fit this pattern painfully well.

Prisons have another disadvantage—they are a heavy financial burden. In 1995, the cost of running the nation's prison system—along with probation and parole departments—is running close to fifty billion dollars a year, up from a mere four billion dollars in 1975. Keeping a juvenile in New York's Division for Youth for a year now costs seventy-five thousand dollars; you could send three students to Harvard for the same money. In many states, new laws mandating longer prison terms have forced local governments into prison construction programs that are the fastest-rising item in their budgets. California has reduced funding for its once excellent state college and university system to help pay for its growing number of prisons. Lowering the quality of higher education cannot be a good crime prevention program in the long run. Add to all this another fifty billion dollars a year for the police, and twenty billion dollars annually for the cost of injuries and deaths caused by firearms, and it takes 120 billion dollars a year to pay for our national violent crime problem. If welfare is a failed, dead-end policy, so too is relying on prison to stop crime. This is not something on which liberals and conservatives need disagree. At the minimum, taxpayers are not getting their money's worth.

But there are better, more effective, and probably less expensive solutions than just building more prisons and handing out longer sentences. One reason for our gloom is that we have forgotten the past. Homicide rates fell consistently across Western Europe beginning in the fifteenth or sixteenth centuries, and the decline accelerated in big cities in the nineteenth century with the coming of the Industrial Revolution. Modern London has a homicide rate only one-tenth what it was in Chaucer's time. New York and Philadelphia were much safer in 1960 than they were in 1850. The good news is that there is nothing fixed in human nature that decrees murder rates. Nor is murder a predestined urban problem.

The crux of our dilemma is that the very things that helped lower rates of violence in the past have become more difficult for us to reapply today. It is no coincidence that the centuries-long decline in murder rates was reversed during the 1960s not only in the United States but in Europe, too. Something fundamental changed. The sixties was the decade in which we cast off the long-accumulated rules of self-control for an exaltation of the individual, a "fatal liberty," Tocqueville wrote in another context. We are now less religious, going to church less often, and sending fewer of our children for Sunday school lessons. The family is being pulled apart by centrifugal forces seemingly beyond our control. In our post-industrial era, jobs are shrinking and the authority of the factory foreman and whistle exert less discipline on us. We are less public-spirited and less willing to spend our scarce tax dollars on public schools to teach students to sit still, obey the teacher, and learn useful skills to compete in the global marketplace.

Finally, more than a century after the end of the Civil War that freed Aaron Bosket, we are still paying the price for the legacy of slavery and racism. It shows in how we think about crime. About three-quarters of all the crimes reported to the police are committed by whites, and there is good evidence that when social, economic, and neighborhood factors are accounted for, there is little difference in crime rates between whites and blacks. But most white Americans instinctively see violence as a black problem—it is they, the ones living in the inner city, the people on welfare, the faces in prison. This makes it easier to call for more police and prisons. But imagine if your child were suddenly transported to the inner city and you could do nothing to remove him from there. All you could do would be to come up with a policy recommendation. You might advocate more cops and jails. More likely, you would want a program that removed guns from the streets, created good jobs, built better housing, and, in particular, made sure your son or daughter lived in a family with good, loving adults.

It is here, the experts are beginning to agree, that we can make a start. Boiled down to its core, everything criminologists have learned about crime in recent research is that most adolescents who become delinquents, and the overwhelming majority of adults who commit violent crimes, started very young. They were the impulsive, aggressive, irritable children who would not obey their parents, bullied their neighbors, and acted out when they got to school. By first and second grade, teachers can usually identify them in class. They find it difficult to learn, and fall behind in school. Because they are accustomed to getting their way by physical force, they see no reason to change. They actually like the way they act, and this makes it increasingly difficult to reverse their antisocial proclivities. After age seven or eight, their cases seem intractable. This was the pattern with Butch and Willie.

When they were boys, psychiatrists wrote them off. Once an antisocial personality, always an antisocial personality, it was believed at the time. But modern research suggests there are positive alternative treatments. Early intervention is the key. Many factors go into producing personality: temperament, the genetic component you are born with; the neighborhood in which you grow up; and perhaps most important, the style of your parents. What the researchers have found is that parenting is not a natural instinct. If everything works out, you learn it at the feet of masters, your own parents. But we are losing parenting in America as mobility and divorce sunder families and fifteen-year-olds who did not have proper childhoods of their own have babies. Inadequate parents, white or black, make children who are more at risk.

Fortunately, psychologists have discovered that some of the missing parenting skills can be taught. Parents can be shown how to keep track of where their children are, what they are doing, and with whom they are playing. If children know someone is watching them and they may get caught, they are less likely to get in trouble. If parents monitor their children more, they are also more likely to spot when something is starting to go wrong. Setting boundaries is essential, so that the child eventually makes these a part of his or her own internal gyroscope. So, too, is consistent, nonphysically abusive discipline. Children who are beaten learn to treat others the same way, using aggression to get what they want. But when parents are instructed in better skills, teachers say the children exhibit fewer discipline problems in school and engage in less lying, stealing, cheating, talking back, and playing hooky. The parents find their offspring less angry, and the children report feeling better about themselves. The magnitude of change in the child, it turns out, is correlated with the magnitude of improvement in parenting skills.

Some model programs to teach these parenting skills, or home skills, are already in place in cities across the country. They take time, and the results can be frustratingly slow, but there are practical ways to extend these programs on a large scale, if we have the political will. Communities, for example, might create the position of a home health visitor, as some European countries already have, to check households where women are pregnant and provide medical advice and family training. This need not be punitive; instead, it should be part of the local government infrastructure, like drinking water is now. When children first register for school and are given physical exams, they could also be checked for signs of physical or sexual abuse and their families could be assigned help. A more drastic measure advocated by some experts is that we start licensing parents to have children just as we require drivers to get automobile licenses. It was not long ago that we thought it essential for couples to take out marriage licenses before living together and conceiving children.

THE TIME HAS ALSO COME to reexamine the American tradition of violence. The dictates of honor were beloved of antebellum white South Carolinians, but as the old code has been transmuted into the strictures of the street, we have unwittingly created a dangerous anachronism. With modern weaponry in the hands of increasingly younger and more desperate children, the rituals of insult and vengeance are a lethal luxury we can no longer afford.

In certain ways, the rest of the globe has come to look more like America since the worldwide upsurge in crime in the 1960s. British homes are now more likely to be burgled than American ones. Cars in France are stolen more frequently than cars in the United States. But in homicide, we retain our longtime lead. In 1991, the most recent year for which figures are available, young men between fifteen and twenty-four in the United States were murdered at a rate of 37.2 per 100,000. That is almost ten times higher than the next closest industrialized country, Italy, and sixty times greater than the homicide rate among the same age group in England. This is not, as some people might suppose, merely a disparity created by the racial composition of our inner cities. When minorities are factored out, America still has a disturbingly disproportionate murder rate.

In the past few years, perhaps guided by the sudden popularity of the term "dissing" in movies and rap music, sociologists and psychologists have begun to recognize the impact of the notion of disrespect. New curriculums, designed to teach alternate, more peaceful ways to settle conflicts, have appeared in thousands of classrooms across the country. Think of the consequences before you act, is their message. You don't have to use your fists, or a gun, when someone insults you. Whether these modern-day civics lessons are effective is unclear. They may reduce pushing in the cafeteria line; by themselves, they may not stop shooting on the street corner.

What is needed is not expensive, and again is not necessarily liberal or conservative. It is a shift in thinking that begins at home, that teaches that respect comes from within, not from worrying about the opinions of others.

This is not to minimize the difficulties in curbing violent crime. But it is helpful to remember how we have succeeded in reducing fatalities caused by drunk driving and smoking. These gains did not come overnight, or by one single magic step. With cigarettes, it has taken years of scientific studies to show the health hazards of tobacco, warnings on cigarette packs by the surgeon general, a ban on television ads, prohibitions against smoking in public places, and most of all, a change in public attitudes that makes smoking less glamorous for young people.

FOR WILLIE, it was too late to change. A few months after he was sentenced for stabbing the prison guard, he managed to break free from a metal chain that locked his handcuffs to a belt behind his back and bashed another guard, Ernest Auclair, in the head, leaving a six-inch wound. At the time, Willie was being escorted out for exercise in a small, carefully guarded yard. He received another twenty-five-years-to-life sentence for the assault, under New York's persistent-felon law. Not long afterward, he threw hot water in the face of yet another guard and could have been given a further life sentence, but the district attorney decided Willie was just having fun at the expense of the prison system. What would one more life sentence do to deter him, especially considering the cost of a trial? He was allowed to plead guilty to a minor charge.

So Willie remains in his specially constructed cell at Woodbourne prison. Some days he expresses remorse for the murders he committed as a boy. They were senseless, wasteful crimes, he now acknowledges. Other times he feels sorry for himself. He has never flown in an airplane, never used a computer, never gotten to be a real father—things that most people take for granted—and he never will. Ironically, he has already served all his time for the attempted assault on Joel Brown, the conviction that brought him back to prison. If he had not attacked his jailers, he would be free. Instead, he still faces three consecutive twenty-five-years-to-life sentences, and given how the parole board feels about him, that means he will spend at least seventy-five more years in prison, until he is one hundred years old.

When he looks out of his cell, through the narrow barred window across the corridor, he can glimpse a patch of farm fields, green with corn in the summer and white with snow in the winter. Those are the boundaries of his universe now. Knowing that he will never get out, he often thinks he is a prisoner on death row, without an electric chair. He would like to die, but he has discovered that committing suicide takes more courage than killing.

His mother, Laura, still works as a security guard, as she has since shortly before Willie murdered the men on the subway seventeen years ago. She has kept what she can of her life in order, building small rituals against the pains fortune sent her. She takes the bus each Thursday after work to do her grocery shopping and visits her aging mother in a nursing home every evening. By the time she gets home, she is exhausted.

Shirley, Willie's bright, vivacious younger sister, never lived up to her early promise and wandered on the streets.

Her daughter, who has a smile as big as Willie's, was in a class for the intellectually gifted. When a visitor dropped by their apartment, she always begged for long, trick words to spell. She was hard to stump. But at the age of twelve, she began playing hooky, and did not come home for days at a time. When Willie, sitting in prison, heard about her, he cried.

Willie's older sister, Cheryl, seemed the least likely candidate to prosper. She had been locked up by the Family Court as a girl, and she had been an alcoholic, living with Charles, the neighborhood enforcer who sold Willie his murder weapon. Then she met Melvin Stewart. His parents were hard workers from the cotton fields of the South, and he had been in the army in Vietnam, which gave him a sense of discipline. After his discharge, he got a job in the post office. The tenement in Harlem where they lived, they decided, with its frozen pipes in the winter, its drug dealers and shootings and its memories of Willie's last arrest, would ruin them. In an act of supreme determination, they moved to a small yellow house in the rural Pocono Mountains in Pennsylvania. For Melvin, it was a two-hour commute each way to his job, but he made the drive every day and Cheryl raised their six children. Over the years, they became active in church, reading the Bible together before dinner.

Now the children play Little League baseball and peewee football, with Melvin as a coach, and Cheryl acts like a cheerleader, jumping up and down. From time to time it occurs to her that she could not be doing this if they had stayed on 145th Street. There were no facilities, and she would have had to look over her head for bullets. Her childhood girlfriend died after being stabbed.

At Christmas, Cheryl and Willie exchange cards, and it makes her sad. She has learned that the descent into violence is not ineluctable, and salvation begins with breaking away from the code of the streets. She also knows a wonderful truth, she tells herself. The family can be rebuilt.

A NOTE ON SOURCES

THERE IS A GREAT WEALTH of primary material on which I have been fortunate to draw. In the interest of space, I have cited specific sources for my information in the notes that follow rather than attempt to list all of them here.

But some particular items deserve mention. The records of Edgefield County, preserved largely in the South Carolina Department of Archives and History, are wonderfully rich. There are full accounts of land sales in Edgefield, mortgages, taxes, and, later, sharecropper liens, all of which helped me to reconstruct the lives of John Bauskett, Francis Pickens, and their slaves who became the Bosket family. The county Coroners' Inquest Reports provide extraordinary data on homicides in Edgefield in the mid-nineteenth century. The papers of John Bauskett and Francis Pickens, contained in both the South Caroliniana Library in Columbia and at Duke University, hold valuable clues to their thinking and to the fate of their slaves. The South Carolina voter registration list of 1868 helped confirm family oral tradition about Aaron Bosket. Equally useful were the federal censuses that recorded how many slaves Bauskett and Pickens owned and, beginning in 1870, made it possible to trace Aaron's life. In Saluda, the criminal court records—with references to Pud Bosket—and the coroners' inquests are still in the county courthouse or at the Saluda County Historical Society across the street. State death certificates provided another way to verify Bosket family accounts about their ancestors. The local weekly newspapers, the Edgefield *Advertiser* and the Saluda *Standard* and *Sentinel*, were a cornucopia of information on everything from slave sales to life on the chain gang.

In Augusta, the annual city directories published by R. L. Polk & Company enabled me to follow the movements of Frances Bosket, her son James, and her grandson Butch, though they were too poor to own a telephone and be listed in the phone book. As I tried to trace the family, moving backward in time from New York to Augusta, an unexpected mention in one of the Polk directories—that Frances was the widow of a man from South Carolina—provided the first clue to where the Boskets had come from.

In New York, the probation and parole reports on Butch furnished a sometimes week-by-week account of his life, complete with interviews with his family members. An especially valuable feature was that these reports often incorporated earlier official accounts from his boyhood that were otherwise lost. Today, overstressed parole agents would not keep such detailed records. Butch's juvenile psychiatric records from Rockland State Hospital made it possible to reconstruct other intimate facts of his life and his relationship with his mother and father.

I was also lucky to obtain most of Butch's adult criminal and prison records. His FBI and Federal Bureau of Prisons files were made available under the Freedom of Information Act, and his Wisconsin Department of Corrections file came as the result of a Wisconsin open records law. Transcripts of his trials turned up in old archives. The Milwaukee Police Department and the Milwaukee County Sheriff's Department located their files on the murders he committed there and his attempted escape from custody in Froedtert Hospital. Butch's letters from prison over the years to Michael Schoenfield gave another glimpse into his mind.

As I researched the sections of this book on Willie, the documentary evidence was even more extensive, running to thousands of pages. For his childhood, there were reports from Wiltwyck, copies of probation reports prepared for the Manhattan Family Court, and the long file kept on Willie by the New York State Division for Youth, often including daily entries from each institution to which he was sent. During this tempestuous period, Willie was seen by many psychologists, psychiatrists, and social workers, and their comments are included in his file. For his adult years, I drew on the transcripts of his trials, and Willie offered copies of his New York State Department of Correctional Services misconduct and medical reports.

Much of the voluminous primary material on Butch and Willie is normally confidential, and it was a rare luxury to have access to it. In some cases, I considered withholding sensitive information, but Willie usually insisted it be published in the interest of telling his true story, and I have respected his judgments.

I have also drawn on interviews with 210 people.

All the dialogue and thoughts attributed to people in the book are real, based on either documents or interviews, or both. Each time a person is speaking, I have tried to indicate the source in a footnote, unless it is repetitious in the same chapter. The only other exception is for Willie himself. Where thoughts are attributed to him, they come from my conversations with Willie in prison.

As indicated in the footnotes, I have benefited greatly from the work of many scholars and writers. Several were especially valuable and need mention. Richard Maxwell Brown, *Strain of Violence: Historical Studies of American Violence and Vigilantism* (New York: Oxford University Press, 1975), showed that Edgefield had a remarkable record of violence that was important to understanding the broader American tradition of assault and murder. Edward L. Ayers, *Vengeance & Justice: Crime and Punishment in the 19th-Century South* (New York: Oxford University Press, 1984), brilliantly illuminated the role of honor in the South and first pointed to the link between white Southern honor and the black concern with respect. Orville Vernon Burton, *In My Father's House Are Many Mansions: Family and Community in Edgefield, South Carolina* (Chapel Hill: University of North Carolina Press, 1985), painted the definitive work on Edgefield social history. And Claude Brown, *Manchild in the Promised Land* (New York: Macmillan, 1965), served as a constant guide. His book remains the best memoir of growing up poor and black in Harlem, but beyond that, Brown's family, like the Boskets, was from South Carolina, and he himself was sent to Wiltwyck at almost the same time as Butch.

NOTES

PROLOGUE

xiii "ANY SO-CALLED CIVILIZED SOCIETY": Willie Bosket letter to the author, March 29, 1989.

1

"BLOODY EDGEFIELD"

3 EARLY EDGEFIELD HISTORY: The best account is the rich personal memoir by John A. Chapman, *History of Edgefield County from the Earliest Settlements to 1897* (Newberry, S.C.: Elbert Aull, 1897).

3 SCOTCH-IRISH IMMIGRANTS: The most comprehensive study is the elegant book by David Hackett Fischer, *Albion's Seed: Four British Folkways in America* (New York: Oxford University Press, 1989), especially pp. 605–15. An older but still useful work is Carl Bridenbaugh, *Myths and Realities: Societies of the Colonial South* (Baton Rouge: Louisiana State University Press, 1952), pp. 119–33.

4 VIOLENCE IN BACKCOUNTRY SOUTH CAROLINA: Richard Maxwell Brown, *Strain of Violence: Historical Studies of American Violence and Vigilantism* (New York: Oxford University Press, 1975), pp. 71–90.

4 "THEY INTRODUCED THE STRAIN": Brown, *Strain of Violence*, p. 73.

4 "ROGUISH AND TROUBLESOME": Brown, *Strain of Violence*, p. 73.

4 "NO CONFLICT WITHIN": Brown, *Strain of Violence*, p. 77.

5 "EACH COLONEL TO RECEIVE": Edward B. McCrady, *The History of South Carolina in the Revolution, 1775–1780* (New York: Macmillan, 1901), p. 144.

5 MAJOR CUNNINGHAM: Biographical details in McCrady, *History of South Carolina*, pp. 467–75.

6 CLOUD'S CREEK MASSACRE: McCrady, *History of South Carolina*, pp. 470–75, and Chapman, *History of Edgefield County*, pp. 30–71.

6 MATTHEW LOVE'S HANGING: David Duncan Wallace, *South Carolina: A Short History, 1520–1948* (Columbia: University of South Carolina Press, 1966), p. 325; also John Belton O'Neall, *Biographical Sketches of the Bench and Bar of South Carolina*, vol. 1 (Charleston: S. G. Courtenay & Co., 1859), p. 36.

6 "CHATTELS PERSONAL": Quoted in H. M. Henry, *Police Control of the*

Slave in South Carolina, reprint (New York: Negro University Press, 1968), p. 7.

6 "THEY ARE, GENERALLY SPEAKING": Quoted in Henry, *Police Control of the Slave*, p. 10.

6 AARON BOSKET'S NAME: He appears for the first recorded time in the 1868 South Carolina voter registration list, Edgefield County, Tenth Precinct, p. 212. The list is on microfilm in the South Carolina Department of Archives and History in Columbia.

6 "WE ARE ALL GOD'S CHILDREN": The phrase was passed on by Aaron's sons to his grandchildren. It was recounted in interviews by Emmie and Tilda Bosket. Local history in Edgefield is remembered with unusual intensity on all sides. Motte Yarbrough, a great-great-grandson of Captain James Butler, was born on land his ancestor had purchased near Mount Willing and talked knowledgeably about the Revolution and Cloud's Creek as if he had been there. Yarbrough was ninety-six years old at the time of the interview.

7 "ALL WAS DESOLATION": Quoted in Robert M. Weir, *Colonial South Carolina: A History* (Millwood, N.Y.: KTO Press, 1983), p. 336.

7 "I DOUBT WHETHER": Chapman, *History of Edgefield County*, p. 72.

7 "BLOODY EDGEFIELD": The notion that Edgefield bred a "syndrome of violence and extremism," strong even for South Carolina, is asserted most clearly in Brown, *Strain of Violence*, pp. 83–90.

7 "GOING TO HOLD COURT": Ulysses R. Brooks, *The South Carolina Bench and Bar*, vol. 1 (Columbia: State Company, 1908), p. 199.

7 "OH MERCY!": Parson Mason L. Weems, *The Devil in Petticoats, or God's Revenge Against Husband Killing* (Charleston: privately printed, 1823).

8 "THE DOCKETS WERE ENORMOUS": Chapman, *History of Edgefield County*, p. 174.

8 SOUTH CAROLINA CRIME RATES: Michael Stephen Hindus, *Prison and Plantation: Crime, Justice, and Authority in Massachusetts and South Carolina, 1767–1878* (Chapel Hill: University of North Carolina Press, 1980), pp. 63–65.

8 EDGEFIELD MURDER RATE DOUBLE STATE AVERAGE: Jack Kenny Williams, *Vogues in Villainy: Crime and Retribution in Antebellum South Carolina* (Columbia: University of South Carolina Press, 1959), p. 4.

8 EDGEFIELD CORONERS' INQUEST REPORTS: Reports for 1844–58 are in the South Carolina Archives.

8 1992 HOMICIDE RATES: FBI Uniform Crime Reports.

9 FIRST QUANTITATIVE STUDY: H. V. Redfield, *Homicide, North and South: Being a Comparative View of Crime Against the Person in Several Parts of the United States* (Philadelphia: Lippincott, 1880). The homicide figures for nineteenth-century New York were supplied separately by Eric Monkkonen, a UCLA history professor who has searched through all the available court and coroners' records as well as newspaper accounts. Over the years, the issue of why the South is so violent has spawned a small cottage industry. The best and most comprehensive single survey is Edward L. Ayers, *Vengeance and Justice: Crime and Punishment in the Nineteenth Century American South* (New York: Oxford University Press, 1984). Hindus, *Prison and Plantation*,

and Bertram Wyatt-Brown, *Southern Honor: Ethics and Behavior in the Old South* (New York: Oxford University Press, 1982), are also thoughtful treatments. A classic pioneering essay, still full of insight, is H. C. Brearley, "The Pattern of Violence," in *Culture in the South*, edited by W. T. Crouch (Chapel Hill: University of North Carolina Press, 1934). Brearley, a native South Carolinian and a sociologist at what is now Clemson University, suggested that the South might be referred to as "that part of the United States lying below the Smith and Wesson line" (p. 678).

9 1933 MURDER RATES: *Historical Statistics of the United States, Colonial Times to 1970*, part 2 (Washington, D.C.: U.S. Bureau of the Census, 1975), p. 414.

9 VIOLENCE SOUTHERN, NOT WESTERN: Ayers, *Vengeance and Justice*, p. 12.

9 "WHITE SAVAGES": Quoted in Ayers, *Vengeance and Justice*, p. 22.

10 "LEX TALIONIS": Fischer, *Albion's Seed*, p. 765.

10 "ROUGH AND TUMBLE": Quoted in Fischer, *Albion's Seed*, p. 737.

10 "BEFORE GOD": Quoted in Williams, *Vogues in Villainy*, p. 33.

10 "PRIMAL HONOR": The term is the coinage of Wyatt-Brown in his erudite *Southern Honor*. Much of my description of honor owes to his work, as well as to that of Ayers in *Vengeance and Justice*, and the brilliant essay by Charles Sydnor, "The Southerner and the Laws," *Journal of Southern History*, vol. 6, February 1940.

11 "TEMPERS WERE SHORT": Lawrence Stone, *The Crisis of the Aristocracy, 1558–1641* (Oxford: Oxford University Press, 1965), pp. 223–25.

11 "THE LAW AFFORDS": Quoted in Ayers, *Vengeance and Justice*, p. 18.

11 WILLIAM FAUX: Quoted in Williams, *Vogues in Villainy*, p. 37.

11 DUELS IN CAMDEN: Williams, *Vogues in Villainy*, p. 37.

12 DUELING OUTLAWED IN SOUTH CAROLINA: Williams, *Vogues in Villainy*, p. 38.

12 "UTTERLY REPUGNANT TO THOSE FEELINGS": John Lyde Wilson, *The Code of Honor or Rules for the Government of Principals and Seconds in Duelling* (Charleston: James Phynney, 1858), pp. 4, 12.

12 LOUIS WIGFALL: For the quarrel at the dance, Clement Eaton, *The Mind of the South* (Baton Rouge: Louisiana State University Press, 1967), p. 289. For Wigfall's fights in Edgefield, Alvy L. King, *Louis T. Wigfall: Southern Fire-eater* (Baton Rouge: Louisiana State University Press, 1970), pp. 18–39.

12 "THERE EXISTS IN OUR COUNTRY": Reverend Arthur Wigfall, *A Sermon Upon Dueling* (Charleston: n.p., 1856), pp. 9–10.

13 "THERE IS NO ONE HERE": Quoted in Ayers, *Vengeance and Justice*, p. 17.

13 GOODE AND CLOUD: Quoted in the Edgefield Coroners' Inquest Reports, July 8, 1851, South Carolina Archives.

13 GEORGE TILLMAN: Shooting at Planters' Hotel from Edgefield Coroners' Inquest Reports, July 21, 1856, South Carolina Archives. Biographical background from Francis Butler Simkins, *Pitchfork Ben Tillman: South Carolinian* (Baton Rouge: Louisiana State University Press, 1944), pp. 29–37. George Tillman's younger brother, Benjamin Ryan Tillman, "Pitchfork Ben," later became the governor of South Carolina and then for many years a U.S. senator. See Chapter 4 for details.

14   ONLY THIRTY-THREE TRIED FOR MURDER: Williams, *Vogues in Villainy*, p. 38.

14   "A SORT OF HONORABLE CRIME": *Report on the Trial of Martin Posey for the Murder of His Wife*, anonymous (Edgefield, S.C.: Advertiser Press, 1850), p. 5. For more on the casualness of antebellum Southern justice, see Bertram Wyatt-Brown, "Community, Class, and Snopesian Crime: Local Justice in the Old South," in *Class, Conflict and Consensus*, edited by Orville Vernon Burton and Robert C. McMath Jr. (Westport, Conn.: Greenwood, 1982); also Sydnor, "Southerner and the Laws."

14   "YOU SEEM": Quoted in John Hammond Moore, "Carnival of Blood: Dueling, Lynching, and Murder in South Carolina, 1880–1920," unpublished manuscript.

14   "MORE DASHING": William Watts Ball, *The State That Forgot: South Carolina's Surrender to Democracy* (Indianapolis: Bobbs-Merrill, 1932), p. 22. Today, Ball's words are celebrated in large letters on a wall in Edgefield's village square.

15   MAJOR POINT OF CONTACT: This observation was suggested in an interview by Professor Lacy K. Ford Jr., of the University of South Carolina.

15   "A BREEDING GROUND": William Francis Guess, *South Carolina: Annals of Pride and Protest* (New York: Harper & Brothers, 1957), p. 229.

16   THE DON QUIXOTE OF SLAVERY: Sumner's speech is quoted in David Donald, *Charles Sumner and the Coming of the Civil War* (New York, Alfred A. Knopf, 1960), pp. 285–86.

16   BROOKS'S REACTION TO SUMNER: Donald, *Charles Sumner*, pp. 288–295.

17   EFFECT OF BROOKS ATTACK: Donald, *Charles Sumner*, pp. 295–311.

17   "EVERY SOUTHERN MAN": Quoted in Donald, *Charles Sumner*, p. 304.

17   "MARSE PRESTON": The slave's recollections are quoted in the extraordinary collection of interviews with ex-bondsmen done by members of the Federal Writers Project in the 1930s. They were published as George Rawick, *The American Slave: A Composite Autobiography*, vol. 2: *South Carolina* (Westport, Conn.: Greenwood, 1972), part 2, p. 295.

18   "PUBLIC OPINION DISTINGUISHES": Quoted in Orville Vernon Burton, *In My Father's House Are Many Mansions: Family and Community in Edgefield, South Carolina* (Chapel Hill: University of North Carolina Press, 1985), p. 364. Burton's meticulously researched book is an invaluable guide to Edgefield history.

2

MASTERS AND SLAVES

19   "HE BOUGHT A NEGRO": Letter from Ann Wadlington to her son Thomas, April 15, 1834, Thomas Ellison Keitt Papers, Duke University Library.

19   JOHN BAUSKETT'S SLAVE PURCHASES: His acquisitions at the Breithaupt estate sale are in the Edgefield District Inventories, 1836–39, pp. 13–26, South Carolina Archives.

19   SHERIFF BOULWARE'S SLAVE SALE: Edgefield *Advertiser*, September 22, 1847, p. 3, South Caroliniana Library.

20   NUMBER OF BAUSKETT'S SLAVES: The total is given in the 1850 slave

census, which formed part of the federal Census program. It makes sorrowful reading. For in keeping with the Southern view that slaves were merely property, the slave census gives no name for any of the bondsmen. Instead, there are only long columns that list each slave's age, sex, and color (black or mulatto). The slaves were truly nonpersons. A holding of 221 slaves would have been very large, because in the 1860 Census, after slavery had grown even more, only eighty-eight planters in the entire South had more than 300 slaves.

20   "NEGROES, NEGROES": Slave dealer's ad appeared in the Edgefield *Advertiser*, February 27, 1851, p. 3.

20   RUBEN: The lineage of Ruben and Aaron Bosket has been reconstructed from stories told and retold by their descendants—interviews with Emmie, Tilda, Clyde, and Ida Bosket—as well as from surviving documents. A few biographical facts about Ruben appear in Aaron's death certificate, dated April 8, 1915, South Carolina Archives. The spelling of the family's name changed repeatedly during the federal censuses of 1870, 1880, 1900, and 1910, as well as in the Edgefield County mortgage and lien books, still kept in the Edgefield Courthouse.

20   BORN IN UPPER SOUTH: Further evidence that many of John Bauskett's slaves were born in the upper South and then sold to dealers to be marched to South Carolina is in the mortality census supplement to the 1850 federal Census. It lists people who had died in the preceding year. All three adult slaves belonging to Bauskett who had died in the previous twelve months were from out-of-state: Ellick, a twenty-two-year-old male born in North Carolina; Frautto, a forty-year-old male slave born in Virginia; and Finny, a sixty-year-old female, born in North Carolina.

20   "THE WOMEN WERE MERELY": Charles Ball, *Slavery in the United States: A Narrative of the Life and Adventures of Charles Ball, a Black Man*, reprint (New York: Kraus Reprint Company, 1969), p. 37.

21   "WE HAD NO CLOTHES": Ball, *Slavery in the United States*, p. 41.

21   "THEY PUT 'EM UP": Rawick, *American Slave*, vol. 13: *Georgia*, part 4, p. 343.

21   LONG-DISTANCE TRAFFIC: In the rich outpouring of studies on slavery in the past twenty-five years, which have added immeasurably to our appreciation of the strength of the African-American family under bondage, there has been little attention to the actual buying and selling of slaves within the United States, a critical part of the slave experience. The data here are from a pioneering exception, Michael Tadman, *Speculators and Slaves: Masters, Traders, and Slaves in the Old South* (Madison: University of Wisconsin Press, 1989), especially pp. 5, 45, 133.

21   RARE TO SURVIVE: Tadman, *Speculators and Slaves*, p. 121.

21   "IT SEEMS TO BE": Ball, *Slavery in the United States*, pp. 14–15.

22   "ONE LUSTY NEGRO": Peter H. Wood, *Black Majority: Negroes in Colonial South Carolina From 1670 Through the Stono Rebellion* (New York: Alfred A. Knopf, 1974), p. 11. More excellent detail on the early contributions of the slaves to South Carolina is in Charles Joyner, *Down by the Riverside: A South Carolina Slave Community* (Urbana: University of Illinois Press, 1984).

22 "THE BARBADIANS": Wood, *Black Majority,* p. 24.

22 "YE WEST INDIES": Wood, *Black Majority,* p. 33.

22 LINK TO BARBADOS: Jack P. Greene, "Colonial South Carolina and the Caribbean Connection," *South Carolina Historical Magazine,* vol. 88, 1977.

22 SULLIVAN'S ISLAND: Wood, *Black Majority,* p. xiv.

22 FIGURES ON SLAVES IN SOUTH CAROLINA: Percentages taken from Peter Kolchin, *Unfree Labor: American Slavery and Russian Serfdom* (Cambridge, Mass.: Harvard University Press, 1987), p. 20, and Hindus, *Prison and Plantation,* pp. xxiv, 246.

23 SOUTH CAROLINA'S WEALTH: Peter A. Coclainis and Lacy K. Ford, "The South Carolina Economy Reconstructed and Reconsidered: Structure, Output, and Performance, 1670–1985," in *Developing Dixie: Modernization in a Traditional Society,* edited by Winifred B. Moore Jr., Joseph F. Tripp, and Lyon G. Tyler Jr. (New York: Greenwood, 1988), pp. 94–98.

23 CULTURE OF CONFORMITY: James M. Banner Jr., "The Problem of South Carolina," in *The Hofstadter Aegis: A Memorial,* edited by Stanley Elkins and Eric McKitrick (New York: Alfred A. Knopf, 1974), p. 68. In the early nineteenth century, the backcountry was given a new more polite name in keeping with its more developed status—the up-country.

23 "COTTON IS KING": Quoted in Lacy K. Ford Jr., *Origins of Southern Radicalism: The South Carolina Upcountry, 1800–1860* (New York: Oxford University Press, 1988), p. 7.

23 THOMAS BAUSKETT: There is a brief biography of Thomas Bauskett in John Belton O'Neall, *The Annals of Newberry,* reprint (Baltimore: Genealogical Publishing, 1974), p. 574. Some of Bauskett's papers are in the William R. Perkins Library, Duke University. The number of his slaves is given in the federal Census of 1810.

23 ANDREW JACKSON: His remark about spelling is quoted in Fischer, *Albion's Seed,* p. 718.

24 JOHN BAUSKETT'S CAREER: There is a sketch of him in the *Biographical Directory of the South Carolina Senate, 1776–1985,* vol. 1, edited by N. Louise Bailey, Mary L. Morgan, and Carolyn R. Taylor (Columbia: University of South Carolina Press, 1986), pp. 109–10. He served three terms in the South Carolina House and two in the Senate. Bauskett's land deals are recorded in the Edgefield County Deeds, South Carolina Archives. Between 1834 and 1859, he made seventy-five transactions in Edgefield County alone, the largest involving 11,423 acres. There is also information on his business ventures in his letters to his father and sister, preserved in the Keitt Papers, Duke, and in his correspondence with Congressman George McDuffie in the South Caroliniana Library. Ernest McPherson Lander Jr., *The Textile Industry in Antebellum South Carolina* (Baton Rouge: Louisiana State University Press, 1969), has an account of Bauskett's textile investment.

24 "OCCASIONALLY SUPERINTEND": Letter from Bauskett to his sister, Ann Wadlington, September 25, 1838, Keitt Papers, Duke.

24 BENJAMIN FRANKLIN: He is named as overseer in the Edgefield Coroners' Inquest reports, March 25, 1852, case of death of "Negro slave named Duke," South Carolina Archives.

24 SLAVES AS COLLATERAL: The mortgage is recorded in the Edgefield County Deeds, Book DDD, p. 560, South Carolina Archives.

24 BAUSKETT'S AMBITIONS: A letter from his son, Thomas Bauskett, to his wife, Sophia, March 12, 1850, indicates John Bauskett's restlessness. The son inquired if there was truth to reports his father had bought property in Charleston and was going to move there. Keitt Papers, Duke.

24 "VALUABLE LAND & NEGROES": Edgefield *Advertiser*, December 29, 1852, p. 1.

25 PICKENS'S PURCHASE: Pickens's acquisition of Bauskett land, Edgefield County Deeds, Book HHH, p. 474. There are indications scattered through Pickens's plantation record book, especially the entries for 1855, that he bought Bauskett's slaves at the same time. The journal is in the Pickens Papers, Duke. The sale was also preserved in the slaves' memory, as noted in interview with Emmie Bosket.

25 FRANCIS PICKENS AND EDGEFIELD: Biographical information in Chapman, *History of Edgefield County*, pp. 144–45.

25 "SHORT AND SQUARELY BUILT": Quoted in John B. Edmunds Jr., *Francis W. Pickens and the Politics of Destruction* (Chapel Hill: University of North Carolina Press, 1986), p. 177.

25 "A STRONG ENFUSION OF ENVY": Calhoun quoted in sketch of Pickens in *Biographical Directory of the South Carolina Senate*, pp. 1272–75.

25 "MY DESTINY TO BE DISLIKED": Quoted in Edmunds, *Francis W. Pickens*, p. 153.

25 "FOR ANY EXTREME": Quoted in Edmunds, *Francis W. Pickens*, p. 12.

26 "WE HAVE A PECULIAR": Quoted in Edmunds, *Francis W. Pickens*, p. 19.

26 "FROM THE DAYS OF MOSES": Quoted in Edmunds, *Francis W. Pickens*, pp. 41–42.

26 TOTAL OF 563 SLAVES: Calculation in *Biographical Directory of the South Carolina Senate*, p. 1272.

26 "MY NEGROES": Pickens's plantation record book, entry for April 29, 1839, Pickens Papers, Duke. His directions for managing his slaves are also in the plantation journal.

27 SLAVES' DIET: Rawick, *American Slave*, vol. 17: *Florida*, pp. 47–52.

27 RACHEL SULLIVAN ACCOUNT: Rawick, *American Slave*, vol. 13: *Georgia*, part 4, pp. 227–28.

27 RUBEN'S MARRIAGE: Interview with Mabel Gibson. The relationship is also reported in Aaron Bauskett's death certificate, South Carolina Archives.

27 "IN DEM DAYS": Rawick, *American Slave*, supplementary series, vol. 4: *Georgia*, p. 663.

28 PICKENS'S MARRIAGE TO LUCY HOLCOMB: Edmunds, *Francis W. Pickens*, pp. 137–39.

28 DANCING WITH THE CZAR: Letter from Lucy Pickens to her sister, Anna Holcomb Greer, April 13, 1860, Pickens Papers, South Caroliniana Library. Edmunds, *Francis W. Pickens*, pp. 140–41, reports the rumors about the paternity of her child.

28 "IN A SOCIETY LIKE THIS": Letter from Lucy Pickens to her sister, April 13, 1860, Pickens Papers, South Caroliniana Library.

28   SALE OF CANE BREAK: Edgefield County Deeds, Book GGG, pp. 170–74. For the Dearing family, see Augustus Longstreet Hull, *Annals of Athens, Georgia, 1801–1901* (Athens: n.p., 1906). Clemson's name became an important one in South Carolina. He provided the money and land to start what is now Clemson University.

28   "I MUST GO HOME": Francis Pickens to M. L. Bonham, April 14, 1860, Bonham Papers, South Caroliniana Library.

29   BOSKET FAMILY SCATTERED BY SALE: Indications that the Boskets were scattered by the sale appear widely in the post–Civil War county records. The Edgefield County Index to Liens, April 20, 1882, Edgefield Courthouse, shows Aaron's brother William Bosket still working on land owned by Mrs. Francis Pickens. The lien records for April 14 and May 25, 1883, also show William working for Mrs. Pickens, but they report that Aaron was laboring for a family near Mount Willing, forty miles to the north.

29   DEARING CHALLENGES PROFESSOR TO DUEL: Henry Norton, "Some Reminiscences of Early Life and Times," in *Papers of the Athens Historical Society*, vol. 2, 1979.

29   $300,000 WORTH OF SLAVES: Listed in Census of 1860, Edgefield District, Saluda Regiment, p. 168.

29   MICHAEL DELOACHE: Chapman, *History of Edgefield County*, pp. 157, 397.

29   "SPARE THE ROD": Edgefield *Advertiser*, May 2, 1849.

29   RANDAL WHIPPED TO DEATH: Edgefield Coroners' Inquest Reports, May 9, 1844, South Carolina Archives.

30   BIBLICAL INJUNCTION OF THIRTY-NINE LASHES: Henry, *Police Control of the Slave*, pp. 53–54.

30   DEATH OF AARON: Edgefield Coroners' Inquest Reports, December 3, 1851, South Carolina Archives.

30   DEATH OF DINAH: Edgefield Coroners' Inquest Reports, May 22, 1849, South Carolina Archives.

31   "AN INVITATION TO PERJURY": Quoted in Hindus, *Prison and Plantation*, p. 132.

31   ONLY SIXTEEN WERE CONVICTED: Hindus, *Prison and Plantation*, pp. 133–35.

31   "HE WOULD NOT CONVICT": Hindus, *Prison and Plantation*, p. 135.

31   RATE OF SLAVE CONVICTIONS BY WHITE JURIES: Hindus, *Prison and Plantation*, p. 144.

31   EXECUTION OF SLAVES: Eighteenth-century figures in Wood, *Black Majority*, pp. 280–81. Nineteenth-century statistics from Hindus, *Prison and Plantation*, pp. 156–58.

31   "ON OUR ESTATES": Quoted in Hindus, *Prison and Plantation*, p. 129. For a thoughtful analysis of slavery's influence on the law, also see Sydnor, "Southerner and the Laws."

31   PROSECUTION OF SLAVES IN COURT: Hindus, *Prison and Plantation*, p. 141.

32   SLAVES AND HONOR: Ayers, *Vengeance and Justice*, quotes a former slave who recalled that his master had taught him to always fight back whenever someone threatened him, p. 133. For more on slaves and honor, see Bertram

Wyatt-Brown, "The Mask of Obedience: Male Slave Psychology in the Old South," *American Historical Review*, vol. 93, no. 5, December 1988, p. 1249.

32 QUARREL BETWEEN ELBERT AND HARRY: Edgefield Coroners' Inquest Reports, December 25, 1858, South Carolina Archives. Fight between Anderson and Baze, April 3, 1863, South Carolina Archives.

32 JOHN BUTLER'S DEATH: Edgefield *Advertiser*, October 31, 1850.

32 MURDER OF DR. WILLIAM KEITT: Letter from Caroline Wadlington Keitt, March 20, 1860, Keitt Papers, Duke.

32 "WE HAVE BUT FEW": Fitzhugh, quoted in Ayers, *Vengeance and Justice*, p. 137.

33 "EVERYONE HERE FEELS": Lawrence Keitt, quoted in Ford, *Origins of Southern Radicalism*, p. 348.

33 "YOU HAVE TO SAY BUT NIGGER": Hammond, quoted in William J. Cooper Jr., *The South and the Politics of Slavery* (Baton Rouge: Louisiana State University Press, 1978), p. 68.

33 "NOBODY COULD LIVE IN THIS STATE": *Mary Chestnut's Civil War*, edited by C. Vann Woodward (New Haven: Yale University Press, 1981), p. 4.

33 CODE OF HONOR EXACERBATED SECESSION CRISIS: For a good analysis of the role of honor in secession, see Cooper, *South and the Politics of Slavery*.

33 "FEAR!": Quoted in W. A. Swanberg, *First Blood: The Story of Fort Sumter* (New York: Scribner's, 1957), p. 82.

33 "IF I KNOW THE PULSE": Quoted in Edmunds, *Francis W. Pickens*, p. 151.

33 "I WOULD BE WILLING": Quoted in Edmunds, *Francis W. Pickens*, p. 152.

34 "WE ARE DIVORCED": *Mary Chestnut's Civil War*, p. 25.

34 "WE HAVE RALLIED": Edmunds, *Francis W. Pickens*, p. 163.

3

AARON

After Freedom

35 UNITED STATES COLORED TROOPS: Edgefield *Advertiser*, July 5, 1865.

35 "DON'T YOU SEE THE LIGHTNING?": Rawick, *American Slave*, vol. 13: *Georgia*, part 4, pp. 230–35, records this as the verse the troops sang as they marched into nearby Augusta, and Aaron Bosket's descendants recalled hearing about a similar song rendered in Edgefield.

35 AARON'S REACTION TO FREEDOM: Interviews with Emmie, Tilda, Clyde, and Ida Bosket.

36 BLACKS OWNED A MERE 2 PERCENT: Burton, *In My Father's House*, pp. 20, 260.

36 SHERMAN'S SPECIAL FIELD ORDER: Eric Foner, *Reconstruction: America's Unfinished Revolution, 1863–1877* (New York: Harper & Row, 1988), pp. 70–71.

36 1868 VOTER REGISTRATION LIST: Aaron's name appears in the roll for Mount Willing Precinct, Edgefield County, in the South Carolina Archives.

36 "IRREPRESSIBLE DEMOCRATS": B. O. Townsend wrote three highly un-

usual and revealing articles for *The Atlantic* under the anonymous byline of "A South Carolinian." They appeared in February, April, and June 1877. Quotation here is from the February 1877 article, p. 192.

37 "OUR COUNTRY IS DEAD": Pickens, quoted in Edmunds, *Francis W. Pickens*, p. 179.

37 EDGEFIELD CIVIL WAR CASUALTIES: Burton, *In My Father's House*, p. 227.

37 "THE FOUNDATIONS OF THE GREAT DEEP": Chapman, *History of Edgefield County*, p. 259.

37 "AS THE BLACKS WERE": Cited in Burton, *In My Father's House*, p. 268.

37 "THE OLD RELATIONS": Townsend, *The Atlantic*, April 1877, p. 470.

38 "TO SWALLOW AN INSULT FROM A NEGRO": Townsend, *The Atlantic*, April 1877, p. 470.

38 "OUTRAGES" REPORTED BY FREEDMEN'S BUREAU: Burton, *In My Father's House*, p. 289.

38 WILLIAM HARDY: Interview with his descendant Carol Bryan.

38 "THE CITY . . . IS INHABITED BY THIEVES": Burton, *In My Father's House*, pp. 297–98.

38 "IT IS DANGEROUS FOR A BLACK MAN": Picksley's complaint is in the Freedmen's Bureau, Monthly Report of Outrages, April 1865–September 1868, microfilm roll 42, pp. 668–72, South Carolina Archives.

39 HOTEL CLERK BEATING GUEST: Joel Williamson, *After Slavery: The Negro in South Carolina During Reconstruction, 1861–1877* (Hanover, N.H.: University Press of New England, 1965), p. 257.

39 "WITH PISTOLS, STICKS AND ROCKS": South Carolina Committee of Investigation, *Evidence by Committee of Investigation of the Third Congressional District* (Columbia: n.p., 1869), pp. 680–82.

39 PICKENS STEWART BEATEN: *Committee of Investigation*, pp. 693–95.

40 "THE KU KLUX KLAN WITH ITS NIGHT VISITS": Townsend, *The Atlantic*, April 1877, pp. 470–71. Foner, *Reconstruction*, pp. 425–59, has a masterful description of the early rise of the Klan.

40 ELECTION OF 1872 RESULTS: Williamson, *After Slavery*, p. 360.

40 "THE EDGEFIELD PLAN": M. W. Gary, "Plan of the Campaign of 1876," in Gary Papers, South Caroliniana Library.

40 HAMBURG MASSACRE: There are vivid accounts in Foner, *Reconstruction*, pp. 570–72, and Williamson, *After Slavery*, pp. 266–73.

41 PRISONERS "TAKEN OUT IN THE STREETS": Matilda Evans, *Martha Schofield: Pioneer Negro Educator* (Columbia: Dupree Printing Company, 1916), p. 47.

42 MURDER OF SIMON COKER: The whole account of Coker's death is taken from Benjamin Ryan Tillman, *The Struggles of 1876: How South Carolina Was Delivered From Carpet-Bag and Negro Rule* (Anderson, S.C.: n.p., 1909), pp. 44–46.

42 "ONE OF THE GREATEST FARCES": Townsend, *The Atlantic*, February 1877, p. 187. Details on the 1876 election in Foner, *Reconstruction*, pp. 574–75, and Williamson, *After Slavery*, pp. 344–45.

42 AARON IN COLUMBIA: He is listed as being in Columbia in the Census of 1870, Richland County, p. 170.

42   MARRIAGE TO ANGELINE: Reported in the Census of 1880, Edgefield County, p. 20.

43   AARON'S DEBTS: The sharecroppers' debts he incurred with several white farmers and Zeke Crouch's store are recorded in the Edgefield County Index to Liens, for 1882, 1883, 1889, and 1891, in the Edgefield Courthouse.

43   AARON'S FREQUENT MOVES AS A SHARECROPPER: The tax records of Saluda County, which was spun off from Edgefield in 1896, clearly demonstrate this pattern until Aaron's death in 1915, South Carolina Archives.

43   VALUE OF AARON'S PROPERTY: The assessed value is reported in the Saluda County Tax Records, South Carolina Archives.

43   "NEGROES HAD NOWHERE TO GO": Benjamin E. Mays, *Born to Rebel: An Autobiography* (Athens: University of Georgia Press, 1971), p. 13. The son of a sharecropper, Mays became president of Moorehouse College and later the mentor of Dr. Martin Luther King Jr.

44   "HE WOULDN'T HURT A HAIR": Interviews with Emmie and Clyde Bosket.

44   "US HAD DE PREACHER": Quoted in Burton, *In My Father's House*, p. 293.

44   BACKGROUND OF TILDA MOBLEY POU: Interviews with Emmie, Clyde, and Ida Bosket. The Census of 1880, Edgefield County, p. 46, records Tilda as married to James Pou.

44   "SHE WAS A NICE-LOOKING GIRL": Interview with Posey Padgett. He was ninety-three years old at the time and still remembered clearly the story of Tilda and William Merchant's relationship.

44   HAMMOND AND HIS SLAVE MISTRESS: Burton, *In My Father's House*, p. 130.

45   AFFAIR OF LUCY PICKENS'S BROTHER WITH FORMER SLAVE: Burton, *In My Father's House*, p. 292.

45   BENJAMIN MAYS'S WHITE ANCESTRY: Mays, *Born to Rebel*, pp. 30–33.

45   "THE MISERABLE COUNTY OF EDGEFIELD": Quoted in Foner, *Reconstruction*, p. 599.

45   "WE HAVE TRIED TO MAKE MONEY": Quoted in George Brown Tindall, *South Carolina Negroes, 1877–1900* (Columbia: University of South Carolina Press, 1952), pp. 170–71.

4

PUD

"Don't Step on My Reputation"

46   PUD AND HANGING OF WILL HERRIN: Interviews with Edna Herrin Williams and Freeman Herrin, a niece and nephew of Will Herrin. Also, interviews with Lois Addy, Mabel Crouch, and Perrine Crouch, all of whom, as young girls, saw the hanging from their houses nearby.

47   "NOW THAT IT IS SETTLED": Saluda *Standard*, December 3, 1908.

47   "MOST OF THE MEN": Quoted in Ayers, *Vengeance and Justice*, p. 237.

47   "THERE COULD NEVER": Quoted in Saluda *Standard*, March 25, 1903.

47   "THESE YOUNGER EBONIES": Saluda *Standard*, October 3, 1907.

47 SHOOTING OF EMANUEL CARVER: Saluda County Coroners' Inquest Reports, September 14, 1908, Saluda Historical Society.

48 "FOR THERE WAS REALLY NOTHING": Saluda *Standard*, October 22, 1908.

48 "DURING ALL THIS": Saluda *Standard*, December 3, 1908.

48 "THE EERIE FEELING": Interview with Lois Addy.

48 RODNEY ETHEREDGE: Interview with his son, Edwin Etheredge.

48 "WELL PLEASED TO SEE": Saluda *Standard*, December 3, 1908.

48 "THE WHOLE FAMILY WAS ANGRY": Interview with Freeman Herrin.

49 "IN ORDER THAT EVERYONE": Saluda *Sentinel*, November 23, 1898.

49 "IN SOME WAYS THE DARKEST": Benjamin J. Brawley, *A Social History of the American Negro* (New York: Macmillan, 1921), p. 298. The classic account of this turbulent period is C. Vann Woodward, *The Strange Career of Jim Crow* (New York: Oxford University Press, 1957). Also useful are David Herbert Donald, "A Generation of Defeat," in *From the Old South to the New: Essays on the Transitional South*, edited by Walter J. Fraser et al. (Westport, Conn.: Greenwood, 1981), and Joel Williamson, *The Crucible of Race: Black-White Relations in the American South Since Reconstruction* (New York: Oxford University Press, 1984), pp. 110–39.

49 BEN TILLMAN: This account is largely drawn from the sympathetic yet clear-sighted biography of Tillman by his fellow native of Edgefield, Francis Butler Simkins, *Pitchfork Ben Tillman*.

50 "WE DON'T PROPOSE": Tindall, *South Carolina Negroes*, p. 87.

50 "THEY ISSUED": Saluda *Sentinel*, January 14, 1897.

50 "GIVE THE NEGRO JUSTICE": Saluda *Sentinel*, January 14, 1897.

50 "THERE WASN'T MUCH": Mays, *Born to Rebel*, p. 22.

51 "A G-D DAMN DOG": *The State*, Columbia, S.C., March 25, 1897. Also, Saluda *Sentinel*, April 1, 1897, and Simkins, *Pitchfork Ben Tillman*, pp. 531–34.

51 SOUTH CAROLINA MURDER FIGURES: These figures are taken from reports by the local prosecutors supplied annually to the legislature and printed in the *Reports and Resolutions of the South Carolina General Assembly*. They are not broken down by race, making it impossible to quantify what proportion of the growth of violence was caused by blacks, though white Southerners believed it was high.

51 SALUDA HOMICIDES: The figures are from the Saluda Coroners' Inquest Reports, in the Saluda Historical Society. Saluda was still a rural farming community. The largest settlement in the county in the first decade of the century, Saluda town, had fewer than five hundred inhabitants.

51 "SALUDA COUNTY HAS MADE": Saluda *Sentinel*, July 6, 1904.

51 "A LARGE AMOUNT": Saluda *Sentinel*, January 21, 1897.

52 MURDER OF JOHN BUZHARD: Saluda *Sentinel*, December 3 and 10, 1896.

52 EUGENE BLEASE KILLS BROTHER-IN-LAW: Saluda *Standard*, September 13 and 20, 1905. Also see the court record, Saluda County Court of General Sessions, Case no. 276.

52 FIGHT BETWEEN JIM TILLMAN AND GONZALES: Simkins, *Pitchfork Ben Tillman*, pp. 379–84; Lewis P. Jones, *Stormy Petrel: N. G. Gonzales and His State* (New York: Columbia University Press, 1973); and Moore, "Carnival of Blood."

53 "PRACTICALLY EVERYONE HERE": Quoted in Moore, "Carnival of Blood," pp. 165–66.

53 "DEPLORABLE CUSTOM": Quoted in Tindall, *South Carolina Negroes*, p. 236.

53 ATTORNEY GENERAL MCLAURIN'S PISTOL: Moore, "Carnival of Blood," p. 176.

54 KILLING OF CAL SMITH: Saluda County Coroners' Inquest Reports, 1896, pp. 1–5.

54 "THE NEGRO FAMILY ARE SATISFIED": Saluda *Sentinel*, December 31, 1896.

54 "EVERY BLACK MAN IN SALUDA": Interview with Roy Holloway.

55 "I THINK I'LL SEE IF IT WORKS": Interview with Beela Herlong, the daughter of Davenport Padgett.

55 "ASSAYED TO WAKE THEM UP": Saluda *Sentinel*, July 27, 1898.

55 CHARLES GOMILLION: Interview with Charles Gomillion. He himself left Edgefield County four years later, in 1916, to go to school in Augusta. Fear was so deeply implanted in him that he did not return to the area until 1990, when he was honored by the Edgefield Historical Society. As a teacher at the Tuskegee Institute in Alabama, Gomillion sued the local county for depriving blacks of their voting rights, a lawsuit that eventually reached the Supreme Court and became a landmark Civil Rights case, *Gomillion* v. *Lightfoot*.

55 PUD'S REACTION TO WHITE VIOLENCE AGAINST BLACKS: Interview with Roy Holloway.

56 "HANGED BY MISTAKE": Fischer, *Albion's Seed*, p. 767.

56 FIGURES ON LYNCHING: Williamson, *Crucible of Race*, pp. 117–18.

56 "BEST CITIZENS, YOUNG AND OLD": The Charleston newspaper's account of Mackey's lynching is quoted in Terence Robert Finnegan, "At the Hands of Parties Unknown: Lynching in Mississippi and South Carolina, 1881–1940," unpublished doctoral dissertation, University of Illinois, 1992, pp. 154–55. Finnegan's study is the most recent and by far the best on lynching in South Carolina. He found that more than half of all the lynchings in the state took place in the old up-country plantation belt centered around Edgefield.

57 "LYNCHED FOR THE USUAL": Saluda *Sentinel*, August 20, 1902.

57 "WE KNEW IF WE FOUND HIM INNOCENT": Interview with B. W. Crouch's daughter, Mabel Crouch.

57 MOST LYNCHINGS DID NOT INVOLVE RAPE: Statistics about the causes of lynching in South Carolina are from Finnegan, "At the Hands," p. 32. He found the same thing to be true in Mississippi—that economic conflicts rather than attacks on white women were the most common origin of lynchings. Another good recent study has reached a similar conclusion about Georgia: W. Fitzhugh Brundage, *Lynching in the New South: Georgia and Virginia, 1880–1930* (Urbana: University of Illinois Press, 1993).

58 "I NEVER FELT AT HOME": Mays, *Born to Rebel*, pp. 1, 34.

58 "NEGROES LIVED UNDER": Mays, *Born to Rebel*, pp. 25–26.

58 "IF HE'D BEEN A MINISTER": Interview with Roy Holloway.

58 "I'M GOING TO WHIP YOU": Interview with Clyde Bosket, a nephew of

Pud's. Clyde's father, Dandy Bosket, who was Pud's younger brother, was one of the other sharecroppers in the incident.

59   "THERE IS NO ADVANTAGE TO LIFE": Interview with Roy Holloway.

59   PUD'S ROBBERY OF STORES: Saluda *Standard*, April 28, 1910. Also the Saluda County Court of General Sessions, 1910 records, indictment and conviction of Pud Bosket.

59   PUD'S ARREST AND ESCAPE: Saluda *Standard*, May 5, June 2, and June 23, 1910.

60   "THE SENTENCE OF THE COURT": Saluda County Court of General Sessions, 1910 records.

60   "THE NEGRO HAS A CONSTITUTIONAL PROPENSITY": Quoted in Tindall, *South Carolina Negroes*, p. 267.

60   CONVICTS WHIPPED TO DEATH: Saluda *Standard*, October 19, 1904, and June 30, 1910.

60   "THE NEGROES ON THE CHAIN GANG": Interview with Floyd Henderson, the son of Warren Henderson. He remembered spending time as a boy with his father watching the prisoners at work, including Pud Bosket.

61   "SO OFTEN WERE THE SLAVES WHIPPED": Townsend, *The Atlantic*, April 1877, pp. 474–75.

61   "IT IS NO UNUSUAL THING": Saluda *Standard*, October 31, 1907.

61   "THERE CAN BE NO DOUBT": W. E. B. Du Bois, *The Souls of Black Folk*, reprint, originally published 1903 (New York: Bantam Books, 1989), pp. 124–25.

62   HOT SUPPERS: Southern whites were often jealous of blacks' ability to enjoy themselves so freely. Henrik Booraem, a teacher and historian in Edgefield, recalled that as a boy he frequently heard older white men say: "I'd rather be a nigger on Saturday night than a white man the rest of the week."

62   "I WENT DOWN TO THE VALLEY": Interview with Roy Holloway.

62   KILLING OF WILLIAM BOSKET: Saluda *Standard*, April 5 and September 6, 1905; also the Saluda County Coroners' Inquest Reports for 1905, pp. 382–84.

62   MAMON BOSKET'S KILLING OF GEORGE DOZIER: Saluda County Coroners' Inquest Reports for 1926; also the Saluda County Court of General Sessions record of Mamon's conviction for manslaughter, February 28, 1927.

62   "THEY SAID PUD": Interview with Mabel Gibson. She was born in 1898 and was a lifelong member of Pleasant Hill church. Virtually all sources agree that fighting and drinking in or near black churches was commonplace in this period in South Carolina. Benjamin Mays, for example, reports it in *Born to Rebel*, p. 14. The Saluda *Standard* reported six cases of killings at churches in the county between 1896 and 1915, several at Pleasant Hill. Describing one such murder, the newspaper said sardonically: "The majority of murder cases between the colored race happen either at country hot suppers or just after some church service when the doxology is still ringing in their ears, although it may not have found lodgement in their hearts." October 26, 1904.

62   PUD'S ARREST FOR GAMBLING: Saluda *Standard*, February 13, 1913.

63   "HE DIDN'T BOTHER NOBODY": Interview with Clyde Bosket, Dandy's son.

63 "PUD JUST THREW": Interview with Clyde Bosket.

63 "DON'T STEP ON MY REPUTATION": Interview with Clyde Bosket.

63 WHITES ABOVE THE LAW, BLACKS OUTSIDE THE LAW: Ayers, *Vengeance and Justice*, p. 234.

63 "HONOR MAY HAVE BEEN EVEN MORE LETHAL": Ayers, *Vengeance and Justice*, p. 235. Ayers is the first scholar to point out the connection between antebellum white Southern honor and the later black concept of respect. My understanding of Pud and his descendants owes much to his insight.

63 BLACK BAD MEN: Two excellent and somewhat varying accounts of the origin and meaning of the bad man in black history are Lawrence W. Levine, *Black Culture and Black Consciousness: Afro-American Folk Thought From Slavery to Freedom* (New York: Oxford University Press, 1977), pp. 406–20, and John W. Roberts, *From Trickster to Badman: The Black Folk Hero in Slavery and Freedom* (Philadelphia: University of Pennsylvania Press, 1989), pp. 171–215.

64 "RAILROAD BILL, HE WENT DOWN SOUF": Quoted in Roberts, *From Trickster to Badman*, p. 172.

64 "THE BLUES IS MOSTLY REVENGE": Cited in Levine, *Black Culture*, p. 214.

64 "I WENT DOWN TOWN": Howard W. Odum and Guy B. Johnson, *The Negro and His Songs: A Study of Typical Negro Songs in the South* (Chapel Hill: University of North Carolina Press, 1925), p. 213.

64 "THEY WERE PURE FORCE": Levine, *Black Culture*, p. 420.

65 PUD'S ASSAULT ON COLEMAN BRYANT: Saluda County Court of General Sessions, 1916 records.

65 PUD LIVING WITH CARRIE HARRIS: Information on Pud's early years comes from interviews with Mabel Gibson, Emmie Bosket, and Ida Bosket. The federal Census of 1900, Saluda County, Huiets Township, pp. 74–75, shows the families of Carrie Harris, Aaron Bosket, and his brothers living close together after being separated for many years.

65 PUD'S MARRIAGE TO LIZZIE: Recorded in the federal Census of 1910.

65 "PUD NEVER STAYED HOME": Interview with Roy Holloway.

65 DEATH OF INFANT CLIFTON BOSKET JR.: His death certificate contains the doctor's diagnosis. South Carolina Department of Health and Environmental Control, 1915, Saluda County, microfilm roll 15, no. 22400, South Carolina Archives.

66 PUD'S FINAL DAY: Interview with Roy Holloway.

66 THE CAR ACCIDENT: Interview with Garrett Langford. Langford, who was out for a Sunday drive with his parents, was in the first car that came upon the scene that day. A remarkably graphic account appears in the Saluda *Standard*, November 13, 1924.

66 PUD'S FRIENDS GET TOGETHER AFTER HIS DEATH: Interviews with Roy Holloway and Emmie Bosket.

• • •

5

JAMES AND BUTCH

Coming Up in the Terry

72 AUGUSTA AND THE CRACKER PARTY: Edward J. Cashin, *The Story of Augusta* (Spartanburg, S.C.: The Reprint Company, 1991).

72 NO "DESIRE OR PURPOSE TO DISCRIMINATE": Edward J. Cashin, *The Quest: A History of Public Education in Richmond County, Georgia* (Augusta: Richmond County Board of Education, 1985), pp. 39–42.

72 FRANCES'S ECONOMIC PLIGHT: Pud's probate court records, on file in the Saluda County Courthouse, detail his poverty.

72 BLACK MIGRATION FROM RURAL SOUTH CAROLINA: Julian J. Petty, *The Growth and Distribution of Population in South Carolina* (Columbia: South Carolina State Planning Board, 1943), p. 64. Also Finnegan, "At the Hands," p. 296.

73 FRANCES'S MOVES IN AUGUSTA: The annual Augusta city directories, published by R. L. Polk and Company, contain invaluable material documenting her movements. Evidence of Frances being evicted is in the bench dockets of the Richmond County Court. For a good description of the Terry in the 1930s, see the guidebook published by the Federal Writers' Project, *Augusta* (Augusta: Tidwell Printing Company, 1938), pp. 49–50.

73 BLACK HOUSEHOLDS HEADED BY WOMEN: The Augusta city directories provide vital information on who was living in each household, block by block, and who was the head of the household.

73 "IT'S JUST THE WAY": Interview with Annie Diggs.

74 JAMES'S VISITS TO UNCLE DANDY'S HOUSE: These accounts are from interviews with Clyde, Emmie, Ida, and Leroy Bosket.

75 JAMES AS A CHAUFFEUR: Interviews with Clyde and Leroy Bosket.

75 NINTH STREET: Interviews with Helen Callahan, Kathryn Callahan, Nellie Callahan, Philip Waring, and Annie Diggs, all former residents.

76 "DADDY" GRACE: James Brown, with Bruce Tucker, *James Brown: The Godfather of Soul* (New York: Thunder's Mouth Press, 1990), pp. 9–27. Brown, like James Bosket, was born in rural South Carolina and was brought to Augusta as a boy.

76 MARIE HICKSON: Interview with Marie Hickson, now Marie Jackson.

77 JAMES BOSKET AND MARIE ELOPE AND THEIR LIFE TOGETHER: Interview with Marie Hickson Jackson.

78 "THE PARENTS WERE TEMPORARILY RECONCILED": The appearance of Marie and James Bosket in the Augusta Juvenile Court is taken from a later probation report for Butch Bosket, prepared for the New York County—or Manhattan—Court of General Sessions, February 18, 1958. The New York probation report incorporated portions of the original Augusta court hearings and orders, which have since been destroyed.

78 JUDGE WOODWARD: Interviews with Marguerite Agee, a former probation officer with the Augusta Juvenile Court, and Rufus J. Lowe, a clerk of the court.

79 "THAT WILL BE A FIVE-DOLLAR FINE": Interview with Charles Gomillion.

79 JAMES BOSKET'S ROBBERY IN WASHINGTON: This was reported in his later New York State criminal record.

79 "I HAVE TO GET AWAY": Interviews with Marie Hickson Jackson and Emmie Bosket.

80 "MISTER, YOU GOT A QUARTER?": Interview with Annie Diggs.

80 LUCY WRIGHT: Interview with Lucy Wright.

81 "THEY DIDN'T ENCOURAGE BLACKS": Interview with Dr. Isaiah E. Washington. The figures on spending per pupil are also from Dr. Washington, who was a school principal in Augusta for twenty-five years.

81 "BY THE TIME I GOT THEM ORGANIZED": Interview with Louise Jackson.

82 TEACHER FOUND BUTCH UNDER STEPS: Interview with Mrs. Ernie Jenkins, another former teacher.

82 "GIT UP HERE": Interview with Annie Diggs.

82 "I'M GOING TO GET": Interview with Annie Diggs.

83 "PUT HIS LIGHTS OUT": Interview with Jeffrey Lockett, a brother of Richard Lockett's.

84 PERCY AND BUTCH: Interview with Jeffrey Lockett.

85 "I TELL MY CHILDREN TO FIGHT": Interview with Annie Diggs.

85 BUTCH'S SCAR, BROKEN HANDS, AND WOUND: Information in Butch's New York State Department of Corrections medical report, June 4, 1958, on his admission to the Elmira Reception Center.

86 JAMES'S ARMY RECORD: Information from James Bosket's army service record, in the National Personnel Records Center, St. Louis.

86 FRANCES TELLS BUTCH TO SPIT ON HIS MOTHER: Interview with Marie Hickson Jackson.

86 "I DON'T HAVE NO MOMMA": Interview with Emmie Bosket.

86 "COMPLETELY UNCONTROLLABLE": The report by the Augusta probation officer, Louise Laney, is incorporated in the probation report on Butch prepared for the Manhattan Court of General Sessions, February 18, 1958.

87 RICHARD LOCKETT'S JUVENILE AND CRIMINAL RECORD: Interview with his brother, Jeffrey Lockett, and information from the Georgia Department of Corrections.

6

BUTCH

The Promised Land

88 BUTCH'S LIFE WITH HIS MOTHER IN NEW YORK: Probation report prepared for the Manhattan Court of General Sessions, February 18, 1958. Also, the clinical summary on Butch prepared by the Rockland State Hospital, December 23, 1954, and a family history Butch gave to the Wisconsin Department of Corrections, July 16, 1963.

89 "NEVER DARKEN THIS DOOR AGAIN": Interview with Edith Kramer.

89 MANHATTAN CHILDREN'S COURT DECISION ON BUTCH: New York County probation report, February 18, 1958.

89 "MISS, YOU DON'T KNOW": Interview with Marie Hickson Jackson.

89 "GOING TO NEW YORK": Claude Brown, *Manchild in the Promised Land* (New York: Macmillan, 1965), p. vii. Like the Boskets, Brown's family was originally from rural South Carolina. He and Butch were almost the same age, and both Brown and Butch were sent by court order to many of the same institutions, starting with the Children's Center.

90 "WITH PROSTITUTES LIVING OVER ME": Reverend Adam Clayton Powell Sr. is quoted in the classic account of the development of Harlem, Gilbert Osofsky, *Harlem: The Making of a Ghetto, 1890–1930* (New York: Harper & Row, 1965), p. 14. Another elegant study is Jervis Anderson, *This Was Harlem: A Cultural Portrait, 1900–1950* (New York: Farrar, Straus & Giroux, 1981).

91 "HARLEM WAS ORIGINALLY": Osofsky, *Harlem*, p. 111.

91 "INHERITED THE TOTAL LOT": Brown, *Manchild*, p. viii.

92 BUTCH'S FIGHTS IN CHILDREN'S CENTER: New York County probation report, February 18, 1958.

92 BUTCH BULLYING YOUNGER BOYS: New York County probation report.

92 BUTCH ORDERED BY JUDGE TO WILTWYCK: New York County probation report.

93 "THOSE POOR LITTLE BOYS": Quoted in Joseph P. Lash, *A World of Love: Eleanor Roosevelt and Her Friends, 1943–1962* (New York: Doubleday, 1984), p. 78.

94 IF ANY PLACE COULD HELP: Wiltwyck had some real success stories. Two of its residents, both there shortly before Butch, were Floyd Patterson, the heavyweight boxing champion, and Claude Brown, the author of the bestseller *Manchild in the Promised Land*.

94 "HELL ON WHEELS": Interview with Edith Kramer. She still retains some of the paintings Butch did in her class. Kramer also wrote two books, based on her experience at Wiltwyck, that describe Butch under a pseudonym: *Art Therapy in a Children's Community: A Study of the Function of Art Therapy in the Treatment Program of Wiltwyck School for Boys* (Springfield, Ill.: Charles C. Thomas, 1958), and *Art as Therapy with Children* (New York: Schocken, 1971).

95 "LOOK, THIS IS ONLY A PAINTING": Interview with Edith Kramer.

96 "I TRUST THREE PEOPLE": Interview with Edith Kramer.

97 JAMES BOSKET'S ARREST IN OHIO: The account of his arrest and conviction for robbery in Ohio is from his record with the Cleveland Police Department.

97 JAMES'S SECOND OHIO ARREST: Cleveland Police Department record.

97 BUTCH'S RELEASE FROM WILTWYCK: Butch's New York State probation file.

97 WILTWYCK FIRST PLACE IN LIFE WHERE HAPPY: Butch's interview with prison psychologist in Wisconsin, in his Wisconsin Department of Corrections file, April 16, 1982.

98 KRAMER THE PERSON WHO HAD THE MOST POSITIVE IMPACT: Letter from Butch to Edith Kramer, July 22, 1980.

98 "THE ONLY REAL SENSE OF FAMILY": Letter from Butch to Bill Ballard, a former counselor at Wiltwyck, April 23, 1980.

98 "BACK TO A HOME THAT WAS NOT A HOME": Letter from Butch to Ballard, April 22, 1980.

98   "A NO GOOD BUM": Butch's comments on his father are contained in his New York State parole file. He later recalled similar memories with a prison psychologist in Wisconsin, in his Wisconsin Department of Corrections file; see entry for March 11, 1963, for example.

98   JAMES BEATS BUTCH: Reported in Butch's New York State probation file and in his Rockland State Hospital file.

98   JAMES INFORMS BUTCH HIS MOTHER IS A PROSTITUTE: Butch to prison psychologists, in his Wisconsin Department of Corrections file, entries for March 11 and July 16, 1963.

99   "HIS NAME IS NOT": Interview with Edith Kramer. The incident is also reported in Butch's New York State probation file.

99   "SEETHING WITH ANGER": Bellevue's evaluation of Butch is recorded in his Rockland State Hospital clinical summary.

100   "ON ADMISSION": Dr. Simon Victor, quoted in Rockland State Hospital clinical summary on Butch.

100   "REMARKABLE UNDERSTANDING": Quoted in Rockland State Hospital clinical summary.

100   CORA MAE JONES AND JAMES BOSKET: Quoted in Rockland State Hospital clinical summary.

100   JAMES SUFFERS FROM SYPHILIS: Reported in Butch's New York State probation file and New York State Department of Corrections file.

100   EFFECTS OF CONGENITAL SYPHILIS: For information on congenital syphilis, I am indebted to Dr. Mary E. Wilson, chief of the infectious diseases department of Mount Auburn Hospital in Cambridge, Massachusetts, and a professor at the Harvard Medical School. See also Dr. King H. Holmes et al., *Sexually Transmitted Diseases* (New York: McGraw Hill, 1991).

101   "DEVELOPMENTAL FACTORS": Dr. S. Vaisberg's findings, dated March 29, 1955, are in the Rockland State Hospital clinical summary.

101   "CONDUCT DISORDER": A good analysis of childhood antisocial behavior is Dorothy Otnow Lewis, "Conduct Disorder," in *Child and Adolescent Psychiatry: A Comprehensive Textbook*, edited by Melvin Lewis (Baltimore: Williams & Watkins, 1991).

101   CONDUCT DISORDER AS A PREDICTOR OF LATER VIOLENCE: For a useful summary of recent research, see John D. Coie and Kenneth A. Dodge, "A Developmental and Clinical Model for the Prevention of Conduct Disorder: The FAST Track Program," in *Development and Psychopathology*, vol. 4, 1992, pp. 509–27.

101   PSYCHOPATHS AND ANTISOCIAL PERSONALITY DISORDER: An excellent guide to the subject is Michael H. Stone, *Abnormalities of Personality: Within and Beyond the Realm of Treatment* (New York: Norton, 1993). A readable introduction for laymen is Robert D. Hare, *Without Conscience: The Disturbing World of the Psychopaths Among Us* (New York: Pocket Books, 1993). Technically, there is a difference between psychopaths and people with antisocial personality disorder. Psychopaths are diagnosed according to their bad traits, such as callousness. Antisocial personality disorder is based on a list of bad acts, such as stealing and fighting. For practical purposes, however, I have used the terms interchangeably.

102 CYCLE OF VIOLENCE: The effect of parental physical and sexual abuse in making children into delinquents and later adult criminals has been amply documented: Cathy Spatz Widom, "The Cycle of Violence," *Science*, vol. 244, 1989, pp. 160–66.

102 DELINQUENT BOYS WITH CRIMINAL FATHERS: This classic study was done by two scholars at Harvard Law School, Sheldon and Eleanor Glueck. Their work has been revived and reanalyzed by Robert J. Sampson and John H. Laub in *Crime in the Making: Pathways and Turning Points Through Life* (Cambridge, Mass.: Harvard University Press, 1993).

103 HERITABILITY OF TEMPERAMENT TRAITS: Stone, *Abnormalities of Personality*, pp. 19, 48–66. There have been some provocative studies of twins in Scandinavia, where the records are better kept than in the United States, that suggest antisocial personality disorder in particular may be genetically transmitted. See *Understanding and Preventing Violence*, edited by Albert J. Reiss Jr. and Jeffrey A. Roth (Washington, D.C.: National Academy Press, 1993), p. 11.

103 "EXCELLENT RECOVERY": Dr. S. Vaisberg, March 29, 1955, in Rockland State Hospital clinical summary.

103 FIGHT BETWEEN JAMES AND BUTCH: Butch's New York State probation file.

104 "I'M SICK": James Bosket's Bellevue Hospital records.

104 DIAGNOSIS OF JAMES AND COURT SENTENCE: Diagnosis of James as antisocial from his Bellevue records. Sentenced to two months in jail from James's New York City police record.

104 BUTCH RETURNED TO ROCKLAND: Butch's Rockland State Hospital clinical summary, April 2, 1957.

104 "I BELIEVED I WAS A BIG MAN": Letter from Butch to the New York State Parole Board, June 6, 1960, in his New York State parole file.

104 "I WENT BACK TO THE STREET": Letter from Butch to the New York State Parole Board, June 6, 1960, in his New York State parole file.

105 MARIE CLAIMS BUTCH PULLED KNIFE: Details about Butch's life in New York after his escape from Rockland State Hospital are from his parole file.

105 "EXTREMELY DISGUSTED": Quoted in the chronological history in Butch's Wisconsin prison file, p. 6, July 16, 1963.

105 MARIE WORKING AT DREAMLAND CAFE: From information Butch gave to his New York parole officer, John A. Taylor, which Taylor included in his report of September 29, 1961, in Butch's New York State parole file. Butch also said Marie was a prostitute in court in Milwaukee, September 30, 1968: Trial transcript, *Wisconsin v. Butch Bosket*, p. 198.

105 "IF YOU DO SOMETHING": Butch's New York State parole file.

105 LIQUOR STORE ROBBERY: Details from the Manhattan Supreme Court clerk's office case file. It includes the police complaints, Butch's confession, the indictments, a psychiatric evaluation from Bellevue Hospital, and the sentencing minutes.

106 JAMES ASKED THE JUDGE: Manhattan Supreme Court clerk's office case file on the liquor store robbery. James's own arrest and conviction on burglary at the time, in his New York City police file.

106 "I NEVER HAD": Butch to staff members who interviewed him at Elmira and Clinton prisons between 1958 and 1960, in his New York State parole file.

106 "I HAVE BEEN A WILD ANIMAL": Butch to C. Watts, May 26, 1960, in his New York State parole file.

107 "FIGURE DRAWINGS SUGGEST": Psychologist's report by Howard Pashens, May 23, 1958, in Butch's New York State parole file.

107 GUNSHOT AND KNIFE WOUNDS: Medical report at Elmira Reception Center, June 4, 1958.

107 "SUBJECT HERE REVEALS": Psychiatrist's report by Dr. Leonard J. Bolton, June 2, 1958.

108 FIGHT WITH INMATE ANDERSON: New York State parole file, February 10, 1959.

108 "FUCK YOU": New York State parole file, March 10, 1959.

108 "A STRONG ARM TYPE": New York State parole file, January 28, 1959.

108 "HIS SPEECH WAS HAZY": Report by Butch's parole officer, February 14, 1961. Other details of Butch's life after his release from prison are also from his parole officer's weekly reports.

108 "HE WAS A CHUNK": Interview with Laura Roane Bosket.

109 "A FEELING OF IMMENSE SIGNIFICANCE": Weekly parole report, June 26, 1962.

7

BUTCH

The Pawnshop

111 "WHO'S DAVE?": This chapter is based largely on three sources. First is the Milwaukee Police Department's investigative file on the murder of David Hurwitz and William Locke, which runs to 449 pages. Second is the transcript of Butch's murder trial in Milwaukee in early 1963. It is 416 pages in length. Third is the transcript of Butch's appeal hearing in Milwaukee in 1968, which adds another 265 pages. Every quotation in the chapter is taken verbatim from one of these three records. Where material is taken from an additional source, I have indicated it with a specific note.

112 "SHOW AUNTIE HOW BIG": A description of the pornographic pictures Butch offered for sale is in his 550-page FBI file, obtained under the Freedom of Information Act.

112 BUTCH'S THEFT OF PORNOGRAPHIC PHOTOS: Butch's activities in New York before coming to Milwaukee and his theft of the pornographic pictures and checks from Evans Color Lab are reported in his New York State parole file, June 20, 1962, to September 5, 1962.

117 URBAN HOMICIDE RATES FALL: The best summary of the new consensus among historians that homicide rates actually declined in America's big cities from 1850 to 1960 is Ted Robert Gurr, *Violence in America*, vol. 1: *The History of Crime* (Newbury Park, Cal.: Sage, 1989), especially pp. 1–79. For Philadelphia, in particular, there is a brilliant study by Roger Lane, *Violent*

Death in the City: Suicide, Accident and Murder in Nineteenth Century Philadelphia (Cambridge, Mass.: Harvard University Press, 1979). For statistics on a number of cities, see Eric H. Monkkonen, *Police in Urban America, 1860–1920* (Cambridge, England: Cambridge University Press, 1981).

118 NEW YORK HOMICIDE RATES DECLINE: New York homicide figures were kindly supplied by Eric Monkkonen, a professor of history at UCLA. He has done exceptional pioneering research comparing coroners' reports, court records, and newspaper accounts of murders to come up with a new, more accurate set of data.

118 DECLINE IN VIOLENCE FROM MIDDLE AGES: Gurr, *Violence in America*, pp. 27–31, offers the best summary of this scholarship.

118 "CIVILIZING PROCESS": Norbert Elias, *The Civilizing Process: The History of Manners* (New York: Urizen, 1978, originally published 1939) and *State Formation and Civilization* (Oxford: Oxford University Press, 1982).

118 AMSTERDAM HOMICIDE RATES: Pieter Spierenburg, "Faces of Violence: Homicide Trends and Cultural Meanings, Amsterdam, 1431–1815," *Journal of Social History*, vol. 27, no. 4, 1994; and figures supplied to author by Spierenburg.

118 BELL, CLOCK, AND FOREMAN: Lane, *Violent Death*, pp. 122–23.

119 SOUTHERN-BORN HONOR FINDS A NEW SPAWNING GROUND: The point that Southern honor was carried northward into the big cities by impoverished African-Americans has best been made by Edward Ayers, *Vengeance and Justice*, pp. 234–35, 274–75.

119 "THE SIGNIFICANCE OF A JOSTLE": Wolfgang and Ferracuti are quoted in Ayers, *Vengeance and Justice*, pp. 274–75.

121 GROWING INCREASINGLY AGITATED: Butch's activities in New York in 1962 and his contacts with his parole officer are from Taylor's parole report.

121 BUTCH PROPOSES TRIP TO CHICAGO: Interview with Laura Roane Bosket.

123 "HERE I AM WITH MY BIG BELLY": Interview with Laura Roane Bosket.

126 JUDGE STEFFES: Interview with Susan Adler.

8

WILLIE

Bad Little Booby

131 NANCY ROANE WORKED LONG HOURS: Interview with Nancy Roane Spates.

131 WESTMORELAND COUNTY HISTORY: *Westmoreland County, Virginia, 1653–1983*, edited by Walter Biscoe Norris Jr. (Marceline, Mo.: Walsworth, 1983).

132 EARLY ROANE FAMILY HISTORY: *Genealogies of Virginia Families from the William and Mary College Quarterly Historical Magazine*, vol. 4 (Baltimore: Genealogical Publishing, 1982), pp. 287–315.

132 CHARLES ROANE'S ARRIVAL IN VIRGINIA: *Genealogies in the Library of Congress, a Bibliography*, second supplement, 1976–86, edited by Marion J. Kaminkow (Baltimore: Magna Carta Book Company, 1987), p. 587.

132   THOMAS ROANE AT MEETING TO PROTEST STAMP TAX: *Westmoreland County, Virginia, 1653–1912,* compiled by Thomas Roane Barnes Wright (Richmond: Whittet & Shepperson, 1912), pp. 40–47.

132   JOHN ROANE'S "UNFORTUNATE END": The family history, by Frank Gildart Ruffin, is reprinted in *Genealogies of Virginia Families,* p. 310.

133   BLACK ROANE FAMILY'S ACCOUNT OF THEIR ORIGINS: Interview with Irving Roane, a great-great-grandson of the John Roane registered as a free black.

133   "JOHN ROANE, NEGRO MAN": *Westmoreland County, Virginia, Register of Free Negroes, 1850–61.* The register is now in the Virginia State Library and Archives in Richmond. Photocopies from the original record book were kindly provided by Conley Edwards, the assistant Virginia state archivist. The entry on John Roane is published with the permission of the Westmoreland County Clerk.

133   FEDERAL CENSUS: Federal Censuses of 1850 and 1860 for Westmoreland County, Virginia, have entries for John and Lucy Lee Roane and their children. The family is then traceable down to Nancy Roane through the federal Censuses of 1870, 1880, 1900, 1910, and 1920.

133   FREE BLACKS IN WESTMORELAND COUNTY: Interview with Inez Johnson, the local expert on African-American history.

133   "I HAVE FOR SOME TIME PAST": *The New York Times,* July 29, 1991, p. 8.

133   "THE PAST IS NOT DEAD": William Faulkner, *Requiem for a Nun* (New York: Random House, 1950), p. 80.

133   LAURA'S CHILDHOOD: Interviews with Nancy Roane Spates and Laura Roane Bosket.

135   LAURA AFTER THE MURDERS: Interview with Gloria Reddick.

136   "OH, LORDY": Interview with Debbie Reddick. Except where otherwise specified, the information about Willie's early years in the rest of this chapter is from interviews with Willie himself or with Laura Roane Bosket, his grandmothers Nancy Roane Spates and Marie Hickson Jackson, his sister Cheryl Bosket, and his neighbors Gloria and Debbie Reddick.

140   WILLIE'S RELATIONSHIP WITH HIS MOTHER: Social workers and probation officers who later visited the family often commented on how Laura compared Willie to his father and how that affected both mother and son. For example, an extraordinarily perceptive report dated August 1975 was written by Carol Hayden, a clinical social worker at the Rockland Children's Psychiatric Center, and a detailed report was prepared for the New York City Family Court by Probation Officer Roger Wrubels, June 16, 1978.

141   HERITABILITY OF TEMPERAMENT: Stone, *Abnormalities of Personality,* pp. 19, 55–59.

141   HERITABILITY OF IMPULSIVE-AGGRESSIVE BEHAVIOR: Dr. Emil F. Coccaro et al., "Heritability of Irritable Impulsiveness: A Study of Twins Reared Together and Apart," *Psychiatry Research,* vol. 48, 1993, pp. 229–42. Also, Jerome Kagan, *Galen's Prophecy* (New York: Basic Books, 1994). Kagan, a Harvard University psychologist, believes that about 25 percent of children are born with an uninhibited temperament, with low heart rates, which means that when they are challenged for violating the law, they do not feel fear. If

raised in a middle-class family, with consistent discipline and in a good neighborhood, they may turn out to be well-liked and successful. But if raised in a family with little discipline and in a neighborhood with many provocations, like high crime rates, they are at risk for becoming delinquent.

141 EFFECT OF PRENATAL STRESS ON YOUNG CHILDREN: Andrea D. Clements, "The Incidence of Attention Deficit–Hyperactivity Disorder in Children Whose Mothers Experienced Extreme Psychological Stress During Pregnancy," *Georgia Educational Researcher*, vol. 9, nos. 1 and 2, September 1992. For a full review of the research, see Lynne C. Huffman and Rebecca del Carmen, "Prenatal Stress," in *Childhood Stress*, edited by L. E. Arnold (New York: Wiley, 1990). While the studies on human children are still considered tentative, strongly documented findings with monkeys and rats show that mother animals subjected to unpleasant stress have offspring that tend to be impulsive, irritable, and lacking in social skills. These studies suggest that environmental stress alters the brain chemicals, or neurotransmitters, of the very young animals, resetting their internal thermostats for aggression. See Susan Clarke and Mary L. Schneider, "Prenatal Stress Has Long-Term Effects on Behavioral Responses in Juvenile Rhesus Monkeys," in *Developmental Psychobiology*, vol. 26, no. 5, 1993.

142 "WHEN MRS. BOSKET FINALLY ADMITTED": Analysis originally made by a team of mental health professionals at the Wiltwyck School, February 1974. Their report has since been lost, but it was picked up and incorporated into the report by Carol Hayden for the Rockland Children's Psychiatric Center, August 1975.

144 WILLIE'S FACE DIRTY WITH TEARS: Interview with Sabrina Gaston.

144 WILLIE WETTING BED: This is noted repeatedly in records of the institutions to which he was later sent; for example, Carol Hayden's report for the Rockland Children's Psychiatric Center, August 1975.

144 TROUBLE IN SCHOOL: Carol Hayden's report for the Rockland Children's Psychiatric Center, August 1975, and report prepared by a probation officer for Manhattan Family Court, April 18, 1974.

144 MRS. HOUSE: Interview with David House, former husband of Mary Lee Jenkins House.

145 EFFECT OF BRAIN INJURY ON VIOLENCE: Dr. Dorothy Otnow Lewis et al., "Neuropsychiatric, Psychoeducational and Family Characteristics of 14 Juveniles Condemned to Death in the United States," *American Journal of Psychiatry*, vol. 145, no. 5, May 1958.

145 THROWING TYPEWRITER: Interview with Willie, and Carol Hayden's report for the Rockland Children's Psychiatric Center, August 1975.

145 CHERYL SENT TO ZAREGA: Interviews with Cheryl Bosket and her girlhood friend, Sharon Parker. Also, the Family Court probation report on Willie, April 18, 1974.

146 WILLIE AT BELLEVUE, 1971: Interview with Dr. Mahin Hassibi, and Bellevue's records on Willie.

148 JAMES'S ARREST FOR KIDNAPPING AND SODOMY: James Bosket's New York City Police Department file.

149 EFFECT OF SEXUAL ABUSE ON CHILDREN: Widom, "Cycle of Violence."

149 SNATCHING POCKETBOOK: Willie's actions at ages eight and nine are drawn from three sources: first, transcript of a hearing in Manhattan Family Court, December 7, 1973; second, Carol Hayden's report for the Rockland Children's Psychiatric Center, August 1975; and third, probation report prepared for the Family Court, June 16, 1978.

149 SETTING MAN ON FIRE IN CENTRAL PARK: Interview with Debbie Reddick.

149 "I FEEL SAD": Interview with Gloria Reddick.

9

WILLIE

"Little Man"

151 WILLIE'S APPEARANCE BEFORE JUDGE FELIX: Transcripts of Willie's hearings in Manhattan Family Court in 1972 and 1973. Additional background from Family Court probation report, April 18, 1974. Also, interviews with Willie; his mother, Laura Roane Bosket; Seymour Gottfried, who was the probation officer in the court when Willie first appeared; Merril Sobie, who at the time was executive officer of the Manhattan Family Court; and Judith Levy Sheindlin, then a city prosecutor, or corporation counsel, and now supervising judge of the Manhattan Family Court.

155 "THE PRESENT PLAN": Quoted in Robert M. Mennel, *Thorns and Thistles: Juvenile Delinquents in the United States, 1825–1940* (Hanover, N.H.: University Press of New England, 1973), p. 8.

155 THREE-QUARTERS OF CHILDREN FOREIGN-BORN: Merril Sobie, *The Creation of Juvenile Justice: A History of New York's Children's Laws* (Albany: New York Bar Foundation, 1987), p. 31.

155 "AT SUNRISE, THE CHILDREN": Quoted in Mennel, *Thorns and Thistles*, pp. 18–19.

156 "BOLTED DOOR, BARRED WINDOW": Quoted in Anthony M. Platt, *The Child Savers: The Invention of Delinquency* (Chicago: University of Chicago Press, 1969), p. 64.

156 "EACH HOUSE IS TO BE A FAMILY": Quoted in Mennel, *Thorns and Thistles*, p. 54.

157 "THE FUNDAMENTAL IDEA": Quoted in Mennel, *Thorns and Thistles*, p. 132.

157 "AS A PARLOR": Platt, *Child Savers*, p. 143.

157 "UNDER OUR CONSTITUTION": Quoted in Laura Kalman, *Abe Fortas: A Biography* (New Haven: Yale University Press, 1990), p. 253.

159 BREAKDOWN OF THE FAMILY COURT: What caused the breakdown of the Family Court system is a much debated issue by lawyers, judges, and children's rights groups. For two thoughtful and well-written accounts of the Manhattan Family Court's problems, with opposite points of view, see Peter S. Prescott, *The Child Savers: Juvenile Justice Observed* (New York: Alfred A. Knopf, 1981), and Rita Kramer, *At a Tender Age: Violent Youth and Juvenile Justice* (New York: Henry Holt, 1988).

159 HALF TO THREE-QUARTERS OF CASES DISMISSED: Interview with Judith L.

Sheindlin, now supervising judge in Manhattan Family Court. Tough, acerbic, and yet fair, Judge Sheindlin has long been regarded as the ablest figure in the Manhattan Family Court.

159 YOUNG PEOPLE SENT AWAY LESS THAN 10 PERCENT OF TIME: Estimate in Prescott, *Child Savers*, p. 109.

160 CRIMINOLOGISTS CITE WILTWYCK: William McCord and Jose Sanchez, "Curing Criminal Negligence," *Psychology Today*, vol. 16, no. 4, April 1982, pp. 79–82. The authors conducted a study of 175 men who had spent at least eighteen months at Wiltwyck between 1952 and 1955 (the period Butch was there) and concluded that Wiltwyck's rehabilitative approach worked. Wiltwyck's philosophy, which the authors termed "disciplined love," resulted in a much lower rate of repeat offenders among its graduates than among graduates of other, more conventional reformatories. By the time Willie was sent there, however, Wiltwyck was no longer able to measure its success because the school could not locate most boys even a few years after they left the program.

160 "IT IS A WONDERFUL": Interview with Ruth Gregory, now Ruth Gregory Geils.

161 A SLICK LITTLE DUDE: Interview with Carol Darden, now Carol Darden Lloyd.

161 ARRUTH ARTIS: Interviews with Arruth Artis and her sister, Sophia Wesley, who was a teacher's aide in Willie's class at Wiltwyck.

163 "RICHARD": Richard is not the boy's real name; I have changed it for reasons of privacy.

163 "MR. JONES, SOME KIDS": Interview with Larry Jones.

165 "I'M NOT EVEN GOING TO LOOK": Interview with Arruth Artis.

167 "THIS IS ANOTHER LULU": Interview with Rose Niles.

168 "PRECOCIOUS, WARM AND EMPATHETIC": Psychological test on Willie done for Wiltwyck by the Westchester County Health Service, 1972.

169 EVERY TIME SHE DID GO: Interview with Laura Roane Bosket.

170 JOEL KATZ: Interview with Dr. Joel Katz. Also, an undated memo by Dr. Katz, "The Wiltwyck School: Enriched Residential Program, A Program for the Intensive Residential Treatment of Adolescents"; and an article by him, "Reduction of Medication and Utilization of a Psychiatric Inpatient Service in a Residential Treatment Center for Children," published in *Wiltwyck Journal*, vol. 1, fall 1974. In addition, there is a vivid description of Dr. Katz and his program at Wiltwyck in Lis Harris, "A Reporter at Large: Persons in Need of Supervision," *The New Yorker*, August 14, 1974.

171 SANDRA OEHLING: Interview with Sandra Oehling, now Sandra Hernandez.

171 WILLIE IN THE QUIET ROOM: Petition written by Sandra Oehling for the Manhattan Family Court, March 22, 1974.

172 "HEY, WILLIE, WHAT'S UP": Interview with Eddie Hay, who was a ten-year-old resident of Wiltwyck at the time.

172 BREAKING INTO VOLKSWAGEN: Interview with Richard Stroh.

173 COULD HAVE BEEN PRESIDENT: Interview with Ruth Gregory Geils.

174 "IT APPEARED TO ME": Dr. Joel Katz, psychiatric note to the Manhattan Family Court, March 22, 1974.

10

WILLIE

The Boy No One Could Help

176 "I MUGGED THIS OLD LADY": Interview with Dr. Mahin Hassibi. Other information on Willie's second commitment to Bellevue comes from Manhattan Family Court probation reports, April 18, 1974, and June 16, 1978.

179 WILLIE AT HIGHLAND SCHOOL: Psychiatric evaluation at Highland, July 19, 1974, and chronological history of Willie's stay at Highland, September 17, 1974, both in Willie's Division for Youth file.

180 HE HAD FABULOUS POTENTIAL: Interview with Marion Beeler.

180 "WHAT STANDS OUT CLEARLY": Psychiatric evaluation at Highland, July 19, 1974, in Willie's DFY file.

181 "I AIN'T SIGNING": Willie's Highland School records, September 20, 1974, in DFY file.

181 WEDDING OF PETER EDELMAN AND MARIAN WRIGHT: *The New York Times*, July 15, 1968.

183 PETER EDELMAN TAKES NEW JOB: Interview with Peter Edelman.

183 THE MASSACHUSETTS EXPERIMENT: Jerome G. Miller, *Last One Over the Wall: The Massachusetts Experiment in Closing Reform Schools* (Columbus: Ohio State University Press, 1991).

183 "WITH THE EXCEPTION": *Newsday*, July 23, 1972.

184 SHOOTING FISH IN A BARREL: Interview with Peter Edelman.

184 LARRY DYE: Kenneth Wooden, *Weeping in the Playtime of Others: America's Incarcerated Children* (New York: McGraw-Hill, 1976), p. 228.

184 NUMBERS OF TRAINING SCHOOLS CLOSED: Speech by Thomas Mullen, then deputy head of the Division for Youth, to the 1978 annual meeting of the National Association of Training Schools and Juvenile Agencies. For a detailed study of the changes in New York's juvenile justice system in the 1970s and 1980s, see Edmund F. McGarrell, *Juvenile Correctional Reform: Two Decades of Policy and Procedural Change* (Albany: State University of New York Press, 1988).

184 EARLY TURMOIL AT BROOKWOOD: Interview with Tom Pottenburgh; also a Division for Youth history of Brookwood prepared for Pottenburgh, January 24, 1978.

185 "HEY, POTTENBURGH": Interview with Tom Pottenburgh.

186 "THE VERBAL AND PHYSICAL ABUSE": Brookwood staff case review, February 19, 1975, in Willie's DFY file.

186 "GOOD MORNING, MRS. GENTILE": Interview with Helen Gentile.

186 "THROWING HAIRYS": Willie's youthful autobiography is written in a vivid, excitable script suggesting the emotions constantly at work in him. It is dated January 22, 1975.

186 "PLAINTIFF BOSKET": Quoted in Prescott, *Child Savers*, p. 202.

187 NAIVE DO-GOODERS: Interview with Tom Pottenburgh.

187 CHUCK NATTELL: Interview with Chuck Nattell. The behavior modifica-

tion program is also described in a report by the school's psychologist, Marvin Reisman, February 10, 1975, in Willie's DFY file.

187 "MOST STAFF FEEL": Bertha Fields in Brookwood's case review, February 19, 1975, in Willie's DFY file.

188 "WILLIE, IN OUR JUDGMENT": Letter to Tom Pottenburgh, January 8, 1975, in Willie's DFY file. There was also another warning on March 3, 1975.

188 "DISHONORABLE DISCHARGE": Interview with Tom Pottenburgh.

188 TIP TO EDWIN CRUISE: Handwritten note by Edwin Cruise, January 7, 1975, in Willie's DFY file. The note is part of extensive material that Cruise kept on Willie between 1974 and 1978 while he was Willie's aftercare worker.

188 "IT IS MY OPINION": Memo by Phil Williams to Edwin Cruise, March 4, 1975, in Willie's DFY file.

189 "WILLIE MAY OR MAY NOT": Memo by Edwin Cruise, March 24, 1975, in Willie's DFY file.

189 "WHAT'S GOING ON": Handwritten note by Edwin Cruise, April 14, 1975, in Willie's DFY file. Phil Williams's abrupt cancellation of his plan to pick up Willie is reported in another memo by Cruise on April 18, 1975. Willie's DFY file also shows that after he had been given the extended leave, Brookwood sent a series of memos to DFY headquarters reporting that he had suddenly shown "remarkable improvement" in his behavior during his last few weeks at the school. These memos are dated April 9, April 10, and April 22, 1975.

189 WILLIE'S ATTACK ON DRY CLEANER: Handwritten note by Edwin Cruise, April 18, 1975, in Willie's DFY file. Laura Roane Bosket's reaction to Willie's outburst is also in the note.

189 CUTTING MAN WITH BOTTLE AND OTHER INCIDENTS: Report by Edwin Cruise, June 13, 1975, in Willie's DFY file. The Family Court's dismissal of the assault charges is in Willie's defense file.

190 "MOTHER! LOOK": Report by Edwin Cruise, December 12, 1974, in Willie's DFY file.

190 CRUISE'S OBSERVATIONS ABOUT WILLIE AND HIS MOTHER: These are contained in a series of detailed reports, September 23 and December 12, 1974; February 15, March 24, April 21, May 1 and 29, June 13, July 9, and September 5, 1975, all in Willie's DFY file.

191 "A TOTAL FAILURE": Report on Willie's surprise arrival by Jay Oppenheim, Highland's assistant superintendent, July 15, 1975, in Willie's DFY file.

191 "HE HAS BEEN BOUNCED AROUND": Carol Hayden's report for the Rockland Children's Psychiatric Center, August 25, 1975.

192 PSYCHOLOGICAL TESTS AT ROCKLAND: Evaluation at Rockland, September 3, 1975. This test is only one in an extensive series performed during Willie's stay at Rockland, August 11, 1975, to September 10, 1975. Willie's file was provided by Rockland State Hospital.

192 "UNSOCIALIZED AGGRESSIVE REACTION OF CHILDHOOD": Diagnosis and analysis by Rockland staff, August 25, 1975.

192 THREE-STEP TREATMENT PLAN: Rockland staff planning conference report, August 25, 1975.

193 TRYON SCHOOL'S REQUEST FOR EXTENSION: Report by Tryon School, October 3, 1975, in Willie's DFY file.

193 MISTAKE BY COURT CLERK: Memo by Edwin Cruise, February 9, 1976, in Willie's DFY file.

194 WILLIE'S ARRESTS IN 1976: Willie's Family Court files.

194 WILLIE'S THIRD ADMISSION TO BELLEVUE: Willie's Bellevue file, March 9–15, 1976. The Family Court probation report, June 16, 1978, also has details on Willie's stay at Bellevue during this period. In addition, interview with Joel Bogart, a teacher in the Bellevue school.

195 WILLIE'S NEW LEGAL AID LAWYER: Interview with Kay McNally.

196 WILLIE'S RECORD IN FAMILY COURT IN 1976: Willie's Family Court file and interview with Kay McNally.

196 AT BRONX STATE HOSPITAL: Interview with Ned Loughran; also, a DFY memo dated February 22, 1987, in Willie's DFY file.

197 SENT TO KENNEDY HOME: Interview with Harriette Godley; also, a letter from David Ruskin of the Kennedy Home to Ed Cruise, December 20, 1976, in Willie's DFY file. Details on Willie's arrest on November 28, 1976, from his Family Court file.

197 ASSAULT ON POLICE OFFICER: Willie's Family Court file, January 10, 1977.

198 "HE CAME WITH A SMILE ON HIS FACE": Memo by Tom Pottenburgh to DFY headquarters in Albany, February 18, 1977. In addition, there are memos written by senior DFY administrators dated February 22 and 23, 1977, agreeing that they had sent Willie on an emergency basis. The fullest account of how Willie was sent back to Brookwood is in a memo by Tom Pottenburgh, October 31, 1977.

198 NEW PROGRAM DEVISED FOR WILLIE: Interviews with Tom Pottenburgh and Phil Williams. Also, memo by Phil Williams, April 22, 1977, and letter from the private psychiatrist, Dr. L. Rack, of the New York Infirmary, February 3, 1977, both in Willie's DFY file.

199 WILLIE'S WORK IN MAINTENANCE SHOP: Interview with Jake Onufrychuk.

199 "I OWE ALL MY THANKS": Letter from Willie to the staff of Brookwood's maintenance shop, in his DFY file.

200 "WILLIE IS JUST LIKE THE SON": Interviews with Minerva and Chuck Woullard.

200 "I FAIL TO SEE": Progress note by Marvin Reisman, April 28, 1977, in Willie's DFY file.

200 POOL CUE ATTACK: Interviews with Bob Pollack and Martin Gallanter.

200 "WILLIE HOLDS A PERVERTED SENSE": Memo by Bob Pollack, June 24, 1977, in Willie's DFY file.

200 "WILLIE HAS BUILT": Memo by Bob Pollack, July 18, 1977.

201 "YOU KNOW, BOB": Interview with Bob Pollack.

201 POTTENBURGH'S EFFORT TO GET WILLIE TRANSFERRED: The effort is outlined in a series of memos, starting with a report by Ed Cruise, June 23, 1977, in Willie's DFY file. Also, an internal memo from Phil Williams to Tom Pottenburgh, June 28, 1977; a memo by Tom Pottenburgh, June 28,

364   *Notes*

1977; and further letters in July and August. The whole process of negotiations is recorded in detail in a memo written for Tom Pottenburgh by Phil Williams, October 31, 1977.

202 SMASHING DOOR AND JUMPING INTO TRUCK: Interviews with Tom Pottenburgh and Phil Williams, and memo by Phil Williams, June 24, 1977.

202 DISPUTE BETWEEN POTTENBURGH AND HONIG: The dispute later escalated into full-scale war. In 1978, the New York State Senate Select Committee on Crime held hearings about her charges, at which she was the star witness. The Division for Youth also conducted its own prolonged internal investigation, ultimately clearing Pottenburgh. My account is based on interviews with both Tom Pottenburgh and Sylvia Honig, her testimony at the senate hearings, and excerpts from a diary she kept while at Brookwood. They were published in the Brooklyn *City Sun*, March 1–7, 1989.

202 "THIS BOY WAS SEEN AGAIN": Dr. Lewis Jarett's psychiatric note, August 31, 1977, in Willie's DFY file. His earlier, more negative reports about Willie were written October 2 and December 17, 1974; January 22 and February 19, 1975; and February 25 and August 2, 1977.

203 "YOU REALLY HAVE TO MEET THIS KID": Interviews with Susan and Alan Raymond. They used footage of Brookwood and Willie as part of a film titled *Bad Boys*, shown on PBS in 1978. The Raymonds won an Academy Award in 1994 for the best feature-length documentary.

203 HE TORE UP HIS ROOM: Sylvia Honig's diary, Brooklyn *City Sun*, March 1–7, 1989.

203 "WILLIE WILL END UP KILLING": Sylvia Honig's diary, Brooklyn *City Sun*, March 1–7, 1989.

11

WILLIE

The Baby-Face Killer

204 MIXUP AT YOUTH DEVELOPMENT CENTER: Interviews with Willie, Phil Williams, and Tom Mullen, then deputy director of DFY. Also, a series of DFY documents, in particular a lengthy memo prepared by Phil Williams for Tom Pottenburgh, October 31, 1977, and handwritten notes by Ed Cruise, September 23 and December 7, 1977.

206 LAURA FIGURED THE DIVISION LET WILLIE GO: Interview with Laura Roane Bosket.

206 "CHARLES": Interviews with Willie, his mother, and his sister Cheryl Bosket, as well as her husband, Melvin Stewart. Charles is not his real name; I have changed it for reasons of privacy.

208 CRUISE BUYS TRAIN TICKET FOR WILLIE: Ed Cruise reported helping Willie out of New York in a memo, April 6, 1978. An unsigned memo by the Henry Street Settlement House, February 15, 1978, gives the same account. Another DFY memo, February 10, 1978, reports Willie's record of poor attendance, drug usage, and fights at Henry Street.

208 "BY ALL MEANS, SEND HIM": Interviews with Minerva and Chuck Woullard.

209 "IF HE DOESN'T GET OFF THE STREETS": Memo by Ed Cruise, April 6, 1978, in Willie's DFY file.

209 HERMAN SPATES'S CRIMINAL RECORD: From his New York State Division of Criminal Justice Services file.

209 ARRESTED AT 207TH STREET STATION: Charges in Family Court probation report, June 16, 1978.

211 "BOOBY, WHERE'D YOU GET THAT WATCH?": Interview with Cheryl Bosket.

212 JUDGE QUINONES POSTPONES CASE: New York *Daily News*, May 19 and June 29, 1978.

214 SHOOTING OF LAMORTE: Interviews with Anthony Lamorte and Willie; also, the two confessions Herman Spates gave to the police, March 31, 1978.

214 OVER THE NEXT THREE NIGHTS: Interviews with Willie and Detective Martin Davin; also, the confessions by Herman Spates.

215 MURDER OF MOISES PEREZ: Interviews with Willie and his sister Cheryl Bosket, as well as the confessions by Herman Spates. Also, the police records of the killing, in Willie's defense file.

215 THE MOST COMPETITIVE GAME OF ALL: After Willie was arrested for the murders, he told a group of four psychiatrists that he viewed each killing as a "competition" in which he had "to win out" in his quest for survival. He believed that in each case he had put himself at risk, and either he had to kill or he would be killed himself. He was very proud that he had won all of these "competitions." Reports by the four psychiatrists, from the Bronx State Hospital, June 30, 1978, in Willie's DFY file.

215 DETECTIVE MARTIN DAVIN: Interview with Martin Davin.

218 "WE KNOW WHERE YOU WERE": Interrogation of Herman Spates from interview with Martin Davin, and the two confessions by Spates, March 31, 1978.

219 HARVEY ROSEN TOOK THE CALL: Interview with Harvey Rosen.

219 "IN THE NAME OF THE PEOPLE": The search warrant is in Willie's Family Court defense file.

220 "WE'VE GOT TO GET UP THERE FAST": Interviews with Martin Davin and Harvey Rosen.

220 LAURA BOSKET AND THE GUN: Interviews with Willie, Cheryl Bosket, Martin Davin, and Harvey Rosen. Laura claims she never knew Willie had the gun and that she offered no help to Davin.

221 "I AIN'T SAYING NOTHING": Willie's comments to Harvey Rosen under interrogation are from handwritten notes kept by Rosen, March 31, 1978, and other documents introduced in Willie's murder trial. Also, interviews with Rosen and Martin Davin.

222 TRIPLING OF VIOLENT JUVENILE CRIME: Report by the Vera Institute of Justice. See the New York *Daily News*, July 9, 1978.

222 JUVENILE JUSTICE REFORM ACT OF 1976: Sobie, *Creation of Juvenile Justice*, pp. 168–69.

222 ROBERT SILBERING ASSIGNED TO FAMILY COURT: Interview with Robert Silbering.

223 "YEAH, THAT'S THE GUY": Interview with Anthony Lamorte.

224 JUDGE EDITH MILLER: Interview with Edith Miller.

224 "YOUNG MAN, WHEN ARE YOU": Interview with Willie.

224 WILLIE'S BEHAVIOR AT SPOFFORD: Interviews with Willie and Harriette Godley, then director of social services at Spofford.

225 "WHAT DO YOU MEAN?": Interview with Kay McNally.

225 "I DON'T CARE ANYMORE": Interview with Seymour Gottfried.

226 IT WASN'T FAMILY COURT THAT HAD FAILED: Interview with Edith Miller.

227 GOVERNOR HUGH CAREY'S REACTION: *The New York Times*, June 30, 1978.

227 SLAP AT PETER EDELMAN: Interview with Peter Edelman.

12

BUTCH

The Prisoner and the Scholar

232 "EVERYTHING PASSES": Quoted in David J. Rothman, *The Discovery of the Asylum: Social Order and Disorder in the New Republic* (Boston: Little, Brown, 1971), p. 97.

232 SILENCE SYSTEM AT WAUPUN: Interview with Walter Birk. Birk was in prison with Butch over a number of years, beginning when they were both in the Milwaukee County Jail soon after Butch committed the two murders there.

232 CELLBLOCK DESIGN: W. David Lewis, *From Newgate to Dannemora: The Rise of the Penitentiary in New York, 1796–1848* (Ithaca: Cornell University Press, 1965), p. 67.

232 "A NUISANCE": Butch Bosket's Wisconsin prison file, entries for May 21 and September 9, 1963. The prison file was made available by the Wisconsin Department of Corrections in accordance with the state's open records law.

233 "THAT GUY'S GOING TO GIVE ME TROUBLE": Interview with Walter Birk.

234 "THE STRONG ARMED TYPE": Butch's Wisconsin prison file, June 24, 1963.

234 "MAKING EXCEEDINGLY GOOD PROGRESS": Butch's first academic report is from an entry in his Wisconsin prison file, September 9, 1963.

235 "MUCH TO MY DISMAY": Butch's Wisconsin prison file, April 11, 1968.

235 "BUTCH HAS ASSISTED": Butch's Wisconsin prison file, August 21, 1970.

235 "THE INMATE EMERGES VERY CLEARLY": Dr. Konstantin Geocaris, in Butch's Wisconsin prison file, June 11, 1968.

236 MICHAEL SCHOENFIELD: Interview with Michael Schoenfield.

238 "*STEPPENWOLF* HAS BECOME A VIRTUAL BIBLE": Butch's letters to Michael and Barbara Schoenfield about *Steppenwolf* are dated May 10, June 13, and October 13, 1981, and February 10, 1982.

238 BUTCH WAS ORGANIZING A RING: The charges against Butch are from the September 11 and 20, 1972, entries, as well as from a lengthy memo of September 11, 1982, in Butch's Wisconsin prison file.

239 ESCAPE FROM HOSPITAL: Memo by Dr. William G. Troyer Jr., in Butch's Wisconsin prison file, November 3, 1972.

239 NOT GUILTY BY REASON OF INSANITY: Butch's Wisconsin prison file, November 21, 1973.

239 DIAGNOSIS SCHIZOPHRENIA: Butch's mental breakdown was chronicled by Dr. Charles Nemeth, a psychiatrist at the Central State Hospital, Butch's Wisconsin prison file, December 1, 1972, and June 13, 1973.

239 "IT DOES NOT APPEAR": Butch's Wisconsin prison file, April 2, 1974.

239 ESCAPE FROM CENTRAL STATE HOSPITAL: Butch's Wisconsin prison file, April 16, 1982. Butch told Michael Schoenfield about the help he got from his woman friend.

240 "PASS $20, $50": Butch's bank robberies in New York and his life during this period are from two major sources, except where otherwise specified. First is his FBI file, which runs to 550 unnumbered pages. Second is a presentencing report contained in his Federal Bureau of Prisons file. It was based, in part, on interviews with him and is especially helpful about his personal feelings at the time.

241 "THESE ARE THE FIRST RECORDED WORDS": Butch's tape was found and transcribed by the FBI. They took it literally and thought he might have robbed banks all across the country and killed a number of policemen. Urgent messages were sent to FBI offices in a dozen cities, but no evidence was found that Butch had robbed any banks except for those in New York or that he had ever killed a law officer.

242 JIMMY AND MARY BLURT OUT WHOLE STORY: Butch's FBI file.

242 BUTCH TRIES TO COMMIT SUICIDE: Federal Bureau of Prisons presentencing report.

242 THOMAS ENGEL: Interview with Thomas Engel.

243 "IT WOULD BE A WASTE": Exchange of correspondence between Thomas Engel in New York and the Wisconsin corrections authorities from documents in Butch's Wisconsin prison file. The internal memo suggesting Wisconsin deceive Engel is handwritten and dated February 26, 1975.

243 THREE STABBINGS A MONTH: Pete Earley, *The Hot House: Life Inside Leavenworth Prison* (New York: Bantam Books, 1992), p. 146.

244 THE COMPUTER ROOM: Interview with Richard Tony Hughes, who was a convict at Leavenworth and worked in the computer program with Butch.

244 "MEDICAL MODEL OF REHABILITATION": Earley, *Hot House*, pp. 49–50.

244 A REMARKABLY RIGOROUS SCHEDULE: Interview with Butch in the *Lawrence Journal-World*, April 27, 1980.

245 AN A IN EACH: Butch's academic transcript, in his Federal Bureau of Prisons file.

245 "IN ALL FACETS": Cellblock case manager D. J. Fitzgerald, in Butch's Federal Bureau of Prisons file, September 3, 1981.

245 "MY PRIMARY INTEREST": Letter from Butch to Michael Schoenfield, January 18, 1980.

246 "PLEASE REMOVE ANY THOUGHTS": Letter from Butch to Michael Schoenfield, February 23, 1981.

246 "AS YOU NOTE SO COGENTLY": Letter from Butch to Michael Schoenfield, February 28, 1981.

246 "HEY, ABOUT DOWNHILL SKIING": Letter from Butch to Michael Schoenfield, April 6, 1981.

247 "AFTER OUR PHONE CONVERSATION": Letter from Butch to Michael and Barbara Schoenfield, July 2, 1981.

248 ROGER BARNES AT LEAVENWORTH: Interview with Roger Barnes.

248 A GREAT ABILITY TO COMPARTMENTALIZE: Interview with Tom White.

249 "WITH HIGHEST DISTINCTION": Letter from Gilbert Dyck, dean of the University of Kansas, to Butch, July 9, 1980, in Butch's Federal Bureau of Prisons file.

249 "WHAT DO YOU THINK?": Decision to elect Butch to Phi Beta Kappa, interviews with Roger Barnes and Scott McNall.

249 "FEW PEOPLE HAVE IMPRESSED ME": Letters by Scott McNall, Robert Antonio, and Norman Carlson in Butch's Federal Bureau of Prisons file.

250 "I POSE ABSOLUTELY NO THREAT": Letter from Butch to Michael Schoenfield, February 1, 1982.

13

BUTCH AND WILLIE

The Warriors

251 WILLIE BOSKET'S FATHER IN WALLKILL: New York *Daily News*, July 23, 1978.

252 REACTION BY THE OTHER WILLIE BOSKET TO NEWSPAPER STORY: New York State parole report on the Willie Bosket in Wallkill, entries of July 24 and 25, 1978.

252 MAMON BOSKET'S TWO CONVICTIONS: Saluda County Court of General Sessions, September 1926, and the sentencing minutes of the New York State Supreme Court, May 10, 1963. The misidentified Willie Bosket was convicted of manslaughter in the first degree and sentenced to eight years in prison on June 2, 1975, according to the Brooklyn Supreme Court clerk's case file.

252 BUTCH CROSSES LAURA AND WILLIE OFF LIST: Butch's visitors list, in Wisconsin prison file. Butch and Laura were divorced in 1971, according to correspondence in his Wisconsin prison file.

252 "A NO GOOD BUM"; "A PROSTITUTE": Butch's Wisconsin prison file, March 11, 1963.

253 BUTCH REFUSES TO ACCEPT MAIL FROM FATHER: Butch's Wisconsin prison file, October 13, 1963.

253 BUTCH'S RECONSTRUCTED HISTORY: Interview with Roger Barnes.

253 BUTCH'S DILEMMA: Interview with Richard Hughes.

253 BUTCH'S FIRST LETTER TO WILLIE: Interview with Michael Schoenfield.

254 "OH, MAN": Interview with Willie.

254 BUTCH'S PHONE CALL TO WILLIE: Interview with Joseph Bertholf, director

of Goshen, and a letter from Reverend Terrence J. Foley to the Catholic chaplain at Leavenworth, October 18, 1978, letter in Willie's DFY file.

254 "HEY, HOW YOU DOING": Interview with Willie.

255 HAD WILLIE INHERITED: Interview with Robert Antonio.

255 WILLIE WAS LUCKIER: Interview with Murray Weiss. Weiss was a reporter for the New York *Daily News* who developed a relationship with both Butch and Willie by phone and by letter.

255 ESCAPE FROM GOSHEN: Interview with Joseph Bertholf, and Middletown *Times Herald Record*, December 27, 1978.

256 "IN A SENSE": Letter from Butch to Michael Schoenfield, December 23, 1980.

256 "I AM DISTRESSED": Letter from Butch to Michael Schoenfield, August 16, 1981.

257 "SINCE I HAVE BEEN CONFINED": Letter from Willie to Butch, April 19, 1982. It was provided by Sylvia Honig, the social worker at Brookwood, who later became friends with both Willie and Butch. This letter is one of several documents Honig kindly gave me when I first began to write about the Boskets at *The New York Times* in March 1989.

258 "ONCE AGAIN I HAVE FOUND": Letter from Butch to Willie, May 21, 1982, also provided by Sylvia Honig.

259 "IN RE YOUR SUGGESTION": A carbon copy of Butch's letter to Laura was preserved with the personal materials he left with Michael Schoenfield.

260 "ABOUT MY SON": Letter from Butch to Michael Schoenfield, August 8, 1982, in Michael Schoenfield's collection.

261 "LISTEN MAN": Letter from Willie to Butch, October 10, 1982, provided by Sylvia Honig.

262 WILLIE AT MCCORMACK: His conduct at McCormack and comments by Nicole Librandi and Susan Yeres are from the transcript of his later trial in 1986 for being a persistent felon.

14

WILLIE

Counsel for the Defense

264 NOTHING CAME OF IT: Interviews with Robert Silbering and Eric Pomerantz.

264 "HOW YOU DOING?": Interview with Willie.

265 MARIE HAYWARD IMPRESSED: Interview with Marie Hayward.

266 CHARLES: Interviews with Willie and his sister Cheryl Bosket.

266 WILLIE TURNS IN CHARLES: Interview with Willie. Also Charles's New York City Police Department complaint and arrest sheet.

268 WILLIE'S RUN-IN WITH JOEL BROWN AND ARREST: Interviews with Willie and his sister Cheryl Bosket, and transcript of the trial that followed with testimony by Brown and his roommate, Isaiah Anderson.

270 "THIS CASE LEAVES ME": New York *Post*, March 21, 1984.

270 PATRICK DUGAN WAS SUPERVISING: Interview with Patrick Dugan.

271 WAITING FOR AN APOLOGY: Testimony by Joel Brown and Isaiah Anderson, trial transcript, *New York* v. *Willie Bosket*, 1984, pp. 67, 78–79.

272 CHERYL BELIEVED WILLIE FRAMED: Interview with Cheryl Bosket.

272 MANHATTAN SUPREME COURT: In New York State, crimes involving a felony are tried before the State Supreme Court. New York's highest court is the New York State Court of Appeals.

272 "IT'S VERY CLEAR TO ME": Alton Maddox in pretrial arguments, trial transcript, New York State Supreme Court, 1984, p. 20.

272 "LET'S GO": Account of fight between Willie and the court officers in transcript of his later trial on charges of assault against them, *State of New York* v. *Willie Bosket*, February 19–28, 1985, pp. 120–593.

273 A VISITING JUSTICE FROM ROCHESTER: Interview with Justice Donald Mark.

273 "THERE IS A PROBLEM WITH THIS CASE": Defense summation by Alton Maddox, trial transcript, 1984, pp. 215–54.

275 "THE ONLY REASON": Sentencing hearing transcript, October 15, 1984, pp. 8–11.

275 "YOUR HONOR, I WOULD LIKE TO ASK": Sentencing hearing transcript, pp. 24–28.

276 MORE THAN TWO HUNDRED ROBBERIES: Deposition in suit brought by Amalia Perez, the widow of Moises Perez, November 12, 1982. In 1989, eleven years after her husband was murdered, she settled out of court with the Transit Authority for $10,000.

276 "YOUR HONOR, HOW CAN": Sentencing hearing transcript, pp. 83–88.

277 "YOU ARE A TICKING TIME BOMB": Sentencing hearing transcript, pp. 91–92.

278 SOKOLOW RECOGNIZED THERE WERE GOING TO BE PROBLEMS: Interview with Stephen Sokolow. Also, transcript of the trial in Manhattan Supreme Court, February 19–28, 1985.

278 "I DON'T BELIEVE": Trial transcript, pp. 594–610.

279 "I DON'T RECALL": Trial transcript, pp. 345–72.

279 "IN MY HAND I HAVE A COPY": Trial transcript, pp. 482–83. Willie borrowed the remark that an indictment could be brought against a ham sandwich from a comment by Saul Wachtler, then the chief justice of the New York Court of Appeals.

15

BUTCH

Free at Last

283 PUT BACK IN WAUPUN: Waupun Program Review Committee, in Butch's Wisconsin prison file, February 9, 1982.

284 "IT'S GOOD TO HAVE YOU BACK": Quoted by Butch in letter to Michael Schoenfield, February 10, 1982.

284 "I AM IN HOSTILE COUNTRY": Letters from Butch to Michael Schoenfield, February 16, June 17, and July 13, 1982, and January 2, 1983.

284 COUNSELED PATIENCE: Interview with Michael Schoenfield.

284 "BRO, FOR NOW": Letter from Butch to Michael Schoenfield, September 6, 1982.

285 "DEAR MR. HINICKLE": Letter from Susan St. Clair to the parole board, July 14, 1983, in Butch's Wisconsin prison file.

286 "WITHOUT QUESTION": Letter from Fred Hinickle to Janice L. Cummings, July 6, 1983, in Butch's Wisconsin prison file.

286 ENOUGH TO SUPPORT FOUR PAROLES: Fred Hinickle quoted in the Milwaukee *Journal*, March 8, 1985.

286 "I AM IN CONTROL": Letter from Butch to Michael Schoenfield, May 25, 1984.

287 COMPUTER PROGRAMMER AT ASTRONAUTICS: Interview with Diane Broadhead.

287 BUTCH AT UNIVERSITY OF WISCONSIN: Interviews with Michael Barndt and Peter Akubeze.

287 PARANOIA AT BAKER HOUSE: Interviews with Richard Ruck, Ervin Heinzelmann, and Michael Schoenfield.

288 "YOUR ENORMOUS EFFORTS": Parole board letter, signed by Marion Winning, in Butch's Wisconsin prison file.

288 "FREE AT LAST": Letter from Butch to Jeremiah Cameron.

289 "NO GREAT LOSS": This and other cynical comments are from letters to Michael Schoenfield, August 26, 1982, May 12, 1983, and January 26, 1984.

289 "SHE WAS A WHORE": Interview with Jeremiah Cameron.

290 "I AM NOT SPIRITUALLY CAPABLE": Letter from Butch to Michael Schoenfield, June 18, 1983.

290 DONNA'S DAUGHTER: Interview with Michael Schoenfield. Kristin is not the girl's real name; I have changed it to protect her privacy.

291 "THE DEMON WHO HOLDS": From the last line of Max Weber's essay, "Science as a Vocation," in *From Max Weber: Essays in Sociology*, translated and edited by H. H. Gerth and C. Wright Mills (New York: Oxford University Press, 1946), p. 156. It was Roger Barnes who thought of the phrase.

291 BUTCH'S ASSAULT ON KRISTIN: This account is from several sources. First, the Milwaukee Police Department's investigative file of the case. Second, the transcript of the preliminary hearing in Milwaukee County Circuit Court, February 13, 1985, on the charge of sexual assault against Butch. There are also court documents filed by Kristin's father and grandmother in a separate civil suit against the county Department of Social Services. In addition, I have relied on the findings of John DiMotto, then the assistant district attorney in charge of the Sensitive Crimes Unit in Milwaukee. It was his view, based on long experience, that the evidence against Butch was very strong. DiMotto is now a well-respected judge in Milwaukee.

293 BUTCH'S NEW LAWYER: Interview with Seymour Pikovsky.

293 "BRO AND SIS": Letter from Butch to Michael and Barbara Schoenfield, April 17, 1982.

294 A DEAD DOG ON ITS BACK: Interview with Richard Hughes, a prisoner with Rodney and Butch at Leavenworth.

294 BRITTON KILLS POLICE CHIEF: *Northwest Arkansas Times* of Fayetteville, and *Washington County Observer* of West Fork, Arkansas, March 21–26, 1981.

295 AN OLD PRISON RUSE: Investigative report by the Milwaukee County Sheriff's Department. Many details about Butch's escape in the rest of the chapter are from this report.

295 ROLE OF GILBERT MICKELSON: From detailed statement by Gilbert Mickelson, in sheriff's report. Account of his personal background comes from statements by his neighbors and a psychiatric analysis by Dr. William Crowley, also in sheriff's report.

297 "GOOD LUCK": Statement by Gilbert Mickelson to sheriff's department.

298 "HI, MR. BOSKET": Interview with Mariellen Kostopulos; also, her statement in sheriff's report.

299 "IT MUST BE ONE OF OUR FRIENDS": Interview with Jim King.

299 "PRISONER ESCAPED": Interview with James Paradinovich; also, his statement in sheriff's report.

301 WATCHING A TELEVISION SHOW: Nancy Hoffman, quoted in the Milwaukee *Sentinel*, March 8, 1985; also in sheriff's report.

301 "ALL THESE WINGS": Interview with Jeremiah Cameron.

16

WILLIE

A Monster Created by the System

303 SWALLOWING TOENAIL CLIPPER: Willie's New York State Department of Correctional Services file, March 16–20, 1985.

304 "LET ME OUT OF THIS CELL": Downstate prison disciplinary reports, March 20, 1985.

304 SET FIRE TO HIS CELL: The accounts of Willie's misbehavior in prison in 1985 and 1986 are taken from three sources: disciplinary reports written by his guards, the transcript of his later trial for arson and assault at Midstate prison, and the transcript of a hearing to determine whether Willie was a persistent felon. These three sources total nearly three thousand pages.

305 "I'M GOING TO GO OFF": Willie's threats appear in persistent-felon hearing transcript, February 19 to March 30, 1987, pp. 73–76.

306 SUPERINTENDENT CHARLES A. JAMES: Persistent-felon hearing transcript, pp. 189–202, 303–27.

307 ONEIDA COUNTY: Interviews with Frank Blando, Steven Fortnam, and Matthew Worth.

308 JOSEPH GULLO WAS MAKING HIS ROUNDS: Willie's arson and assault trial transcript, October 21–31, 1986, pp. 53–297.

309 OFFICER PETER BEREZNY SAW: Arson and assault trial transcript, pp. 315–402.

309 ONEIDA BRINGS CRIMINAL CHARGES: Interview with Steven Fortnam,

Oneida County assistant district attorney; also arson and assault trial transcript, p. 467.

310 FORTNAM OFFERS PLEA BARGAIN: Interviews with Willie, Steven Fortnam, Judge John T. Buckley, and Frank Blando, Willie's public defender.

311 WILLIE'S OPENING: Arson and assault trial transcript, pp. 13–25.

312 WILLIE'S CLOSING: Arson and assault trial transcript, pp. 842–49.

312 "YOU DID A GREAT JOB": Interview with Judge Buckley, and arson and assault trial transcript, p. 950.

313 BLACK LIBERATION ARMY RAID: Interview with Judge Buckley, and persistent-felon hearing transcript, February 19, 1987 to March 30, 1987, p. 3.

313 "THE DEFENDANT DENIES": Persistent-felon hearing transcript, p. 11.

314 LETTER TO PRESIDENT REAGAN: Persistent-felon hearing transcript, pp. 140–68.

314 SHAKIM ALLAH: Persistent-felon hearing transcript, pp. 350–57.

314 TERRANCE JONES: Persistent-felon hearing transcript, pp. 594–640.

315 HERMAN SPATES: Persistent-felon hearing transcript, pp. 749–97.

315 "YOU'VE TRIED AS GOOD A CASE": Persistent-felon hearing transcript, pp. 1023–24.

315 "A LONG TIME BLACK PEOPLE HAS BEEN PERSECUTED": Persistent-felon sentencing hearing transcript, March 31, 1987, pp. 12–14.

317 "THEY TRIED NONVIOLENCE": Handwritten notes by Matthew Worth; also, typed report Worth made for himself after the incident.

320 STABBING OF EARL PORTER: Testimony of Earl Porter and Sharon Moseley, stabbing trial transcript, Ulster County, February 14 to April 19, 1989, pp. 157–97, 307–20.

320 DELORES TRIPPARDELLA'S ACCOUNT: Statement to the Ulster County Grand Jury.

321 SHANK PUNCTURED PORTER'S LUNG: Stabbing trial transcript, pp. 102–10.

321 "THIS TRIAL MEANS NOTHING": Stabbing trial transcript, pp. 26–32.

322 TRYING TO LEGENDIZE HIMSELF: Interview with Donald Williams.

323 "ON APRIL 16TH, 1988": Stabbing trial transcript, pp. 330–32, 403–12. In his letter, Willie could not resist exaggerating the length of the weapon he had crafted.

323 EVERYONE IN NEW YORK STATE: Stabbing trial transcript, pp. 421–24.

324 THE JURORS' REACTION: Middletown *Times Herald Record*, February 2, 1989.

324 "THIS IS THE PART": Stabbing trial transcript, pp. 481–83.

324 "YOUR OPINION IS NOTED": Stabbing trial transcript, pp. 485–87.

ACKNOWLEDGMENTS

M Y FATHER, Lyman Butterfield, was a historian. John Adams and Thomas Jefferson were the men he believed in, and he had a deep faith in the importance of going back to the beginning of something to find the original facts. You could not be raised in his house without imbibing his reverence for the power of history. It was his inspiration, I now realize, that sent me searching into the eighteenth and nineteenth centuries to find out why late-twentieth-century America has become plagued with violence.

This enterprise also clearly owes a primary debt to Willie Bosket. I would never have thought of undertaking the book, nor would it have been possible, without Willie's help. Willie wanted to know the whole story of how he had come to be, in his phrase, "a monster created by the system." Altogether over the past five years, I spent almost two hundred hours talking with Willie in his special isolation cell at Woodbourne state prison. He also encouraged members of his family to talk to me, and most did, painful as the memories were for them. They included his mother, Laura Bosket; his sister Cheryl; his grandmothers, Marie Jackson and Nancy Roane Spates; and his neighbors, whom he called "cousin," Gloria and Debbie Reddick. No doubt parts of the book will make them uncomfortable, but I am honored that despite our differences they entrusted me with their story.

In addition, Willie gave me hundreds of pages of documents he had accumulated about himself, starting with his juvenile criminal records. When necessary, he wrote letters giving me permission to examine otherwise confidential files about him and his father, opening more doors for me. As I discovered information about his past and began to uncover the Bosket family's history, I shared the material with Willie. But at no time did he attempt to influence what I wrote. For all Willie's cooperation, I am deeply grateful.

It is impossible to list all those who have given me help or information.

I have cited in the notes many of the more than two hundred people who spoke with me, often repeatedly, as interview subjects, and my obligations to them are manifold.

Certain specific debts must be acknowledged by name. In South Carolina: Bettis C. Rainsford generously introduced me to the rich heritage of Edgefield and proved that Southern hospitality is a living tradition. Ida Bosket and her family patiently helped me find Willie's lost link to his South Carolina ancestors. Mary Parkman proved an enthusiastic guide to Saluda and an indefatigable researcher, saving some local documents from destruction. In Columbia, George C. Rogers Jr. and John Hammond Moore offered wise counsel and gracious hospitality. George L. Voght, the director of the South Carolina Department of Archives and History, and Allen H. Stokes Jr., the librarian of the South Caroliniana Library, went beyond the bounds of duty in steering me through the vast resources of their institutions.

In Augusta: Edward J. Cashin was an invaluable guide to local history, and his wife, Mary Ann Cashin, the librarian of Augusta College, pointed me to key materials for the Boskets' years in her city. Helen Callahan showed me where Butch Bosket was born, just down the block from her home, and located the Boskets' neighbor, Annie Diggs, a great raconteur. Philip Warring and Ruth Crawford took time to improve my understanding of the history of African-Americans in Augusta.

In New York: My foremost obligation is to Robert Silbering, a tireless, big-hearted ally, who spent many hours explaining the intricacies of New York State's criminal justice system and who helped direct me to important criminal files in public records. At the outset of my work, Sylvia Honig offered encouragement and furnished some key original documents, including letters between Willie and his father, Butch. Kathy Erickson helped arrange my initial visit with Willie. Matthew Worth, who himself had been working on a biography of Willie, graciously turned over all his material to me when he opted instead for a career as a lawyer. Claude Brown, as a graduate of Wiltwyck, provided valuable advice and tracked down Edith Kramer, who had taught both him and Butch. Kramer showed me Butch's artwork and allowed me to reproduce it. Judge Judith Sheindlin permitted me access to the Manhattan Family Court and instructed me in its workings. Betty Schack made contacts for me in the state's juvenile justice system. Leonard G. Dunston, the director of the Division for Youth, kindly gave me access to Willie's files and allowed me to talk to agency officials who had worked with Willie. Dr. Dorothy Otnow-Lewis, a leading psychiatrist, took time to visit Willie and offer me her expert counsel. At Woodbourne, Reverend Hector Chiesa, the prison chaplain, was a sympathetic intermediary to Willie.

In Wisconsin: I am profoundly indebted to Michael Schoenfield and his then wife, Barbara, who shared their memories of Butch and gave me access to their collection of 120 letters from Butch. In Milwaukee, Susan Adler was energetic and resourceful in tracking down the transcripts of Butch's trials there and in sharing her encyclopedic knowledge of the city's courts. Erwin Heinzelman helped re-create Butch's time in Baker House. Sheriff Richard Artison graciously gave me his department's investigative report on Butch's final escape attempt and consented to my interviewing his deputies involved in the shooting. Deila Comer and June Lippert provided a lesson in Milwaukee's geography.

In Kansas City, Mark Fleisher was a thoughtful host and arranged for me to tour Leavenworth. In Texas, Roger Barnes spent time recalling his sessions as one of Butch's prison professors and drove me to visit Richard Tony Hughes in Bastrop Federal Correctional Institution. In Boston, Dr. Mary Wilson explained the complexities of congenital syphilis. To all of these people, I am indebted in many ways.

I am also deeply grateful to my editors at *The New York Times*, Joseph Lelyveld and Max Frankel, who took an interest in the project and gave me time to write the book. I particularly wish to thank the Harry Frank Guggenheim Foundation for a generous grant that helped me finish the research and writing. The foundation plays an important and generally unrecognized role in trying to understand and stop violence.

Along the way, I benefited greatly from the advice of a number of scholars of Southern and South Carolina history whom I would like to thank, though they may not agree with my views: Fitzhugh Brundage, Orville Vernon Burton, David Donald, Walter Edgar, John B. Edmunds Jr., Terence R. Finnegan, Lacy K. Ford Jr., J. William Harris, Charles Joyner, Lawrence S. Rowland, and Michael Tadman.

For research assistance, which helped save me vast quantities of time, I am especially grateful to Julia Case, Norma Gransee, Barbara Hale, Brent Holcomb, Pam Jenkins, Jennifer Kushner, Helen Milliken, Rowena Nylund, Lewis Ramsey, and Harold Roby. For helping locate court and criminal records, I thank Murray Butcher and Martin Horn.

My agent, Carol Mann, was a constant and enthusiastic supporter. Jonathan Segal, my editor, provided a judicious admixture of patience, firmness, and literary insight.

And from my heart, I want to thank my wife, Elizabeth Mehren. She made great sacrifices of time, sought to make my writing more elegant, and was a loving companion. Her help was inestimable.

INDEX

Fox Butterfield is the author of *China: Alive in the Bitter Sea*, which won the American Book Award (now known as the National Book Award). He graduated *summa cum laude* from Harvard University, where he also received a master's degree in East Asian studies. After further graduate work in Taiwan, he became a foreign correspondent for *The New York Times*, and was a member of the *Times* reporting team that won the Pulitzer Prize for its publication of the Pentagon Papers. He has been stationed in South Vietnam, Japan, Hong Kong, and China—where he opened the paper's Beijing bureau in 1979—as well as in Boston, New York, and Washington, D.C.

He is currently a national correspondent for the *Times*, writing about crime and violence. He lives with his wife and three children near Boston.

A NOTE ON THE TYPE

The text of this book was set in Plantin, a typeface first cut in 1913 by the Monotype Corporation of London. Though the face bears the name of the great Christopher Plantin (ca. 1520–1589), who in the latter part of the sixteenth century owned, in Antwerp, the largest printing and publishing firm in Europe, it is a rather free adaptation of designs by Claude Garamond made for that firm. With its strong, simple lines, Plantin is a no-nonsense face of exceptional legibility.

Composed by Crane Typesetting Service,
Charlotte Harbor, Florida
Printed and bound by Quebecor Printing Martinsburg,
Martinsburg, West Virginia
Designed by Robert C. Olsson